Social History of Africa

THE REALM
OF THE WORD

Social History of Africa
Series Editors: Allen Isaacman and Jean Hay

THE REALM
OF THE WORD

LANGUAGE, GENDER, AND CHRISTIANITY IN A SOUTHERN AFRICAN KINGDOM

Paul Stuart Landau

HEINEMANN
Portsmouth, NH

DAVID PHILIP
Cape Town

JAMES CURREY
London

Heinemann   James Currey Ltd.   David Philip Publishers (Pty) Ltd
A division of Reed Elsevier Inc.   54b Thornhill Square   PO Box 23408
361 Hanover Street   Islington   Claremont 7735
Portsmouth, NH 03801-3912 London N1 1BE   Cape Town, South Africa
Offices and agents throughout the world

Every effort has been made to contact the copyright holders for permission to reprint borrowed material where necessary. We regret any oversights that may have occurred and would be happy to rectify them in future printings of this work.

The author and publisher wish to thank those who have generously given permission to reprint borrowed material:

LMS photographs reprinted by permission of The Council for World Mission, London, United Kingdom.

ISBN 0-435-08963-3 (Heinemann cloth)
ISBN 0-435-08965-X (Heinemann paper)
ISBN 0-85255-670-5 (James Currey cloth)
ISBN 0-85255-620-9 (James Currey paper)

Library of Congress Cataloging-in-Publication Data
Landau, Paul Stuart, 1962–
        The realm of the Word : language, gender, and Christianity in a
    Southern African kingdom / Paul Stuart Landau
            p. cm. — (Social history of Africa)
        Includes bibliographical references and index.
        ISBN 0-435-08963-3 (alk. paper). — ISBN 0-435-08965-X (pbk. :
    alk. paper)
        1. Ngwato (African people)—Missions. 2. London Missionary
    Society. 3. Missions—Botswana. 4. Botswana—Church history.
    I. Title. II. Series.
    BV3630.B25L36 1995
    306.6'76883—dc20
                                              94-24942
                                                   CIP

British Library Cataloging in Publication Data
Landau, Paul Stuart
    Realm of the Word:Language, Gender, and Christianity in a
    Southern African Kingdom. — (Social history of Africa Series)
    I. Title. II. Series.
    306.676883

Cover design: Jenny Jensen Greenleaf
Cover Photo: Mr. Mokakapadi Ramosoka and the late Mrs. Mosele Ramosoka, of Lerala, photographed by the author in June 1990. Paul Landau's shadow appears bottom, center.
Printed in the United States of America on acid-free paper
99 98 97 96 95 EB 1 2 3 4 5 6 7 8 9

In memory of Samuele Makara

CONTENTS

ACKNOWLEDGMENTS

Researching and writing this book was a long process, extending from 1988 to 1994. During that time, I received help from too many people to thank them all individually, but I would like to name some. First, my adviser and longtime teacher, Jan Vansina. With enthusiasm and a startlingly broad expertise, Jan guided my progress throughout the project. He advised, cautioned, and exhorted me, not only in person but in a constant stream of letters to Botswana. He recognized and encouraged what was best in the work, and even more, what was best in the parts of myself I wished to express through it. He did these things even amidst circumstances that would have distracted lesser men. For more than can be contained in these words, I thank him.

Jeffrey Butler and Stanley Greenberg first interested me in South African history at Wesleyan University. Jeff told me, "Not all power flows out of the barrel of a gun," at a time when the opposite postulate was much more in vogue than it is today. Stan Greenberg has gone on to demonstrate the maxim in his work for the White House. Steve Feierman first set me on the track of religion and ideology back in 1984; he helped me thrash out my topic and gave me very useful advice on how to do research before he left Wisconsin in 1989. Neil Parsons, now in Cape Town, befriended me at the University of London and displayed a spirit of open-handed generosity and good humor that represents what is best in academe. He shared his own material with me, including his excellent Ph.D. dissertation, but more, he shared his time, his energy, and his home. This book owes him a large debt, and its title harks back to his 1972 booklet, *The Word of Khama*. Isaac Schapera took the time to meet with me, and gave me material from his own (voluminous) private research notes. Shula Marks welcomed me to the Institute of Commonwealth Studies and twice invited me to deliver a paper before her seminar there. This was quite important: I felt, for the first time, like a member of the southern Africanist scholarly community. She also read several chapters of the manuscript, and gave me good advice. Finally, Jean Hay, my editor, by combining forthright critiques with personal encouragement, made this a better book. My thanks to her, and to Allen Isaacman, for their thoughtful reviews.

"Pro" Nthobatsang and Gabriel Selato helped me during my researches in Serowe, in 1988-1989. Thanks and very best wishes go to them both. In and around Lerala, in 1990, Baruteng Onamile was my assistant and my friend. Baruteng proved to be a man with both patience and common sense superior to my own. If the world were turned about, he could have written a better book than this one. Thank you, Baruteng.

The following people extended their gracious hospitality to me: Joan Reeves in Gaborone; Janet Jennings, and Mrs. Oagaletse Phiri and MmaNtho in Serowe; Rachel Mathare and Samuele Makara of Lerala; Prudence and Dave Holton, Donatella Rovera, and Martin Ass in London; Isla Brown in Scotland; Tefetso Mothibe and his family in Lesotho; and John and Olive Rutherford in Greystoke, Cumbria, in what used to be called Westmorland, England. I would also like to express my appreciation to Gay Seidman, Crawford Young, David Henige, and especially Steve Stern, for his very helpful written comments. Thanks also to Barb Davis of the U.S. Peace Corps, to Barolong Sebone, and to vice chancellor of the University of Botswana, Thomas Tlou.

For my SeTswana I am indebted first to Daniel Kunene, who introduced me to southern African languages, and to Jennifer Yanco and Part Themba Mgadla. Other people who hosted, taught, encouraged, or critiqued me are David Coplan, Michael Crowder, Terence Ranger, Stanley Trapido, Kristen Vallow, Richard Werbner, Christopher Whann, and Marcia Wright, who included me in her graduate seminar; fellow students and faculty at the University of New Hampshire, Columbia University, the University of London, Boston University, and the University of Wisconsin; and among these latter, special thanks to Nancy Rose Hunt, who read and commented very helpfully on two chapters, and Cathy Skidmore-Hess, who read the whole in its previous dissertorial incarnation. Thanks also to Claudine Vansina and Judy Cochran for kindness and untrumpeted labors.

The photographs in this book that are protected by copyright come from the collection of the Council for World Mission (London), which retains all rights to their use. I thank the Council for permission to publish them. Many people were involved in the production of the book, but I would like to thank Gail Miller of the School of Oriental and African Studies in London and Paul Shustak, who gave me his time and skill to produce the two graphs.

For funding I am grateful for a Fulbright grant administered by the Institute of International Education of the United Nations, and for a Fulbright grant from the United States Department of Education. For institutional privileges extended to me, my thanks go first to Sekgoma T. Khama and the Khama family for permission to use their family archives for scholarly purposes. Secondly, I thank Columbia University; the Union Theological Seminary of New York; the School of Oriental and African Studies, and the Institute of Commonwealth Studies, both of the University of London; Selly Oaks College in Birmingham, England; the Khama III Memorial Museum and its staff, especially Ruth Forkhammer, in Serowe, Botswana; the United Congregational Church of Southern Africa; the Botswana National Archives; the University of Botswana, and the government and people of Botswana. Finally, I would like to thank my parents, Sidney and Sarah Landau, both for their support and for having intellectual pursuits that moved me, often irritably, closer to my own. As is customary, while sharing credit, I take responsibility for all faults and errors that inevitably occur here.

Ke a leboga.

GLOSSARY

Owing to the nature of my arguments, the truest definitions of SeTswana terms are left to the main text. For easier reference, however, this glossary is offered.

Names, Places, and Peoples and Their Prefixes:

Kaa, *Kalanga*, *Khurutshe*, *Ngwato*, *Seleka*, *Tawana* and other such capitalized radicals designate ethnicities, languages or dialects, or political affiliations.

Tswana is the overarching term for those speakers of the *Sotho-Tswana* language group who reside in the northern Cape and in Botswana, and for others who apply it to themselves.

Mo- followed by a capitalized radical (for example, *Tswana*) means a person of that ethnic, linguistic, or political affiliation.

Ba- followed by (e.g.) *Tswana*, means people (plural) of that affiliation.

Mo- and *ba-* are also the prefixes for terms for human beings generally.

Ma- is the rude version of *Ba-* when prefixed as *Mo-* and *Ba-* to ethnic radicals. It connotes inferiors.

Se- is a prefix that often denotes language or dialect; hence, *SeTswana*.

Mma- or *-mma-* means "mother of," but in the past also connoted kingship or chiefship as a territorial title. Hence M*maLebogo*.

Ga- means "land of" or "country of." Hence Gamma*Ngwato*.

Goo- (regional usage) means "place of." Hence Goo*Tau*, the village.

Baka- (regional usage) means "the people of," like the SeTswana *Ba-*. Hence BakaNswazwi, Nswazwi being a hereditary chiefly title.

Other Words Used More Than Once in the Text:

The following terms are listed alphabetically by first letter (not by radical), for the convenience of the general reader.

badimo: the ancestors (plural of *modimo*)
badumedi: believers (plural of *modumedi*)
bakeresete: Christians (plural of *mokeresete*)
baruti: teachers, preachers, senior Christians (plural of *moruti*)
beng: masters (plural of *mong*)
bogadi: brideprice

xi

bogobe: the Tswana staple, a breadlike mash
bogwera: male initiation rites
bojale: female initiation rites
bojalwa: beer
dikaelo: catechumen classes, examples (plural of *sekaelo*)
dikgotla: courts (plural of *kgotla*)
dingaka: priest-healers (plural of *ngaka*)
kgomo (pl: *dikgomo*): cattle
kgosi (pl: *dikgosi*): ruler
kgotla (pl: *dikgotla*): central court; politically, neighborhood or village
Lefoko la Modimo: Word of God
lesotla (pl: *masotla*): locally tilled royal farmland
letsema: "First fruits" seasonal ceremony
lotshwao: herd's ear mark, baptismal "mark"
mafoko: words (plural of *lefoko*)
masimo: agricultural lands
matimela: lost or wayward cattle
matshego: blessings (plural of *sego*)
modimo: god
modumedi (pl: *badumedi*): believer
mokeresete (pl: *bakeresete*): Christian
molefoko (pl: *balefoko*): person of the Word
mong (pl: *beng*): master
morafe (pl: *merafe*): nation, village, kingdom
moroka: rainmaker
moruti (pl: *baruti*): teacher, preacher, senior Christian
mosadi (pl: *basadi*): woman, usually married woman
motlhanka (pl: *batlhanka*): servant
motse (pl: *metse*): village
ngaka (pl: *dingaka*): priest-healers; - *ya, - tsa kgosing*: of the rulership
phalalo: the tithe
phuthego: congregation, gathering; from *go phuthega*: to gather
pula: rain (and Botswana's currency)
sego (pl: *matshego*): blessing, gourd
sekaelo (pl: *dikaelo*): catechumen class, example
sekole (pl: *dikole*): school
Selalelo: Holy Communion
thuto: education, Christianity, literacy, civic knowledge
tumelo: faith, "religion"

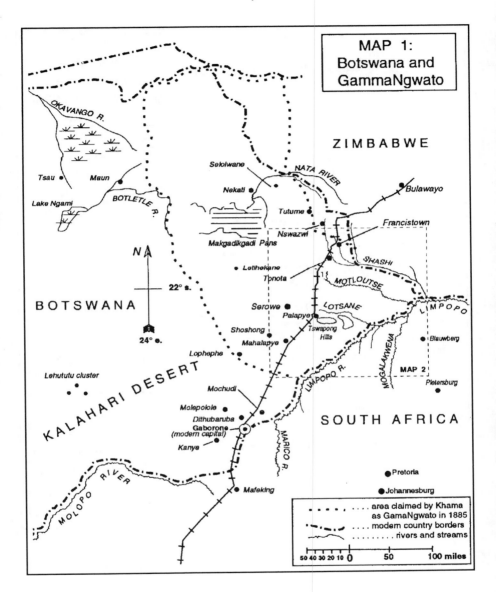

MAP 1:
Botswana and
GammaNgwato

OKAVANGO R.

ZIMBABWE

Tsau   Maun

Lake Ngami

BOTLETLE R.

Selolwane

Nekati

Tutume

NATA RIVER

Bulawayo

Francistown

Nswazwi

Makgadikgadi Pans

SHASHI

N

22° s.

Letlhakane

Tonota

MOTLOUTSE

BOTSWANA

Serowe

LOTSANE

Palapye

LIMPOPO

24° e.

Shoshong

Tswapong
Hills

Blauwberg

Mahalapye

Lophephe

MOGALAKWENA

MAP 2

Lehututu cluster

Pietersburg

Mochudi

Molepolole

Dithubaruba
Gaborone
(modern capital)

Kanye

LIMPOPO R.

MARICO R.

SOUTH AFRICA

KALAHARI DESERT

Pretoria

Johannesburg

MOLOPO RIVER

Mafeking

. . . . . . area claimed by Khama
           as GamaNgwato in 1885
. . . . modern country borders
. . . . rivers and streams

50 40 30 20 10 0   50   100 miles

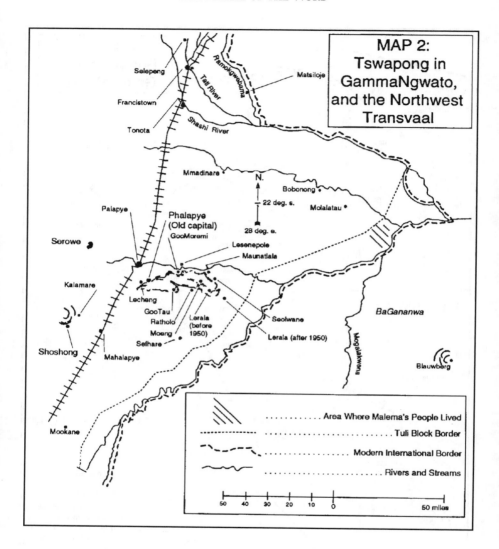

MAP 2: Tswapong in GammaNgwato, and the Northwest Transvaal

INTRODUCTION
HUMAN BEINGS, LANGUAGE,
AND RELIGIOUS CHANGE

Satan, why do you walk with me?
What is my sin?
What is my sin?
What is my sin?
Go from me, Satan![1]

It was a June morning in 1990, in Lerala, a village in the Tswapong Hills of eastern Botswana. I was sitting in front of my house, a veritable oven of concrete roofed with zinc-iron, rare among Lerala's cool red-earth rondavels with their battered thatch. I sat on the low ledge surrounding the house, waiting for Baruteng, my friend and my assistant, who was helping me with my intrusive fieldwork. After he arrived, we went into our routine, sitting together facing the dirt yard and the rising sun, and transcribing the recordings of yesterday's interviews. It fast became midday. When the sun reached a certain height, it drew enough of a slanting shadow under the eave at the side of the house to offer us shade there, and we were about to move. Before we did so, and with the glare of the sun whiting away my view, I heard some children singing in the yard. It sounded like they were repeating the name Satane, or "Satan." Blinking, I turned to Baruteng, and as I commonly did, asked him what was going on.

"Ke bana hela. Ba a tshameka." ("It's just some children. They're playing.") They were singing a skipping song, the one printed above. Their words meant little as they sang, to them or to anybody else. Yet as forgotten sentiments, as signs marking another time, they were interesting to me, the outsider. After more than a year in Botswana, I had never before heard any mention of Satan, and here were girls singing the name.

The village of Lerala grew up on the margins of several different larger political entities in Botswana, all of which interested Christian missionaries more than the village itself. These missionaries, particularly those of the London Mis-

---

[1]   Satane o tsamaya le nna ke eng? / Molato ke eng? / Molato ke eng? / Molato ke eng? / Tswa mo go nna Satane! For a few other skipping rhymes, see J. D. Corkish, "Some Notes on Children's Skipping Rhymes," *Botswana Notes and Records* 3 (1972), 37–39.

sionary Society (LMS), brought Satan with them. Although the LMS surely discouraged people in Botswana from speaking the name *Satane*, in earnest or in jest, it could hardly determine what real Christians in villages said. On the other hand, the LMS, like most missionary societies, assumed that Africans provided a natural focus for Satan's attention, and saw BaTswana as essential sinners. BaTswana were people of wild birth and dark color who, in the order of things, lived like children unknowingly close to evil. A skipping song of real children preserved this implied message, much as such songs preserve archaisms all over the world.

At the same time, the message was altered, divested of its gravity, merely by resounding in the raised voices of playing children. Their naming of Satan took him over. In the song, he was a nuisance one could banish like a wandering dog; in the more complex word games of adults, Satan rarely made an appearance. Tswana Christians rarely dwelled on fire and brimstone.

To draw a rather obvious conclusion, in the general proliferation of pronouncements from missionaries—a discourse, if it can be so called, fraught with contradictions—certain elements proved less attractive to adults than others. Satan became a name on a schoolgirl's lips. Perhaps we might make a list of where other ideas and figures went, too. Such a project would have to take into account that utterances shift their meanings depending on how and where they are uttered. Why, one would need to ask, did missionaries' messages reflect and refract meaning, wind about circuitous paths, and sometimes dissipate into the meter of hopscotch? How did men and women distil the Good News into something good for (some of) them? This is an important question for southern Africans, among whom Christianity and literacy are dual colonial legacies of great depth. It is perhaps most important of all for the subjects and citizens of the Ngwato kingdom.

Exactly what this term "Ngwato" designates, and designated, and when it did so, will be a subject for later discussion. It can be stated now that the Ngwato kingdom, or "GammaNgwato," best translated as the land of Ngwato authority, was at its widest coincident with most of Botswana's Central District, covering a great deal of the arable and grazing land of Botswana. This book treats the history of Christianity in that place, from the beginnings of the kingdom in the 1850s, up to its demise in the late 1940s. Yet I attempt much more than this, nothing less than a social and political history of the making of the kingdom. I approach Christianity as a polymorphous construction built from the practices of actual people, and argue that it cannot be understood apart from the reorganization of politics, gender, and status in GammaNgwato itself.

Overall, the book will develop two linked theses that help structure the emphases in the narrative as a whole. First, it will be shown that an originally tiny "Ngwato" polity wrested a form of ecclesiastic statehood from the expressions and habits propounded by a missionary society, expanded its own tenuous loyalties into a kingdom, and flourished for decades in the environment of British imperialism. Missionaries wished to control the meaning of being a Christian without having to articulate its built-in contradictions. The disharmony within their stance was in part that of any successful ideology: it refused resolution in the interests of mass appeal. In GammaNgwato, the Ngwato king harnessed this feature of Christianity and expanded the kingdom through it. Because the administrative elements of the kingdom comprised but a part of its ultimate field of authority, I have called GammaNgwato at its widest a "realm" and sometimes a "regime" of the Word. This realm constructed its hold on its citizens through their varied participation, as we shall discover. Institutionally, however, it can be seen as having relied on the LMS, and the Church nominally under its care; on the transformed authority of the Ngwato *kgosi*, or Tswana ruler; and on the requirements of British "Indirect Rule."

The literary, legal, and Christian implications of "Word," though all critical, were in fact its facets: it was a single, ineffable thing, an unimpeachable and unknowable pronouncement. Yet this book also envisages the Word as a way people had of beholding the particular, integrative mode of power in the kingdom, which carried Christianity along with it. The Word moved unevenly through the capital's male royalty, among commoners of middling status, and especially, ramified amidst women. And it gave rise to an ideology of loyalty, status, civility, citizenship, and, ideally, a faithful Christianity. The ideology, not only spoken but worn in modes of dress, consumed in teas and soaps, and enacted in other behaviors, is best expressed as *thuto*, which is often glossed simply as "learning," more or less the import it has today. Yet *thuto* was an omnibus of meaning, allowing the interplay of imperial, local, and royal motives. With *thuto*, the Ngwato kingship proliferated and legitimated a realm of authority throughout the territory that the Bechuanaland Protectorate obligingly mapped for it.

The book thus focuses on how African Christians constructed a political realm of power. Secondly, and more extensively, it argues that they succeeded because of a complex social alliance between Ngwato royalty, clergy (missionaries and Tswana preachers), and most of all, Tswana women; and that the administration of the British Protectorate stood behind their efforts. Missionaries wrote for the king and doctored the bodies of his subjects in the capital. From that capital town, the king disbursed a great field of literate, relatively wealthy people, many of them members of the royalist LMS Church; and the king sent teachers and evangelists, men of the Word, to each corner of the kingdom. As women began visibly and audibly to participate in Christian work, they also embodied the efforts of the king to reorder his kingdom's *thuto*, its institutions, its modes of association. They helped contain and direct elements of the changing world as it pervaded his domain. As communicants in both senses, women configured the norms of loyalty in every town and village. Church became a new forum for reproducing the body politic; it permeated the Tswana town's male political space (the *kgotla*), and behind church walls, took on many of the *kgotla*'s integrative functions. The other informal male social arena was the beer-drink; women's grasp of *thuto*, together with royal fiat, attacked and crippled this institution. Women's citizenship, as one may call it, changed the social enactment of gender wherever it took root, upset ethnic and gerontocratic hierarchies, and transformed the meaning of BaNgwato, stretching what was once a minor ethnonym over and across a kingdom.

At the same time, the realm always had many dimensions. Christians were not all the most tractable subjects, either of Ngwato authority or colonial officialdom. By providing a transcendent appeal, Christianity offered a way to oppose the patriarchal or ethnic domination within villages and homesteads, and often benefitted the direct authority of the king, but Christians occasionally fought the kingdom itself. Thus, thuto always threatened to detach from its political source, and militants embraced the language of the regime only to contest its power. When they did, the British bolstered the king's efforts to reassert control over the Word and to reestablish *thuto*'s rooted unity.

The Ngwato realm, a realm of the Word, never stabilized. In a sense, the meaning of the Word itself only crystallized around the conflicts of its beholders. Two critical points emerge here. The first is that Christianity, even the Christianity of a mission, was made and remade in many places; in the centers of the region's constellations of power, and in tiny villages and farmlands. The second is that people's religion and politics only existed in those habituated, yet changing, expressions (meaning perceived actions as well as perceived words) that lay embedded in the region's living languages.[2] Christianity grew through dynastic quarrels, the manner in which the soil was tilled, and the clinical practice of pulling teeth; a kingdom's power lay in Sunday school hymns, evangelical sermons, and the arrangement of church pews.

Religion and Language

The quintessential secularizing tradition of social science has long had trouble coming to terms with the emotions, the inwardness, of what was taken to be religion. Despite the great importance of the historiography of African religions, and moments of crystal lucidity, the field embraces a confused legion of problems. For one, alongside any study of traditional African religions, there is the no longer silent question of whether it makes sense to speak of transcultural "religion" as a heuristic category at all. Because the issue has been complicated by subjecting "tradition" as an analytic term to scrutiny, "traditional religion" is now more of a conundrum than a starting point.[3] In practice, some historians have written of religion as an indivisible aspect of general cultural change and even of social, political, and economic change.[4] Others, and sometimes the same people, have presented religion as something in and of itself, something emotive and spiritual, cathartic, prescriptive, and manipulative, in short as a separate entity. "Religion is a sphere at least that has definable characteristics and without it we are lost," says one author.[5]

Depicting religion is an issue not only about definitions but also about meaning itself, as many have recognized. In the best and clearest attempt at definition,

---

[2]   See Paul Ricoeur, "The Model of the Text: Meaningful Action Considered as a Text," *Social Research* 38 (1971), 529–62, reprinted as Chapter 7 in Ricoeur, *From Text to Action: Essays in Hermeneutics II* (Evanston, IL, 1991).

[3]   "Tradition" has wilted somewhat under harsh light. Although it may yet recover in altered guise, it no longer means a kind of ever-receding priorness, and its commonsense meaning has been subtly inverted by some analysts. See Terence O. Ranger and Eric Hobsbawm, eds., *The Invention of Tradition* (Cambridge, 1983), and Jan Vansina, *Paths In the Rainforests* (Madison, 1990), 257–60.

[4]   For instance, Wyatt MacGaffey, *Religion and Society in Central Africa* (Chicago, 1986); Monica and Godfrey Wilson, *The Analysis of Social Change* (Cambridge, 1945); Karen Fields, *Revival and Rebellion in Central Africa* (Princeton, 1986), and David Lan, *Guns and Rain* (Berkeley, 1985); Wim Van Binsbergen, *Religious Change in Zambia: Exploratory Studies* (London, 1981).

[5]   For instance, Terence Ranger's challenge to the field in, "Religious Movements and Politics in Sub-Saharan Africa," *African Studies Review* 29, 2 (June, 1986), 1–71; Jean Comaroff, "Healing and Cultural Transition: The Tswana of Southern Africa," *Social Science and Medicine* 15B (1981), 367–78; J. D. Y. Peel, "The Pastor and the Babalawo: The Interaction of Religions in 19th c. Yorubaland," *Africa* 60, 3 (1990); and I. M. Lewis, *Ecstatic Religion* (Harmondsworth, 1971). The quote is from E. Bolaji Idowu, *African Traditional Religion, A Definition* (Maryknoll, NY, 1973).

Geertz describes religion carefully as a "system of symbols which acts to . . . establish powerful, pervasive, and long-lasting moods and motivations" in people. He begins filling in the content of his model by looking at "symbol," but he does not hesitate over "system." If religions are really systems that act and explain, then it is also true that one cannot easily ask most of their beneficiaries about them, if only because "religion" is a word in English (and other Latinate languages). Although seemingly trivial, the problem points to a profound epistemological difficulty, because the word and concept "religion" took shape in the late medieval period along a particular branch of Western thought. As Europeans first inspected unfamiliar territory in the east and then overseas, confronting the unsettling specificity of the Catholic faith, they made religion as a universalizing category to show what newly encountered non-Christian people lacked. Hence, if religion is a system of symbols, it is so precisely because it is a system unimaginable to a part of its users—those in whom anthropologists are most interested. What then unifies and integrates the symbolizing phenomena of religion? I would argue that in the end, it is their unreal nature. Whatever else is described by referring to domains of transcendent truths, they assuredly call down the same orbit of terms implied by the vernacular past of the word "religion."[6]

An alternative mode is to begin openly with a reflexive question: What does religion really signify for Western scholars, as a word in common usage? Here one has at least a fuzzy answer, its shape embracing abstractions like faith, hierarchy, doctrines, and ritual. In practice, whether desired or not, such terms set the tone for an inquiry into "religious history" and shadow other more deliberate definitions. They compel a view not just of God and Church, but of African ancestors, "mysterious" rituals and institutions, and reverent demeanors, as religious. Because one cannot refigure the deployment of common words, in a sense such phenomena must be called religious. Clearly, not many Africans at first shared this colloquial version of religion with Europeans. Eventually, if and when such a notion became translatable into African cultures, it did so as part of an historical process. (It did not, for example, simply materialize with the appearance of the Word as written.)[7]

The problem of translation arises most critically in describing a real process of "religious change." The project itself seeks "religious" precedents for present usages. Surely, however, it cannot be supposed that a particular application of an adjective, a descriptive decision, will find some sort of meaningful explanation in forces coming out of the African past. On the other hand, the European act of translation began long ago in southern Africa. At first, there was the assertion that Africans had no religion, properly speaking. Soon enough, however, Europeans began giving names to aspects of southern African behavior they called religious. Looking at BaTswana, for example, what might otherwise be called "invoked ancestors" became demons, and *dingaka* ("priest-healers") aware of the ancestors' presence were termed sorcerers. These are extreme examples of a process in which this book must still partake. Ignoring for a mo-

---

6   Clifford Geertz, "Religion as a Cultural System," Chapter 4 in *The Interpretation of Cultures* (New York, 1973), 90–91 esp. For the encounter producing religion, see J. R. S. Philips, *The Medieval Expansion of Europe* (Oxford, 1988).

7   The changes that Jack Goody suggests in *The Logic of Writing and the Organization of Society* (Cambridge, 1986), if illuminating, often seem too abrupt.

ment the benefits or drawbacks of particular decisions in translation, it is difficult to escape the feeling that the bestowal of names is itself a classical part of colonizing. It was an appropriation, a rearrangement, and a publication of other peoples' meanings, and it was followed by a patent denial of authorship. If the act of translating was acknowledged, it was as a technical process, an exchange of morpheme for morpheme, with context merely a dim backdrop. Rarely was there an awareness of how translation shifts the use of language as it proceeds, and how it subordinates what it touches. Many anthropologists deplore the way their discipline has legitimated this renaming, and recently their work constantly alludes to it—just as once it could only function by denying it.

Denials of colonial power in general were central to the European study of the Other, but nowhere did they sow more seeds of future confusion and paradox than in the study of the Other's religion. Take, for example, the specific question of whether BaTswana before colonialism had "a high God." The question seems strangely enigmatic: How can one know? In this vein, G. C. Oosthuizen devotes an analysis to whether the term *Moya* in independent Churches means "Holy Spirit."[8] These appear to be deep philosophical issues, and perhaps in the end they are. It is also possible, however, that they are "philosophical" matters in the sense that Wittgenstein intends when he tells us that much philosophy is brought about by wrongly formulated questions. In Oosthuizen's question of whether *Moya* means the Holy Spirit, the idea "means" shyly stands in for a simple equivalence. One can then see that "Was *Modimo* God, is *Moya* the Holy Spirit?" are problems in the field of Divinity. For historians, such issues hold little promise of verification, especially since the anthropological school of diffusionism and the Hamitic hypothesis lost their currency. Historians, as opposed to theologians, must avoid treating religious beings as transcultural universals: the "high God" is the questioner's God, the "Spirit" the questioner's Spirit: they are ready-made decisions of translation, not evidence.

Of course there are problems with this approach beyond its avowed atheism. As universals are thrust aside, it becomes easy to lose one's way, and once lost, it is hard to turn back, as signpost after signpost fades from view. The notion of a people having a "cosmology" also begins to look suspect, much like their having a God. As Jack Goody has noted, structuralists envision cosmologies, in their analytic, literate essence, as lying somehow close to "observed" life.[9] The nature of the link between the cosmological image and life, however, is problematic. It commonly leads to the balanced opposition: Was African Christianity "determined by the structure of 'basic' cosmology" already in place, or was it given shape by missionary teachings?[10] The enigmatic

---

[8]   G. C. Oosthuizen, "The Aetiology of Spirit in Southern Africa," in G. C. Oosthuizen *et al.*, eds., *Afro-Christianity: Religion and Healing in Southern Africa* (Lewiston, NY, 1989). If aspects of Oosthuizen's work appear outmoded, this is not to denigrate his thorough scholarship, for instance in his invaluable *The Theology of a South African Messiah: An Analysis of the Hymnal of "The Church of the Nazarites"* (Leiden, 1967).

[9]   Jack Goody, *The Domestication of the Savage Mind* (Cambridge, 1977), Chs. 4 and 5 especially.

[10]   Robin Horton, "On the Rationality of Conversion, Part I," *Africa* XLV, 3 (1975), 220; Richard Gray, "Christianity and Social Change in Africa," *African Affairs* 77, 306 (January, 1978), 98–99. At the time, of course, this debate was quite fresh! The question of traditional ideas persisting is asked eloquently by Bengt Sundkler, *Bantu Prophets in South Africa* [1948] (London, 1961), passim, and more simply by Oosthuizen, who views what he calls "Afro-Christianity" as an intellectual act of syncretism between an ideal faith and real culture. See Oosthuizen, "The Aetiology of Spirit in Southern Africa."

quality of this opposition derives from the incommensurate natures of "teachings" and the diagrammic vision of tradition. Never the twain shall meet.

Perhaps cosmologies are best placed at the level of the individual, to be configured by and for him or her. As cognitive systems, they might act upon other systems, intersect, and persist through time.[11] Hence Terence Ranger wrote, in an influential volume, that in Masasi, Tanzania,

> Men [i.e., people] inhabited a whole series of intermediate "systems" of belief and practice, each combining elements in different ways, and each to be seen not so much in terms of "syncretism" [with the Masasi Christian mission's ideologies] as in terms of its ability to meet the religious, and social and political, needs of individuals.[12]

This focus on what people themselves show through their behavior and expressions is something to be emulated. Africans could not at first encounter "Christianity," an alien ideology. Neither BaNgwato nor any other people are theologians *ex nihilo*: Christianity existed for them in bits and pieces. Still, Ranger's systems are so nebulous as almost to be unnecessary. In their initial meetings with evangelists, BaTswana heard many different kinds of messages, with little backing up those messages except the status of their bearers. Immediately following the translation of the Bible into SeTswana by Robert Moffat and his assistants in 1830–1838, missionaries and African evangelists began to mediate this protean text, refracturing it all over again.[13] The Tswana activity of learning about Christianity and determining its social and political performance was then a series of collective and contradictory acts of creation. People took what was alien into familiar societal roles and frameworks, which they then transformed or exploded. They managed and developed the messy results, and elaborated new needs as old ones were met.

In contrast to the direction of the appropriation I am suggesting, Jean and John Comaroff call the development of notions such as *moruti* (teacher-evangelist) and *modumedi* (Christian), a "commandeering of everyday terms" *by* European hegemonists. Such "subtle acts of appropriation . . . traced the hardening outlines of a symbolic order that was already beginning to cast a shadow over Tswana cultural identity." The symbolic order, which is responsible for the commandeering, was part of the way European power constituted itself. Elsewhere the Comaroffs argue that the Tswana Christian, or *modumedi* (one who "agrees" or believes, they point out), "identifies with an explicit, systematic faith," proffered by missionaries. That faith remained a part of the colonial symbolic order until it was later

---

[11]   Cf. A. R. Radcliffe-Brown, *Structure and Function in Primitive Society* (New York, 1952), 195.

[12]   Terence Ranger, "Missionary Adaptation of African Religious Institutions: The Masasi Case," in Terence Ranger and I. N. Kimambo, *The Historical Study of African Religion* (Berkeley, 1972), 221.

[13]   J. O. Whitehead, *Register of Missionaries* (London, 1877), 44. Examining "the interpretive situation" for how southern Africans read the Bible would surely be an interesting project here; Edward Said, "Opponents, Audiences, Constituencies and Community," in Hal Foster, ed., *The Anti-Aesthetic, Essays on Postmodern Culture* (Port Townsend, Wash., 1983), 142; and Roger Chartier, "Texts, Printing, Readings," in Lynn Hunt, ed., *The New Cultural History* (Berkeley, 1989), 154–75. In this regard, see Lamin Sanneh's notion of translation, as expressed in *Translating the Message: The Missionary Impact on Culture* (Maryknoll, 1990). Sanneh seems to assume a constancy (called Christianity), so long as the Bible is speakable in a new language. What ends up being read and spoken is, *ipso facto*, to be called Christianity; but to see this as the critical concern, one needs to have faith oneself.

reconfigured by African independent Christians. "In the precolonial world, by contrast, 'cosmology' diffused itself through the fabric of social existence."[14]

The dichotomies that emerge here, revolving about the ability to name, ultimately privilege one division: between "the Tswana" and a (many-layered) colonial presence. It is an important dialectic. Yet these very entities must now be queried and disassembled. Certainly the Tswana Christian said her faith was Christianity, and just as certainly she could rarely quantify Tswana cosmology; but it does not follow that she was given the first and "lived through" the second. The opposite may be as true. In the colonial world, "mission" Christianity also was diffused—and existed—through the fabric of social existence. Little girls gave a name to the devil. The problem as I see it is that BaTswana have to be recognized as generating their own conflicts, and so their own history, albeit within an evolving field of behaviors simultaneously beholden to colonial desires. The mutable symbolic order, and especially Christianity, belonged to European interests in somewhat the same way, after all, that Tswana cosmology belongs to the Comaroffs.[15] Just as the social scientist gives a name to, and so brings into being, cosmology, other configurations of power allowed Africans themselves to give a name to aspects of their faith, and at times to the whole of it.

My argument over perspective with the Comaroffs, possible only because I have been greatly enriched by their work, leads me to a generalization. Historical events do not transpire on the margins of change nor as its outward index, but themselves constitute and reconstitute practice, language, "cosmology," and Christianity.[16]

Sacred Power

Up to now, I have mostly been attacking *a priori* definitions of religion in southern Africa, either hidden or manifest.[17] Yet it would be quixotic to claim that this sort of insistent recontextualization must, or should, replace the work of those scholars who divide human experience into the sacred and the profane. As Mircea Eliade writes, one can scarcely imagine "how the human mind could function without the conviction that there is something irreducibly *real* in the world."[18] This is Eliade's notion of the sacred, which touches Geertz as well, and is thus the terrain on which one finds religion. If I understand him, it would seem that a far greater portion of 19th century Tswana life was sacred than contemporary English life. The spread of Christianity in southern Africa, with its relegation of "religion" to behavior tied to Church, may have desacralized culture.[19]

---

[14]   Jean and John L. Comaroff, *Of Revelation and Revolution: Christianity, Colonialism and Consciousness in South Africa*, Vol. I (Chicago, 1991), 218–19, and 152.

[15]   *Ibid.*, and Chapter 6; and Comaroff, *Body of Power*, Chs. 3 and 4. (Or, one might say, the way Tswana law belongs to Isaac Schapera.)

[16]   A point made by David William Cohen, most recently and effectively with E. S. Atieno Odhiambo in *Burying SM: The Politics of Knowledge and the Sociology of Power in Africa* (Portsmouth, NH, 1992).

[17]   Others have made similar points. See, for example, Mary Douglas's chapter on Evans-Pritchard's Nuer Religion, in her *Evans-Pritchard* (London, 1980).

[18]   Mircea Eliade, *The Quest: History and Meaning in Religion* (Chicago, 1969), Preface, quoted in Eliade, *A History of Religious Ideas*, Vol. 1 (trans. W. R. Trask), xii; see also Eliade, *The Sacred and the Profane* (Chicago, 1959), 12.

[19]   Indeed, through this desacralization religion then becomes the thing that may in fact *not* be real.

Gabriel Setiloane has dealt with these issues for BaTswana in enlightening fashion. I have not, and have taken a different approach. This is because, to begin with, the notion of sacred or numinous *power* is vague. Questions of power are central to forthcoming discussions, and unfortunately, despite attempts to qualify and describe a sacred power in Eliadean or Weberian terms, few scholars agree on one set of applications for it.[20] Moreover, this book abjures sacred and profane as an *a priori* division because colonial officials, missionaries, and Ngwato people competed in precisely this domain.[21] That is, they alternately contested, misjudged, and realigned one another's definitions of this supposedly evident duality. Sometimes they forgot about it altogether. As I will show, for both the people who became citizens of GammaNgwato and their colonizers, it was power itself that tended to erase the line between the spiritual and the material.

If power is something reproduced moment by moment, it makes sense to look at the ways its subjects enroll themselves in disciplinary projects so that they participate in making power. The small reordering of gesture, dress, association, speech, and identity that occurred daily in GammaNgwato organized BaTswana both according to European hierarchies and to Ngwato ones, neither set to the exclusion of the other.[22] This book nevertheless rejects some elements of this Foucauldian conception of power as too amorphous. Historians must be careful, as surely not every society underwent a transformation parallel to that of early modern Europe: punitive spectacles and panoptical inspection existed side by side in the concentrically organized Tswana town; authority rested on external rules and even, at times, on the enlistment of subjects in "the establishment of truth."[23] Secondly, it is not nonsense to say that the colonial government or Tswana sovereign "had" power, and that power could be abrogated at the political level. This does not release us from looking at the constituent rivulets of power that informed such authority, but if authority is deprecated in its constituted form, it becomes nonsense to speak of power at all.[24]

Elite Autonomy and Local Autonomy

Most of the recent work on Christianity in Africa has quite justifiably been concerned to explain and chart the explosive growth of independent churches led by Africans in the twentieth century, and it is this literature in which many of

---

[20]   Gabriel Setiloane, *The Image of God Among the Sotho-Tswana* (Rotterdam, 1976). For instance, see the lack of agreement between scholars in the special edition of the *Journal of Ritual Studies* 4, 2 (Summer, 1990), devoted to the matter, and Barbara Holdrege's "Introduction: Towards a Phenomenology of Power," in the same issue.

[21]   Cf. Fields, *Revival and Rebellion*, 197.

[22]   Here I am drawing on my reading of Michel Foucault; see Sources. Other scholars have used Antonio Gramsci's conception of cultural hegemony to similar profit, as do Jean and John L. Comaroff, *Of Revelation and Revolution*, Introduction; and Steven Feierman, *Peasant Intellectuals: Anthropology and History in Tanzania* (Madison, 1990), Introduction.

[23]   Michel Foucault, *Discipline and Punish* (New York, 1979), 184.

[24]   Nancy Hartsock has a similar argument in "Foucault on Power: A Theory for Women?," in Linda J. Nicholson, ed., *Feminism/Postmodernism* (New York, 1990), 168, 170 esp. She draws on Michel Foucault, *Power/Knowledge* (New York, 1980), 83, 85, 97. Thanks to an anonymous reader for this reference.

the debates mentioned here are found. From Bengt Sundkler's pioneering *Bantu Prophets in South Africa* (1948) onward, scholars have discussed perceived and real discrimination in mission churches. To this they have contrasted independent churches, and highlighted their reestablishment of a continuity with elements of culture too often isolated and suppressed by Western missions. In this context, scholars have rightly stressed the independent churches' "instrumental" focus and use of "faith healing," as such practices hark back to the function of indigenous priest-healers. Independent churches have often been viewed as a result of the search for "community," a search especially prevalent when older forms of societal integrity fall apart, as was frequently true in South Africa.[25] Parallels can be found in urban Lusaka or Lagos, and in besieged peasant communities in Zimbabwe or Kenya. The spiritual communities of independent churches offer a place of "belonging," define their members' identities, and anchor social and even economic life in a supportive institution. In their congregations, people create a version of "home" where the ugliness and attitudes that accompany colonial discrimination or economic hardship are screened out. Some scholars have shown how in South Africa, so-called "Zion" churches help people to organize for success, or at least survival, in the outside world. Jean Comaroff has argued that these churches actually oppose the "dominant, neo-colonial social order," and by transforming the signs of subjugation in the symbolism of the body, they protest and even defy their oppression.[26]

The summary above is a simplification of the very ideas that have greatly enabled my thinking. At the same time—and to give now my theoretical discussion above a more pragmatic application—the grounds on which those ideas have been elaborated are rather fragile. Historical reconstructions of missionary churches have been weakly articulated, and the vision of the relations of power within them is correspondingly static. The limited degree of autonomy possessed by the handful of African leaders in mission or independent churches hardly indicates even the most basic features of local congregational life. Women exercised power without official positions. As later chapters illustrate, when individual parishioners changed their affiliation to independent churches—a shift that in the end became common in southern Africa—they did not necessarily redefine their identity or alter their practices. And here generalizing from South Africa north into Botswana compounds the problem. Even on the face of it, the kingdoms of Botswana at the turn of the century had as much in com-

---

[25]   Inter alia—this is not a review of the literature—see the oft-cited J. R. Coan, "The Expansion of Missions of the African Methodist Episcopal Church in South Africa, 1896—1908" (Ph.D. dissertation, Hartford Seminary Foundation, 1961), and also David Barratt, *Schism and Renewal in Africa* (Nairobi, 1968); J. D. Y. Peel, *Aladura: A Religious Movement among the Yoruba* (London, 1968); John Mbiti, *African Religions and Philosophy* (New York, 1969); MacGaffey, *Religion and Society*, and Gabriel Setiloane, *African Theology* (Cape Town, 1986).

[26]   For instance, Martin West, *Bishops and Prophets in a Black City* (Cape Town, 1975); J. P. Kiernan, *The Production and Management of Therapeutic Power within a Zulu City* (Lewiston, 1990); Richard P. Werbner, "The Argument of Images: from Zion to the Wilderness in African Churches," in Wim van Binsbergen and Matthew Schoffeleers, eds., *Theoretical Explorations in African Religion* (London, 1985); Martinus Daneel, *Quest for Belonging: An Introduction to the Study of African Independent Churches* (Gweru, Zimbabwe, 1987); and Jean Comaroff, *Body of Power, Spirit of Resistance* (Chicago, 1985). The quote is from Jean Comaroff, "Bodily Reform as Historical Practice: The Semantics of Resistance in Modern South Africa," *International Journal of Psychology* 20 (1985), 551.

mon with kingdoms in the central and west African savannahs as they had with most besieged African polities in the Cape and Transvaal. Most of all, in order to see who held power under missionary auspices, one must find out what power meant to diverse Africans with diverse motives. It is hoped that this book suggests a productive way to refocus on these questions.

Texts, Human Beings, and Use

Can expression be "read" as a text, and read apart from the intentions of the speakers? The question and its attendant debates, already familiar in some branches of history, are now being heard throughout African studies. Seen as text, discourses become a single level in interpretation, and the material existence of a form or an event becomes irrelevant before its discursive construction.[27] Increasingly, scholars have focused on the component imagery of the European depiction of Africa; increasing attention has also been paid to understanding oral discourses generated by Africans. By treating seriously rural and non-elite Africans' expressions of self, in written and oral media, Westerners might mitigate the sin of writing their history in institutions and with resources from which they are removed.[28]

In the chapters that follow, the focus often will be on Ngwato idioms of expression. Language was the medium in which political and religious allegiences were forged, and it changed constantly. Expressions concerned with good and lawful behavior drew both on previous Ngwato patriarchal expectations and on Christian doctrines; they were redeployed and regenerated in turn by both Christian and nonbelieving subjects of the king. Within them, key tropes "turned" and channelled broadly understood messages.[29] For example, talking about "drinking beer" and "gathering cattle" became figures of speech and were used in new ways to illuminate aspects of Christian and royal messages. Conversely, new phenomena such as text-based teaching, the church bell, and women's hats also became figures, redirecting and altering prior meanings. This is a specific way of saying that, to have larger resonance, expressions about "Christianity" had to find elements of Tswana society and culture to resonate with; and that this resonance was mobile rather than stationary, following the lineaments of power.

---

[27] See Haydon White, *Tropics of Discourse* (Baltimore, 1978), Ch. 11 esp.

[28] Drawing on James Clifford, "Introduction," to James Clifford and George E. Marcus, eds., *Writing Culture: The Poetics and Politics of Ethnography* (Berkeley and London, 1986), 10. For recent work and debate on African orality and history, see David W. Cohen and E. S. Atieno Odhiambo, *Siaya: The Historical Anthropology of an African Landscape* (Athens, Ohio, 1989); Leroy Vail and Landeg White, *Power and the Praise Poem* (Charlottesville, VA, 1991); Belinda Bozzoli, with Mmantho Nkotsoe, *Women of Phokeng* (Portsmouth, NH, 1991); Luise White, "Vampire Priests of Central Africa: African Debates About Labor and Religion in Colonial Northern Zambia," *Comparative Studies in Society and History* 34, 4 (1993), 746–72; and see David Coplan's plea in "Eloquent Knowledge: Lesotho Migrants' Songs and the Anthropology of Experience," *American Ethnologist* 14, 3 (1987), 413, and his *In the Time of Cannibals: Word Music of South Africa's Basotho Migrants* (Chicago, 1994). Finally, Jan Vansina's revised *Oral Tradition as History* (Madison, 1985) is of continued, enduring relevance.

[29] To an extent, every piece of language is a trope. Thus Henry Louis Gates discusses race itself as a sort of trope, and the image of "the talking book" is also a (specific) literary trope in African-American fiction; Henry Louis Gates, *Figures in Black* (Oxford, 1987), xxxii, 249.

With such textual concepts, it is of paramount importance to recognize that tropes and images do not themselves act. Discourse must not obscure historical agency. The usages in Christianity happened at the plows, pens, mouths, and hands of people; of royals, aristocrats, commoners, and foreigners, men and women all.

So how might we approach religious change, seen in its fullest historical context? We have rejected the misreading of translation that decants particular signifiers (thought, religion, cosmology, system) and tracks them backward in time in an imaginary metamorphosis. Alternatively, like the best efforts to date,[30] we might immerse ourselves in recontextualized and contextualizing Tswana usage. In this lies Ludwig Wittgenstein's essential thesis that *meaning resides in use*.[31] Rather than burden this introduction with a discussion of my understanding of Wittgenstein, I hope to do justice to his contribution in the arguments that follow. Throughout them, it will be seen that locating use is an historical project, in that all past usage is initially comprehensible only in its own time and place, and in the translated language of that time and place.[32] The book is therefore unapologetically historical. The concept of the subject (the doer) is granted equal status to text (the done), and in a narrative format. The distrust of narrative in colonial studies is peculiarly a fear of assuming what Ernest Gellner calls a "cultural location," a stationary viewpoint from which to judge and depict subjects. Let us leave ourselves open to the inevitable criticism that comes from judging.[33]

*   *   *   *   *

The body of the book is divided in two parts, corresponding in Part 1 to the center of the regime—its capital town—and in Part 2 to its peripheral villages. Such a division has a dual resonance in Tswana history. First, nineteenth-century BaTswana lived, wed, threshed, celebrated, and debated social and political issues affecting their livelihood in agro-urban towns, in which the kgo*si* or ruler had his administrative and judicial court. The towns moved (and took new names) when their environments began to decay, so usually their arable lands lay nearby. Their cattle posts, on the other hand, might lie some distance away from town. For much of the lean season before the harvest, the greater half of the people lived at these second homes at their posts in the veldt, drinking milk and tending the cattle. The richest senior men of the Ngwato town, most often royals or "aristocrats" (as one might call relations of the king clearly apart from the ruling house), often loaned

---

[30]   Many authors, including Geertz, Peel, and Sundkler, have certainly approached the issue in this vein. See also W. James and D. Johnson, eds., *Vernacular Christianity* (New York, 1988), Introduction.

[31]   As elaborated especially in Wittgenstein, *Philosophical Investigations,* trans. G. E. M. Anscombe (New York, 1958), and additionally in his *On Certainty* (Oxford, 1967) and *Zettel* (Oxford, 1967), both trans. by G. E. M. Anscombe.

[32]   I view decontextualized and etymological word-meanings with, I think, much more caution than do the Comaroffs. For instance, *go sega* certainly signifies the act of severing both sorghum stalks ("to reap," *Body of Power,* 65) and the umbilical cord. But so does the English "to cut"; and you *sega* a melon, also. Hence my stress on usage.

[33]   Ernest Gellner, "The Mightier Pen?" review of Edward Said, *Culture and Imperialism* (London, 1992), in the *Times Literary Supplement*, February 19, 1993.

cattle to people in smaller, distant villages, which then became their *de facto* posts. These villagers tended the beasts, lived off them, and kept a portion of their off-spring; by doing so, they accepted some subservience to their patrons in the capital, who toured the posts at their leisure.

There is a further, equally important, meaning to the division between center and periphery. As the following narrative will show, the territory of the Ngwato kingdom grew well beyond what the loaning of cattle had ever accomplished. Christianity and literacy became the means for the extension of the king's authority to distant villages that had scarcely recognized it before. Therefore, the two parts of the text connote a chronological division as well as a spatial one. Although the time frame of the book is often violated to round things out, Part 1 begins in the 1850s and ends in the 1920s, and Part 2 moves from the early 1900s to the 1940s and a bit beyond. In the 1850s, there was no kingdom aside from a very populous town. In the 1920s, the vast stretch of Central District was spoken of as GammaNgwato.

Part I (The Center of the Kingdom) begins with Chapter 1, which looks at the making of new forms of monarchical authority in the capital town of the BaNgwato. Although rumors and hymns were perhaps the disembodied vanguard of Christianity, it was in the turmoil of the 1850s that the rulers of the northern Tswana mini-states first confronted missionaries. In the context of exploring the conversion to Christianity of the Ngwato prince Khama, an historicized meaning is sought for both the "Word" (*Lefoko*) and "Christian learning" (*thuto*). Critical to the later development of Christianity in the kingdom, Khama headed a "cult of the Word" that found a clear function in the competitive realm of politico-spiritual power. The chapter concludes with a reading of early royal rain-prayers, examples of the expression and constant remaking of the king's authority under the Word of God.

Chapter 2 peruses the careers of the major missionaries in GammaNgwato. Its central section narrates the conflict between the LMS, which sought to place its Ngwato mission in a regional southern African "union" of congregations, and King Khama and the Church, which sought to place all Christians in the Ngwato "District" under the authority of the capital's congregation. The key contest helped define the shape of the realm of the Word by diminishing and coopting the influence of the missionaries, and calling into being a useful "misunderstanding" with the LMS about who had power, and why.

Chapter 3 addresses the ongoing transformation of the ethos of the new teachings (*thuto*) and their changing signification, from 1860 up to about 1920. Demographically, the practice of *thuto* shifted from the men of the cult of the Word to some of the town's commoners, and then from men to women. During this long period, the associations and implications behind *thuto* changed as a product of Ngwato and colonial negotiation. The question of who became a Christian and why was answered more and more broadly. This was only possible, however, because the king and his missionary undertook basic political, economic, and ecclesiastical reforms in the kingdom that are herein related.

Why did the Ngwato Church come to be populated overwhelmingly by women? Chapter 4 depicts the complex social dynamic by which the Ngwato Church was so redefined. Critical to this discussion is the regime's prohibition of "beer," which was configured severally by the motives of the king, for whom beer became a symbol of disloyalty; by women's elite ideology of "temperance"; and by changes in the mode of production and so in the balance of power within the household. It is argued that prohibition, and the prominence of women in the Church, were linked aspects of the way the realm of the Word evolved a coherent and gendered means of power.

Part II (The Periphery of the Realm of the Word) begins with Chapter 5, a transitional chapter that addresses the meaning of the biological body and the social body to BaNgwato, to missionaries, and to Tswana preachers. How and where people "located" pain and wellness indicates much about the social function of Christian congregations. Missionaries often took up the scalpel and forceps, as they were predisposed to a medical role by their apparent similarity to African priest-healers. The surgical medicine of missionaries, with its interior focus, conflicted in a profound way with the Tswana notion of "health," which was a status held in reference to the community at hand: communities the realm intended to fracture and assimilate.

African preachers have been lightly represented in the literature on the missionary spread of Christianity in Africa. Chapter 6 focuses explicitly on the central role of BaTswana in Christianity's growth, and so *ipso facto* on the provision of personnel for the authority of the Ngwato realm of the Word. Drawing on oral research and unexplored correspondence in SeTswana, I argue that African preachers and teachers, *baruti*, were far more important in restructuring "missionary" Christian life than a handful of missionaries. They carried with them a vocabulary and a set of standards that represented the kings's authority, and so reproduced nodes of the kingdom's power all over GammaNgwato.

Power in the realm of the Word flowed in more than one direction at once, and sometimes the discourse of the king was appropriated and found in altered guise to be dangerously seditious. When Christian subjects thus rebelled in GammaNgwato, the kingship tried to force them, and especially the women among them, to submit, and received colonial support in the effort. This is the subject of Chapter 7, which argues that just as the kingdom devalued ethnicity as a mode of identity, substituting *thuto*, it relied on the Bechuanaland Protectorate's primitive understanding of ethnicity to accomplish its state-enforcing aims.

The meaning of larger historical forces within small villages can only be explored through oral field research. Chapter 8 makes a sustained effort to trace the subtle interplay of kin, family politics, and the shifting consciousness defining a village's relationship to Christianity and Ngwato authority, as represented by powerful Ngwato evangelists and King Khama's Church. Building on previous chapters, I explore the associations people made (and make) between authority, the ancestors, Christianity, and colonialism. The king's Word emerges in its most mediated form, still recognizable, yet clearly ripe for fragmenting into the variety of independent churches that arose on the borders of the kingdom after 1950. Following chapter 8 is a conclusion and epilogue drawing together the many arguments of the book and suggesting a comparative framework.

Source Material and Archives

Attention to both words and the Word has been critical from the start of this project, and I have relied as much as possible on retrievable instances of the written language and speech of the Ngwato kingdom itself. Besides becoming much of the subject matter of the book, this material also provided the better part of its narrative content. A venerable methodology in the field of history, even a definitional one,[34] such a use of contemporaneous written expressions still bears remarking in the historiography of Africa. In GammaNgwato, because my starting point is the construction of a new sort of written learning (*thuto*), it was particularly appropriate to seek out written texts generated by elites and common folk. Foremost among them became the Ngwato regime's correspondence (mainly 1880s to 1940s) now housed at the Khama III Memorial Museum in Serowe. (It and all the material discussed here are listed under "Sources" at the end of the book.) Most of the texts are in nonstandardized written SeTswana, and reading them occupied about half my time in Serowe, from December 1988 to June 1989. Michael Crowder and Neil Parsons first consulted some of this material when it was still dispersed in the keeping of the Ngwato royal family, but I believe I am the first historian to have made full use of it. Secondly, in October 1988 and October, November, and December 1989, and for much of the time from October 1990 to January 1991, I worked in British archives and libraries, mainly in the School of Oriental and African Studies in London. There, I combed through all the original London Missionary Society reports, incoming letters and other materials touching GammaNgwato, and I read the primary school readers and lesson-books published for southern African missionaries. I also consulted archives in Selly Oaks College, Birmingham, England, and the Botswana National Archive, in Gaborone, where, in addition to missionaries' writings and government officials' reports, I found old jottings, receipts, Tswana and magistratical court reports, Bible students' personal histories, school reports, and complaints to authorities in SeTswana and English. In Serowe's old LMS church, and in the possession of its resident preacher, I found baptismal and marriage records, *ad hoc* certificates of marriage, a book of minutes of deacons' meetings, and medical books. The LMS's SeTswana Bible and its main hymnbook also were primary written sources.

The other kind of material critical for the making of this book came from people's mouths. I lived in Botswana for over fourteen months, from November 1988 to June 1989, and January through July of 1990, during which my SeTswana improved greatly from its classroom baseline. Besides having innumerable conversations, I listened to, recorded, and transcribed songs, Christian hymns, and over a hundred interviews, both in Serowe in the first half of 1989, and then, most profitably, in the Tswapong Hills, where I lived in the village of Lerala from March into July, 1990. Helping me in this work were "Pro" Nthobatsang, Gabriel Selato, and, in Lerala, Baruteng Onamile. People's personal reminiscences supplied me not only with versions of history, but with examples of Christian practice and linguistic usage, ideology, and attitudes, and, in rural Tswapong, with competing, genealogically enwrapped oral traditions. Such histories reside mostly in the aging voices of illiterate men, and are today disappearing as a genre, to be replaced by other forms of knowledge about the past. This book will be one of them.

---

[34]   E.g., see William H. Dray, *Philosophy of History* (Englewood Cliffs, NJ, 1993), 106.

PART I

THE CENTER OF THE KINGDOM

The first part of this book is mainly concerned with the capital town of the Ngwato kingdom. This town was the center of Ngwato political life and the seat of expanding Ngwato sovereignty. Its location shifted from Shoshong to Phalapye in 1889, and in 1902 from Phalapye to Serowe, where it remains today. At that point new settlers came to Shoshong, adjacent to the old capital's ruins, while along the railway line arose the new town of Palapye—spelled and eventually pronounced a bit differently than Phalapye. Therefore when I mean the center of the kingdom, I will sometimes refer simply to "the Ngwato capital" or "the town" to avoid confusion.

1

Khama III and the Word of God

Before we enter the main body of this narrative, perhaps it is best to step back and ask a few preliminary questions. What can be said about southern Africans in and around the Kalahari Desert before white people came among them? In particular, when was it that people were "first" exposed to what they would later call Christianity? The answer is largely a matter of conjecture.

Rumors

Centuries before they met people of the central and eastern Kalahari in the early 1800s, Christian Europeans had traded with Bantu-speaking peoples in ports off the southeast coast of Africa, established plantations on the Zambezi River, and settled the southern interior of the Cape.[1] News of their presence and, perhaps, their words may well have travelled into the interior ahead of them. African men and women surely talked to one another about the upheavals of the 1810s and 1820s in the Cape and around Delagoa Bay, but even before then, "Mambari" slave traders of mixed race may have brought Portuguese guns, and perhaps ideas, far south of the Zambezi.[2] Although noted in the 1840s, it may have been much earlier that the Kwena (Tswana) chiefship began regularly buying beads from itinerant "yellow men" with long hair. Third-hand news from distant parts might have echoed bits of what coastal evangelists, whether Portuguese, Dutch, or English, were repeating far away. These fragments would have changed their shape quickly, as hearsay tends to do; for any one bit of information, new prefaces and additions

---

[1]   In the early sixteenth century, the late sixteenth century, and the beginning of the eighteenth century, respectively.

[2]   Henry H. Methuen, *Life in the Wilderness, or Wanderings in South Africa* (London, 1846), 146; see also Wilmsen, *Land filled with Flies*, 96. Wilmsen has recently told me of his and James Denbow's suspicions that Islam touched southern African culture before Christianity; after all chicken bones, beads, and pottery from the Indian Ocean trade have been found from the earliest cattle-complex sites in the northern Transvaal. We await their new book. For a related study, see J. Matthew Schoffeleers, *River of Blood: The Genesis of a Martyr Cult in Southern Malawi, c. 1600* (Madison, Wisc., 1992).

3

would cover incongruities, familiar names would "explain" orphaned parts of narrative, and the hard edges of the unknown would smooth over like sea-glass. It is possible that even inland peoples like BaTswana caught some of these fragments, with no marks of their provenance, flowing quietly in the currents of southern Bantu culture.

There is some, but not much, evidence for such early borrowing. It is difficult to know what to make, for instance, of the "Ngoma-Lungundu" (so-called Drum of Mwali) traditions collected in the 1930s by the South African anthropologist van Warmelo. These traditions seem a trifle too much like the biblical Exodus, and in light of van Warmelo's diffusionist biases (he believed in a diaspora of "the Venda," subgroups of whom he explicitly compared to the Jews), one is tempted to ignore them. *Ngoma* was apparently an analogue Ark of the Covenant, from which God spoke; on the other hand, it was also, really, a drum used by a broad spectrum of peoples in southern Africa, displayed and beaten in major ceremonies of renewal and celebration. The most that can be said is that one should not discount the possibility that biblical themes entered the Venda elite's "traditions" of *Ngoma*'s past use before the translation of Exodus into the Venda tongue.[3]

There are also intriguing variants on the widely distributed cosmogonic depiction of a Man-God "creator" of southern African humanity, the One-Legged one. In Hurutshe (Tswana) versions, a certain "Thobega" was a man, an earthly ruler, who was killed and then "became a God." Alternately, as the Transvaal government's 1905 survey has it, the BaHurutshe knew a Deity called "Modimo [God?] Thobega," who made himself known as "Moroa Mogaloatsela"; *Morwa* means son.[4] The missionary William C. Willoughby heard the following tradition in the 1890s, from Hurutshe people in the Marico-Ngotwane River uplands: A boy named Thobega disappeared; later, a man looking for stray cattle found someone who *resembled* the missing boy, but was not him. "I am Thobego[sic]-a-Patshwa Tintibane, the one-legged god," said the stranger/boy. "I lived with you long ago." And he wished people to come hear him utter prophecy.[5] Especially in translation, "boy" establishes only that this Thobega was unmarried. In short, a mimetic copy, an image, of a disappeared shepherd re-emerges as the creator deity. Thus the Thobega tales appear to reflect the Christ story, but clearly the problem is figuring out how old the stories are.

There are other snippets, most tied to the so-called "Transvaal Ndebele," some of whom traced their descent from the southeast coast and to a northward migration dating from the eighteenth century, before the rise of the Zulu kingdom. Re-

---

[3]   Van Warmelo's informant, E. Mudau, supplies a detailed genealogy of his sources, who were mostly elderly non-Christians. See N. J. van Warmelo, ed., *The Copper Miners of Musina and the Early History of the Zoutspansberg* (Pretoria, 1940). For Ngoma in general, see John M. Janzen, *Ngoma: Discourses of Healing in Central and Southern Africa* (Berkeley, 1992). I myself heard *ngoma* drums being used by Tswana-speaking people. They are called *dikgomana* or *dikomana*, and the ceremonies are called *komana*. SePedi-speakers called their similar rites *kgoma*. Janzen evidently missed this example of what he calls the Ngoma discourse (see his pages 36, 76). The shift from "ng-" to "k-" or "kg-" from Nguni languages to Sotho-Tswana is common.

[4]   P. L. Breutz, "Tribes of the Marico District," *Ethnological Publication No. 30* (Pretoria, 1955); and Transvaal Native Affairs Department, *A Short History of the Native Tribes of the Transvaal* (Pretoria, 1905), 11.

[5]   William C. Willoughby, *Nature Worship and Taboo* (Hartford, Conn., 1932), 37. I cannot decifer *mogaloatsela*, although Neil Parsons has told me it may refer to the Portuguese as being "people down the road." *Thobega* has its roots in "broken," as in imperfect.

lated peoples live throughout northern Tswana towns today, and probably have for over two hundred years. They carry sub-identities such as "MaLete," "BaPedi," and "BaGananwa," and are sometimes called Matebele by other BaTswana. While some particulars stand out, like a close parallel to the Jacob and Esau story, it is again mostly impossible to isolate specifically "Christian" elements from hoary traditions at such a great remove.[6] The same caveat certainly applies to less tangible changes in ideas about sin (*molato*), spirit (*mowa*), or a creator figure. Nonetheless, to the question of whether echoes of early coastal tales survived in inland Tswana polities, we might hazard a hesitant yes. Just as importantly, such questions are part of the reason that the historical place of a "traditional" Sotho-Tswana *Modimo*, a distant, "high God," is impossible to fix.[7]

Even close to the time of arrival of evangelists on northern Tswana ground, we are reduced to guesswork. There is a good possiblity that bits of Christian hymns spread faster than the hymnbook itself, moving north from the Cape. Later on, surely, Ngwato people would hear new hymns sung not at the behest of missionaries, but on informal visits to neighboring congregations when fetching water, working in a distant kinswoman's fields, or looking for a meal during the lean season. Not long after hymns, but in many places before the inland advent of missionaries, there came itinerant Christians, some of whom had earlier known European missionaries.[8] It is only for the middle of the nineteenth century that we can begin to speak with more confidence.

Identities

A second preliminary question must be addressed as one begins to examine the more recent past. What were the groupings, ethnic or otherwise, by which people

---

[6]   N. J. van Warmelo, "The Ndebele of J. Kekana," *Ethnological Publication No. 18* (Pretoria, 1950). Some of the same elements also appear in BaKhurutshe traditions, and BaKhurutshe (related to the BaHurutshe, as their name suggests) had prolonged contacts with the BaNgwato. See N. J. van Warmelo, *Transvaal Ndebele Texts, Ethnological Publications Vol. I* (Pretoria, 1930); Vivian Ellenberger, "DiRobaroba Matlhakolatsa ga Masodi-a-Phela," *Transactions of the Royal Society of South Africa* XXV, 1 (1937), 1–72. There seems to be a complex web of identity connecting "MaTebele" in the northern Transvaal with BaLovedu and VaVenda, but the name MaTebele itself probably once connoted mercenary fighter, and may later have been lent to Mzilikazi's distantly related aristocratic followers as "Ndebele." Cf. Julian Cobbing, "The Ndebele State," in J. B. Peires, ed., *Before and After Shaka: Papers in Nguni History* (Grahamstown, S.A., 1981), 166–77, and Neil Parsons, *A New History of Southern Africa* (London, 1982), 44.

[7]   Perhaps *modimo* as a *fons et origo* singular for *badimo*, the ancestors, long existed in some form. Suspicions arise when we read that BaTswana seem to have used the term *Modimo* much as Westerners use the word "God" in expletives when referring to fate. The only truly important function ascribed to *Modimo*, as opposed to *badimo*, was His ultimate control over the heavens and hence, rain. See Isaac Schapera, *Tribal Innovators* (London, 1970), 129, on the difficulty of getting at an "original" conception of *Modimo* after years of evangelism; Setiloane, *Image of God*, 77–86, while interesting, does not convince otherwise. See Janet Hodgson, *The God of the Xhosa* (Cape Town, 1982), for an extended treatment of the subject for the Xhosa, and Henry Callaway's traditions concerning the High God for the Zulu, in *The Religious System of the AmaZulu* (Cape Town, 1970, 2nd printing), 1–99.

[8]   Later in the 1880s, for instance, one such man established regular services in a remote village twenty miles north of Lehuhutu in the Kalahari; LMS SA Journals, 4/17, S.A. 1891–2, letter, 2/ or 27/2/1892 (illeg.). Compare this with the activities of roving Methodists or Ranters in remote English Fens towns of the 1810s, R. W. Ambler, "From Ranters to Chapel Builders," in W. J. Sheils and D. Wood, eds., *Voluntary Religion: Studies in Church History*, Vol. 23 (Worcester, 1986), 319–37.

identified themselves? The terms Kwena, Tswana, Ngwato, and BaNgwato have already been mentioned. What did they mean? In part, in the 1840s, Ngwato meant one of many mobile polities in the eastern Kalahari. At that time, those who considered themselves Ngwato, at least as one of several identities, comprised a population in the mere hundreds. By way of contrast, in 1920 they numbered somewhere near 100,000, and the word Ngwato denoted among other things a fixed territorial regime, ruled through overlapping threads of kinship, monarchical representatives, and village and ecclesiastic notables. Ngwato also came to name the colonial "district," composed mainly of lightly administered magistracies; the district border mapped the furthest extent of the kingdom's authority.

In the mid-nineteenth century, however, Kgatla, Tlokwa, Tlhaping, Kwena, Rolong, Kgatla, Hurutshe, Ngwaketse, and the nascent Tawana state were equally important polities. Those north and west of the Limpopo and Molopo Rivers (see map), as opposed to those lying south of the Molopo, later became part of Botswana and are often treated together as a group, but it was only the later history of their colonial interactions, and cartography, that spread their core ethnonyms across such a broad territory. In the 1840s, "the BaNgwato" are best imagined as one of these small regional identities, all of which changed quickly in the next decade and all of which were multivalent and overlapping.

Bearing in mind that the prefix *Ba-* denotes the plural "people [of]," and *Mo-* the singular "person," identity nevertheless lay first of all within one's village: Ba*Lerala*, Ba*Lophephe*. Often, however, village names were those of patrilineages; hence, *Nswazwi* village, Goo*Moremi* village. Secondly, if we separate the issue, identity lay in patrilineal descent from an ancestor, real or putative: thus BaPedi, BaKaa, BaTalaote, etc. The "Ngwato" lineage at the core of what would become the larger polity of the same name was another example. (Indeed, in this vein, the BaTawana "derive" from the BaNgwato, and, more distantly, the ancestors of the BaNgwato and BaNgwaketse royal lines branched off from the BaKwena.) As the 1850s progressed, another layer of identity was vested in affiliation, and here again we find BaKwena, BaNgwaketse, and BaNgwato—this last as time went on sometimes given as BammaNgwato or BagammaNgwato—naming the spreading political affiliations subordinate to the patrilineal core. In addition, socioeconomic status sometimes merged with descent, producing "ethnicities" like BaKgalagadi, MaTswapong, the caste-like group MaSarwa, and perhaps even "batlhanka" (servants). By the 1860s, one might be a MoKaa and a loyal MoNgwato as well as a Mo*Shoshong*; one might be distantly MoKwena (but not, perhaps, live in a ward designated -*kwena*) and be a MoNgwaketse; one might be a MoTswapong, but be a *motlhanka* among BaPedi. The identities of these examples are not layered in the same ways.

Kalanga is another problematic identity. In GammaNgwato after 1850, it contracted, and after 1900, it lay beneath a great many "BaNgwato," but in the centuries before it had shifted and expanded so as to engulf other identities. Its mother tongue was and is closely related to Shona. MaSarwa, especially in the nineteenth century, spoke *inter alia* a language of the non-Bantu panoply called Khoisan. With these two exceptions, however, no affiliation in what is today southern, central, and eastern Botswana or the northern Cape differed greatly in its language from any other. Inclusively people spoke SeTswana, a language that missionary orthography standardized after breaking off SeSotho from "Sotho-

Tswana," a southern Bantu subfamily.[9] The unity of SeTswana made it easier for a person to change political allegiances. Indeed, the BaNgwato, BaNgwaketse, and BaKwena positively encouraged immigration. In their towns, within a few generations, married men might take their grandfather's political adaptation as their birthright. Even as they thereby raised their status, they proudly wore their shadow identities like invisible epaulets.

Finally, women married in and out of all these groups. Like men, they kept their previous identities half submerged. Unlike men, however, they relied on their husbands to bear their public ethnonyms for them; if and when women bore children, they became known by the personal names of their own first offspring: MmaOaja, MmaKelapile.

It should be clear that no discussion of tribes or ethnic groups would be adequate to such a situation. From the 1830s onwards, and particularly in the 1850s, Tswana polities sacrificed continuity and tradition for warfare, expansion, trade, evangelization, and social transformation. A complex mixture of ivory hunting, cattle rustling, and slave raiding, of the land-hungry migration of mixed-race folk and then *Voortrekkers* into Natal and the Transvaal, and of the consolidation and expansion of regimental Nguni kingdoms—preeminently the Zulu—pressed onto Kalahari BaTswana.[10] As we return to the topic of how the interior people of south-central Africa encountered Christianity, it is just this turbulence that allows us some clarity. For in the midst of the upheavals of the nineteenth century, and as part of them, were literate European men and women, who wrote letters and kept notes.

A fair number of these Europeans wrote about Sekgoma, the Ngwato *kgosi* or ruler, and about Khama, his eldest son (born around 1835). From the 1850s onward, their work began a respectable corpus on Khama. As a result, Khama attained "world-wide prominence" (in Professor Isaac Schapera's words), "as a zealous convert to Christianity" and as a chief steadfastly loyal to Great Britain.[11] The story told by travellers, traders, and hunters, and especially missionaries was surprisingly constant. Especially in the retelling, it took on a compact and stereotyped form. Indeed, the story can be summed up in a few sentences, and it provides a good point of departure for understanding the arguments of this book.

The Missionary Narrative

Khama and his brother Kgamane befriended Europeans, and learned from their civilized ways. The two young men converted to Christianity after they became convinced of its moral rightness and potential for their tribe. Their calling led them to fall out

---

[9]   Tore Janson and Joseph Tsonope, *Birth of a National Language: The History of Setswana* (Gaborone, 1991), 38–40.

[10]   I am alluding to the terms of the lively debate begun by Julian Cobbing in the mid-1980s, expressed in his article, "The Mfecane as Alibi: Thoughts on Dithakong and Mbolompo," *Journal of African History* 29 (1988), 487–519, and addressed and challenged subsequently by Elizabeth Eldredge, Carolyn Hamilton, and a host of other scholars. As many of their contributions are only now reaching publication, I have not attempted to cite them.

[11]   Isaac Schapera, "The Political Organization of the Ngwato of Bechuanaland Protectorate," in Meyer Fortes and E.E. Evans-Pritchard, eds., *African Political Systems* (London, 1940), 56.

with their father, Chief Sekgoma. Circumstances pressed down on them, and they were sorely tempted to compromise their faith. Ultimately Khama had to thrust aside the patriarch, who in the end became a scheming and loathsome figure. After showing himself to be a backslider and an opportunist, Kgamane also had to be pushed away. Khama then assumed the chiefship of an expanding Ngwato domain, which grew into a multi-ethnic but nonetheless still somehow tribal enclave of safe passage, lawful and pleasant demeanors, and reasonably good hunting. As nearly all writers represented him, Khama thenceforth remained a model African, a loyal colonial chief, Christian, steady, and beloved by his people, in implicit contrast to what was called to mind by the word "Zulu." In sum, Khama's ascension itself came out of a struggle between his "Christian spirit and ethic" and Sekgoma's unsavory, depraved, and brutal heathenism: between Africa's dim past and its bright colonial future.[12]

Regional Instability and the Politics of Conversion

There is some truth in this story. Khama did rule in place of his father before it was his time to succeed, and did so in the period of his assimilation and fashioning of his personal Christian faith. The two activities were intimately related, as missionaries and travellers suggested. In contrast to their narrative, however, I will argue that Khama and his allied kinfolk themselves actively constructed just the sort of Christianity that promised political might. Within it, they produced a means to power especially suited to the colonial age coming upon all southern Africa.

To the south of GammaNgwato, Sechele's Kwena capital provided an important first view for Khama of what southern Africa's future might look like. Kgosi (Chief, Ruler) Sechele wore Western clothing even before Dr. David Livingstone, his famous tutor, had set eyes on him. He got Livingstone to baptize him in October of 1848, but he was writing to London gun-makers years before. An autodidact, he not only read and wrote, but collected Western paraphernalia and often put European cuisine on his table. Nonetheless Sechele had to rule his people while under virtual siege. The Boers, Dutch- and Huguenot-descended farmers from the Cape, had formed a factious settlement on his eastern side. The Kwena border with this South African Republic (ZAR) was merely an area of hostile stalemate. One result of this situation was that Sechele received a flood of refugees, and his kingdom grew explosively. In 1852 the Marico division of the ZAR therefore attacked him in force. A minor incident during the war illustrates the fragile role of Christianity within the topsy-turvy frontier of Tswana—Boer relations. During a momentary lull in fighting while negotiations proceeded, a resident African teacher-

---

[12] J. C. Harris, *Khama the Great African Chief* (London, 1922), 67. This is much as the following: Norman Goodall, *A History of the London Missionary Society, 1895–1945* (Oxford, 1954), 244–45; Edwin Lloyd, *Three Great African Chiefs* (London, 1895), 34. Lloyd says much the same in *Report of the London Missionary Society*, No. 91, 1884–1885 (London, 1886), 124. E. W. Smith, *Great Lion of Bechuanaland: The Life and Times of Roger Price, Missionary* (London, 1957), 143–4; D. R. Briggs and J. Wing, *The Harvest and the Hope: The Story of Congregationalism in Southern Africa* (Johannesburg, 1970), 162; and, to a lesser extent, J. Mutero Chirenje, *A History of Northern Botswana* (London, 1977), 94, 97. A notable exception is Anthony Sillery, *John Mackenzie of Bechuanaland, A Study in Humanitarian Imperialism* (Cape Town, 1971), 33–35. See Q. N. Parsons, "The Image of Khama the Great–1868 to 1970," *Botswana Notes and Records* 3 (1971), for a broad treatment of Khama's hagiography.

evangelist (*moruti*) delivered a Sunday sermon; among the audience of BaKwena stood a good number of appreciative Boers. On Monday, however, the Boers made the *moruti* flee for his life as they taunted him for his European clothing. In the final battles, Boers captured and enslaved hundreds of women and children.[13]

Because of these difficulties, Sechele decided to appeal to London; in December of 1852, he made it to Cape Town in an audacious attempt to reach the Queen of England. After failing to arrange an ocean passage, he conceived the idea of blunting any further attacks from the ZAR by hosting a white missionary in his domain. For this purpose, he eventually turned to the ZAR itself, and in July, 1857, he secured five Hermannsburg Society Lutherans: a minister, a schoolmaster, his wife, an artisan, and his wife. They had an unhappy reception from the people, because the BaKwena associated them with the slave-raiding war five years earlier. Sechele himself soon disclaimed responsibility for their presence and began calling them "these Boers." However unpopular the German Lutherans were, their teachings found some purchase. In addition there was at least one practicing Tswana *moruti* in Kweneng,[14] and two after Kgosi Sechele became one himself, preaching to his people in a chapel adorned with the names of his ancestors.[15]

Meanwhile, Robert Moffat, the London Missionary Society missionary, travelled north to visit Mzilikazi of the Ndebele kingdom and win this renowned and feared ruler to Christ. The Ndebele lived in an accretive settler state; their ruling Khumalo lineage had left the Nguni heartland in Natal during the disturbances associated with Shaka's conquests, and Mzilikazi frequently raided surrounding peoples for cattle. In addition to evangelizing the Ndebele, Moffat had a secondary purpose for his intrepid journey. He wanted to try to secure the release of the Ngwato Kgosi Sekgoma's senior brother, who had been held captive after a raid some years earlier. Naively believing his mission to be one of peace, restoring a throne upended by regional warfare, Moffat was actually the tool of a conspiracy between treacherous Ngwato men and Sechele of the BaKwena. Through Moffat, the exiled brother, Macheng, was returned with his partisans to GammaNgwato, where they displaced Sekgoma from the Ngwato *kgotla*. In return for Sechele's crucial support, Macheng diverted part of the expanding north-south wagon trade from Shoshong, his own town, southward to Dithubaruba, the capital town of

---

13   F. Jeff Ramsay, "The Rise and Fall of the Kwena Dynasty of South-Central Botswana, 1820–1940" (Ph.D. dissertation, Boston University, 1991), 100–112, and David Livingstone, *Missionary Correspondence, 1841–1856*, ed. Isaac Schapera (London, 1961), 219. The *moruti*, Mebalwe, was left by Livingstone in 1850. Wilmsen, *Land Filled with Flies*, 98, gives figures for the expansion of Tswana polities, but their precision is quite misleading.

14   Livingstone, *Missionary Travels and Researches*, 135; Livingstone, *Family Letters*, Vol. 2, 48; Moffat, *The Matabele Journals*, 194; Smith, *Great Lion*, 161–64. The *moruti* was probably Paul, a Livingstone assistant (see Livingstone, *Family Letters*, Vol. 1 [London, 1956], 116); this is perhaps the same Paul as Hendrick Paulo who, with Jan Khatlane, was a Lutheran "lay reader" and assistant, but I am not sure. See Ramsay, "Rise and Fall," 80, 114, and Chirenje, *History of Northern Botswana*, 71, 84. The Rev. Schroeder and Herbst, the artisan, both died of fever in Dithubaruba in 1863.

15   Sechele preached after Livingstone had officially "suspended" him from the membership of the Kwena Church; Ramsay, "Rise and Fall," 83ff.; John Mackenzie, *Ten Years North of the Orange River: A Story of Everyday Life and Work among the South African Tribes* (London, 1871), 109.

16   Neil Parsons, "Economic History," 117. The Rev. Hepburn later noted that Macheng drove the trade to the south, but opined that he did so because of his poor skills at regulating it (*Twenty Years*, 117); I am surmising that it was the intended plan. For the Ndebele, see Julian Cobbing, "The Ndebele State," 166–77.

Kweneng.[16] Sekgoma and his royal household then went into exile. They moved to Dithubaruba, in response to a well-timed offer by Sechele.

In the confused Kwena milieu in which they found themselves, the members of the Ngwato royal house entered into their first sustained exposure to Christian ideas and practices. The royal house was prepared for such exposure, since they had experienced the words and actions of Kwena Christians even before the exile. They had long kept up their old genetic ties to the BaKwena through alliances and intermarriages, and their dealings with them must have told them considerably more than the fleeting, if ballyhooed, visits of Dr. Livingstone and Robert Moffat to Kgosi Sekgoma in the early 1840s. Now, in their uncertain refuge in Kweneng, Khama and his mother's family continued to learn about *Lefoko la Modimo*, the Word of God.[17] Khama later recalled,

> we found three German missionaries [*baruti*] . . . and we heard the Word of God from them. There was a school [*sekolo*] at Mokwena. We asked if it would be wrong for us to study [*ithuta*] there; and the *moruti* said, no, study if you want to. Sechele did not like this, but he would not forbid us. So we studied, and we begged that one *moruti* should come with us, when we were called by the BagammaNgwato to return home. So, it was there that we encountered the teaching [*thuto*].[18]

Why did Khama and his brother Kgamane, along with their maternal uncle Mogomotsi, move so fast toward the new teaching? It must be remembered that the newness of *baruti* (evangelists) in their experience meant that there had been little practice in speaking about *baruti* or their habits. There were few given meanings for "*moruti*" beyond the vague "teacher of the Word." On the other hand, there was among southern Africans an ancient social role of ritual expertise, that of the priest-healer or "specialist," in SeTswana, the *ngaka* (plural, *dingaka*). In trying to understand Khama's interest in Christianity, we must place that interest in the culture he lived in. *Ngaka* provided a base upon which to elaborate the emerging differences in the activities of *moruti*.

Dingaka sought to restore a sense of balance and power to their "patients," both within the human community and in the wider social matrix, which included people and their ancestors. *Dingaka* treated both corporeal and extracorporeal problems of a serious nature: one did not go to them for a skinned knee, but one might well do so to safeguard one's integrity in a volatile or dangerous situation. For Khama and his kin, removed from the proximity of their larger community, the teachers of the Word represented an esoteric variation of this field of expertise. Finally, Sekgoma's tolerance for foreign ritual specialists had been broad, and he had long imported eclectic *dingaka* from far away into GammaNgwato during Khama's boyhood. Khama must have accepted the natural diversity of specialists' power at an early age.

---

[17] The first missionary stationed in Shoshong found that Khama and Kgamane already knew how to read. They may also have had copies of Moffat's New Testament. Andrea Mignon, "Ein Vorkolonialer Missionsversuch in Botswana: Eine ethnohistorische Studies zur Geschichte der Hermannsburger Mission bei den Balete/Botswana im 19. Jhd." (Ph.D. dissertation, University of Vienna, 1989), 47–50. Thanks to Ms. Mieke Ziervogel for helping to translate; and Sillery, *John Mackenzie*, 33.

[18] A. J. Wookey, ed., *Dinwao Leha e le Diplolelo kaga Dico tsa Secwana (History of the Bechuana)* (Vryburg, LMS, 1913), 60–61, my trans. Thanks to Isaac Schapera. Khama, presumably making a mistake as he spoke fifty years later, identified one of the Dithubaruba Lutherans as the Rev. Schulenburg.

In learning to apprehend and give name to what was new, BaNgwato first appreciated what was familiar to them, that which they had experience in expressing. The efforts of missionaries and Tswana *baruti* to offer a remedy for "suffering and evil" overlapped with Tswana conceptions of illness and health. Life (*botshelo*) and healing (*go alafa, go fodisa*) had huge fields of meaning, and it makes sense that one of the earliest recorded sermons by a Tswana *moruti* implied that faith in God protected against malaria. As we shall see, nearly all early missionaries to the BaTswana dispensed medicine and visited the ill as part of their ministry, indelibly marking the whole scope of Christian activities with the *ngaka*'s concern with physical and emotional health.[19] A final point is that Khama might initially have spent more time with Tswana *baruti* than with missionaries, even in Sechele's town. Khama later attributed his own faith to "the teaching and example" of a *moruti* named Kgobadi, one of many Christian BaTswana who passed unrecorded through Tswana towns in the 1840s and 1850s. And on his way up to visit Mzilikazi's Ndebele kingdom in August 1857, the Rev. Moffat had left the BaNgwato a *moruti* named Sehunelwe.[20]

Despite parallels with *dingaka*, much distinguished the ritual expertise offered by *baruti* from the start. Like Kgosi Sechele of the BaKwena, the teachers of the Word of God, both dark- and light-skinned, carried signs of association with European traders from the south who were then arriving and even settling in Shoshong.[21] *Baruti* dressed only in cloth, carried "books," and even wore spectacles. In contrast, the Ngwato *kgosi*, Sekgoma, eschewed woven cloth and was the greatest *ngaka* in GammaNgwato, renowned down through the Kalahari and the Transvaal.[22] Khama chose the new path and became a *moLefoko*, a person of the Word.

New Priest-Healers Arrive in the Ngwato Town

Sekgoma and his family returned to his capital town at Shoshong from Kweneng in 1859. With Sechele's unpredictable aid, he drove away Macheng in a violent *coup d'état*. Clearly influenced by Sechele's experience, he then requested his own Hermannsburg Society missionary. During his family's exile, Sekgoma had seen the firearms missionaries were able to secure for Sechele through their Cape trad-

---

[19] James D. Hepburn, *Twenty Years in Khama's Country* (London, 1895), 43–44; Caroline F. Seeley, "The Reaction of the BaTswana to the Practice of Western Medicine" (M.Phil, London School of Economics, 1973), 78, 88ff.; Thomas Tlou, "Khama III—Great Reformer and Innovator," *Botswana Notes and Records* 2 (1970), 99. Tlou asserts that to the rank and file, "*dingaka* and missionaries were species of the same genus."

[20] "Our South African Ally—King Khama," *Pall Mall Gazette* (London), 21 October 1893, also cited in Parsons, *Word of Khama*, 2. None of the early missionaries in Shoshong mention Kgobadi. See "Khobare" in *The Chronicle of the LMS*, 34 (Vol. 5, n.s. 50) (February 1896), 39 (thanks to Neil Parsons for citation); he was the Rev. Ashton's assistant in Dikhatlong, to the south in Kweneng. He died in 1896 at about age eighty. I have not examined the Hermannsburg Missionary archives. Sechele's preacher was "Paul" mentioned above and in Mackenzie, *Ten Years*, 109; Anthony Sillery, *Sechele* (London, 1954), 123; and see J. L. H. Burns and J. Sandilands, *100 Years of Christianity among the Bamangwato* (Lobatsi, Bechuanaland Protectorate, 1962), 24, and Harris, *Khama*, 24.

[21] The establishment of Protectorate government would come later, in 1885.

[22] See also Richard Gray, "Christianity," in Andrew Roberts, ed., *The Cambridge History of Africa*, Vol. 7 (Cambridge, 1986), 147.

ing contacts, as well as the immense security their presence offered. Although he was not personally interested in the Word, Sekgoma had no reason to censure the family of his senior wife Keamogetse when they involved themselves in its teaching, or *thuto*.[23]

Thus Heinrich Schulenburg, a Hanoverian woodcutter, came from Natal alone to Shoshong in July 1859.[24] Khama and Kgamane greeted him and immediately brought him a sheep to slaughter, and Sekgoma received him in a large crowd. The Rev. Schulenburg attracted about thirty children for his morning Bible classes. Some Ngwato men could already read in 1859, and Schulenburg tried to make assistant teachers out of them. His normal services were held outside the *kgotla*, which as a "political" space—and the official center of the town—was reserved for married men. Most of his students were young people and women.[25]

Sekgoma soon had Schulenburg request gunpowder and munitions from the Boers in the ZAR, and good relations obtained between the missionary and the people. On the 15th of April, 1860, Schulenburg baptized Mogomotsi, Khama's young maternal uncle. On the 6th of May, he baptized Khama and Kgamane, only his fifth and sixth such sanctified conversions. In April, 1862, he baptized Gobitsamang Tshukudu, and on the 22nd of May he married her to Khama, in the first such ceremony in Shoshong. In wedding her, Khama rejected Seakametse Pelotona, a young woman with whose family Sekgoma had long before begun the process of Tswana "marriage." Seakametse eventually went to live with another Ngwato man, but Khama may have left her with child.[26]

Schulenburg and all Hermannsburg missionaries in Bechuanaland were dismissed by their Society after a complicated disagreement, although Schulenburg stayed in Shoshong as a local trader. Meanwhile a drought, a famine, and a major smallpox epidemic wracked the town. It was in this inauspicious period that the London Missionary Society (LMS) first placed two permanent missionaries in Shoshong. The Rev. Roger Price and his wife Elizabeth arrived on 1st May, 1862, and the Rev. John Mackenzie and his wife Ellen came in June. They found there a

---

[23]   Smith, *Great Lion*, 165. For Sechele's receiving guns through Livingstone, see David Livingstone, *South African Papers, 1849–1853*, ed. Isaac Schapera (Cape Town, 1974), 43. Kelethokile Raditladi, in BNA S.598/ Z, Simon Ratshosa, "My Book," 90ff., supports this interpretation. There were other reasons Sekgoma, like many Tswana *dikgosi*, favored having a missionary. Robert Moffat's aid to the BaTlhaping in their struggle against the invading BaKololo in 1823 was surely known to him, as the BaKololo had also dispersed his grandfather's small chiefdom around the same time. See Chirenje, *History*, 37; and Neil Parsons, "Settlement in East-Central Botswana, ca. 1800–1920," in *Settlement in Botswana* (Gaborone, 1980), 118.

[24]   Mignon, "Ein Vorkolonialer Missionsversuch," 37, and Parsons, "Khama III," 18.

[25]   Mignon, "Ein Vorkolonialer Missionsversuch," 47. Interview: The Rev. Johane Lenyebe, b. 1917, Serowe, May 1989, pointing out a walled space in old Shoshong used for *thuto*.

[26]   Mignon, "Ein Vorkolonialer Missionsversuch," 48–50; and WCW/795, Copy of Schulenburg register. Although some others may not have been BaNgwato, three of the first four are there recorded as: Serole (4/3/60), Mogomotse Manyeli [sic] (15/4/60), Impedi [Mpedi] Morapedi (15/4/60). Serole was age "17." Ages here were rough. Mogomotsi, if he was the same Mogomotsi (this seems certain from subsequent mentions) as Khama's uncle, was older than the "28" years given for him at his baptism. His son Boetse, Khama's first cousin, was baptized at age "20" on 25/5/62; Khama's brother Seretse, age "18," was baptized 27/4/62. Thanks to Isaac Schapera, private communication, 24/12/90, citing the W. C. Willoughby Papers, and his interviews in the 1930s with Edirilwe Seretse Sekgoma and Rampodu Segolodi Kgama I.

congregation of about twenty people. Both Mackenzie and Khama were twenty-seven years old.[27]

The changeover from Hermannsburgers to the LMS would not at first have seemed momentous to most BaNgwato. The Rev. Schulenburg taught scripture, delivered sermons, and tended the sick; Mackenzie and Price stepped into the same roles.[28] Yet Mackenzie soon sought to increase his stature. Arriving in Shoshong during the heaviest part of the smallpox outbreak, he drew some fluid from a child with "a mild form," and according to his own account, recklessly went to work inoculating Sekgoma's sons and other royalty.[29] He and Price also pulled teeth, treated wounds, and gave out novel but probably useless doses of various chemicals. As he later wrote,

> I began to find that my knowledge of medicine increased my influence with the people. . . . The successful treatment of a case of fever in a near relative of Sekhomé became widely known; and I found that native doctors themselves came to me for advice.[30]

Mackenzie was known simply as "Redman," ostensibly because of his sunburned color, but perhaps also because red connoted ambivalent power and change in an *ngaka*'s practice.[31] His reputation grew. Redman disconcerted people by refusing to divine with pieces of bone like some *dingaka* did, but Sekgoma still sent him patients. One of them submitted to a painful eyewash and went about loudly proclaiming that Redman had "charmed" pure water to make it "powerful."[32]

BaNgwato beheld the missionaries' power in more subtle ways as well. For instance, "Sunday" was defined as a special day because of the ill luck said to fall on those who worked while the Christians were attending to their Word. To non-Christians, Sunday represented a half-understood danger to their health; the "agreers" (*badumedi*) or "Word people" (*baLefoko*) had taken for themselves one day in every seven. By way of contrast, we may note Elizabeth Price's remark to Khama's

---

[27]   It is not clear whether the Hermannsburgers were dismissed for compromising their faith in some way, or because of their resentment over their society's financial strictures. Chirenje, *History of Northern Botswana*, 82–84; Mignon, "Ein Vorkolonialer Missionsversuch," 56–65, 67. Mackenzie advised the LMS to hire Schulenburg, but in an unserious fashion (LMS SA 32/A/3, J. Mackenzie, R. Price and R. Moffat to A. Tidman, 20/2/61). Isaac Schapera, personal communication, 24/12/90, cites Willoughby as reporting twenty baptized converts; but by 1861 Schulenburg said he had baptized only eight people, in a letter to the LMS cited by Chirenje, 83.

[28]   LMS SA 33/B/2, R. Price to A. Tidman, Linokane, 22/2/64. Schulenburg went on to the BaLete in the Transvaal in 1864. He retired in 1872, and wrote that the common beliefs of the BaTswana were "pathetic" and such that "no healthy person could comprehend." Mignon, "Ein Vorkolonialer Missionsversuch," 99, citing H. Schulenburg to T. Harms, 4/7/1872.

[29]   Mackenzie, *Ten Years*, 252–53.

[30]   Ibid. 265–66; 380.

[31]   Una Long, ed., *The Journals of Elizabeth Lees Price* (London, 1956), 99; Mackenzie, *Ten Years*, 111. Redman or "red-person" is Mohibidu; the famed hunter Gordon Cummings was also called by this name. "Whites" in general were initially known as "reds," for their color, but Mohibidu was a proper name for Mackenzie, and this *may* have reflected the meaning of red in SeTswana color-symbology, in that red was associated with change and the Janus-face of power. I will refer to Mackenzie as he was commonly known, Redman, when it seems appropriate. Cf. Anita Jacobson-Widding, *Red-White-Black as a Mode of Thought* (Uppsala, 1979), 179 esp., in revision of Victor Turner; and Harriet Ngubane, *Body and Mind in Zulu Medicine* (London, 1977), 127.

[32]   Mackenzie, *Ten Years*, 265–66. The word for "powerful" Mackenzie uses is *bogale*, or "fierce."

mother when Khama had taken ill. She told the old woman not to worry, since *"nothing ill"* can ever really befall believers, "come life or death."[33]

The prominent *dingaka* of Shoshong were not idle. They sought to broaden their own self-definition to accommodate Price and Mackenzie in their ranks. Their top-ranking peers sat in the central *kgotla* and had their talents put to use by Sekgoma, just like the missionaries. Some of them argued that they "prayed" to God "by the herbs and plants of the field . . . [while] the white men were taught to pray from the books."[34] State-level *dingaka* were quite willing to include novelties like books and prayers in their own professional repertoire. Khama's Christian brother Kgamane insisted only that a missionary not be placed in a junior position to any other *ngaka*.[35] One may assume that at first only the missionaries sought more than this.

At the top of the hierarchy of *dingaka* and missionaries sat Sekgoma himself, the chief *ngaka* of the realm, assisted by his *dingaka tsa kgosing*: the priest-healers of the rulership (*kgosing*). These senior men functioned as public health officials. Their authority extended to the founding and relocating of villages, the demarcation of agricultural lands, and the production of rain to water them. They sanctified seeds, which were then distributed and planted by the people, and they issued ecological prohibitions and directions during the planting season.[36] They guarded the health of the *kgosi's* person and supervised the reproduction of society itself through their direction of *bogwera* and its feminine counterpart, *bojale*, the generational rituals of instruction. In the *bogwera*, which included circumcision, the *dingaka* helped define the role of a mature man and the shape of the social universe expected to form around him. Top *dingaka* exercised these duties in idioms that were at once "spiritual" and "material,"[37] and embodied a field of power inherent to the *kgosi's* authority, feared and respected throughout its realm. Chief among these men under Sekgoma was Pelotona Tidimane, a MoNgwato of royal descent. Pelotona's importance can be judged by the fact that Mackenzie thought him the second- or third-ranking senior man in the town.[38] It is no coincidence that the woman Khama had discarded when he married his Christian wife was Pelotona's daughter.

The development of Christianity thus threatened Pelotona and the *dingaka tsa kgosing* in Khama's actual behavior. As missionaries courted the Ngwato princes, they insisted on the universal exclusivity of Christian "truth," whatever that was. Moreover, Christianity asserted a connection with the central *kgotla* in the metaphors that developed to compose its very expression.[39] We can see this both in the

---

[33] Mackenzie, *Ten Years*, 473; Long, *Journals of Elizabeth Lees Price*, 161; Price's emphasis. For Sunday's enforcement, see Tlou, "Khama III," 99.

[34] Mackenzie, *Ten Years*, 472 (quote), 380.

[35] *Ibid.*, 386; Kgamane told a *ngaka* who had come to change Mackenzie's hearthstones that it was "arrogant presumption . . . to offer your priestly aid to a man like Makense, or to any of his nation."

[36] Mackenzie, *Ten Years*, 381, 385. Cf. Gloria Waite, "Public Health in Precolonial East-Central Africa," *Social Science and Medicine* 24, 3 (1987), 197–208.

[37] See Jean Comaroff, *Body of Power*, 86, for an excellent discussion of *bogwera*, and W. C. Willoughby, "Notes on the Initiation Ceremonies of the Becwana," *Journal of the Royal Anthropological Institute* 39 (1909), 228–45, which she also cites; Thabo Fako discusses the *ngaka's* idioms in this way in his "Historical Processes and African Health Systems: The Case of Botswana" (Ph.D. dissertation, University of Wisconsin—Madison, 1984), 389.

[38] Mackenzie, *Ten Years*, 415–16; Isaac Schapera, *Rainmaking Rites of Tswana Tribes* (Cambridge, 1971), 117.

[39] T. O. Beidelman, *Colonial Evangelism* (Bloomington, Ind., 1982), 14.

imagery in the discourse of the Word, and in the development of the concept *thuto* to connote the ethos of the emerging group, or cult, of the Word.

The Teaching of *Thuto*

A handful of young, aristocratic, and male Christians took reading lessons in the Rev. Price's home. Increasingly Kgosi Sekgoma's presence, as he came looking for medicine or other favors, was deemed a "nuisance."[40] Khama and his scholastically more gifted brother Kgamane would come and "write til evening," scratching their mysterious codes on boxes, planks, or walls.[41] These were lessons in *thuto*, the practice of reading and writing, and the largely scriptural content of the new medium. The tutorials increasingly appeared as an alternative to being trained in the highest arts of the *ngaka*, normally the duty of an heir, and so their centrality represented a momentous decision for Khama. Although literacy itself seemingly excited Kgamane, the same cannot be said for Khama, who according to his nephew, a *moruti*, "was not much of a bible reader." But Redman tied Christianity to the two princes, and actually talked of "the God [*Modimo*] of Khama and Kgamane," implying an opposition with Sekgoma's faith in his ancestors (*badimo*).[42] This was a revolutionary statement during this period of disease and hunger, when Sekgoma and his *dingaka* had failed to relieve the land of the 1862–1863 drought or the smallpox epidemic that afflicted most households in the town.

At the center of the emerging Christian group was Mogomotsi, Khama's young maternal uncle; his sister and Khama's mother, Keamogetse, who attended services (Mrs. Price thought her a "secret" Christian); Kgamane; several other brothers; and Mogomotsi's own immediate family. This was an expanded natal house, a mother's brother/sister's son cabal. Such an enatic alliance typically competed against houses that were related to it through the patriarch or, as in this case, even against the patriarch himself.[43] Khama and Kgamane rejected the possibility of lessons in royal and priestly duties from their father or his own *dingaka tsa kgosing*, like Pelotona; instead, by mastering what became known as *thuto*, "teachings," they constructed an alternative to the mode of power that such lessons would have offered.

Their situation of this new mode in a natal house differed from the normal route. *Bogwera*, the "initiation school" superintended by *dingaka*, broke men away from the confines of their mother's house before ushering them into political society.[44] In contrast, the early baptisms fixed the unity of Khama's natal house,

---

40   Long, *Journals of Elizabeth Lees Price*, 77.

41   *Ibid.*, 145, 155.

42   BNA S.598/Z, Simon Ratshosa, "My Book," Kelethokile Raditladi, 90ff. William D. Mackenzie, *John Mackenzie: South African Missionary and Statesman* (London, 1902), 143–44.

43   In fact such mother's brother–sister's son relationships are often defined through alliances; see Comaroff and Comaroff, "The Management of Marriage in a Tswana Chiefdom," in Eileen Krige and John L. Comaroff, eds., *Essays on African Marriage in Southern Africa* (Cape Town, 1981), 44.

44   W. C. Willoughby, "Notes on the Initiation Ceremonies," reports a myth of *bogwera*'s origin in which a woman devises *bogwera* for her husband. After she initiates him, he confers with his male friends; they too go to be initiated. In the end, they come back and kill her "in the midst of their regiment" formed out of her initiation of them. Taking the new knowledge for themselves, they leave other women to reinvent only a secondary and derivative form of initiation for girls.

and indeed, the Christianity of his paternal half-brothers always remained suspect to him. The modes attending the cult were not all new, however. In 1864
Redman and Price had two district "schools." Price was assisted by Kgamane
and two or three other Christians in his itinerations to the north of Shoshong,
while Redman went with Khama and Mogomotsi to teach at the Phaleng settlement in the west. This teaching duplicated the usual co-supervision of *bogwera*
by initiated adolescents.[45] *Thuto* was evangelistic at its core, and Khama introduced himself to many of his people through it.

The etymology of *thuto* is related to the fact that *baruti* and European missionaries lived within the large central towns of the BaTswana. Outside
Bechuanaland, missionaries in Africa most often set up stations away from indigenous communities, but Tswana demography made this practice unwork-
able. By 1866 Shoshong, the Ngwato capital, had perhaps 20,000 or 30,000 residents. Political allegiance was spatially represented in the ranked, concentric,
and planetary layout of *dikgotla* (the plural of *kgotla*). The term embraced the
residences around each *kgotla* as well, herein called wards. For much of the agricultural year, people lived out on farmlands or even farther away, at the cattle
posts of their household. Their *kgosi* lived much like other prominent household heads, although he received tribute not only from his extended family, but
from the entire town and, when possible, from beyond it.

As missionaries learned SeTswana and as future *baruti* learned about Christianity, they negotiated an evangelical usage of terms reflecting the preeminence
of the town (*motse; morafe* in the restricted sense; or politically, *kgotla*). People
gathered in the town (*go phuthega*) when they had food, after the harvest, to
live their social and political lives as a *morafe*. The town—with its emblem, the
kgotla—was a political invention, and people lived there in season, even when
doing so caused them some economic hardship. In times of true famine, people
"scattered" in search of food. The Christian congregation, called a *phuthego*, therefore coopted the kernel of social life, and located its own opposite in being lost,
alone, and unsatisfied, in living like an animal. The only previous institutional
use of the word *phuthego* appears to have been with reference to the assembly
of people in a *kgotla*.[46]

At the same time, because BaNgwato were agro-pastoralists, evangelists
called on the image of Christ as the "Good Shepherd." One regional *moruti* in
another polity even told surprised Tswana aristocrats that they were sheep.[47]
The gathering of wayward herd animals was both practically and metaphori-
cally linked to the concentration of people, and non-Christians were compa-
rable to *matimela*, lost cattle. Herds of cattle, like the town itself as a social
entity, were shepherded and collected by their male master. Cattle embodied
and cemented human relations in BaTswana's social lives, at the top of which
was the *kgosi*, presiding over both the central kraal for lost cattle and the

---

[45]   Long, *Journals of Elizabeth Lees Price*, 161.

[46]   See, for example, John Iliffe, *The African Poor: A History* (Cambridge, 1987), 79–80; and Chirenje, *History of Northern Botswana*, 206. The South African government was not unaware of these associations in picking the name Bophuthatswana for the Tswana bantustan.

[47]   Diphukwe's sermon of 1877 is the earliest recorded that I have found; it is also cited with regard to malaria, above: Hepburn, *Twenty Years*, 43–44.

kgotla.[48] Using intersecting verbal imagery, Christians built a discourse reflecting their own involvement with the town.

Although some meaning attached to the term *thuto* among BaNgwato in the 1840s, its usage was reconfigured in the 1860s. The lessons that Khama received from the missionaries, and himself taught, the literacy within the lessons, and the text of the Bible itself were all eventually called *thuto*. *Thuto* has come to mean "education," and even "civilization," which points to its close connection with *rutegile*: both words stem from *go ruta*, to teach.[49] Importantly, *rutegile* also meant "civilized" in the sense of *civitas*, being enmeshed in the social and political nexus of the Tswana town, physically represented by the *kgotla*. In addition, the verb *go ruta* quickly began to denote "to preach," and so *thuto* meant sermon, a lesson, or a preaching. By inextricably linking the second set of these meanings with the first, *thuto* encoded a Christian hegemony. Its application to any of the messages of Christian evangelists bonded the association between evangelism and the town. Hence *thuto* held out great promise to Khama; after being raised on a cattle post, he now helped plot *thuto*'s discursive path straight toward the *kgotla*. The power along this vector was the Word of God.[50]

The Word of God

From the start, evangelists, unlike *dingaka*, spoke to Khama and other enquirers about what they called *Lefoko la Modimo*, the "Word of God." This was their primary means of self-identification: preachers of the Word who made people of the Word. How was the concept derived? Clearly missionaries drew the phrase indirectly from the notion expressed by John at the start of his gospel: "In the beginning was the Word, and the Word was with God, and the Word was God" (John 1:1). The "Word" of God was the sign-as-thing-signified, possessed of the ambiguity and inner tension of a core symbol.[51] Not only is the Creation a *speaking* ("And God said . . ." Gen. 1: 3, 6, 11) and a *naming* ("And God called the light Day, and the darkness he called Night," Gen. 1:5), but it is the Incarnation itself: "And the Word was made flesh, and dwelt among us . . ." (John 1:14). Lastly, and perhaps most importantly, the Word reflected the prominence of literacy in the Nonconformist Protestant tradition. Out of these associations, inchoate as they were for

---

48 In the 1860s Kgosi Sekgoma I lent cattle to commoners to bind them to his personal rule. This system, *kgamelo* or "milk pail," was a local adaptation by the Ngwato royal house of the system found throughout southern and central Africa, called in SeTswana *mafisa*. Isaac Schapera, *Handbook of Tswana Law and Custom* (London, 1970), 67ff. and 246ff. For the *kgosi* as shepherd, see Simon Roberts, "Tswana Government and Law in the Time of Seepapitso, 1910–1916," in Richard Roberts and Kristin Mann, eds., *Law in Colonial Africa* (Portsmouth, N.H., 1991), 167–84, and Adam Kuper, "The Kgalagadi *lekgota*," reprinted [from 1971] in A. Kuper, *South Africa and the Anthropologist* (London, 1989); see also Hoyt Alverson, *Mind in the Heart of Darkness* (New Haven, 1978), 124ff. In any Christian shepherd imagery, of course, there is also a direct reference to the language and idioms of the Bible.

49 Comaroff, *Body of Power*, 62.

50 WCW/742, "Khama's own account of himself," in W. C. Willoughby's hand.

51 Simon Prickett, *Words and The Word: Language, Poetics and Biblical Interpretation* (Cambridge, 1986), 164ff.

many missionaries, came the implication that Christians could somehow pattern their selves according to His Word.[52]

What did *Lefoko* ("Word") come to mean in actual Christian usage? It did not mean a piece or part of speech. That sense of "word," in which speech is laid out horizontally, anesthetized, and cut into parts, was alien to *Lefoko*. Even now, in Botswana, one has difficulty asking what a certain "word," as opposed to a thing, means.[53] *Lefoko* was preeminently associated with orality. According to Malcolm Guthrie, its root in Proto-Bantu is **pung*, which connotes the movement of air. Still, here it is wise to note that the root of "spirit" in Hebrew, Latin, and Greek is also "wind" or "breath."[54] That being said, in SeTswana, *go foka* (or *hoka*) today means, among other things, to blow. *Lefoko* was once nearly synonymous with *lentswe*, which is now translated as "voice." "The *kgosi*'s word is law" in SeRolong SeTswana was "*Lentswe la kgosi ke molao,*" and in Solomon Plaatje's collection of proverbs, *lentswe* and *lefoko* are alternatives in, "A word once uttered can never turn back, only a pointed finger can."[55] A common rhetorical device among BaNgwato was and is to say "I have but one *lefoko*, and that is," followed by a perhaps lengthy pronouncement or decision. Whereas "I cannot speak [*bua*]" expressed defeat, "I have no *lefoko*" connoted disapproval or disdain. "Have you no word [*lefoko*]?" Rev. Hepburn asked Sekgoma in 1875, "Are you determined to speak only with guns?" "No, I have no word," Sekgoma replied.[56] *Mafoko* (the plural of *lefoko*) were stronger than *puo*, speech, and meant news or matters of purported significance. Woman spoke as often as men, but the male expectation that they "leave the *mahuku* to men alone" referred to political affairs. *Mafoko* carried weight. When one "acted" with words, as in calls for rain or in healing activity, one certainly used *mafoko*.[57]

---

[52]   See William Hunt, *The Puritan Moment* (Cambridge, 1983), 118.

[53]   See Jack Goody's unhappily titled work, *The Domestication of the Savage Mind* (Cambridge, 1978), esp. 114. The difficulty alluded to is clear from any examination of early SeTswana writing. See also Malcolm Guthrie, "Bantu Word Division," 1–31, in M. Guthrie, *Collected Papers on Bantu Linguistics* (Middlesex, 1970), esp. 6. It may be argued that nouns are spoken to children as words, as when pointing at a dog or chair; but this sort of usage is a hidden copulative, a so-called "ostensive definition."

[54]   Malcom Guthrie, *Comparative Bantu*, 4 vols. (Farnborough, 1967–70), CS 1602 (read "pong"), "fan, winnow." *-fokh*, SeTswana, would then be an old derivation (cf. *hoka*, to blow); Jan Vansina, personal correspondence, 10/11/90. See also Owen Barfield, "The Meaning of 'Literal'," in his *The Rediscovery of Meaning, and Other Essays* (Middletown, Conn., 1977), 32–43; and Owen Barfield, *History, Guilt and Habit* (Middletown, Conn., 1979), 36–48.

[55]   John L. Comaroff and Simon Roberts, "Rules and Rulers: Political Processes in a Tswana Chiefdom," *Man* n.s. 13, 1 (1978), 26; and Solomon Plaatje, *Sechuana Proverbs with Literal Translations and their European Equivalents* (London, 1916), 50, 51, nos. 282, 292.

[56]   Hepburn, *Twenty Years*, 29. See also LMS SA 84/5, "Khama's Jubilee": "A word for my son: I do not know him."

[57]   K III D/30/82, Khama to Tumedisho Maruapula, Serowe, 6/7/12, D/31/75, Khama to Rauwe Sekoko, Serowe, 22/7/13, H/59/"1921," Sekgoma Khama to Khama, Serowe, 16/7/21, and TK Papers A/1 Moses Holonga to Tshekedi Khama, Bokalaka bo Mfhafsha, 5/6/34, for use of the word *mafoko* as "a message or decision of import." Margaret Kinsman, "'Beasts of Burden': The Subordination of Southern Tswana Women, 1800–1840," *Journal of Southern African Studies* 10, 1 (1983), 49, quoting an article in the *Grahamstown Journal* from 1834; Plaatje, *Proverbs*, 55. See Goody, *Domestication*, 46; Seeley, "The Reaction of the BaTswana," 39; and Robin Horton, "African Traditional Thought and Western Science," *Africa* 37 (1967), 50–71, 155–187, for a wider discussion.

Under the missionaries, *lefoko* changed its connotations to embrace literacy and texts, and was associated with *thuto*. Evangelists not only taught reading but linked literacy with the power of *Lefoko* even in the context of healing and health. According to Livingstone, Sekgoma asked him to "change my heart. Give me medicine to change it, for it is proud, proud and angry, angry always." Dr. Livingstone offered him the New Testament, the paradigm of *thuto*.[58] As Jean and John Comaroff remark, "Protestantism was the faith of the book, in that it required the convert to make a self-conscious commitment to 'the word,' that is, to a textualized truth." Another historian even translates "*Batho ba lefoko*" as the classic "People of the Book."[59]

Before and after the introduction of literacy by evangelists, then, the term *lefoko* both denoted an utterance and connoted power and importance in social life. In certain usages, its force and weight grew further as *Lefoko la Modimo* came also to signify literacy. Khama's natal-house alliance learned their *thuto* using the SeTswana Bible, while exiled in Sechele's town. Until the late 1870s, most BaNgwato had only the Bible and then the hymnbook as texts. In the Bible, the Word of God was fundamentally instrumental;[60] in the Bible, one read God's *mafoko* (words), which promised power over one's destiny and, as preached by *baruti*, protection against malign forces in this life. The Gospels, Psalms, and hymns were *mafoko* in every sense, being pronouncements, binding truths, and utterances abetting specific manifestations of God's power.

It was critical that "*Lefoko la Modimo*" entered Ngwato usage when only a tiny minority of BaNgwato, the royal cult of "the Word," were literate.[61] To the non-literate, Christianity-and-literacy—in other words, *thuto*—was confined in its full possession to devotees of this cult. They were then "of the Word" and might derive benefits in health, status, and power from it. The cult and the Word defining it were also tied to the presumed power of missionaries (in their identity as whites and an odd sort of *dingaka*) through shared signification in manners, expression, and clothing.[62] *Lefoko la Modimo* thus implied esoteric, male authority, action upon the world, the half-seen power of the Bible and other texts, and the realm of white people. Khama and other early Ngwato Christians of the cult, for their part, shared this sense of the power of *Lefoko* and found new applications of *mafoko* to their world.

---

[58] Livingstone, *Missionary Correspondence*, 19 (3 July, 1842). Later this story passed into missionary tradition; LMS SA Reports 4/4, E. Lloyd, Shoshong 1912–13.

[59] Comaroff and Comaroff, "Christianity and Colonialism," 14; Chirenje, *History*, 41 (noting LMS SA, 32/A/5, J. Mackenzie to A. Tidman, 27/6/1862); J. T. Brown, *Setswana Dictionary*, "Bible," 357. See also WCW/374, offprint, *The Chronicle of the LMS, Supplement* (n.d.), A. J. Wookey, "Literature for the Bechuana": "the Word of God is becoming the book of the people." For a related discussion, see Comaroff and Comaroff, *Of Revelation and Revolution*, 226–29.

[60] See Isaiah 55.11 for another example. S. J. Tambiah, "The Magical Power of Words," *Man* (n.s.) 3 (1968), 183.

[61] My main objection to Goody's arguments on the effects of literacy is that he does not clarify *where* it is in a liminally literate society that one can find the changes in cognition he describes. See also his *The Logic of Writing and the Organization of Society* (Cambridge, 1986); and Jan Vansina, *Oral Tradition as History* (Madison, 1984), 120–22 and *passim*.

[62] I will take up the theme of dress in my discussion of changing patterns of conversion. According to Mackenzie, in 1860 "less than a half-dozen" BaNgwato wore Western dress, whereas by 1877, when "most young men" studied *thuto*, most people wore Western-type clothing, WCW/795, offprint of J. Mackenzie, "The Bamangwato Mission, A Retrospective," in *The Chronicle of the LMS*, January 1877.

The Cult of the Word Mobilizes and Fights

It was the nature of the cult of the Word as led by Khama and his uncle that it increasingly attracted men as inquirers, most from within the princes' age-regiments.[63] During the 1860s, this cult and its priest-healers, "Redman," Price, and various *baruti*, repeatedly insulted Sekgoma. Puzzled, for a long time the *kgosi* maintained his calm.[64] The first sally against him had in fact been Khama's marriage in 1862 to the daughter of the very senior traitor Tshukudu, who in 1857 had conspired to betray Sekgoma and stormed the *kgotla* in the coup that brought Macheng to power. Once Khama's insulting marriage was accepted, Khama publicly derided his father's rituals in preparation for war with the Ndebele. Then, when Khama left to fight, seasoning his men for later battles, he felt it prudent to store his belongings at the Prices' home rather than in his own house near Sekgoma's *kgotla*.[65] Sekgoma ignored this trend, even weathering Khama's rejection of his gift of cattle taken during the Ndebele skirmishes. At some point, Mackenzie "pleaded" with the *kgosi* to abolish *bogwera*, and "admitted that I wished the people to leave him as priest, [but] to be subject to him as commander." Mackenzie thus explicitly asked the Ngwato ruler to halve his authority according to increasingly invidious distinctions. In 1863 Kgamane prevented his fiancée, whom he personally educated, from attending the *bojale* rites. Moreover, she was none other than the second daughter of Tshukudu. When Khama fell ill that same year, Kgamane stood against his father and insisted that the Rev. Price, rather than the *dingaka tsa kgosing*, minister to his brother. Sekgoma still kept his peace but could not disguise his mounting irritation; he came to Price mainly to have his rifles repaired, a service for which he paid in livestock. Sekgoma's sons now "unwaveringly resist[ed] and reject[ed] his authority" when it interfered with their "duty as Christians," and Sekgoma grew "increasingly bitter" against the missionaries.[66]

The barrage of challenges to Sekgoma culminated in a calculated attack on a central pillar of the *dingaka*'s and the *kgosi*'s authority, the *bogwera*, or male initiation rites. In April 1865, Khama and Kgamane worked to convince three of their brothers to boycott the *bogwera* rites, and all of them refused to accompany their father to the ceremony of their younger brother's age-group.[67] Sekgoma cajoled, became angry and confused, promised his throne to those sons who obeyed him, and then threatened everyone, young and old, who attended classes in *thuto*. The numbers of such students correspondingly shrank to those aristocrats who hitched

[63]   Khama was circumcised in the *bogwera* of around 1850, and Kgamane in 1852; they led the age-regiments emerging from these rites, the MaFolosa and MaTsosa. Parsons, *Word of Khama*, 1; Isaac Schapera, *Handbook of Tswana Law and Custom* (London, 1970), 313.

[64]   Chirenje, *History of Northern Botswana*, 94.

[65]   Mackenzie, *Ten Years*, 362; Long, *Journals of Elizabeth Lees Price*, 127.

[66]   LMS SA Personals, Mackenzie papers, 2/1, J. Mackenzie to A. Tidman, Shoshong, 24/1/1863; Mackenzie, *Ten Years*, 285, 378; Smith, *Great Lion*, 146; Long, *Journals of Elizabeth Lees Price*, 130, 135–36, 143, 156, 160, 162. The *dingaka* probably diagnosed Khama as having *dikgaba* (see Seeley, "Reaction of the Batswana," 39), caused by Sekgoma's bad feelings, as they required the *kgosi* to "bathe."

[67]   Jane Sales, *The Planting of the Churches in South Africa* (Grand Rapids, Mich., 1971), 86; Lloyd, *Three Great African Chiefs*, 36. Lloyd obscures the fact that many Christians in other missions argued that *bogwera* was not unChristian, writing only that "Khamé knew that it would be wrong, for any Christian man, to go to a heathen ceremony, and so he refused."

their fortunes to Khama. Sekgoma intimidated waverers with his stature as supreme *ngaka*, and the missionaries spent a year with no increase in Christian interest "whatsoever." The lines were drawn.[68]

Pelotona Tidimane, the other *dingaka tsa kgosing*, and senior allies of Sekgoma escalated the conflict by insisting that Khama honor his previously arranged marriage to Pelotona's daughter, who had since had children.[69] Khama refused, of course, and again announced his independence in matters "connected with the Word of God." Sekgoma broke down, and made a half-hearted attempt to kill his son. He was thwarted, and his brother-in-law Mogomotsi wrung despairing concessions from him, but the war had only begun.

After the Prices left in 1866, the *dingaka* began to attack Khama with sorcery. Khama wisely avoided techniques proscribed by the missionaries for protecting himself, which would have diluted his stature among them. Such consistency was not shown by all his allies, such as his wife's father, Tshukudu, the senior man with the best reason to fear Pelotona, nor by Khama's non-Christian followers in his age-regiment.[70] According to Mackenzie, they nervously suggested that while the "Word of God no doubt threw its protection" over Christians, it did not safeguard non-believers.[71]

In March, Sekgoma's party occupied Khama and Kgamane's dwellings. Khama's partisans, essentially the cult of the Word (Mackenzie said "almost all my congregation")[72] and its allies from Khama's and Kgamane's age regiments, retreated to the Shoshong Hills. They fell under the command of Khama and Mogomotsi and were helped by several white traders. On the mountainside, they camped, appropriately, behind the ruined walls of the old Hermannsburg church. Opposed to these men were Sekgoma, his senior counsellors, the *dingaka tsa kgosing* and other important *dingaka*, and the bulk of the people. The gravity of the ensuing battle to Pelotona and his peers can hardly be overstated; as *dingaka*, they stood to lose all rank in the kingdom if they were defeated. In his role as Redman, Mackenzie secured permission to preach to Khama's men after a tense service in Sekgoma's *kgotla*; he showed his books to the *kgosi*, who was surrounded by "thirty or forty" of his top *dingaka*, saying, "these are my weapons; you need not fear letting me go."[73] Redman followed this pattern for six Sundays, only hearing later from a girl studying *thuto* that Sekgoma's party had debated whether to kill him. Sekgoma's mother had accused her son of cowardice, pointing out that Redman "visits your sons to strengthen them." Of all Sekgoma's partisans, it was Pelotona Tidimane who most agitated for Redman's immediate assassination; Sekgoma overruled him.[74]

---

68   Mackenzie, *Ten Years*, 413; oral tradition at the turn of the century recognized Khama's provocation of his father: Khama refused to give Sekgoma the royal due of the heart of the slaughtered giraffe, WCW/QNP, Additional Documents (WCW/742).

69   *Ibid.*, 415–16; and Anthony Dachs, *Papers*, 28–29 (J. Mackenzie to A. Tidman, Shoshong, 19/3/1866). Sekgoma knew full well that the LMS's rules prohibited polygamy.

70   He was later assassinated by Sechele; Mackenzie, *Ten Years*, 433.

71   Mackenzie, *Ten Years*, 422.

72   *Ibid*, 425.

73   *Ibid.*, 431; Redman was also thought to have been bringing ammunition to Khama.

74   *Ibid.*, 436.

Eventually Khama and his men bargained for a conditional surrender and returned to the town; Mackenzie wrote of the returning warriors that "they remained steadfast to their principles. One explanation they gave of this new kind of life was, that I was a potent wizard, and had cast my spells upon the young chiefs and the other Christians."[75] This appreciation partly accounts for his freedom of movement; Mackenzie did not write carelessly, and the antecedent to the pronoun "they" embraces Christians as well as non-Christians. Nonetheless, Mackenzie was not only Redman, but also a white, tied by his race and manners to the half-seen might of the south, and so after the battle Sekgoma also renewed his acquaintanceship with him.

In fact the *kgosi* came quickly to dire straits again. During the conflict, he had sent word to Macheng to return to Shoshong as an ally. Macheng finally arrived with a contingent of about 150 Kwena men, but only after Khama had already surrendered. He therefore assumed his place in the *kgotla* with little trouble. Finding life as a subject uncomfortable, Sekgoma fomented a coup that misfired, "repaired to the missionary's house," and then fled the town.[76] Commencing to rule with more caution than he had previously shown, doubtless aware that his earlier despotism had unseated him, Macheng employed Mackenzie as his secretary. His subsequent years as *kgosi* were fairly stable ones.[77]

Mackenzie went on furlough in early 1869, however, and Macheng's situation at once grew awkward, for Mackenzie left Khama and Kgamane in sole charge of the cult of the Word. Between 1869 and 1871, with no missionary present, the cult grew into a sort of "teaching Church." Attendance in schooling and services increased more than ever before, as Khama built the morale of young enquirers and directed them as their prince. More than this, he made his junior brothers deacons, and thereby strengthened the connection between being a Christian and being one of his followers. When Redman/Mackenzie returned from furlough in 1871, with the Rev. James D. Hepburn (who would serve from 1871 to 1892), they met with a warm reception and found a great demand for new Bibles.[78] Unsurprisingly, however, relations between the new Church and Macheng were deteriorating. In 1872 Macheng remarked that "there was another [king] in town—the Word of God; and Macheng was not first in rank, but second."[79]

Finally, in August of that year, Khama and the cult of the Word rose up, young men killed Macheng's Ndebele councillors, and Macheng fled Shoshong. Thus, twelve years after his baptism, Khama ruled GammaNgwato. The experience was

---

[75] *Ibid.,* 451. In this context Mackenzie alludes to their goodness in spite of "all their failings and mistakes."

[76] *Ibid.,* 451.

[77] Macheng had had many partisans in GammaNgwato; J. P. R. Wallis, ed., *The Matebele Mission: A Selection from the Correspondence of John and Emily Moffat and David Livingstone and Others, 1858–1878* (London, 1945), 64, 71; Chirenje, *History of Northern Botswana,* 99; see John Mackenzie, *Day-Dawn in Dark Places* (London, 1883), 257–64, for another description of the war. For Mackenzie as secretary, LMS SA 35/C/2, Kuruman, J. Mackenzie to J. Mullens, 26/1/69; and A. Dachs, *Papers,* 90–93 ("Macen" to Sir P. Wodehouse, Governor of the Cape of Good Hope, Shoshong, 29/3/1868).

[78] Mackenzie then gave Khama and Kgamane a £10 gratuity for their "work." LMS SA Personals/2, J. Mackenzie, Una Long catalogue, 2/10/1871; LMS SA 36/3/C, J. Hepburn to Mullens, Shoshong, 13/9/1871; Hepburn, *Twenty Years,* 186.

[79] Dachs, *Papers of John Mackenzie,* 34 (Mackenzie to Mullens, Shoshong, 2/7/1872).

yet another prelude to his future reign, as the Church had not yet attained the strength or status required to legitimize Khama and his cohorts; but the trend was clear. Khama's brother, Kgamane, turned against him, piously attacking Khama for "allowing" the disenfranchised *dingaka tsa kgosing* to make rain on their own, as if a Christian king must forbid such ceremonies outright. Such a threatening maneuver from within the cult of the Word itself was the first warning that the Word provided a whole vocabulary of power, and so could express interests antithetical to those of the king. In political terms, Khama was hemmed in from both sides, so he effected the return of his disruptive father Sekgoma from exile less than six months after taking power.[80]

The maneuver backfired as a ploy to buy time, because Sekgoma and Kgamane immediately conspired against him. Khama withdrew his partisans from Shoshong to prepare for a decisive onslaught. During the ensuing two years, his faction attained formidable size: both Hepburn and Mackenzie comment that large numbers, even "most," young men then followed the Word of God, and Hepburn called Shoshong a town of "a few old men" during Khama's absence. In fact Christian and non-Christian women and children stayed in Shoshong as neutrals. In 1875 they witnessed a battle about the mission houses and central kraal, again involving a contingent of BaKwena, in which several men died. One child recalled how afterwards "our fathers [walked] over the battlefield picking up the dead and wounded men and taking them to the minister, Rev. Mackenzie."[81] The Christian party won, and Khama again sat in the *kgotla*. This time he stayed there for fifty years. Satisfied with his work, Mackenzie left GammaNgwato shortly afterward to continue his political life. The Rev. Hepburn's first act under Khama's monarchy was to suspend Kgamane from the Church.[82]

---

[80]   Julian Mockford, *Khama King of the Bamangwato* (Oxford, 1931), 66.

[81]   Hepburn, *Twenty Years*, 15, 19, 26–28; Dachs, *Papers of John Mackenzie*, 34 (Mackenzie to Mullens, 2/9/1872); WCW/795, offprint of John Mackenzie, "The Bamangwato Mission, A Retrospective," in *The Chronicle of the LMS* (January 1877); Ramsay, "Rise and Fall," 144; WCW/804 [Confessions], R. K. Mogodi, 3.

[82]   Hepburn, *Twenty Years*, 33. Neil Parsons has argued that Khama's final and successful conquest of GammaNgwato in 1875 had an economic rationale. Macheng spent his formative years among the Ndebele and accelerated his own downfall by applying the Ndebele system of kingly ownership of all cattle. Parsons writes, "it was a similar question of cattle ownership, royal or personal, that led to the final *coup* by Khama against his father in 1875." Neil Parsons, "The Economic History of Khama's Country," 117 and 20n. The source for this (and Briggs and Wing, *The Harvest and the Hope*, 162) is Rev. Hepburn's report that Khama demanded the "cattle and women" of his rebelling party in 1875 (Hepburn, *Twenty Years*, 27–29). Khama later reorganized the rules and practice of cattle-holding to grant unrestricted ownership to the commoners whose borrowed royal cattle had put them in the king's debt; years later he commented that this was because the old system had caused trouble for his father. Schapera, *Tribal Innovators*, 169; Parsons, "Economic History of Khama's Country," 117, noting BNA J.978A, Khama to H.C.

But I read the sources differently. However important disputes over cattle were, they were perennial and do not constitute an explanation. First, according to Hepburn, the cattle and women Khama demanded had only recently been taken in warfare by Sekgoma's partisans as wagons fled to Khama's camp on the Boteti River. Secondly, in his recollection of his father's "trouble," Khama seems to be arguing only that his father acted stingily in loaning cattle *within* the terms of the venerable Ngwato system; as if his temperment alone caused the problem (Parsons, *Image of Khama*, 2–3). Khama did legislate on cattle-holding, but retroactively, and perhaps as late as 1907, while claiming his reforms were much older (K III Papers, B/10/"Lophephe Book," 13/6/07 and 14/6/07, and B/10, *Verbatim Report of the Enquiry Held at Lophepe* [sic], on June 19th, 1907 by Captain Daniel).

We might pause here to ask why Khama went to so much trouble to steal his father's rule. Would it not have come to him soon enough anyway? No, not necessarily. From the early nineteenth century on, the laws of primogeniture in Tswana politics were often violated in practice.[83] Khama's lineage was filled with usurpers. Sekgoma himself had not acceded to power in a "legitimate" way and had murdered three of his own male kinsmen, ostensibly over a difficulty with cattle.[84] Even so, Macheng got in his path. Thus Khama could scarcely have known whether he would become *kgosi*, or whether his succession would be forever delayed. He was forty years old when, after the staccato series of coups just described, he did succeed.

Missionary discourse permeated Khama's methods and aims, and Khama and his generational partisans shaped that discourse as it opened a gate to the *kgotla*. Power formed a critical element in Khama's Christianity, and Christianity lay in the crux of his rule. This was never a stable arrangement, however, and had constantly to be renewed. The early practice of rainmaking illustrates some of the mechanics of its incessant reassertion.

"Rain Falls on All Sides"

As the power of the Word of God deepened and the replacement of the *dingaka tsa kgosing* proceeded, Christians coopted many of their "ritual" practices.[85] Redman agreed first to help devise a Christian version of the ceremony in which the *kgosi* initiated plowing (*letsema*); during Khama's brief reign in 1872, Redman instituted the 33rd, 65th and 100th Psalms as substitutes for "heathen" intonations mentioning the ancestors.[86] In years to come, thousands of people would gather for this annual ceremony. Similarly, a mass prayer of "thanksgiving" replaced the "first fruits" ceremony described by many ethnographies of southern Africans. Previously in this ritual the *kgosi* would "bite" (*go loma*), and anoint himself with, parts of a gourd, the first crop to mature at harvest time. The men identified as belonging to the dominant lineage then tasted the fruit in strict hierarchical order. Connections to this rite and to *letsema* persisted in the general language of Christianity. To sanctify or "bless" the harvest is *go segofatsa*, a word Robert Moffat placed into the vocabularies of generations of Christians by choosing it in his translation of the Beatitudes. The same word is still used to invoke ancestral benevolence in non-Christian agricultural rites. Its root, *sego*, means gourd, the first fruit.[87]

After Christian invocations had been placed in these ceremonies, Redman gloated that "Inasmuch as every chief has a right to choose the nation from whom [*sic*] his son shall receive his doctors or priests, Sekgoma had only exercised [his]

[83] See John L. Comaroff, "Rules and Rulers: Political Processes in a Tswana Chiefdom," *Man*, n.s. 13, 1 (1978), 1–20, for the ethnographic view.

[84] G. E. Nettleton, "BaNgwato," in Isaac Schapera, ed., *Ditirafalo tsa Merafe ya Batswana be Lefatshe la Tshireletso* (SeTswana) (Cape Town, 1954), 78.

[85] Schapera, *Tribal Innovators*, 121–26.

[86] Mackenzie to Mullens, Shoshong, 2/9/1872 in Dachs, *Papers of John Mackenzie*, 39–40.

[87] Gourds and related tubers also remained important in actual cultic practices in the Tswapong Hills. See W. C. Willoughby, *The Soul of the Bantu* (New York, 1928), 226, 248–50; Comaroff, *Body of Power*, 67; J. O. Whitehouse, *Register of Missionaries* (London, 1877), 44.

. . . right in choosing for his son a missionary."[88] It was a choice the *kgosi* and his counsellors regretted. The *dingaka tsa kgosing* never regained their position in the *kgosi's kgotla*, just as Pelotona had feared. The next generation, however, recouped. While Khama opened each morning *kgotla* with Christian prayers, among those standing beside him was Pelotona's son Kuate, a Christian *moruti*.[89] At the same time, missionaries were still expected to act like "doctors or priests," and the Rev. Hepburn soon would remark that his medicine chest was "feared" and "avoided."[90] Half-hidden continuities flowed over abrupt ruptures.

As the making of rain had perhaps been most critical to the power and status of Pelotona and other *dingaka tsa kgosing*, the Christians created a Christian replacement for it, too: prayers. Before Khama's succession, the cult of the Word's rainprayers challenged Sekgoma in particular, since he himself had been a famed rainmaker.[91]

BaTswana assumed a natural mimesis between harmony in human affairs and the harmonizing gift of rain; if the peace of community was threatened, then rain would not fall and the crops would die. In times of drought, human relations were reworked to bring them into hierarchic harmony. Kgosi Sekgoma would look for behavior unbecoming to the season, such as reaping too early or picking unripe fruit, and redouble his attention to his ancestors' seeming wants. In one severe drought (probably that of 1862–1863), Sekgoma led the entire community of royal Ngwato men in slaughtering a black ox on the grave of his great grandfather, roasting it in place, and eating it—in order of seniority from first to last—and beseeched the ancestors to allow rain to fall. If acrimony tainted the *kgotla*, rain techniques had a diminished effect.[92] Now, just as rain rites fell only to royal Ngwato men, rain prayers fell to the mostly royal, male cult of the Word. What Redman, Hepburn, and Khama and his fellow Christians had done was to replace the words of ancestral rituals at the core of the body politic with another Word uttered by the next generation of the same people.

The early Christian prayers were exclusive. The missionary officiated as priest alongside the cult, and from a distance, the mass of the people saw the form and visual signs of past occasions. In 1876, in the aftermath of war and hunger, a drought arrived that led people to demand that Khama publicly produce rain for the people. At the same time, devotees of Mwali, the high God whose cult was based in the Matobo Hills to the north, attempted to establish more of a foothold in Shoshong. Some BaNgwato were already Mwali adherents in the 1850s, as were most of the

---

88 LMS SA Personals 2/5, John Mackenzie, 11 September [1876?]. Mackenzie had an affinity for Tswana customs born of his own childhood memories of life in the Scottish Highlands, *Ten Years*, 137, 387 ("Baal's Fire Day"), etc.

89 WCW/475, R. W. Thompson, *L.M.S. Special Visit to South Africa, August, September and October 1892* (Cape Town, 1893), 7.

90 Quote, WCW/374, offprint, *Chronicle of the London Missionary Society*, February 1878.

91 R. Haydon Lewis, "The Black Man's Gift," *The Chronicle of the London Missionary Society*, Vol. 28 (N.S.) (1920), 286; Schapera, *Rainmaking Rites*, 118–20; W. C. Willoughby, "Notes on the Totemism of the Becwana," *Journal of the Royal Anthropological Institute* 35 (1905), 302–303.

92 WCW/384, W. C. Willoughby, "On the Relations of a Heathen Man to God," 4, reports this as the "last great rain-making ceremony" the BaNgwato held. Schapera, *Rainmaking Rites*, 92, 120, 29–31. For acrimony and drought, a widespread equation, see also Randall Packard, *Chiefship and Cosmology: An Historical Study of Political Competition* (Bloomington, Ind., 1981), 6, 68–70, and Elias C. Mandala, *Work and Control in a Peasant Economy* (Madison, Wis., 1990), 74–75.

expanding resident Kalanga-speaking population.[93] Ironically, Mwali had probably taken advantage of the breaking of Sekgoma's *dingaka tsa kgosing*. Khama and Hepburn consulted, and then mounted a week of rain-prayers to defend against the Mwali resurgence, while also targetting the Ngwato *dingaka* who were still practicing. After a short time, Hepburn saw an approaching storm and exulted, "God has heard our prayers." At the same time, he added an element of folk meteorology to his thanks: "God's hot sun has been making rain for us; and now this last Sunday evening, rain clouds have gathered on the mountain across the valley." A good rain began and astonished everyone by falling for twenty-seven days. The extraordinary soaking weakened Mwali's support, and signalled the end of the other *dingaka*'s rainmaking at the state level.[94] A new public ritual was born.

What were the Christian rain prayers like? In seeking to make rain by means of *mafoko*, in hymns or songs, the Christians adopted existing discursive forms for their activities. In times past, girls went out to sprinkle the borders of agricultural lands, *masimo*, with medicines to create boundaries for rain. They sang as they worked:

> Where is the water, o attractor [of rain],
> A drop of rain water, attractor,
> A drop of rain water?[95]

The "attractor" or puller (*mogoge*) is otherwise unnamed, but was some conduit to the elements above. In the old LMS hymnbook *Dihela*, there are hymns composed for the purpose of praying for rain. They are still used in this way today by the United Congregational Church of Southern Africa or UCCSA, the heir of the LMS in southern Africa, as well as by today's independent churches.

> Rain falls on all sides
> With God's blessings [*matshego*]
> If you make it rain for all,
> Then us, make it rain for us,
> We too, we too.
> And us, make it rain for us,
> We too, we too.
>
> Savior, don't pass us over
> When You are out on Your search;
> Seek us, Keep us
> You, we trust to You,
> To You, to You.[96]

---

[93] W. C. Willoughby, *The Soul of the Bantu* (New York, 1928), 275.

[94] Hepburn, *Twenty Years*, 131–36, 171. Caroline Dennis, "The Role of *Dingaka*," 58. Rainmakers were reduced to adjuncts to the missionaries in this regard; LMS SA Reports 4/4, E. Lloyd, Shoshong 1912–13.

[95] "Metse a kae, mogoge wee, / Tlhokoloa ya metse a pula, mogoge wee, / Tlhokola ya metse a pula?" in Schapera, *Rainmaking Rites*, 86; Schapera's translation. I recorded a metrically similar song in Tswapong: "Morokola metse a pula, mogoge / Gogo a-weee, mogoge / Goga a-weee" (repeat). Interview: Senior women singing, 19 May 1990, GooMoremi. The translation of *morokola* was given to me vaguely as "a sort of bird," and may be similar to the lightning bird that Callaway's Zulu informants discussed, Callaway, *Religious System of the AmaZulu*, 381–33; 407.

[96] J. Mackenzie, "Pula ea na ntlheng cotlhe," No. 195, first and third verses, *Dihela*, 175; my translation. Despite spelling changes, these are the same hymns as in the original *Dihela Tsa Tihelo ea Modimo* (Kuruman, South Africa, 1894), compiled by "Robert Moffat [and] other teachers," i.e., *baruti*.

This hymn asserts the universal saliance of God, as opposed to the limited domain of lineage ancestors, while at once suggesting the communality of Church members. The root of the word for "blessings" is, as we saw, *sego* or calabash. Jesus is thus enlisted in the dispensing of fertility and abundance as the essence of his favor.

To state the most general point, in Christian as well as non-Christian thought, asking for rain was felt to influence its presence. Although even (perhaps) non-Christians felt that rain came from some power Above, early Ngwato Christians continued to use ritual and "prayer" in vitally pragmatic ways.[97] Perhaps "rain falls on all sides" was a universalist rebuke to the hubris of specifying the rain's parameters, but, if so, it was a weak one given the whole of the prayer ("seek us"). Here is another:

Give us heavy showers
Pour out raindrops;
Good rain,
That is very gentle, not like spears;
A washing of the earth;
A female, heavy rain
In this time.[98]

Typical of many hymns, this one used SeTswana expressions to render its message clearly. Rainmaking as a whole is shown here to be a gendered activity. The *moroka* (rainmaking *ngaka*) and the prayer-leader were men, and evoked a male "seeding" or provocation of rain. While the performance of the *moroka* was half-concealed, it was an activity undertaken for the political community, and Christian rain-prayers were a publicly generative ceremony. Both rain rituals and prayers thus fell under male authority, although men in both cases were often implored and manipulated by greater numbers of married women (*basadi*). In contrast, married women in southern Africa had long been most responsible for actual production, especially in areas where the hunt had dwindled in importance.[99] The association of *basadi* with arable farming was tied to their control over reproduction, a hoary sociobiological symbolism to be sure. The language of the hymn reflects these permutations.

Almost certainly, their authors (in these cases, John Mackenzie and Edwin Lloyd, a missionary in Shoshong from 1884 to 1892) derived the hymns in part from their prayers with Ngwato Christians. Some of these hymns came from the mouths of Khama and his fellows in the 1860s and 1870s. In the verse following the one above, Lloyd uses baptism as a metaphor to link Christianity with rain, and by implication with the Tswana notion of "cooling" (*go hodisa*) associated with water, healing, and stability:

And all these hearts, every one,
Are completely dry,
    But through sinning;
Wet [or baptize, *kolobetsa*] the heart
With Your spirit,

---

[97] As opposed to Robin Horton, "African Conversion," *Africa* 41, 2 (1971), 85–108.

[98] E. Lloyd, *"Pula,"* No. 379, second verse, *Dihela* (Cape Town, 1973), 347; my translation. See also J. Mackenzie, "Me thobo e tla nna en[g]?," No. 328, *Dihela*, 301, in this regard. Cf. Steven Feierman, *Peasant Intellectuals* (Madison, 1990), 81.

[99] On hunting, see John M. Mackenzie, "The Natural World and the Popular Consciousness in Southern Africa: The European Appropriation of Nature," in Preben Kaarsholm, ed., *Cultural Struggle and Development in Southern Africa* (London and Portsmouth, NH, 1991), 14 esp.

Khama with his chief advisers, 1882. Unknown photographer. Reproduced courtesy of the Council for World Mission, London.

Hear this request
Our Father.[100]

From what we know of Lloyd, he surely did not develop such metaphors himself. Nonetheless, it was by this means that the missionaries, half in and half out of their roles as *dingaka*, insinuated new ideas into older discourses. From Khama's point of view, rainmaking was a way for him and his Christian allies both to channel missionary behavior and to constitute their own authority in profound ways.[101]

Postscript to 1875

Old Sekgoma lived on until 1883, a Lear-like figure in somewhat demented condition. Kgamane, himself bitter, remarked that Khama had left his father "with nothing, not even a dog."[102] After all, Sekgoma was deposed by his son, under the righteous gaze of the bearers of values and ideas he never mastered: in the West, such is the stuff of tragedy.

A final point is critical to understanding Khama's conversion. Any attempt to locate his true religious feeling as opposed to his "cynical" motives founders on an erroneous assumption: that Khama from the start viewed *thuto* and *Lefoko* as demarcating a separate sphere for human activity, with its own *raisons d'être*. This was not the case. Unlike his father Sekgoma, Moshoeshoe of Lesotho, Sechele of Kweneng, or other Sotho-Tswana rulers, Khama never faced the problem of whether to "become" a Christian while in power—when Sekgoma had, he told his missionary, "Sir, you do not know what you are asking."[103] Inseparable from the development of the cult of the Word into a Church was the fact that the cult served the ambitions of the heir. Such usage fairly defines Khama's "conversion."

Managing and restraining the Church itself, however, was another problem altogether. Ngwato Christians wished to make the Church their own, but missionaries often had the same notion. We now turn to their conflict.

---

[100] E. Lloyd, *Dihela*, 379. Dry, or *omile*, is used to describe the state of the country in the first verse, so it has associations with heat. See Comaroff, *Body of Power*, 68, 200.

[101] One of Schapera's royal informants told him in 1935 that "Khama was blessed by God, and whenever he prayed for rain in the morning, it was sure to fall that very afternoon or evening," Schapera, *Rainmaking Rites*, 140. For more on the meaning of "rain" as a sort of trope, see my "When Rain Falls: Rainmaking and Community in a Tswana Village, ca. 1870 to Recent Times," *International Journal of African Historical Studies* 26, 1 (1993), 1–29.

[102] Hepburn, *Twenty Tears*, 237. WCW/810, W. C. Willoughby, "Notes taken on Letters to my Wife," 15/2/1898. BNA S.1/13, Notes on Kgotla Meeting (29/7/1898), Kgamane Sekgoma. Kgamane and Khama were estranged at the time of the quote, and Kgamane remained closer to his father than did Khama after the latter took power.

[103] Even Sechele, the *kgosi* of the BaKwena, was a "backslider" in the eyes of the LMS, and Sechele knew the Bible well. Moshoeshoe hesitated to fully embrace Christianity, since it entailed the political and emotional ramifications of relinquishing all wives but one: Leonard Thompson, *Survival in Two Worlds—Moshweshwe of Lesotho, 1786–1870* (Oxford, 1970), 92, 97–98. Quote: Mackenzie, *Ten Years*, 468; Mackenzie gives this as "*Monare*, you do not know what you say," followed by Sekgoma's oft-quoted comparison of conversion with combatting the Ndebele "single-handedly." My version is more colloquial and probably to the point, from the likely "Ga o itse se o se buang/botsang."

2

Missionary Labors: The Struggle to Master the Church

In subsequent chapters we are concerned with the meaning of the behaviors through which the nexus of the Ngwato Church and state grew. But it is just as necessary, and just as intriguing, to look into the history of how Europeans and Africans produced an environment in which behavior might be given meaning. Who and what determined that one set of actions and expressions would be accepted over another, as good, or Christian, or lawful? What allowed missionaries to be powerful or kept them weak? Who molded the discourse of the Word as it developed? This chapter addresses these questions. The answers are to be found not only in the substance of the hegemonic discourse of a looming Europe, transforming all it touched, but more centrally in the *substantive* relations between people who depended on one another for their livelihoods and daily routines, cagily stealing glances at exterior powers, but living on African soil.

If the LMS directors believed that the BaNgwato in the 1880s and after were subjects of their stewardship, residing in one of several LMS "districts," for the people of GammaNgwato, the missionaries' Society largely remained an epistolary entity. In contrast to the LMS, the Ngwato Church, as I am calling it,[1] was an indigenous institution. Yet all through its history the Ngwato monarchy and representatives of the LMS contested its management. At the center of the conflict lay two different views of the nature of the Christian community, different enough to make ambiguity and "misunderstanding" absolutely necessary for the maintenance of the LMS's presence in GammaNgwato.

The following narration is built around the careers of GammaNgwato's main missionaries after Mackenzie; most cycles of conflict ended in the expulsion of one or more of them. An essential argument emerges from their experiences: whether missionaries attached themselves to the king, sought to reform the Church, or op-

---

[1]   In GammaNgwato, if it became necessary to distinguish the Ngwato Church from others, it was known popularly as both Kereke ya ga Khama (Khama's Church) and Lontoni (after "London").

posed the basis of the kingdom's rule, they were suffered only insofar as their presence strengthened the logic of power in the Ngwato realm of the Word.

The Peril of Intimacy with the King

The Rev. James Hepburn came to Shoshong in 1871 at the close of Mackenzie's furlough. Although Hepburn was a fervent proselytizer, in twenty years he met with scant success in broadening the membership of the Church. He remained with the BaNgwato until their capital shifted to Phalapye in 1889, and then left Phalapye under a cloud of dashed hopes in 1892.

This did not mean that Christian rituals lacked participants. Attendance at the seasonal prayers in the *kgotla* was massive. Available figures date from a later period, but they are suggestive for the 1880s on. The *letsema*, the king's announcement of the plowing season, drew about 10,000 people as a Christian service in the *kgotla* in 1900; around 7,000 attended the annual plowing service on the last Sunday in October 1907, and 8,000 came to the rain-prayers in 1908; large crowds followed suit in major villages outside the capital that by 1900 owed allegiance to the king. In the 1870s and 1880s, Hepburn found men and women making an extra effort to attend Sunday prayers during the weeks of planting. Likewise, Khama's annual permission to reap was given within the services of a heavily attended national prayer in the *kgotla*.[2] In cycles of danger, celebration, or adversity, townspeople flocked to the Church just as they would have attended another public assembly; but for a long time, this marked the extent of most people's interest.

Almost as a symptom of his inability to broaden the basis of the Church, Hepburn retreated into his role as Khama's state adviser and priest-healer. Anchoring his authority in the Ngwato kingship, he correspondingly decreased his dealings with the European world and seldom wrote to the directors of the Society. In 1877 he noted that Khama and his brothers practiced the "laying on [of] hands" to bless *baruti* (teacher/evangelists) sent by the Church outside the capital. The LMS placed this bit of intelligence in their *Chronicle*, unconcerned that to lay on hands, "*go baya diatla*," literally meant "to ordain" in SeTswana (borrowing from Congregational usage), a responsibility officially denied to Khama. In 1880 Hepburn wrote to the LMS to complain of insufficient funding in justifying his reliance on Ngwato contributions, and asked only not to be "hindered" by the directors. As part of his withdrawal into Ngwato society, Hepburn acted as an intermediary for Khama, in *his* dealings with both the wider world.[3]

Helping Hepburn's retreat into Ngwato politics was the fact that the 1880s were a critical period for Khama. Once again Boer settlers, this time from the northern Cape,

2   Schapera, *Tribal Innovators*, 121, citing W. C. Willoughby to LMS, 4/10/00; LMS SA 68/4, A. Jennings to R. W. Thompson, Serowe, 29/10/07; 69/4, E. Lloyd to Cousins, Shoshong, 9/10/08 and 9/11/08; 71/3, E. Sharp to Thompson, Serowe, 29/7/09.

3   James Hepburn, *The Chronicle of the LMS*, Vol. 20 (1882), 73; Idem, *Twenty Years in Khama's Country*, 169; K III Papers, A/2/47, E. Farrell to J. Hepburn, Crocodile River, 21/11/88; and A/2/64, Goold-Adams to Khama, 22/11/1889; A/1/13, T. Shepstone to Khama, 9/12/1879, asserting (in English) that Sekhukhune and Cetwayo were destroyed because they "treated the Queen as an enemy"; A/1/10, T. Shepstone to J. Hepburn, 31/12/1878, asking for information; C/13/20, [B.S.A.C. Police lieutenant] to J. Hepburn, ca. 1890, and A/3, J. Willoughby (B.S.A.C. Police) to J. Hepburn, Matloutsie, 25/6/90.

threatened Tswana rulers. The British government used John Mackenzie's services to produce a protectorate south of the Molopo River in 1884. Fearing a German-Boer alliance through the Kalahari, the British then sent an expedition under Charles Warren to secure agreements from Khama and other *dikgosi* to extend the border northward a year later. The result was a "Crown Colony" of territory, British Bechuanaland, south of the Molopo (about 26° S. latitude); and north of this river, the Bechuanaland *Protectorate*, extending up to 22°. Such a mapping prepared the way for new forms of bounded control over a vast area. Open and unmarked, flat, the Protectorate's savannahs were to be woven through not only with resident magistrates, district officers, and merchants, but also with headmen, *baruti*, and Christians who had to be put in the service of the *kgosi*—now no longer a *kgosi* but a king. Eventually the Church would play a pivotal role in "imagining" this new community, and it is in this context that Khama's subsequent struggles with his missionaries must be seen.[4]

Hepburn went on furlough in 1884, and emulated Mackenzie by placing the Church entirely in Khama's hands. Upon his return, accompanied by the Rev. Edwin Lloyd, he saw that the Church had contracted to a "very little" group of Christians, embroiled in political intrigue. In 1886 Hepburn turned to the Tawana state in Ngamiland, in the northwest of the Protectorate. There he had earlier attempted to establish a branch of the Ngwato Church under Khama's enthusiastic sponsorship, but on this second visit, his efforts came to nothing (as discussed in Chapter 6). Shortly after reentering the Ngwato capital, he began to display signs of what the directors would later view as fatigue.[5]

During Hepburn's absence, the Rev. Lloyd had taken charge of all Shoshong, but he soon returned to supervising the BaPhaleng, a people on their way to becoming Ngwato. In 1888 Lloyd arranged to construct a church building in their neighborhood. As an immigrant group, so-called *bafaladi*, the BaPhaleng still maintained some corporate identity in their designated ward, which lay a fair distance west from Khama's *kgotla* and from the meeting place of Hepburn's congregation. Regardless of whether or not Khama had originally approved Lloyd's plan, he soon expressed the fear "that two or more churches will divide the town."[6] 1889 was already a divisive year; Khama had made plans to move his capital to the Tswapong Hills, but a drought prevented the necessary harvest and caused a partial famine. With Hepburn as his scribe, Khama even wrote to Lobengula of the Ndebele in 1890, to beg for the privilege of buying grain for the BaNgwato. In these dire times, with Hepburn still a close and indispensable adviser, Khama communicated his dissatisfaction with Lloyd to the directors of the Society. Lloyd later came under censure in an LMS circular (which Hepburn displayed to him) and protested angrily to the directors.[7]

---

[4]   Parsons, *A New History*, 163–64; and see Anthony Sillery, *Botswana, A Short Political History* (London, 1974), Chs. 5 and 6. My phrase here points to Benedict Anderson's marvelous book, *Imagined Communities*, rev. ed. (New York, 1991).

[5]   *Report of the London Missionary Society*, Vols. 91, 92, and 93, Shoshong; Parsons, "Khama III," 198–99; R. Lovett, *The History of the London Missionary Society, 1795–1895*, Vol. 1 (Oxford, 1899), 639.

[6]   *Report of the London Missionary Society*, Vol. 38 (for 1888), 202. Quote: LMS SA 46/1/D R.H. Lloyd to R. W. Thompson, Shoshong, 12/7/89. Lloyd served from 1886 to 1892.

[7]   "I have great hunger. We had no harvest," wrote Khama, K III Papers, D/27, Khama to Lobengula, Phalapye, 23/9/1890. Khama gave the request to J. S. Moffat to give to Lobengula "so he won't think I am acting as a spy in his country." Three years later, Khama sent a regiment to help Col. Gould-Adams's forces in carriage, in the conquest of Lobengula's kingdom, but abruptly withdrew them at the start of plowing season; *South African Affairs in Matebeleland, Mashonaland and the B.P., Correspondence* (Bluebook), Sir H. B. Loch to Marquess of Ripon, Cape Town 15/11/1893. Quote: LMS SA, 46/2/A E. Lloyd to R. W. Thompson, Shoshong, 1/7/1889.

Nonetheless, Hepburn's few letters to the LMS in this period did not inspire confidence. Upon the death of Khama's first wife, MmaBesi, Hepburn sent the puzzling message, "Everything disorganized and I must reorganize everything." It was then that Khama moved his capital from Shoshong northeast to Phalapye in the Tswapong Hills. In January 1890, Hepburn wrote a formal letter to Lloyd and sent a copy to the LMS. The letter protested with alarming ambiguity that Khama was "not unconscious of the clear distinction I have always maintained between his own proper Chieftainship and the kingship of Christ." It also criticized Lloyd for building the Phaleng church in Shoshong without asking Khama's permission. The situation in GammaNgwato appeared to be reeling out of control to the Bechuanaland District Committee (BDC) of the LMS as it met at Kuruman, in British Bechuanaland.[8] What was going on up north?

The BDC passed a set of fruitless motions designed to define and pay African evangelists so as to bring them under firmer control, and in this connection began to query the status of the Ngwato Church. It noted that "no contribution [from the Church] had been made for some time to the Society," and that the "Native Teacher [Pule, Hepburn's right-hand man] whom we sent there does not draw his salary from us[, and] . . . we are at a loss to explain the exact position which this Church now holds" in relation to the Society. Hepburn failed to respond in an appropriate manner: instead, he saw the BDC's disquiet as stemming from another missionary's carping over an admitted £84 debt he owed, which he likened to "a poisoned spear" causing "fear and shame."[9]

The relationship between Hepburn and Lloyd had completely soured. On 13 June 1890, Khama wrote (with Hepburn's help) to ask for Lloyd's removal. Lloyd reacted by impugning Hepburn's competence and his loyalty to the LMS. Vaunting his own efforts for the BaPhaleng, Lloyd noted that Hepburn had never built a new church in Shoshong. Lloyd echoed the LMS's concern with Pule, which Lloyd himself must have instigated, musing that Pule "seems to have no connection with our Society." Moreover, the Rev. Hepburn was "unhealthy."[10]

It was indeed Hepburn's behavior that convinced Khama to postpone his dismissal of Lloyd. Shortly after moving with the BaNgwato to the new capital at Phalapye, Hepburn turned with a vengeance to constructing a respectable church building. Materials proved difficult to acquire without LMS financing, which Hepburn lacked the diplomacy to solicit. Consequently he demanded that Ngwato royals sell cattle and give him money. Moreover, he refused to employ the laborers in the regiment sent by Khama on the grounds that most of them were not Christians. Although this was in line with Nonconformist practice in England, it subverted the church's status as a Ngwato

---

[8]   First quote: LMS SA 46/2/C J. Hepburn to R. W. Thompson, Phalapye, 16/12/1889. Second: LMS SA 47/2/A, J. Hepburn to E. Lloyd, Phalapye, 2/1/1890. After the founding of the Protectorate in 1885, the BDC accounted for both it and British Bechuanaland, administered from the Cape Colony.

[9]   First quote: LMS SA 47/1/B, BDC meeting, Kuruman, 4/3/1890; emphasis in original. Second: LMS SA 47/1/C, J. Hepburn to W. Thompson, Phalapye, 9/4/1890 and 3/5/1890.

[10]   LMS SA 47/1/D, Khama to W. Thompson, Phalapye, 13/6/1890; 47/2/A, E. Lloyd to R. W. Thompson, Kanye, 7/7/1890. Lloyd went so far as to suggest that Hepburn had approached the Dutch Reformed Church!

project.[11] Hepburn's effort to disengage from Khama was supported by several of the king's relations, especially his half-brothers, the Church deacons
Mphoeng and Raditladi. In their account, Khama reacted to Hepburn's maneuvers by calling the congregation to his *kgotla* and telling them, "It is I who
have summoned you, including you Christians; I don't mean Hepburn's congregation—of that I say nothing—I mean my own." Hepburn then suddenly
gave up, bidding goodbye to the Church, despite Deacon Mocwaedi's implor-
ing him to "plough" the garden of Christ as usual.[12]

After Hepburn had left for London to consult with the directors, Khama dispatched letters (now using a Ngwato amanuensis) after him. Khama told both the
high commissioner at Cape Town and the LMS directors that Hepburn was coming
to bear false witness against him. According to the king, Hepburn wanted to separate Phalapye's Christians from the "heathen" and rule over them. Khama soon
marshalled most Church members to write a long complaint precisely to that effect. The Rev. Lloyd succeeded in ingratiating himself with the king in early 1892
and entered the war of words as a second secretary. In a frenzy of textual activity,
Khama let it be known that Hepburn's return would "set the town on fire and
destroy both Church and Chieftainship." Indeed, many deacons encouraged the
Rev. Hepburn. In addition to Mphoeng, Raditladi, Mocwaedi, and their followers,
Khama's only son, Sekgoma, was very close to the Reverend and his wife.[13]

Khama proceeded to confiscate and probably destroy all the Church's records.
The king then sent a final message to Hepburn in Cape Town, delivered to him by
a son-in-law. It read, "Now the Church is mine. Let all discussion end."[14] The BDC
met in May 1892, in a spirit of outrage, and rallied to Hepburn's defense:

It is quite evident that the Chief's action arose in great measure, if
not wholly, from a desire on his part to be paramount, not only in the

[11]   Rhodesian National Archives, "Phalapye, March 23, 1894," marked "[29]" and "handwriting of W. C.
Willoughby, apparently copied from ms. by Tiro," courtesy I. Schapera (my trans.), 6–7: hereafter "RNA,
23/3/1894." In England at the time, "Members and their minister usually formed a Chapel Committee
which directed the building in all its aspects. Finance was obtained from collections," Roger Dixon and
Stefan Mathesias, *Victorian Architecture* (London, 1978), 230–31; thanks to Sarah Landau. The Victorian
Gothic structure only opened in Phalapye after Hepburn's departure. Its facade is still standing in the
woods near Lecheng, Botswana.

[12]   Rhodesian National Archives, "Phalapye, May 24th 1895," hearings on Mphoeng and Raditladi affair,
courtesy of Isaac Schapera (my trans.), 2; LMS SA 48/1/D, J. Hepburn to R. W. Thompson, Phalapye, 7/
10/1891; J. Hepburn to R. W. Thompson, Phalapye, 4/11/1891; LMS SA 49/1/A, "Mocwaidi's version,"
in E. Lloyd to R. W. Thompson, Phalapye, 13/1/1892.

[13]   High Commissioner Loch hoped Hepburn would return and reestablish amicable relations with the
king, but was alarmed enough to dispatch Assistant Commissioner Surmon to Phalapye to head off "any
difficulties" that Khama might have with other Europeans. K III Papers, A/4/11, H. B. Loch to Khama,
Cape Town 24/11/1891; LMS SA 49/1/A, E. Lloyd to R. W. Thompson, Phalapye, 13/1/1892 (incl. quote);
and telegram, Khama to LMS, Phalapye, 12/1/1892; WCW/804, W. C. Willoughby, "Khama's Disputes,"
encl. Church members to LMS, Phalapye, 13/1/1892; Mrs. J. D. Hepburn, *Jottings* (London, 1928), 40–41;
LMS SA 50/1, A. J. Wookey to R. W. Thompson, Wynberg 8/3/93, and 49/1/B, Khama and council to
LMS, Phalapye, 5/3/1892.

[14]   WCW/475, *Special Visit to South Africa during August, September and October 1892. Report of Rev. R. W.
Thompson, Foreign Secretary* (For use of the LMS Directors only), 4, 5 esp. Despite his finality, the king sent
Rev. Hepburn £1,000 that same March, and asked that his old friend keep the huge sum—equivalent to
several years' pay—for his personal use. Some of it, in fact, went to pay Hepburn's debts for the construction of the church.

management of the affairs of his own tribe as such, but also in matters purely ecclesiastical. It has further been made evident during these meetings that this same spirit prevails throughout the whole of Bechuanaland. . . .[15]

But if the local BDC roared like a lion, the LMS itself went in like a lamb. In September, Wardlow Thompson, the LMS foreign secretary, came with the old missionary Roger Price to investigate the situation in Phalapye. Thompson had heard from Hepburn that Khama was bitter and blamed the Rev. Mackenzie for leading him into a Protectorate that he now despised. Whether the news was true or not, the secretary felt it best to defer to the king, and thus wrote that Hepburn had become "overstrained by disease." Yet the Rev. Price, who had tutored not only Khama but also his half-brothers, gave two of these brothers a hearing. Raditladi and Mphoeng told him that Khama's rule had become an obstacle to the Kingship of Christ. In his measured conclusion, Secretary Thompson therefore attributed the trouble in Phalapye to "misunderstanding" and issued an ambiguous hash of pronouncements.[16]

By May 1892, Khama had renewed his call for the LMS to remove the Rev. Lloyd from his kingdom, which it subsequently did. Lloyd and Hepburn then ended their comic-opera feud; Lloyd confessed that Hepburn's failure to sign a resolution congratulating him on his marriage had wounded him long ago. He penitently begged the directors to destroy all his backstabbing letters. The Rev. Hepburn, unfortunately, never recovered from his trials and suffered "a complete breakdown," dying in Cape Town in 1895. Khama kindly asked Hepburn's widow to come with her family and live in Phalapye, but she declined. Only Lloyd and his family would return, years later.[17]

The Missionary as King's Minister

The Rev. William Charles Willoughby first wrote to the LMS in 1882. The LMS sent Willoughby to Lake Tanganyika, where he briefly became Mirambo's unfortunate missionary, and became sufficiently ill with malaria to be sent home. Nine years later, after a time in the ministry of a Congregational church in Brighton, he arrived in Phalapye in June 1893. He was thirty-six years old. An elementary school teacher named Alice Young came with him and his wife to superintend seven Ngwato teachers and 190 children in the town's central *sekole* or school. As an early signal to these missionaries, Khama personally contrib-

15   LMS SA 49/1/A, BDC Report, Taungs 3/5/1892; also quoted in Parsons, "Khama III," 19n, 199, from *Report of the LMS* (1892).

16   K III Papers, B/2/47, J. Hepburn to R. W. Thompson, Phalapye, 24/10/1890; WCW/475, Rept. of R. W. Thompson, "Special Visit to South Africa . . . 1892," and Rhodesian National Archives, "Palapye, May 24th, 1895," 3.

17   LMS SA 49/1/B. E. Lloyd to R. W. Thompson, Vryburg 13/5/1892. When Lloyd had married the daughter of an LMS missionary, Hepburn had not joined other missionaries in resolving that she was "a fit and proper person" to be his wife. First quote: WCW/804, W. C. Willoughby, "Khama's Dispute," encl. J. Hepburn to R. W. Thompson, Wynberg 23/3/1892; LMS SA, 50/4/C, Mrs. Hepburn to R. W. Thompson, Wynberg 21/12/1894; 53/1/A J. Brown to R. W. Thompson, Taungs 1/1/1896. Second quote: Mrs. J. D. Hepburn, Jottings (London, 1928), 41.

uted to the congregation the central symbol of Church, its bell. *Tshipi*, or bell, is the SeTswana for "iron," but as a metonym, *tshipi* also meant both "the church" and "Sunday."[18]

The Church that Willoughby found in Phalapye apparently operated autonomously; there is no extant documentation. Instead of supplying him with a list of members, Church leaders told him that "they know pretty well who ought to come [to Communion] and who ought not." Takers of Communion amounted to fewer than 200 people. Willoughby lamely instructed the deacons to do what they could to prevent "unworthy persons" from taking the sacrament, but since he knew nothing about his charges, he had no way to check their standards against his own. Furthermore, he spoke no SeTswana. He did receive occasional help from John Smith Moffat (Robert Moffat's son), the assistant commissioner in Phalapye, and Moffat, an ordained minister, helped him translate sermons. But Willoughby confined his initial impact on the Church to introducing raisin-water as a substitute for wine in the sacrament.[19]

Willoughby was not, however, a man to stand idle. Besides the medical work the BaNgwato pressed on him, as he learned SeTswana, he became Khama's secretary and political advisor in a greater capacity than any missionary before or since. Willoughby's personality strangely echoed that of the king. Both were dour men who eschewed luxury to the point of asceticism.[20] Both missionary and king took careful note of their detractors; an indication of this trait can be found in Willoughby's bound volumes brimming with cuttings of reviews of his later books, each pasted down and annotated in his hand. Both men spoke their mind, held grudges, lost their tempers, and craved personal loyalty. If "all the people feared" Willoughby, much the same was true of Khama.[21]

In 1894 Willoughby wrote that "I am unfortunately blessed (?) [*sic*] with a kind of mania for order and method," and happily noted that Khama—what a difference from Mirambo's attitude!—"has sent me *all his papers* to look through that I may be better . . . able to advise him." Adding that his "real work" would not suffer, he commenced the job of writing and copying down all Khama's correspondence into a book of carbon papers.[22] But from the start, the ambiguity of Willoughby's position embroiled him in dynastic and religious disputes. In 1895, Mphoeng and Raditladi, whom we recall helped "ordain" *baruti* in the 1880s and sided with Hepburn in 1891, decisively broke with Khama. When the Khama stood up and told what he called "the Old Church" to teach their *thuto* outside his country or not at all, Willoughby supported the king. Yet as an impartial LMS represen-

---

18   LMS Candidates' Papers, 1796–1899, Box 17, W. C. Willoughby material; Box 18, A. Young; LMS SA 50/2. W. C. Willoughby to R. W. Thompson, Phalapye, 3/7/1893; LMS SA Reports 2/4, W. C. Willoughby, Phalapye, 1894 (20/3/1895); 3/1, W. C. Willoughby, Decennial review of mission work, Phalapye, 1/1/01.

19   LMS SA 50/2, W. C. Willoughby to R. W. Thompson, Phalapye, 7/8/1893.

20   E.g. LMS SA 69/3, W. C. Willoughby to R. W. Thompson, Tiger Kloof 15/9/08.

21   LMS SA Personal/6, W. C. Willoughby. Willoughby several times struck or beat BaTswana while headmaster of Tiger Kloof Missionary College, 1905–1915, and Khama was also known to strike subordinates in anger. Quote: LMS SA, E. Lloyd to R. W. Thompson, Shoshong, 20/8/09; also quoted in Parsons, "Khama III," 279.

22   LMS SA 51/2, W. C. Willoughby to R. W. Thompson, Phalapye, 22/9/1894; Idem., 21/7/1894. K III Papers, D/27, is a typical bound book of correspondence on onionskin.

tative, Willoughby also channelled reports from his detractors to the directors, at least one of which openly criticized him and Khama.[23]

Willoughby mostly helped Khama in his dealings with traders, admirers, and the press; but sometimes he dealt directly with the Protectorate administration. In 1895 Britain's Colonial Office tentatively planned to transfer the new Protectorate to the administration of Cecil Rhodes' chartered company, the British South Africa Company (BSAC). The very fate of the Ngwato kingdom hung in the balance, and so that year Willoughby accompanied Khama, Bathoeng (of the BaNgwakgetse), and Sebele (of the BaKwena) to England to agitate against the plan. This was the height of his secretarial service; he planned the logistics of much of their campaign and returned to Phalapye exhausted. There his labors only continued, as the following communiques, all in Willoughby's translations and penmanship, attest.

> *Khama to High Commissioner (1895).* I hear it said that the police are going along the Macloutsie [*sic*] to its source thence they will look towards Nata making a boundary and I enquire whether you know about this matter why is my country divided I wish to know.[24]
> *High Commissioner to Khama.* [It is] necessary for customs and administration purposes to make a line between Chartered Company administration and High Commission administration [but this will] not affect . . . tribal rights.[25]
> *Khama to High Commissioner.* What is administration. Is it not government. I don't understand how one part of my country can be under the government of the Queen and another part under the government of the Company. I see what the government of the Company is like by the way my men have been treated by the Company's policy of which I sent you an account by cartpost. End.[26]

In negotiating a northern boundary for the kingdom, Willoughby spent three weeks researching and writing a thirty-odd-page speech for Khama to deliver. The president of the "Boundary Commission" used its wording in his judgement.[27]

For these acts Willoughby received scant thanks, since Khama felt he had exceeded his authority in promising land to the BSAC on which to lay a line of rail.[28] Willoughby wrote,

---

[23] LMS SA 52/1/B, "Church members" to LMS, Phalapye, 16/3/1895, in W. C. Willoughby's hand. See Chapter 3 for this conflict.

[24] K III Papers, A/5/2, encl. in Assistant Commissioner to Resident Commissioner, Phalapye, 25/?/1895.

[25] K III Papers, A/5/4, encl. in Resident Commissioner to Khama, n.d.

[26] K III Papers, A/5/5, encl. Assistant Commissioner (Phalapye) to High Commissioner, n.d. Khama was referring to some men he had sent to the Rhodesian mines, K III Papers, A/1/3, Sanyon to Khama (1878?): "My heart was sore when I heard of the hunger they had suffered." By 1896 Khama refused to send men to the mines, C/15/9, Khama to West & Whitworth, Koffyfontein Mines, Ltd., Phalapye, ?/?/1896.

[27] W. C. Willoughby, "Review of Five Years' Work ...," 14. For another such example, see BNA H.C. 130/2, Khama to H.C. (Milner), Serowe, 28/8/00. For treatments of British-Ngwato political negotiations, see Paul Maylam, *Rhodes, the Tswana, and the British* (Westport, Conn., 1980), Neil Parsons, "Khama III," and Sillery, *Founding a Protectorate*.

[28] *South African Correspondence Relating to the Visit to this Country of the Chiefs Khama, Sebele and Bathoen* (London, 1896), Bluebook, 2, no. 5.

King Khama. Studio portrait, probably 1895. Reproduced courtesy of the Council for World Mission, London.

I have had quietly to resist the attempt to make the Missionary a kind of interpreter and private secretary to the Chief. And I am bound to give it as my opinion that this political work has not been of the slightest assistance to my proper Missionary Work, but rather the reverse. . . .[29]

29 K III Memorial Museum, Q. N. Parsons/W. C. Willoughby Papers, W. C. Willoughby, "Review of Five Years' Work at Phalapye, 1893–8," 15.

His position in Phalapye grew difficult. Each successive conflict with or on behalf of the king—and there were many—wore down Willoughby's self-definition as autonomous European minister and made his agenda part of the Ngwato political scene. In 1897, he wrote to his wife (who had escaped to the healthful air of the Cape) about a major conflict between Khama and his first son, Sekgoma:

> So far, Sekgoma takes my advice, which is simply to bear all and remain silent, feeling sure that time will help him if he is oppressed by his father, as he says. Last week he wanted to tell the High Commissioner about it. . . . But I kept him quiet. It is a source of anxiety to me; for if there is another row, I cannot repair the injury as I did before. The worst of it is, they think I am in favor of the [king] because I preach the gospel of endurance; and the [king] thinks I am in favor of them because I warn him of the consequences of a row.[30]

By November, Willoughby feared that Khama would try to exclude certain of his son's partisans from the Church, and he prepared for a "battle" with the king. Willoughby would not permit the church pulpit to be used "for any such purposes" as partisan politics. Somehow he failed to recognize that his own similar activities, his arrangement of cited texts to convey political messages in church, and his opposition to the king's desire to exclude subjects from services were themselves political. Eventually, Khama began to impugn his loyalty.[31]

From October 1896 through 1898, an atmosphere of tension and even fear pervaded the capital as supporters of Khama's fully grown son Sekgoma conspired and grumbled. The old cult of the Word again fractured. Much of the Christian Ngwato aristocracy had been exiled with Mphoeng and Raditladi; now a good many wealthy Church members backed Sekgoma's ambitions. The Rev. Willoughby, safely in sight of his coming furlough, chose this period to apply himself to reforming the Church. Willoughby wanted to impose bureaucratized standards for entering and rising through the Church's membership, and the king gave his blessing.

GammaNgwato's *fin de siècle*, discussed in the next chapter, left a mixed legacy for the Ngwato Church. Willoughby's missionary secretariat marks a significant, if rough, divide. Before 1900, the Ngwato Church essentially denoted a smallish group or cult in the capital, organized from the inside out. The resident LMS missionary was its priest and the king's secretary. The autonomy of the polity was fairly intact. After about 1900, the Ngwato "district" mapped in 1895 by the British began to resemble a true kingdom. Within it the Church expanded, growing in importance as the Protectorate government gnawed away at the kingdom's administrative func-

30 WCW/QNP "Additional Documents" (WCW/742, now lost), W. C. Willoughby to Mrs. Willoughby, Phalapye, 24/9/1897. For more on Sekgoma's conflict with his father, see Paul Landau, "Preacher, Chief and Prophetess," *Journal of Southern African Studies* 17, 1 (1991), 1–22; and Parsons, "Khama III," 210–15, 375–81. Willoughby's conflicts with Khama involved rinderpest, famine relief, land tenure, dynastic prerogatives, and access to Protectorate officials. In 1897 Willoughby fenced off the mission and asserted rights to the local spring, irritating Khama so much that he avoided the missionary for months.

31 "Battle": QNP/WCW "Additional Documents," W. C. Willoughby to Mrs. Willoughby, 20/11/1897; 27/11/1897; and see WCW/795, Sekgoma II to W. C. Willoughby, Palla Road, n.d. (1899?), SeTswana, in which Sekgoma addresses Willoughby as "my beloved friend." WCW/810, W. C. Willoughby, "Notes taken from my letters," for January, 1898; and *Ibid.*, W. C. Willoughby to Mrs. Willoughby, 30/4/1898; LMS SA W. C. Willoughby to LMS, Phalapye, 19/5/1897.

tions, as they had been previously construed. The missionary then became only one protagonist among many in negotiating the path the Ngwato Church would follow.

Upon Willoughby's return from furlough in 1900, the king greeted him warmly. Khama looked years younger. An unobtrusive missionary had acted in Willoughby's stead, and Khama had recently married his fourth wife, the last of a series, a youthful mission-educated schoolteacher named Semane. With Willoughby came Ella Sharp, a young woman who would teach and supervise the main LMS school in GammaNgwato for the next thirty years. The Church regained its stability and grew markedly over the next few years; Khama made generous presents to the Church through his missionaries, and Willoughby and Khama drew closer once again.[32] In 1902 Khama shifted the capital to Serowe, where it rests today; Willoughby left in 1903. Although he had been GammaNgwato's most successful missionary in many ways, his efforts left him emotionally divided. In 1902 he wrote that "the native of the Protectorate is at heart a slave, and a slave is the same thing as a despot with the other end upwards." Yet Willoughby became known as a despot himself during his subsequent tenure as the first principal of the LMS College in the Cape. Thus his last letter to Khama upon leaving southern Africa in 1916 was heartfelt:

> So I greet you my lord, and bid you farewell *ka pula* [by rain, e.g., fruitfulness]. We have seen many years together and we are not young anymore in this world. However I will always remember you and your words, your good deeds, and all the friendship we received from you.[33]

His last interview with the directors upon his retirement in 1919 contains the following reflection: "The genius of Bantu thought and life was not akin to Congregationalism, and was largely alien to it. Bantu life denied the principles of equality and freedom."[34] The tension in the statement is palpable. But it flowed naturally enough from the contradictions inherent in the missionary's mediating role.

The Broker of Misunderstanding

Albert Jennings was born in Camberwell, England, in 1871, the year James Hepburn had come to GammaNgwato. Jennings was "born again" as a teenager, and he became a fervent evangelist.[35] In October, 1903, he arrived in Serowe with his wife Mabel, after completing his first tenure at the Barkly West station in the Cape. His

[32]   Parsons, "Khama III," 206–207; Khama gave £1,120 to Williams, and £1728 to Willoughby; LMS SA E. Lloyd to R. W. Thompson, Shoshong, 20/8/09.

[33]   First quote: BNA S.178/1, W. C. Willoughby to H. Williams, Serowe, 7/9/02. Second: K III Papers G/50/55, W. C. Willoughby to Khama, 21/12/16, excerpt, SeTswana.

[34]   LMS SA, Southern Africa Committee Minutes, Box 4, W. C. Willoughby, "Interview with Rev. W. C. Willoughby upon his retirement," 23/6/19. Statement was later partially retracted.

[35]   LMS Candidates' Papers 1796–1899, Box 17, A. Jennings to LMS, London 10/12/1896; A. Jennings to Johnson, London 14/2/1898; Testimony (rec'd 27/5/1896); and the Rev. R. V. Price to LMS, Nottingham 26/12/1896.

appearance coincided both with drought and hunger and with yet another period of friction between the London Missionary Society itself and Khama. Part of the problem lay in the Society's negotiations for Ngwato land on which to build the LMS College, but a far deeper reason for the conflict was the LMS's persistent attempt to coopt and regulate the Ngwato Church.

The Society long wished to standardize its rules in southern Africa. In 1896 Willoughby had called for a regularization of the disbursement of Church members' contributions, *phalalo*, under Bechuanaland District Committee auspices. In 1899 the BDC (under Willoughby, J.T. Brown, and A.J. Wookey) met and sent a circular to all Tswana Churches, marked for the attention of both believers and nonbelievers (*ba e seng ba thuto*); among other things, it instructed BaTswana on how to raise their children and solicited money for schools. In 1907 the first LMS "Bechuana" Native Advisory Committee of seventy-six delegates met during the BDC meeting at Kanye, coinciding with government efforts to form a secular Bechuana Native Advisory Council, a body with the very same acronym. Willoughby meanwhile stepped up his agitation for freehold land tenure. Each of these maneuvers threatened the independence of the realm of the Word.[36]

Insofar as the Rev. Jennings understood these conflicts, he supported the Ngwato king, and went so far as to attack Willoughby's character. While the LMS pursued its agenda, Jennings helped King Khama try to regularize and hierarchize the Ngwato Church within his demarcated territory. After the capital had shifted from Phalapye to Serowe, the outstanding discontinuity in this regard was the separate status of the Shoshong Church and its outstations. Shoshong still had its own European missionary, Howard Williams (1902–1907). A muted conflict had pitted "interfering" Serowe deacons against the Shoshong congregation's separate status. In late 1906, Jennings and Khama, in the interests of the Ngwato agenda, asked the LMS that Serowe and Shoshong no longer be treated as two equal stations.[37]

Nonetheless, Edwin Lloyd returned to GammaNgwato and took the Shoshong post in 1908. Lloyd did so over the protests of the BaPhaleng, the residents of the west side of the village, for whom he had had a separate church built back in 1889. Phaleng Christians objected that Lloyd had tried to cut them off from the BaNgwato. In contrast, the BaKaa of Shoshong had no problem with Lloyd. Khama had given one of his daughters in marriage to their chief, Tshwene, the most important leader in the village of Shoshong next to Khama's reconciled brother Kgamane. Tshwene was also a member of the Church at Shoshong. Not surprisingly, as late as 1910 the Rev. Lloyd sensed that the BaKaa exhibited "more spiritual life" than the BaPhaleng.[38] Knowing all this, when Khama

[36] Parsons, "Khama III," 281, 184n, W. C. Willoughby to LMS, 29/6/1896. WCW/374, *Go Ba Diphuthego tsa LMS tse di mo Becwaneng*, SeTswana. In fact, the conference became a forum for pointed Tswana complaints about the LMS; WCW/374, *Mahoko a Phuthego ba LMS*, Kanye, 1907, SeTswana; LMS SA 71/3, E. Lloyd to R. W. Thompson, Shoshong, 20/8/09.

[37] LMS SA 60/4, W. C. Willoughby to LMS, Serowe, 28/8/02; 67/5, A. Jennings to Cousins, Serowe, 13/11/06. The main concern at the time was that A. J. Gould, whom Khama justly accused of misbehavior among the BaKhurutshe at Tonota, would not take over the post.

[38] LMS SA 74/5, E. Lloyd to Hawkins, Shoshong, 9/7/12. The identity "BaKaa" was a dispersed one with "origins" around the Shoshong Hills. The BaPhaleng had moved from Shoshong to Phalapye with the rest of the capital's people but had been resettled in Shoshong at the turn of the century; there were ca. 1,600 BaKaa, and ca. 1,400 BaPhaleng in and near the village. LMS SA 57/16, H. Williams to LMS, Phalapye, 4/7/00; 72/8, E. Lloyd to R. W. Thompson, Shoshong, 17/8/10.

overruled the BaPhaleng's objection to Lloyd in 1908, he seized on their more fundamental demand, that "between Shoshong and the capital, there should be no two sets of
regulations. Let there be one set of Church laws for [the] land of Khama, as we are all
the children of the Serowe Church and wish its laws to be applied to all the village
churches."[39] Khama made this his own precondition for Lloyd's arrival, and the Rev.
Jennings was happy to second it. Henceforth all Serowe's Church laws, including bans
on beer-drinking and Jennings' notion of proper marriages, were to be enforced as king-
dom-wide Church law in Shoshong and every other village within reach.

Jennings then went on furlough for two years and opted to leave his work in
the hands of the "Native Church." While Khama was left exercising a free hand in
Church affairs, the "South African District Committee" (SADC) convened. The SADC
was an outcome of the LMS's desire to reorder their mission field, and was composed of missionaries from stations throughout southern Africa. The new body
called a "native" conference for all Tswana Churches in April 1910, which the "native" Ngwato delegates boycotted. The SADC then considered the conference's recommendations in its draft of a "Scheme for the Unification of the London Missionary Society in Bechuanaland," put forth in 1910. The "Scheme" sought to systematize
regional Church policy along the same lines as the SADC.[40] It escaped no one's
notice that 1910 was also the year South Africa united into a sovereign state, having assimilated British Bechuanaland and the Tswana peoples south of the Molopo
River.

Although few of the unified regulations proposed in the Scheme were offensive to BaNgwato, the critical problem was the mere fact of their existence. The
SADC straddled South Africa and the Protectorate, equalizing all Tswana polities
within itself, and levelling Tswana hierarchies within LMS districts. The Shoshong
station, for instance, would have a voice proportionate to its membership but on
the same level as that of Serowe, the Ngwato capital town since 1902. The Ngwato
District, with its creeping "Congregational principle," would drape itself over the
Ngwato kingdom and slowly smother it.[41]

This was not all. The SADC redrew the Scheme in 1911, in the aftermath of the
birth of the Union of South Africa, and in view of the likelihood that the Union
would incorporate the three High Commission Territories (Basutoland, Swaziland,
and the Bechuanaland Protectorate). It *now* proposed that southern African LMS
Churches, including Ndebele Churches to the north, not only unify, but also join
the Congregational Union of South Africa (CUSA). An official circular requested
all Protectorate LMS Churches to consider the idea. In Serowe, the Rev. Jennings
received the circular from a Ngwato student home from the Cape for the Christmas holidays. Jennings promptly placed the matter before the Church, as he wrote
to F.W. Hawkins, the LMS foreign secretary in London:

> [I gave copies] in the first instance to the Deacons at the Deacons Meeting
> on Dec. 23rd . . . and reminded them that we had discussed the subject

---

[39]   "BaPhaleng" response in LMS SA 67/? Jennings to Thompson, Serowe, 3/6/07; *Report of the London
Missionary Society*, Vol. 39 (1889), 127.

[40]   LMS SA 69/1, A. Jennings to W. Thompson, Serowe, 23/1/08; WCW/787, *Report of the First Purely
Native Conference of Delegates from the Bechuana Churches*, April 1910, 2; LMS SA 72/6, Scheme for the
Unification of the London Missionary Society in Bechuanaland, 1910.

[41]   LMS SA 72/6, Scheme for Unification, 1910.

from time to time during the past two or three years and I explained to them carefully that it was a matter for the church's discussion and decision as to whether or no the Serowe church should join in the Unification Scheme. . . . I had requested the Deacon who was in charge of the [Church subdivision] in which Khama lives [t]o show him the Circular when the Deacons received their own copies, and I made many personal attempts to speak with the Chief on the subject unsuccessfully. . . .[42]

A struggle had begun over the social space that would set the parameters for discussion. Jennings wished the Church to reflect upon and define (or undefine) itself, in deacons' meetings and on Church territory. His original, albeit swiftly revised plan had been for a deacon to show the circular to the king as if he were any other Church member. Khama, on the other hand, was offended that Jennings had not sought him out in the central *kgotla*, and recognized the consideration of the scheme as a matter of state.

On Tuesday morning the 9th of January I went early before breakfast to visit the Kgotla, and found the Tribe [i.e. Ngwato senior men] assembled there in excited discussion, and on the way home passed a number of men proceeding to the Magistrate's court. At nine o'clock, the Magistrate sent a letter to me requesting me to come over to the Court-house to hear what a Deputation of the Tribe sent by Khama, had to say to me about the circular. . . . I was met by about twenty men nearly equally divided between members of the Church and outsiders. . . . Khama was absent.[43]

Khama used the magistrate's "court" as an adjunct forum to the *kgotla*, one that Jennings would be obliged to attend. At the court, Jennings discovered that the "Church members had been charged by the heathens with trying to cut off the [king] from the Church, including an attempt to agree to join the Union of South African States, in defiance of the [king]. . . ." While non-Christians backed the status quo, Church members were divided between those who wanted at least to discuss the circular within the Church, and those who "absolutely refused to touch the subject in a church meeting."[44] The group of headmen appearing before the magistrate was Khama's response: half the headmen were nonbelievers, but all of them spoke with one voice. Monaheng, an important Church member, said:

We do not like the idea of the Union of the Churches of the London Missionary Society. We are afraid of these circulars as they suggest the separation of the Church members from our Chief and Headmen . . . we also do not like to be separated from our Chief and Headmen as we do not know how they interfere with the Church.[45]

Monaheng here referred to a particularly damaging passage in the circular. The English text, which many young people could read, said that Union with CUSA

---

[42] LMS SA 74/3, A. Jennings to Hawkins, Serowe, 14/1/12 (misdated 1911); and long quote: 74/3, A. Jennings to F. H. Hawkins, Serowe, 19/1/12, 1, 2.

[43] LMS SA 74/3, A. Jennings to F. H. Hawkins, Serowe, 19/1/12, 1, 2.

[44] *Ibid.*, 2.

[45] LMS SA 74/3, A. Jennings to F. H. Hawkins, Serowe, 19/1/12 (enclosing) Minutes of the Magistrate's Court, 9/1/12.

would "secure the freedom of the church [sic] from the interference of Chiefs and Headmen," and that Union regulations would be "binding on every Church."[46]

Deacon Ntwetwe echoed Monaheng's attack and added that "we understand that after the Union of the Churches has taken place we [would] have to be bound together, and what has been bound cannot free itself from its bonds." Headman Gagoitsiwe then rose to speak; had the proceedings occurred in Church, as Jennings wished, he would not have done so, since he was not a Christian. Gagoitsiwe propounded the view that Church laws in fact emanated from King Khama; as laws of the realm, they had to be considered equally beneficial by non-Christians.[47]

Although Jennings tried again to have Khama visit him at home, the struggle over venues ended with his visit to the king in his public *kgotla*. Khama received him coldly and accused him of allowing the scheme to go forward without first discussing the issue with him. Khama argued that he and others had "been looking for a long time for external signs of what they knew as the internal desire of the missionaries, . . . to divide the Church from the State." But *dikgosi* would not stand to be divorced from the Church. "Most of the Church members and inquirers were headmen and their children. Did we want two churches, one for the headmen and chiefs and the other for the common people?"[48]

The Rev. Jennings persisted in his assertion that considering the circular was "solely a business for the Church members." Alluding to Willoughby's insensitivity, Jennings argued that Khama had been misled by the provision about the "interference of chiefs" and the use of the word *kopano*, or union. It was only by the oddest coincidence that the term sounded like the *kopano* of South Africa, he explained, which Khama justifiably feared. Yet Jennings now got his bearings. Although "the whole agitation was based upon misunderstanding," he wrote, his "private opinions largely coincide with those of the tribe on the matter."[49]

The way forward now became clear. On Sunday, Khama reversed himself and ordered every Church member to come and "consider" the issue as Jennings wished, in Church. Predictably, Church members voted unanimously against the scheme for union. On Monday morning, Khama could afford a conciliatory posture. "Khama

[46] LMS SA 72/6, Scheme for the Unification of the London Missionary Society in Bechuanaland, 1910, my italics. The SeTswana (and the SeNdebele printed beside it) read that Union "will help *the Churches* to protect the faith [or beliefs] and purely ecclesiastical things from the annoying [or troubling] of destructive chiefs and headmen, who upset the churches." An internal memo to the SADC's meeting also stated the need to gain control of "Native"-run Churches. LMS SA Committee Meetings Box 3, 14/10/11.

[47] "Our [king] has well protected our interests. He has abolished circumcision [the bo*gwera* ceremonies] and has protected our children from being spoilt [i.e., has proffered Christian education to most headmen's children], and saved us from strong drink. We have no complaint against our [king] because what he does not approve of, the Church also does not approve of. We mean we are one with our [king]." *Ibid.*

[48] *Ibid.*

[49] LMS SA 74/3, E. Lloyd to Hawkins, Shoshong, 14/2/12; and see Maylam, *Rhodes, the Tswana, and the British*, 64, 151. Jennings hoped to mollify Khama by confiding that the "interference" reference was mainly directed at the BaTswana of the Cape. But in fact one is hard pressed to understand Jennings. Could he have not known the thrust of the South Africa Act of 1909, which provided for the conditional inclusion of the High Commission Territories? Khama was informed in that year that GammaNgwato would likely move into South African hands, and wrote a letter protesting the Union as the South Africa Act passed on 31 May 1910; see Ramsay, "Rise and Fall," 316, n234; and LMS SA 74/3, A. Jennings to F. H. Hawkins, Serowe, 19/1/12, Minutes.

again went over the subject in the Kgotla, from the point of view of my speech the day before. He completely changed his attitude and . . . [faulting the deacons,] exonerated me from any blame."[50]

Here Khama gave Jennings a way of saving face in the midst of the failure of an LMS policy. We need not be so credulous. It is apparent that Khama and his aristocratic allies had every reason to oppose a congregational union in southern Africa. First, Khama objected to the LMS's clear desire to extract the Church from the matrix of his kingdom. Nor could he allow the issue of whether there was to be a viable Ngwato Church itself become a matter for consideration in deacons' meetings. The Church housed critical elements of Ngwato monarchial authority and provided a means for its exertion (as we shall see), and the SADC had shown threateningly that it operated on the same level, in an idiom both political and religious. Thirdly, it was very reasonable indeed to see Church union, codified or not, as a prelude to the discorporation of the kingdom and its fractured inclusion in the Union of South Africa.[51]

In Ngwato politics, the unification scheme was obnoxious for additional reasons. Non-Christian headmen opposed the scheme, and in fact the LMS, because both threatened to provide Christian headmen with a second patron, whereas they would keep but a single appeal to the king. Under their pressure, Christian headmen relinquished such treasonous thoughts. Finally, the absolute elimination of the "interference of headmen" was not in Khama's interest, given the high percentage of aristocratic men still holding Church membership.

It was not long before Jennings began to sense a tumble in his prestige with the king.[52] King Khama understood the utility of multiplying his links to chiefs and headmen, not ending them, and he opposed the ecclesiastical rules coming from the LMS which threatened to do just that. A consideration of the downfall of the Revs. Edwin Lloyd and Albert Jennings, which transpired during and after the "crisis" over the scheme, further illuminates this dynamic.

The Marrying Missionaries

One of the key issues in ecclesiastical policy was how to provide the sacrament of marriage. Marriage underpinned the community missionaries wished to create: monogamous, individuated, and even mutually competitive family units headed by public, productive men and private, reproductive women.[53] At the same time, even after Khama had discouraged polygamy, Tswana marriage remained largely a processual form of family alliance. Christianizing marriage was complicated. In

---

50 *Ibid.*, 6, my emphasis.

51 As Deacon Ntwetwe said, "this Church Union we fear will *lead to* the Union of the countries to which we have already objected." LMS SA 74/3, A. Jennings to F. H. Hawkins, Serowe, 19/1/12, Minutes, my emphasis.

52 LMS SA Reports, 4/3, A. Jennings, Serowe, 1911.

53 Jean and John L. Comaroff, "Home-Made Hegemony: Modernity, Domesticity, and Colonialism in South Africa," in Karen Tranberg Hansen, ed., *African Encounters with Domesticity* (New York, 1992); and see Kristin Mann, *Marrying Well: Marriage, Status and Social Change among Educated Elites in Colonial Lagos* (Cambridge, 1985), 35–52, and Margaret Strobel, *European Women and the Second British Empire* (Bloomington, Ind., 1991), 53 ff. esp.

practice, the Rev. Hepburn had married and divorced Ngwato Christians in Church; then, for a while, deacons sanctified marriages and Khama decided Christian divorces as he did non-Christian ones; then, in 1895, the British high commissioner for South Africa issued a proclamation that, according to Willoughby, made it "necessary for any marriage celebrated by a Minister of Religion in the Protectorate, to be registered in the usual way." This placed Christian divorce in the sticky province of British Courts. Willoughby then fashioned himself as a champion of individuated "rights" for brides and grooms, to "protect these young people in their struggle" with their seniors. His position was somewhat fatuous. From 1895 to 1898, he performed only fifteen marriages.[54]

It was the Rev. Jennings who decided in 1904 (leading a trend in the LMS) that no MoNgwato would be admitted to Church membership who had not been married in "European law." At the same time, he simply began marrying Church members in good standing who had already been wed in Tswana practice, which most village deaconates had required for membership as a signification of adulthood. Soon Jennings was performing the marriage sacrament for even casual Church enquirers, and journeying outside Serowe for the purpose. On a single day in 1904 Jennings married twenty-six couples at once. Marriage became an evangelical technique. According to Jennings' own figures, he married 655 couples during his eleven-year tenure, while the Church roll grew threefold.[55]

In the outline for the first (1910) Bechuanaland "scheme" were several strong, albeit not always clear, guidelines on what was and was not required for couples already "married in Nature"—the LMS term that lumped Tswana marriage together with mere concubinage. In this outline, Christian marriage was strongly encouraged for all couples entering, or remaining in, the Church. But almost immediately the LMS faced the fact that it had no license to perform legal marriages at their stations in the Cape Province: the new Union of South Africa did not recognize the ministerial status of LMS missionaries, since they held no denominational title.[56] The London Missionary Society, although Nonconformist and largely "Congregationalist," was not a "Church." The 1911 scheme proposed to solve this problem by making LMS missionaries marriage officers of the "Congregational Union of South Africa."

As we have seen, Ngwato opposition prevented the scheme from taking effect. One consequence, however, of the promulgation of the *Ngwato* Church rules for GammaNgwato brokered by Jennings in 1908 was that Lloyd immediately began marrying couples upon his arrival in Shoshong. Under Jennings' practice, Shoshong's Church members had been rendered "not legally married to their wives." Lloyd married four or five couples per week—always, for some reason, on Mondays.[57]

---

[54]   Isaac Schapera, *The Tswana* [1953] (London, 1966), 41; Jean and John L. Comaroff, "The Management of Marriage in a Tswana Chiefdom," in Krige and Comaroff, eds., *Essays on African Marriage*, 33ff.; WCW/ 810, "Notes taken . . .", W. C. Willoughby to Mrs. Willoughby, Phalapye, 26/2/1898; and W. C. Willoughby, "Review of Five Years," 21.

[55]   For marriage, see Isaac Schapera, *Married Life in an African Tribe* (Harmondsworth, 1971). LMS SA 64/ 29 A. Jennings to LMS, Serowe, 28/7/04; Jennings' numbers do not quite accord with the record; LMS SA 76/3, A. Jennings to F. H. Hawkins, 8/6/14.

[56]   LMS SA Reports, A. Jennings to F. H. Hawkins, Serowe, 3/9/12.

[57]   LMS SA Reports, 4/2, Serowe, for 1908 (E. Lloyd, 1909); quote, Reports 4/1, Shoshong, 1913 (E. Lloyd, 1914).

Between 1911 and 1913, then, Jennings and Lloyd worked rather feverishly under a dual and conflicting mandate: their authority came on the one hand from the Ngwato Church, and on the other, matched the sensibility expressed by the LMS's technically defunct Scheme for Union. At first this duality was of little concern to the king. Perhaps what unveiled its contradictory implications was the return, by 1910, of the descendants of many of the aristocrats he had exiled in the 1890s.[58] Khama wished to integrate these people, many of whom were Christians, into his kingdom smoothly, but they had not yet been brought into line with new Church rules, including the requirement for "legal" marriages. They would have to be informed that they had been living in sin and be married alongside their juniors.

In this delicate climate, Edwin Lloyd had on at least one occasion solicited advice from Khama on whether to perform a marriage. In July 1912 he blundered, however, and refused to sanctify the marriage of the BaKaa Kgosi Tshwene's younger brother to Tshwene's daughter Goakohile. Since Tshwene was Khama's son-in-law, Goakohile was Khama's granddaughter; now she would be transformed into a concubine and barred from Communion. Worse, Lloyd's refusal threatened to shake the loyalty of the BaKaa. He recognized the gravity of the matter and wrote to Khama to justify himself.[59]

Khama replied in a long and crushing letter. He expressed astonishment as to the "new practice" of forbidding kin-linked marriage. He pointed out that LMS missionaries found many such niece-uncle couples upon their arrival in GammaNgwato, and freely admitted them into the Church. Even Lloyd, Khama noted archly, had perhaps unwittingly married many close relations and continued to do so even today. Khama then broadened his attack to Jennings, who had by then married hundreds of Christians and enquirers throughout the kingdom; he accused "you ministers" of marrying couples merely as "a means of collecting money . . . which pays you." From the famous "Christian chief," this slander came with surprising casualness. The king closed in specious praise for Lloyd's decision and wished him well.[60]

This was more than the conservatism of an aging man. Khama wanted his missionaries to wield the marriage sacrament in accordance with the interests of his regime: specifically, as a dispensation of identity from both Church and state. It made homesteaders out of men, and *basadi*, "adult women," out of females. As a cap to the processual entanglements of Tswana marriage, it inserted the kingdom's Word in a communal function: very few persons underwent Christian marriages with partners purely of their own choosing, no matter what missionaries thought. Its misuse imperiled the capital's relationship to men like Tshwene, tied to Khama by their membership in Church, and sometimes by blood.[61] As it was, the marriage

---

58   LMS SA Reports, 4/2, A. Jennings, Serowe, 1909.

59   K III Papers, D/29/42, Khama to E. Lloyd, Serowe, 10/5/11; D/30/72a, E. Lloyd to Khama, Shoshong, 6/7/12.

60   K III Papers, D/30/77, Khama to E. Lloyd, Serowe, 18/7/12, SeTswana. Khama here referred to marriage fees, though he knew that committees like the BDC decided on the use of funds.

61   Khama also had a daughter married to the Talaote *kgosi*. Thomas Tlou, "*Melao ya ga Kgama*: Transformation in the 19th c. Ngwato State" (M.A. thesis, University of Wisconsin, 1969), 26. Bozzoli, *Women of Phokeng*, Ch. 5, supports the notion that church people were no more likely than others to challenge their parents' prearranged marriages—despite Khama's own history.

sacrament had to move among the intersecting ties of local and state power, but both Jennings' marital evangelism and Lloyd's officious delicacy cut them apart.

The Church is Made Whole

Jennings had first realized that there was trouble between himself and the king the previous year, during Khama's 1911 Baptismal "Jubilee." Held in 1911 after a year's delay, the event brought "under review . . . the main essentials of Christianity as exemplified in the life of the Chief Khama" in the fifty years since his conversion.[62] In it the king deliberately placed missionaries, traders, and administrators on the same footing. Jennings' next sign came in August 1912, when he tried and failed to secure for the LMS a title deed to the church that, after years of effort, was finally being built in Serowe. Simon Ratshosa, a confidant of Khama's, later castigated his efforts as unseemly and duplicitous, and called Jennings' blueprint "a mere goods-shed with open sides for ventilation."[63]

In order to "out-maneuver" the anti-LMS faction in Serowe, whom he saw as secondary-school-educated young men like Simon Ratshosa, Jennings had to return to Khama all monies and supervisory capacity over the church. A better architectural design had emerged, partly from Khama's own ideas gleaned during his visit to England. Moreover, the king had raised a further £8,000 by recriminalizing the use of beer and imposing strict fines on miscreants. As he had done in Phalapye, Khama once again purchased and contributed the church's bell, the actual and metaphorical apex of the church; but now its built space itself returned to the possession of the kingship.[64]

By mid-1912, Jennings had arrived at Hepburn's earlier realization. If only by virtue of popular acclaim, he wrote, "Khama is the state and the state means Khama. Khama also means Church, and it is natural that in the eyes of both Church members & heathen, the Church means—Khama! He and I both agree that it is not so. . . ."[65] Certainly. Yet a month later Khama wrote to express openly his disenchantment with Jennings. At the end of 1912, the LMS's new Foreign Secretary trundled off to southern Africa. As he neared Serowe, Secretary Hawkins heard rumors of Ngwato hostility and so prepared to capitulate on all points. Khama was almost eighty years old and chronically dyspeptic. He did not mince words: while the LMS directors had always been his "fathers," their agents "have long been in the country but they have not benefitted the country in any way."[66]

---

[62]   LMS SA Reports, 4/3, A. Jennings, Serowe, 1911.

[63]   BNA S.598/2, S. Ratshosa, "My Book," the section marked "Religion," unpaginated. Jennings had contracted the Church's construction to a Bulawayo architect without Khama's permission.

[64]   The cornerstone was laid by Resident Commissioner Panzera, an Anglican. Jennings felt like he was "eating dust." LMS SA 74/5, A. Jennings to Hawkins, Serowe, 10/8/12; K III Papers F/39/22, A. G. Martin, rec't to Khama, 12/12/13. Khama also bought other furnishings for the Church (K III Papers F/ 39/41, Bailey to Khama, n.d.).

[65]   LMS SA 74/4, A. Jennings to F. H. Hawkins, Serowe, 23/5/12; quoted in Parsons, "Khama III," 286.

[66]   K III Papers, D/30/70, Khama to W. C. Willoughby, Serowe, 29/6/12; G/50/20, [Khama?] to Capt. G.A. Merry, Serowe, 5/2/13; G/50/88, Khama to LMS, n.d. (1913–14). Thompson, the previous foreign secretary, had written Khama in November 1912 in a late defense of the Union Scheme, espousing the separation of Church decisions from Tswana kings; K III Papers, G/50/15, R. W. Thompson to Khama, London 17/11/12.

After discussions in this vein, Secretary Hawkins, having to do something, inspected Lloyd's ministry and found it wanting. In view of Lloyd's past unpopularity in GammaNgwato, and because he had also been dismissed by the LMS from Kanye in 1906, Hawkins' job was clear. It was made easier by the Lloyds' peevishness, the barbed wire around their yard, and a locked house gate. The Rev. Lloyd deprecated such things as red herrings. He felt that his troubles came from Kgosi Tshwene, from the time he had refused to marry Tshwene's "daughter to her own uncle."[67] Nonetheless, the foreign secretary decided that Lloyd would have to leave the Society. Furthermore, the Rev. Jennings also would be transferred. As in 1890, a fresh start meant removing Khama's missionaries. King Khama, "while he was undoubtedly friendly to the Society, . . . was not anxious that its influence should become too strong. He is a very astute man." Hawkins ventured further: "It is the utmost importance that the Society endeavor to obtain the previous approval of Khama to the steps it proposes to take."[68]

In July Khama came forth with a ferocious, if superfluous, diatribe against Lloyd, similar to his earlier attacks on James Hepburn. The bad news was then broken to Lloyd, who was smitten, and took months to reply. It seemed he had nowhere else to go. He would not take his furlough to "save face," and instead filed a flippant report in which he ridiculed Hawkins' obesity: at one steep crossing with the wagon, he wrote, "we off-loaded the Foreign Secretary; & well it is that we did so, for the borrowed oxen were in excellent condition and very fresh."[69] And Lloyd's missionary career came to a close.

No one from London was to take his place in Shoshong. Hawkins and the LMS now heeded Khama's wish to place the Shoshong station under a "Native Minister" directly beholden to the central congregation in Serowe.[70]

A Last "Misunderstanding"

The LMS delayed action on Jennings' departure due to organizational and financial difficulties. In 1914, W. C. Willoughby himself brought the word to Jennings in Serowe. Willoughby then held the chair of a diminished SADC, and on the 10th March he visited Khama to secure approval for a last-ditch effort to institutionalize the LMS in Serowe. There was to be an extensive redeployment

---

[67]   Lloyd had also had earlier troubles with Rev. Hepburn, of course. WCW/469, W. C. Willoughby, draft of "Report of Deputation to Kanye, July 1906"; LMS SA, F. H. Hawkins, "Strictly Private and Confidential Supplementary Report," for use of the SADC only (London, 1913), 7. Lloyd in fact raised the question of marriage "between close blood relations" at an SADC meeting, but no action was taken, LMS SA 75/3, Minutes of SADC annual meeting, Tiger Kloof 7/3/13–19/3/13, 6.

[68]   Jennings also resented Khama's control of the Church and looked forward to his death, LMS SA 67/3, A. Jennings to R. W. Thompson, Serowe, 2/2/06; and F. H. Hawkins, "Strictly Private," 23--24.

[69]   K III Papers, G/50/22, Mrs. Lloyd to Khama, Serowe, 12/7/13; the grievances included allegations that Lloyd "did not teach nicely," "refused to baptize children," and spent too much time herding his own cattle with the stock of the congregation in Shoshong. LMS SA Reports, 5/1, Shoshong, 1913 (E. Lloyd); LMS SA 75/3, F. H. Hawkins to R. W. Thompson, Tiger Kloof 22/3/13.

[70]   LMS SA, South African Committee Meeting, Box 4, 5/1/13; LMS SA, F. H. Hawkins, "Report ... Nov. 1912 to March 1913," 64. The minister placed in Shoshong was probably Peter Gaeonale.

of experienced personnel, Willoughby explained, which would result in five missionaries (including a "European, male" school teacher, and the old school-teacher Ella Sharp) residing in Serowe.

Khama was taken aback. Unbeknownst to Willoughby, he wrote that very evening to the LMS requesting an unseasoned missionary, whom he could more easily mould.[71] Willoughby told Jennings to convoke Serowe's congregation the next day at the morning hour Khama had suggested. Once the meeting began, however, Willoughby found that the Church had already come to a decision at sunrise. For some reason, Willoughby spoke in English and Tom Brown interpreted. The missionaries, he lectured, were "servants loyal to our King [Christ]," but were willing to treat Khama in a special manner:

> Other Churches will not be told by the Executive, but you are told in this way . . . Mr. Hawkins was here [in 1913]. He and the Chief talked together. What these two chiefs said, we do not know. . . . [But] he is putting five missionaries down here.[72]

The Church disagreed. Deacon after deacon objected that they had not been consulted beforehand. Modisaotsile, a son-in-law of Khama, concluded, "The Church is unable to receive five missionaries. The reason is that the missionaries said, Let all the people of the LMS Church be one Church. We refuse the union of the Churches. We are afraid."[73] Few people could have forgotten that Willoughby and Brown had spearheaded the 1910 drive to unify all Churches. Moreover the Ngwato Church refused to deal with territorial groups like the SADC, whose very existence was an infringement on its liberty.[74] Yet Willoughby must have felt he had a special claim to the king's confidence. The two men had maintained a correspondence even under the pressure of political conflict. None of their many contretemps had derailed their mutual commitment, for instance, to religious conformity in Serowe. Now Willoughby professed bewilderment at the Serowe congregation's attitude and said that it must surely be based on misunderstanding.

> [As for] union of the Churches . . . we have nothing to do with this at all, unless [it] means a union of the churches *within the Mangwato territory under Chief Khama's control.* That we do mean to effect. The words we once spoke in regard to [Union] are dead.[75]

Of this the Church made sure. Willoughby's presence was called an affront, and the congregation stalled with interminable deliberations. Khama was courteous but clear, and Willoughby gave up. His report merely suggested to the SADC that it forcibly remove Lloyd, who clung grimly *post mortem* to his

---

[71]   K III Papers, G/50/31, Khama to LMS, Serowe, 10/3/14; LMS SA 76/2, W. C. Willoughby and J.T. Brown to F. H. Hawkins, Serowe, 21/3/14.

[72]   *Ibid.*

[73]   *Ibid.*

[74]   Willoughby refrained from sending the SADC a copy of his report. Brown had previously written, "we have had in the past, notwithstanding our District Committee, independency in its extremist form," in supporting the 1910 Bechuanaland Scheme, LMS SA, Reports 4/3, Kuruman for 1910 (J.T.Brown).

[75]   LMS SA 76/2, Willoughby and Brown to Hawkins, Serowe, 21/3/14, my emphasis.

Shoshong home. It was apparent that Khama would expand his Church and the provision of its *thuto* at a pace dictated by BaNgwato, not by missionaries.[76]

The Outcome of Struggle

Each missionary to the Ngwato kingdom realized, to a greater or lesser degree, that his livelihood depended on the good will of the Christian king and the Church. The Revs. Hepburn, Willoughby, and Jennings, as individuals, were caught between their idealized role and this reality of their restrictive dependence on the king.

For the LMS, the peculiar instability of its relationship with Khama and the Ngwato Church made it necessary to rotate or discard missionaries, and to cast this practice as normal and periodic. This renewal permitted the LMS to stay in the Ngwato kingdom; but for Ngwato Christians, the LMS was really only a prophylactic for the regime of the Word, giving it international resilience. Few doubted that Khama would jettison the LMS if he wished. Although such an arrangement thwarted the LMS's social and political agenda in the Ngwato kingdom, it served Ngwato political autonomy well. Thus Jennings' mediation of the LMS's attempt to denationalize its mission was doomed to fail.

Looking ahead, this relationship with the LMS would persist into the 1940s, always in flux and under strain. The Ngwato Church continued to defend itself against the LMS, much as it did against other denominations. Non-Christian headmen continued to demand a say in the "state" affairs of the Church.[77] In his confidential report to the directors in 1913, Secretary Hawkins called the Ngwato Church "self-supporting" and "independent," and the next year the LMS *Chronicle* commented, "In a very true sense Khama is head of the Church as well as head of the State." Khama's wife, Semane, meanwhile became the senior deaconess and led evangelical forays outside Serowe. The Rev. Haydon Lewis, Khama's new missionary, wrote,

> 1915 has tended to the development of a sense of unity among the whole of the Mangwato Churches . . . in a sense we have simply brought matters affecting the local policy of the church into line with the general policy of the tribe.[78]

---

[76] Ibid; LMS SA 76/2, Khama to F. H. Hawkins, Serowe, 24/3/14; the only local European doctor died soon after, which may explain Khama's subsequent receptiveness toward a medical missionary; 76/3, E. Sharp to Hawkins, 18/5/14. There had also been a further rumor of the coming union of the Matebeleland and Ngwato Churches under CUSA auspices, and Khama suspected Jennings of authorship. K III Papers, E/32/9 Khama to W. C. Willoughby, Serowe, 7/7/14; and similar letters, E/32/29, Khama to W. C. Willoughby, Serowe, 30/9/14, and Khama to W. C. Willoughby, 1/10/14; LMS SA 78/1, R.H. Lewis to Hawkins, Serowe, 12/2/16.

[77] Church members continued to demand their Communion tickets be in SeTswana, not both SeTswana and Ndebele; the deacons felt that any other arrangement would "lend colour to the idea that the Missionaries were going to squeeze the Churches into Union," LMS SA 75/3, J. T. Brown to Thompson, Kuruman 24/1/13; LMS SA Annual Meeting of the SADC, 1914, 15. In 1916 non-Christian headmen rebuked Khama for not consulting them on the rebuilding of the church, LMS SA Reports 5/2, Serowe, 1916 (R.H. Lewis, 1917).

[78] LMS SA Reports, R.H. Lewis, Serowe, 1916.

The LMS plan to unify Church policy across the boundaries of Tswana states was handily transformed into a unification of missionary policy within the Ngwato kingdom. This allowed the old king to stand aloof. Khama "neither claims nor would be allowed" any official authority in the Church, the Rev. Lewis assured the directors. But as the Rev. Cullen Reed, who briefly served as Lewis's co-missionary, put it,

> the work cannot be divided. The whole of it centres in the church at Serowe and the deaconate there, as does the tribal life in the kgotla [sic] there. The whole also looks to the Chief [Khama] for political direction, if not for spiritual also, and the connection with Serowe is *vital and constant*.[79]

The "whole of it" is best called the realm of the Word. In 1922 men and women gathered for a sedate rejoicing, the "Jubilee" anniversary of the aging reign of the aged King Khama. The leader of an age-regiment (*mophato*), in the ancient and mutable southern African tradition of courtly praise, thanked the venerable LMS for its labors. His words sum up the themes of this chapter.

> The Missionaries . . . first brought the light among our tribe. You taught us to humble ourselves before the British Government. We are here in tribal dress so that you may see the fruits of your labours. You have helped our Chief. He always tells us that. He reigns through the Church. His reign is established on God.[80]

Ripe understatements, accusations couched in self-deprecation, these were common coin in Tswana speeches. Here the notion of ruling "through the Church" is coupled to a gesture to the regiment's "tribal dress," in allusion to several paradoxes. Missionaries had facilitated the aims of imperial government from the start, thus humbling the BaNgwato. Yet they had also served the power of the Ngwato monarchy. They had labored in a growing Church of Ngwato Christians, rehearsing new behavior and scripting alien values; yet BaNgwato claimed the Church outright as their own institution, and missionaries knew it. Everyone was aware that in southern Africa, Christians had worn Western clothing for a long time. Regimental "tribal dress" was an invention, a sign for the ambivalence of what missionaries had simultaneously opposed and championed. Some regiments wore Scots kilts.

The Church itself did not stand still, and it changed greatly after 1900. As it fought for and won the right to itself, as it were, its character emerged through a different process of contestation and compromise. Both the composition of the Church and the very meaning of being a Ngwato Christian were matters for ongoing negotiation, of a subtler kind than that pursued by delegations and foreign secretaries. This is the subject of the next chapter.

---

[79]   LMS SA 79/1 C. Reed to F. H. Hawkins, Serowe, 23/9/16. My emphasis.

[80]   LMS SA 84/5, Leader of the "Yellow Regiment," 23/7/22, in R. H. Lewis, notes on the Jubilee Celebration, "Khama salutes his Missionaries." Lewis's original translation is even more direct: "as [Khama] himself is always telling us, when he says, 'I govern by means of the Church.' Truly his government is founded upon God." LMS SA Reports, 84/3 R. H. Lewis to F. H. Hawkins, Serowe, 30/7/22.

3

How the Meaning of Thuto *Changed: Status, Literacy, Cattle, and Nationalism*

> *Chiefs long ago were true believers, and loved the Church very much;*
> *not those of nowadays: they are utterly outdone by commoners.*
> Mrs. Setuhile Sebina, Ngwato Christian[1]

From the moment *thuto* (loosely, teachings) germinated in the kingdom in the early 1860s, the ethos of the term was shifting. Such a viscosity can be freeze-framed and represented in demographic terms, especially with regard to the gender and background of Christians, and this chapter does so, following trends into the 1920s. During that same period, however, the very meanings within *thuto*—its signs, implications, and accidental properties—also changed, negotiated and renegotiated in the margins between Ngwato and colonial demands. Neither of these two sorts of transformation would be possible, however, without the institutional and ecclesiastical reforms of the turn of the century, occasioned by dynastic and colonially abetted crises. This chapter, then, is about the relationship between history and signification in the making of the realm of the Word.

The Demographics of Thuto

As a gendered quantity, *thuto* at first split between the female enquirers' classes assembled under the Rev. Schulenburg in 1860 and the almost exclusively male club of Christians initiated into full membership. In a patriarchal and polygamous milieu, the call to congregate under an empowered man or an omnipotent Master seemed directed toward women and children; but the Christian "faction" of the

---

[1]   Interview: Mrs. Setuhile Sebina, Serowe, 28 Feb. 1989. "Commoners" is the diminutive of *batho*, people.

town as stewarded by Price and Mackenzie embraced most young men. So long as there was no stable division between Church members and enquirers, the core of the Church remained the Khama-aligned cult of the Word. The greater part of Hepburn's congregation continued to be high-born Ngwato men; many were half-brothers, cousins, or other kin of Khama, while others had close marital ties to such men.[2]

The situation was very different in other Tswana towns, where women always outnumbered men in LMS congregations. In 1862, for instance, Mackenzie noted that Montsiwe of the BaRolong, in opposing the Christians in his town, attempted to "terrify . . . the females who, he knew, animated" all other Christians.[3] In GammaNgwato, on the other hand, the king himself animated other Ngwato Christians. In the 1890s, and even after the turn of the century, the capital town's congregation was still mostly married men. The Rev. Williams, in Phalapye from 1898 to 1899, noted that while "the thuto (gospel) is quite an adjunct of national life . . . [only a] small proportion of women" even attended services.[4] The Church roll probably reflected this imbalance all the way up through 1906 or 1907.

Thuto was not confined to Church services, however, but also pertained to school, or *sekole*. At first, of course, little distinguished evangelism and schooling in practice. Of the early *baruti* (teachers) in the 1870s, eight of twelve were close relations of Khama, and all were Church members. In the *kgotla* or "ward" schools established in the capital as early as 1878, Raditladi commented that "People rejoice to hear the Word of God."[5] By 1892, the Ngwato capital had five "day" schools, typical for the Tswana polities. The schools taught a few hundred out of the town's population of thousands of children. In 1900 the BDC enjoined BaNgwato, "Coerce your children into going to school."[6] Yet the spread of *thuto* in this way was slow; it did not seem a thing for children.

Neither catechumen classes nor day- or Sunday-school were restricted by age or periods of attendance. Therefore, the younger sons of Christian families, who tended to stay at the cattle posts caring for their family's wealth, often returned to school intermittently or later in life. The Church sent books out to cattle posts, but formal schooling was set into the stability of the town. In general, attendance depended on the constant interplay between missionaries' expectation of a regular,

---

[2] Dachs, *Papers of John Mackenzie*, 34 (Mackenzie to Mullens, 2/9/1872); WCW/795, offprint of John Mackenzie, "The Bamangwato Mission, A Retrospective," in *The Chronicle of the LMS* (Jan. 1877); see also Hepburn, *Twenty Years*, 26–28.

[3] LMS SA 32/4/C, J. Mackenzie to J. S. Moffat, "BaNwato" 24/6/1862.

[4] LMS Reports 3/1, Phalapye, 1898 (H. Williams, 1899).

[5] Rhodesian National Archives (now Zimbabwe National Archives), "Phalapye, March 23, 1894," marked "[29]" and "handwriting of W. C. Willoughby, apparently copied from ms. by Tiro," courtesy Isaac Schapera (hereafter "RNA 23/3/1894"), 1, 6. With the spread of primary schools, the distinction between *moruti* and plain *tichere* (teacher) did arise, but since both would be Church-goers, the difference between them was often seen as one of rank.

[6] WCW/374, *Go BaDiphuthego*, LMS circular, ca. 1899: "Kgarametsang bana ba lona ba ee sekolen[g]." See too Chirenje, *History of Northern Botswana*, 161; R. W. Thompson (London Missionary Society), *Special Visit to South Africa, August, September, October 1892* (Cape Town, 1893), 6; Parsons, "Khama III," 249; LMS SA Reports, School Report, Serowe 1915 (E. Sharp, 1916). See also Part Themba Mgadla, "Missionary and Colonial Education among the Bangwato: 1862–1948" (Ph.D. dissertation, Boston University, 1986), 160, 261, 267; at least in the 1920s, the Standards cost one pound per year, 252.

TABLE 3.1: THE NGWATO CHURCH, 1897 TO 1915[7]

Year		Confirmed Membership	In School Boys	Girls	In Sun. School	Relevant events

The capital at Phalapye, usually including outstations if figures are known

Year		Confirmed Membership	In School Boys	Girls	In Sun. School	Relevant events
1893		200				
-						
1897		402	142	162	311	Rinderpest
1898		496	141	151	n.a.	
1899		557	1050	49	728	S.A. War leads
1900		553	1095	119	2180	to outdoor, *kgotla*
1901		544	1148	1327		classes

The capital at Serowe, and all outstations, including Shoshong

| 1902 | | 564 | 1076 | | 1255 | |
| 1903 | | 600 | n.a. | | n.a. | Drought |

Shoshong is separate station; Se = Serowe and outstations, Sh = Shoshong and outstations

1904	Se	418	132		n.a.	Drought, marriages as
	Sh	275	255	390		evangelical method
1905	Se	555	340	243		Drought, marriages
	Sh	279	360	490		
1906	Se	796	364	200		
	Sh	341	365	337		
1907	Se	862	493	200		
	Sh	341	348	330		
1908	Se	n.a.	n.a.	n.a.		
	Sh	262	28[1]	60[1]		
1909	Se	922	259	938		Return of exiles
	Sh	269	269	202		
1910	Se	972	n.a.	n.a.		Missionary conflict
	Sh	n.a.	n.a.	n.a.		with king
1911	Se	873	276	94[1]		Drought
	Sh	293	179	302		
1912	Se	n.a.	n.a.	n.a.		Bad Drought
	Sh	359	172	407		
1913	Se	932	415	410		Drought
	Sh	431	360	570		

Shoshong and its figures merge with Serowe

| 1914 | | 1715 | 220[2] | 350[2] | | 255 Herero Christians |
| 1915 | | 2247 | 1040 | 2460 | | enter and are rec'd |

Notes: n.a. = not available. [1] Not including outstations. [2] Excluding Shoshong?

---

[7]   Compiled from the published *Reports of the London Missionary Society*; JR LMS/S 3, Communion register; and LMS SA Reports and correspondence. The numbers are not exact, and varied throughout the year. What constituted an "adherent," "outstation," and "schoolchild" varied widely.

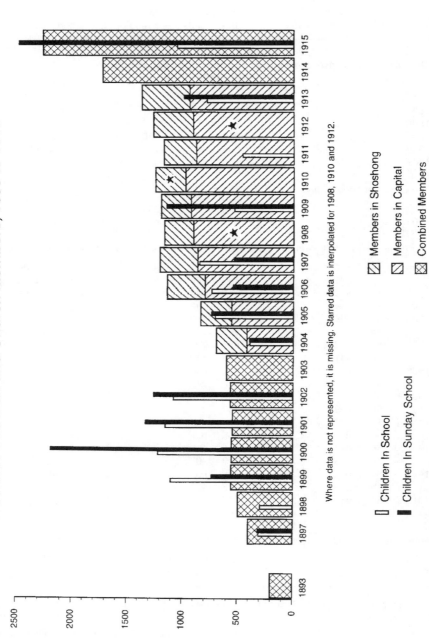

School Children and Church Members, 1893 to 1915

Where data is not represented, it is missing. Starred data is interpolated for 1908, 1910 and 1912.

Children In School
Children In Sunday School

Members in Shoshong
Members in Capital
Combined Members

TABLE 3.2: THE NGWATO CHURCH, BY SEX, 1900 TO 1903[8]

Year	Membership at Phalapye		Catechumens at Phalapye	
	M	F	M	F
1900	M 179	F 113	M 30	F 25
1901	M 177	F 117	M 59	F 53
Jan. 1902	n.a.	n.a.	M 58	F 53
Dec. 1902	n.a.	n.a.	M 60	F 117

Note: n.a. = not available

abstract school year, the flexibility of Tswana seasonal labor, and the variability of the rains.[9]

Girls, who grew up at home, attended school more regularly than boys. Ngwato families may have been discouraged from sending their boys to a school presided over by a woman, and white missionaries themselves felt that Ella Sharp's sex was unfortunate.[10] Most importantly perhaps, the provision of *thuto* to interested souls in the 1860s had established a pattern that prevented anyone from guarding its perimeters. Schooling eventually affected all *thuto*. After Christian parents began sending their girls to school, commoners, people of recent non-Ngwato extraction, and even dependent households moved to acquire *thuto*. The wives, mothers, and daughters among them joined Ngwato youth in catechumen classes; their daughters entered *sekole*.[11]

Table 3.1. and Graph 3.1 show that children's numbers in school (and hence in the catechumenate) peaked around 1900–1901. During the South African War, the church building was transformed into a fortress, and school moved directly to the king's *kgotla*. The excitement this must have generated accounts for a sharp rise in enrollment. The figures suggest that parents hesitated before sending their daughters into this space, but soon the school relocated to the church. Table 3.2 shows that 1902 was a critical year; women and girls outnumbered men and boys in the catechumenate, by two to one. This may have been a resumption of an earlier trend.

---

8   JR LMS/S 3 Communion register.

9   Interviews: Mrs. Balatheo Moloi, Serowe, 17 Nov. 1988; Mr. Radiphofu Moloi Sekgoma, b. 1902, Serowe, 20 Nov. 1988; Mr. L.G. Baruti, b. 1902, Baruti ward, Serowe, 8 Nov. 1988, English; and Chirenje, *History of Northern Botswana*, 162-3; LMS SA Reports, 2/?, J. Hepburn to R. W. Thompson, Shoshong 11/2/1887; 4/2, Serowe for 1909 (A. Jennings, 1910); 4/3, Serowe for 1910 (E. Sharp, 1911); LMS SA 46/1/A, E. Lloyd to R. W. Thompson, Shoshong 13/1/1889; 77/2, E. Sharp to F. W. Hawkins, Serowe, 8/2/15.

10   LMS SA 65/?, E. Sharp to H. W. Thompson, Serowe, 8/9/04; and H. Williams and A. Jennings, Minutes of the BDC, 26/10/04, cited in Mgadla, "History of Education," 259, and see 262–65. Women teachers had been accepted in the labor market in turn-of-the-century England. Male teachers, many from Tiger Kloof, came and went rather quickly through Sharp's staff, perhaps because neither Khama not the Church paid them; Bessie Head, *Serowe, Village of the Rain Wind* (London, 1981), 19, interview with Rannau Ramojababa, retired schoolteacher, then aged eighty.

11   LMS SA Reports, 3/2, Serowe for 1903 (A. Jennings, 1904): Sunday school, being the lowest route of approach to the Church, attracted mainly children, but some adults, "most of [whom] attend no other service and include the off-scouring of the town," came as well; and LMS SA Reports 3/1, Phalapye for 1899 (H. Williams).

Five to eight years later (1907–1910), Church membership reached a plateau. The school population rose again in 1913–1916; and a similar number of years later, the Church membership rose, partly in response to the increasing school body (even discounting 255 Herero refugees who gained immediate membership in the Church). Such six-year intervals correspond to the time that typically elapsed between the baptism of school-going catechumens and their subsequent Church confirmations, often directly after their marriages. In 1908 the average age of Christian bridegrooms was thirty-one, and of brides twenty; in 1917, the ages were thirty and twenty-one, respectively. These averages are elevated by the fact that some couples had probably already set up house together, married in SeTswana practice.[12]

Putting aside all caveats, we can surmise that a core of pubescent girls matured into the Church's membership. From 1908 onward, the Church became younger and was increasingly dominated by literate, recently married women.

Such figures provide glimpses at a complex process. To fathom what the transformation of the Church entailed, not only for its relatively elite membership but for the kingdom as a whole, we must broaden our scope. *Thuto* might be read, not just in books, but as part of the social history of Christians. It flowed through the life of the Church, connecting the town, the kingship, the lives of distant villagers, and Christians' inward selves. Yet *thuto* also divided people, and showed unevenly in their dress and their comportment, signs of the political and economic distinctions among them.

Clean and Haberdashed

The mark of a Christian from an early date was a suit of Western clothing. Khama first accepted his in 1852, from an itinerant white hunter. By 1876, according to Mackenzie, only the poor, the dependent, and the conservative dressed in the leathers of the old style; and, although he felt no need to mention it, so did most women. The missionary described all these people as "unclothed."[13] Why did the lack of Western fabrics mean being "unclothed"? Ann Hollander notes that for six centuries, the Western world has worn not merely a covering, but "clothing that creates a form, a visual arrangement made up of . . . the combined movements" of overlapping shapes of fabric and body parts.[14] To missionaries, the absence of these structuring forms meant undress, a lack of individual closedness; in much the same way, the absence of rectilinear enclosures for nuclear families suggested loose and

---

[12] UCCSA Papers, Marriage Register 2 (Serowe, Nov. 1906–April 1912), Marriage Register 3 (Serowe, May 1912–Jan. 1920), average of 140 couples each sample, 1908 and 1917–18. This does not take into account marriages obviously made in couples' declining years to sanctify long-passed SeTswana marriages, which would further raise these numbers.

[13] Parsons, *Word of Khama*, 1--2, citing James Chapman, *Travels in the Interior of South Africa* (London, 1868); 112; H. Depelchin, *Journey to Gubulawayo*, 130, and Samuel Blackbeard to May Blackbeard, ca. 1930, copy in possession of Dennis Blackbeard; orig. in Grahamstown archives, South Africa; Dachs, *Papers of John Mackenzie*, Mackenzie to Mullens, Shoshong, August 1876.

[14] Ann Hollander, *Seeing Through Clothes* (New York, 1978), quote 85; and 83, 381. Thanks to Kristen Vallow. See also Hilda Kuper, "Costume and Identity," *Comparative Studies in Society and History* 15 (1973), 356.

promiscuous relations between groups. Turning this relationship around, the Word itself "clothed" Africans. As Robert Moffat wrote:

> The same Gospel which had taught [BaTswana] that they were spiritually miserable, blind, and naked, discovered to them also that they needed reform externally, and thus prepared their minds to adopt those modes of comfort, cleanliness and convenience. . . . Thus, by the slow but certain progress of the Gospel principles, whole families became clothed and in their right mind.[15]

Dirtiness and nakedness both served to blur the edges of the ideal Victorian categories of home and person; but while dirt was unwanted, it was seen as integral to Africa, with its undifferentiated "tribes" and communal customs. In this context, Khama stood out for European writers mainly because he, conversely, was recognizable. As Mrs. Knight-Bruce wrote in a revealing metaphor, Khama "has emerged out of the dust storm that turns so much African history into a dull confusion. . . ."[16] From an imperial distance, it seemed irrelevant whether the confusion belonged to Africa or Mrs. Knight-Bruce.

On a basic level, anything unfamiliar demands the contours of a boundary, even if egoistically drawn, in order to be pictured: this cognitive requirement did not depend on having a colonial mentality.[17] In the setting of southern Africa, however, Nonconformist missionaries went further and linked the Other's quality of being unknown to sin and deviation. Was not a "visible" definition of personhood (like Khama's) central to the notion of the Christian, who had to make a personal commitment of faith? Without such a definition, the African receded into the foggy mass of heathendom. Christian commitment came as a confession, a discussion of oneself; catechumen and enquirer both were *baipoledi*, "self-tellers." Without personal expression, one was a tribesman, as early ethnographers confirmed. Frantz Boas noted, "The more primitive [a tribe] is, the greater is the number of restrictions that determine every action," obliterating the individual will.[18] Hence when missionaries and their charges in GammaNgwato called sin *ditiro tsa bosilo*, acts of filth—darkening and cluttering the self—they spoke on several levels at once.

Sin was equated not only with the unknown, but also, on another level, with the past. Europeans' ignorance of precolonial Africa was reified as a quality of darkness, physically lurking before enlightenment. When LMS Foreign Secretary F. H. Hawkins came to South and Central Africa he travelled, like so many before him, *Through Lands That Were Dark*. They were dark indeed to the European gaze: the pall covered "written" Africa as an automatic and perpetual qualifier.[19] The trope

---

15   Robert Moffat, *Missionary Labours and Scenes in Southern Africa* (New York, 1847), 334–35. Moffat later noted that BaTswana were "not partial to bathing," and recommended that missionaries teach "cleanliness in their persons and homes," LMS SA 32/3/B, R. Moffat to Tidman, Kuruman 23/12/1861.

16   L. Knight-Bruce, "Kame," *Murray's Magazine* V, 28 (1889), 453 (452–65), cited in Q. N. Parsons, "The Image of Khama the Great, 1868–1970," *Botswana Notes and Records* 3 (1971). See Albert Memmi, T*he Colonizer and the Colonized* (Boston, 1976), and more generally, Mary Douglas, *Purity and Danger* (London, 1967).

17   This forms part of Ludwig Wittgenstein's reasoning, which I am bearing in mind, in *Philosophical Investigations*, trans. G. E. M. Anscombe, 3rd ed. (New York, 1958).

18   Franz Boas, "The Aim of Ethnography" [1888], in Boas, *Race, Language and Culture* (New York, 1940), 633.

19   F. H. Hawkins, *Through Lands That Were Dark: Being a Record of a Year's Missionary Journey* (London, 1914).

was an ancient one, reflected in the medieval Christian discourse of Light and Darkness. Perhaps more discomfiting was the way Ngwato Christians absorbed this
imagery. In a soliloquy on "custom," Kelethokile Raditladi, an ordained *moruti* and
nephew of Khama, mused, "Why should we go into the mud when we have been
cleansed? Why look back while we are holding the plough?" Mrs. G. Sethebogeng
recalled to me the hymn that led her to Church: "I was lost—I was filthy in a way
not cleansed by water—I was washed clean in Jesus's blood." When the time came
for her confirmation, she confessed that she had "feared being in darkness."[20] In
linking BaNgwato with missionary discourse, tropes like dark or dirty were potent
precisely because they declared a unity of meaning while conveying situational
and particular ideas. Mrs. Sethebogeng's negation of light was not identical to that
of the LMS, but they seemed to speak the same language.

Dirtiness pervaded England too, whose "masses" were similarly unwashed
sinners. The English census of 1851, taken at the height of Congregationalist Church
growth, revealed a disturbingly irreligious working class.[21] Like BaTswana, they
might begin their salvation with a simple "washbucket" and a clean shirt. At the
same time Moffat issued the statement just described, a home mission in London
distributed the pamphlet, "Dirt: and a Word about Washing."

> Wash your whole body over every morning; and put on clean clothes
> as often as you can. You could soon afford plenty of clean shirts and
> sheets, if the publican gave you back your money. . . . An habitually
> dirty man can hardly be religious. . . . Cleanliness in person prepares
> for purity of heart, and for a reception of the life-giving principle of
> the Gospel.[22]

Missionaries in southern Africa kept to these interlocking sentiments in subsequent decades, thus supplying *thuto* with a physical presence, however ill-defined.
Cleanliness was not immediately and univocally corporeal; the economy of commodities, including soap, grew only after the turn of the century.[23] Nevertheless,
the Rev. Willoughby, who wore white cotton shirts and a black frock coat, com-

---

[20]   BNA S/598/2, K. Raditladi, in S. Ratshosa, "My Book," Part 2, ca. 1930, 90; Interview: Mr. Lebogang
Bolokeng, b. 1920, Serowe, n.d. The Rev. R. K. Mogodi also mentions (1910) those "of whom it is said,
'They were washed clean but they have gone back and rolled themselves in the mud,'" which suggests
some currency for the phrase (in ZKM, Tiger Kloof Ordination Examinations ca. 1910, Roger K. Mogodi,
6).

[21]   R. Currie, A. Gilbert, and L. Horsley, *Churches and Churchgoers: Patterns of Church Growth in the
British Isles since 1700* (Oxford, 1977), 25, 29, 34; Table 2.3. The earliest Dissenting movement to spread
the gospel to "the unenlightened parts of the world," as the first LMS meeting put it, came in tandem
with the Essex association of Congregational ministers' revolutionary decision to evangelize domes-
tically. See Deryck Lovegrove, "Idealism and Association in Early 19th Century Dissent," in W. J.
Sheils and D. Wood, eds., *Voluntary Religion: Studies in Church History*, Vol. 23 (Worcester, 1986), 303–
18; quotes, 304 and 307.

[22]   W. C. Clayton, *Ipswich Temperance Tracts, No. 228, ca. 1850,* in R. J. Helmstadter and P. T. Philips, eds.,
Religion in Victorian Society, A Sourcebook of Documents (Lanham, Md., 1985), 341.

[23]   Tim Burke, "'Nyamarira That I Loved': Commoditization, Consumption and the Social History of
Soap in Zimbabwe," *Collected Papers on the Societies of Southern Africa in the 19th and 20th Centuries,*
Vol. 17 (Institute of Commonwealth Studies, University of London, 1991); and Burke, "Lifebuoy Men,
Lux Women" (Ph.D. dissertation, Johns Hopkins University, 1992); Burke's Chapters 2 and 3 discuss
issues of cleanliness and hygiene for Southern Rhodesia. Explicit programs for bodily hygiene had to
wait for the twentieth century, when soap began to be marketed actively in Southern Africa, 91.

plained about the soiled cuffs of his deacons in 1898, and the Rev. Williams wished for "a more decent care for the body." The BDC's Scheme for Union asked district missionaries to discuss with regional *baruti*, among other concerns, "the personal cleanliness of all its members."[24]

The appearance of some Ngwato Christians, and Khama especially, did satisfy missionaries, hunters, traders, and other observers. Khama acted to generate their perspective, as Neil Parsons has pointed out. He spoke quietly, and held his six-foot frame erect; he seemed pensive; he ate with a fork.[25] In 1879 we have a pleased description of Khama's dress and that of his counsellors in the *kgotla*:

> [Khama] squatted on his heels, in the midst of his people, like the very least of his subjects, [and] bore no mark of his royal dignity, except for a big feather fastened in his soft felt hat of British make. His garb recalled that worn by one of our good Belgian Burghers during the summer: unpolished leather shoes, brown trousers, a flannel shirt, and a light jacket of English material.[26]

Men were to avoid both "nakedness" and sartorial flair. Although a desire to purchase goods was certainly a mark of civilization for Nonconformist missionaries, BaNgwato and other southern Africans were expected to temper new habits with modesty. The following description by F. H. Hawkins in 1914 echoes the passage above: in Khama's home there was a

> large old-fashioned drawing-room table [and] . . . a light folding table on which was a richly framed autograph portrait of Queen Victoria, which she had given to the Chief in 1895. On this table also stood a very large blue enamel milk-pail full of milk and a bottle of vinegar . . . on the walls were portraits of Royalties.[27]

Ideally BaNgwato were to become loyal European yeomanry, while remaining safely African. They were to shun the urbanism that Nonconformists especially distrusted and that they knew so well.[28] Further, missionaries not only asked for this transformation, they wanted its origins to remain partly obscured. The *natural* state of a Christian underclass was a primitive worker-peasantry, at

---

[24]   LMS SA 85/2, S. Ratshosa to J. C. Harris, Serowe, 15/5/23; LMS SA Reports, 3/3, Shoshong for 1904 (H. Williams, 1905); LMS SA 72/6, Scheme for the Unification of the London Missionary Society in Bechuanaland, 1910; WCW/"In Remembrance of Me."

[25]   Khama: J. Chapman, *Travels in the Interior of South Africa*, I (Johannesburg, 1868), 112, cited in Parsons, *Word of Khama*, 1–2; Dachs, *Papers of John Mackenzie*, 89 (J. Mackenzie to J. Mullens, Shoshong, 27/1/1868). See also Parsons, "The Image of Khama."

[26]   Quote: Depelchin and Croonenberghs, *Journey to Gubuluwayo*, 128. Although the remarks come from a Catholic and continental perspective, English Nonconformists shared much the same Romantic bent.

[27]   Hawkins, *Through Lands That Were Dark*, 50.

[28]   As Jean and John L. Comaroff discuss, in *Of Revelation and Revolution*, esp. 71--73. It is worth noting that Sechele of the BaKwena failed to capture this precise middle ground and therefore became a slightly comical figure in the 1880s, with his spectacles and dyed-black hair, silver tea set, and crumpets. See Ramsay, "The Rise and Fall of the Kwena," 116; Walter Kerr, *The Far Interior* (London, 1886), 27; and Thomas M. Thomas, *Eleven Years in Central Africa* [1873] (Bulawayo, 1970), 48. W. C. Willoughby, *Tiger Kloof: The LMS's Native Institution in South Africa* (London, 1912), 78, rhapsodizes precisely about the pupil "discovering his own clumsiness [i.e., with tools], learning to respect, and possibly to envy, the skilful," etc.

home with the wood plane and plow. An inflorescence of qualities supposedly followed after the "seed"[29] of the Gospel had taken root and grown, as a single process.

In Pierre Bourdieu's terms, missionaries thus held the "domestic acquisition of cultural capital," preferably hidden, to be far better than "learning." The working compromise was to neaten up domestic life and teach it in the classroom, while scorning scholastic culture. When missionaries fostered "educated" attitudes through their own teaching, they despised their students as inferior poseurs. For instance, the Rev. Jennings felt that much anti-LMS agitation in 1910 originated from (as he put it) "half-educated" youth. "Half" is key: such people seemed hybridized, and threatened a state of being that missionaries held as natural and undivided, but which, strangely, could never quite be put into words. Such knots of meaning made missionaries' vision of proper African dress as precise as it was banal, yet it somehow eluded articulation.[30] Both too much and too little "dress" connoted something akin to what Adolph Loos termed "ornament," which he saw as the results of misdirected labor: on the one side, the naked but beaded heathen, on the other, the lavish and vain dandy. One might object that missionaries did not theorize about labor; still, the space between the dandy and the heathen was collapsed, in accordance with the missionary desire that African production outpace consumption by a very small margin: rural Africans were perpetually to remain in an interim state. Poised between universal ideals and actual subordination, between clarified individual wills and assumed conformity, they would always be subject to criticism.[31]

Thus the sign of a MoNgwato's "natural and clear" social station was tenuous and hard to discern in practice, at least until we leave the realm of middle-class missionaries' perceptions. In fact, clothing found other meaning in the vicissitudes of Ngwato society. In some cases, BaNgwato understood parts of the British symbology of attire too well; they knew, for instance, that tropical English woolens physicalized an adherence to codes heedless of comfort or pleasure. After all, how comfortable were Khama's flannel shirts and three-button jackets in the Kalahari summer? In hindsight, one better comprehends Tshekedi Khama's sartorial taste during the ceremony of his suspension in September 1933. In the sweltering, after-

---

[29] Chirenje, *A History of Northern Botswana*, 170, citing J. Hepburn to R. W. Thompson, Shoshong, 11/2/1887; LMS SA Reports, 4/1, Shoshong, 1907 (E. Lloyd, 1908). For instance, a catechumen in the 1870s, Sechagawe, read Genesis and threw it away; he now returned to the fold; the "seed" merely lay dormant until it finally "begins to spring up into life." For John Mackenzie, conversion was "the yellow harvest field," and the missionary (himself) "the husbandman on the wild furze-covered moorland," *Ten Years*, 264. See also Jean and John L. Comaroff, *Of Revelation and Revolution*, 80.

[30] LMS SA 74/3, A. Jennings to F. H. Hawkins, Serowe, 19/1/12; LMS SA Reports, 3/1, Phalapye Mission Outstations, 1900 (H. Williams, 1901); 3/3, Shoshong for 1904 (H. Williams, 1905). See Homi Bhabha, "Of Mimicry and Man: The Ambivalence of Colonial Discourse," *October* 28 (1984), 125–33; Nicholas Thomas, "Colonial Conversions: Difference, Hierarchy and History in Evangelical Propaganda," *Comparative Studies in Society and History* 34 (1992), 377; Pierre Bourdieu, *Distinction: A Social Critique of the Judgement of Taste* (London, 1984), 76; and Jean and John L. Comaroff, "Home-Made Hegemony," 26.

[31] Adolf Loos, "Ornament and Crime," 1908, in U. Conrads, *Programs and Manifestoes on 20th Century Architecture* (Cambridge, Mass., 1970), 20: "What is natural to the Papuan [read "any uncivilized people"] and the child is a symptom of degeneracy in the modern adult. . . . The evolution of culture is synonymous with the removal of ornament. . . ." One could just as easily find statements from other fields of aesthetics encoding the same industrial ethic.

noon heat, the regent king faced the military and legal apparat of the Protectorate buttoned to the neck in a heavy overcoat.[32]

For BaNgwato, clothes also reflected Ngwato gradations of power and status. Western dress was not worn wrong, but worn differently. Hats, for instance, in addition to being a useful item in themselves, fast took on a symbolic load.[33] With certain other pieces of clothing, hats signified a subtle prestige, and for men, the Ngwato Church was one forum for such worldly displays. Yet Ngwato regiments had long worn feathery headgear. When Khama left his ambitious brother Kgamane in charge of governing in 1883, Kgamane tried to provoke the senior men of the *kgotla*, including Christians, to wear plumage set into their hair. Upon his return from preparatory maneuvers against the Ndebele, Khama interpreted this act as seditious. Such was the quality of the line separating heathenism and usurpation from Christianity and loyalty: a layer of English felt between a feather and the head.[34]

As Saint Paul had admonished, no adornment should be worn in Church, and women, not men, should cover their heads in deference to man and God. Most married women, *basadi*, accordingly wore plain scarves from an early date.[35] These scarves soon became consistent markers of marital status in the midst of services, visibly mapping the position of their wearers in the pews. From the Rev. Hepburn's time, Christian men brought hats and pegged them or held them in the church. Tensions accompanied such trivial signs and gestures. A boy had missed a season of school; would his father keep his usual seat? A new Christian mother had not wed in Church; where was her signature blue headkerchief? Not every young man had the cash to purchase a new hat, nor did each woman have the "suitable" clothes expected for major rituals.[36] When it came time to baptize six men of servant status from the backwater villages of the Tswapong Hills, other Christians ventured to help them out, but Hepburn felt that he had to "restrain" them from purchasing hats for the Tswapong men. The Ngwato masters of the men would be offended, and anyhow, servants must not get "puffed up." On a herd boy's head, a hat became an absurdity, paralleling "mistresses providing ostriche feathers for English maids. And yet it was quite natural that Christians should have fallen into the mistake, for who among them had seen a Church member come to Church without a hat."[37]

These sorts of "mistakes" were not uncommon and remind us that status was renegotiated in church each week. There, missionaries' social expectations were

---

[32] Michael Crowder, *The Flogging of Phineas McIntosh: A Tale of Colonial Folly and Injustice, Bechuanaland, 1933* (New Haven, Conn., 1988), 90.

[33] Schapera, *Praise-Poems*, 133–34; retranslation of *utla* suggested by Julie Croston, "Crocodile Snatch the Boer Child's Hat: Historical Use of Tswana Praise-Poems," Paper presented at the African Studies Association annual meeting, Denver, Colo., 1987.

[34] Isaac Schapera, *Bogwera: Kgatla Initiation* (Gaborone, 1978), illustration; Depelchin, *Journey to Gubuluwayo*, 126; Mbako Mongwa, "The Struggle," 63; and see Hilda Kuper, "Costume," 365. For Kgamane: Edwin Lloyd, *Three Great African Chiefs*, 76; BHP, Box "Ntbks", Bk. 1; *Annual Report of the LMS*, 91st year (1885), 124 ("Shoshong").

[35] 1 Tim. 2:8–15; 1 Cor. 11:1–16. See Ruth Borker, "To Honor Her Head: Hats as a Symbol of Women's Position in Three Evangelical Churches in Edinburgh," in Judith Hoch-Smith and Anita Spring, eds., *Women in Ritual and Symbolic Roles* (New York, 1978); thanks to Nancy Hunt.

[36] Cf. Setiloane, *The Image of God*, 188.

[37] LMS SA Reports, 2/1, Shoshong of 1886 (J. Hepburn, 1887).

sometimes confounded. The Rev. Willoughby, who thought himself scrupulously impartisan, nonetheless wryly noted to himself how "the Bechuana array themselves in an odd lot of misfitting English clothes . . . and it is really absurd to see the close-cropped woolly heads of our native women under English hats."[38] The debate was not confined to inward racist musings. From the start, "masters" (*beng*) argued to the Rev. Mackenzie that to teach (*ruta*) dependent inferiors "was to cause them to run away." As we have seen, Ngwato Christians were by and large masters rather than servants in the 1880s and 1890s.[39] Many Christians were wealthy, and Ngwato tradesmen and transport drivers in the north-south wagon trade were likely to attend services. By the 1910s the old aristocratic prejudices weakened to exclude only hereditary cattleherds and MaSarwa servants, but we can hear in *Moruti* Lenyebe's words an echo of an earlier, generalized attitude toward commoners. Some *beng*

> did not like [the cattleherds] to become Christians, it was jealousy, but they did not appreciate it at all. They [herders] were minor people and . . . the masters said it would only waste their time . . . [even some Christian masters] regarded a *moruti* like the enemy, who came and spoilt their MaSarwa by teaching them to be like their masters.[40]

The matrix for elitist fears, as for the symbolism of the hat, was the actual aristocratic core of the membership of the Church. Status and power were always serious matters for them. In 1895, the aristocratic nature of the Church received its first genuine blow as the cult of the Word fractured and split. This crisis significantly accelerated the democratization of *thuto* and the evolution of a larger realm for the Word.

Revolt and the Dissolution of the Cult of the Word

In 1895 Khama accused three of his half-brothers of conspiring against him; in turn, they accused the king of "persecuting them," explained Willoughby, "for preaching the gospel to the serfs; [and said] that Khama hated them because they objected to his acting as Chief in the Church."[41]

Khama correctly associated his brothers and their followings with the "old Church" under the Rev. Hepburn.[42] Here the sources tell us mainly about men. Raditladi, the father of the *moruti* Kelethokile, was at the core of the rebellious group; he had criticized Khama after the Hepburn affair three years before in 1892. His faction varied in composition, but its center included Mphoeng, Tiro, Tumedi, Motlhapise, Morwa, and Kuate. Raditladi and Mphoeng were Khama's

38   W. C. Willoughby, *Native Life on the Transvaal Border* (London, n.d. [ca. 1899]), 25.

39   LMS SA Reports, 2/1, J. Mackenzie to R. W. Thompson, Kuruman, 17/2/1882.

40   Interview: The Rev. Johane Lenyebe, b. 1917, Serowe, May 1989. [This and all material from my interviews is given a ragged right margin to distinguish it from other sources on sight.] In Ngamiland even Christian masters were not "willing to let [BaKoba] be married lawfully, for they say that will set them free from slavery," LMS SA 89/1, Sandilands to Hawkins, Serowe, 8/1/27, Kgasa extract No. 19; and Parsons, "Economic History of Khama's Country," 118.

41   WCW/QNP, W. C. Willoughby, "Review of Five Years' Work at Phalapye, 1893 to 1898," 14.

42   LMS SA 51/2/B, W. C. Willoughby to LMS, Phalapye, 16/3/1895.

half-brothers, Morwa was a son-in-law, and Kuate was a cousin on Khama's mother's side; all were prominent Church members. Kuate had accompanied Rev. Hepburn to Ngamiland before he and his younger brother Gadilebane fell afoul of the king. Their father was none other than Pelotona Tidimane, Sekgoma's chief *ngaka*, whose daughter Khama had put aside for a Christian wife. The cult of the Word was indeed a close-knit group, and Tumedi, a wealthy MoKhurutshe,[43] was perhaps the only man central to the dissenting faction with a non-Ngwato lineal identity.

In a deposition made before Sidney Shippard, the new "resident commissioner" for the Protectorate, Raditladi explicitly linked the emerging rift in the cult of the Word to the twenty-year history of the Church's evangelism, in which at least he and three of his peers had been frustrated participants. The "serfs" mentioned by Willoughby above were Tswapong Hill villagers. Raditladi's argument was that Khama had consistently disrupted the spread of *thuto* among them through an undue concern with his own position in the Church.[44]

There was truth in the assertion. Khama feared that providing *thuto* freely to subaltern adults outside his capital would change its meaning and detach it from his kingship. According to Raditladi and his faction, in January 1894 (with Willoughby temporarily absent) the king told them they were "spoiling my people with the new teaching."[45] In March, before Tiro and Morwa left to teach in Maifala and Malete in Tswapong, Khama accused them of confiscating Tswapong grain and ordering Tswapong people to cut wood for them at Tiro's and Morwa's cattleposts. April 1894 again saw Tiro, Morwa, and most likely Tumedi fearful of teaching, as they innocently put it, "those who would learn singing [hymns], and sewing and knitting."[46]

But Khama's suspicions of evangelical abuse were not far-fetched. The "serfs," the "MaTswapong" among whom the aristocratic evangelists preached, were hill dwellers destitute of money or their own cattle, and BaNgwato used them as servants and herders.[47] After 1875, royals in charge of the major wards in the capital were given official responsibility for Tswapong communities; the resulting mix of political and economic domination led the Rev. Lloyd to write that "Matswapong are 'owned' by Bangwato head-men, that is, they are their slaves. Each master owns a few of these people. If they should be successful hunting, they must give up to their master the whole produce of the hunt . . ."[48]

---

43   LMS SA, 53/?, W. C. Willoughby to LMS, Phalapye, 18/3/1896; Parsons, "Khama III," 201.

44   RNA 23/3/1894.

45   LMS SA 52/1/B, Church members to LMS, Phalapye, 16/3/1895.

46   *Ibid.*, 16.

47 Although it is considered offensive by some, I use the term *Ma*Tswapong, because almost no Tswapong person, nor MoNgwato, says or ever said *Ba*Tswapong. Secondarily, the very designation as a collectivity is a Ngwato creation, and BaTswapong just legitimizes the ethnicization of a status distinction. Chapter 8 deals explicitly with the Tswapong Hills.

48   Quote: LMS SA Reports, Shoshong (E. Lloyd) 1/1/1887; and Mackenzie, *Ten Years*, 366; K III B/10, "Verbatim Report of the Enquiry held at Lophephe, on June 19, 1907, by Captain Daniel"; and WCW/734, W. C. Willoughby, "Notes of Tour in the Cwapong and Cweneng Hills," 1896. According to Motswaedi Dimpe, other groups living outside the capital were also placed under royals, though what this entailed is not clear; M. Dimpe, "Batswapong-Bangwato Relations: The Politics of Subordination and Exploitation, 1895-1949" (University of Botswana Student Research Essay, 1986).

Khama suspected Raditladi's reconstruction of *thuto* might turn initiates away from him as the kingdom's supreme Christian; the evangelists "were drawing these people into their service. [But] the Matswapong are my people."[49] In 1899 similar worries helped Khama decide that royal BaNgwato might no longer collect "grain, skins, feathers," and other levies from the MaSarwa families attached to their cattle posts. But at the moment, according to the biased accounts of Raditladi's allies, Khama merely laid personal claim to the whole of *thuto*: "Don't you know me? I will edify you. Don't you know it is I who have taught you these books here? That the people teaching you [the king's kin], I was the one who taught them?"[50]

In the ensuing arguments, the Rev. Willoughby remained loyal to King Khama; in lieu of his support, Raditladi and Mphoeng confided in John Smith Moffat, Robert Moffat's son. As Moffat was an ordained minister, they attended "prayer meetings" in his home, taking refuge in the special discourse of the king. Moffat's involvement was provocative, as in 1891 he had left the LMS to become the first assistant commissioner in GammaNgwato (Phalapye) for the Protectorate, a post that irked Khama, who had to apply to Moffat's office even to buy rifle ammunition. Accused by Khama of betrayal, Moffat oddly exclaimed, according to the king, "If the Bamangwato have forsaken me, if the white men have forsaken me . . . it is better that God take me out of the world."[51]

In this maelstrom of politico-religious anxiety, the king did not speak much about evangelism or *thuto* when accusing Raditladi, Kuate, Tiro, and others of transgressions. He and his close allies—at that time, his son, Sekgoma, and his secretaries, Simon Seisa and Ratshosa Motswetla—instead argued that "Spiritous liquors and [indigenous] beer are the causes of this quarrel."[52] Chapter 4 discusses the evolution of Khama's prohibition and its gendered meaning. Here it is enough to note that those who abstained from all alcohol, including—most difficultly—*bojalwa*, home-brewed beer, pledged a complete allegiance to the moral and political order underpinning the king. Khama's half-brothers, Mphoeng and Raditladi, failed to do so. Khama therefore represented their elusive debate with him as, tropically, alcoholic insubordination: "I charge Raditladi and Tiro with drinking liquor, causing the present quarrel and communicating with the government without letting me know."[53]

Khama repealed his unpopular ban on home-brewed *bojalwa* at the last minute in 1895, so as to diminish Mphoeng and Raditladi's ranks. Nevertheless, the resident commissioner decided to allow Mphoeng and Raditladi to resettle in "disputed territory" with their followers. Among perhaps one or two hundred adults

[49]   PRO 21/6/1895, and Schapera, *Tribal Innovators*, 89. Especially worrying to Khama was Raditladi's injunction that Christians "fear not them that kill the body," i.e., kings: LMS SA 52/1/B, Church members to LMS, Phalapye, 16/3/1895; RNA 23/3/1894, 20.

[50]   RNA 23/3/1894, 18. Khama was addressing Christians in Ratholo.

[51]   Neil Parsons, *A New History of Southern Africa* (London, 1982), 179; quote: PRO 21/6/1895, 31–32.

[52]   PRO 21/7/1895, 14. Seisa had been a government interpreter at Gaborone's for four years before 1893, BNA HC.130/2, Acting R.C. Mafeking to H.C., 16/11/1900.

[53]   PRO 21/7/1895, 17.

were thirty-odd members of the Church, including its richest and oldest believers, original members of the cult of the Word.[54]

Cattle Rendered Metaphoric: A New Elitism

If the cult of the Word had remained a loosely codified group, it would not have stopped fragmenting, and any dissenting part of it would again and again have used the Church to vie with the king. Indeed, this was a dangerous probability. The Rev. Willoughby had been bothered by the highhandedness of the some Church men for some time, and even commented that the greatest adulterers might be found among them, because they had "concubines," or illicit second and third wives, in keeping with their station. A conflict between rich and poor Christians surfaced during the rinderpest epizootic, when Willoughby's protocol in distributing aid ignored the social register.[55] The king thus seconded Willoughby in 1896, when he decided "to begin a new list of Church members. I have issued books of Communion Tickets to members, and have made a law concerning contributions to the Church fund."[56] It was the start of his rationalization of the Church mentioned in Chapter 2. Willoughby excluded the poor from the new tithe, but he considered them quite rare, even after 1896–1897, a period of rinderpest, hunger, and general distress. He endeavored to treat "all candidates [to membership] alike with regard to rank," and to reject the type of discrimination embraced by Hepburn in the affair of the hats.[57] For his part, Khama was sensible to the expansive nature of Christian doctrine, and he now turned away from the old royal-aristocratic conception of the cult of the Word and embraced the idea of a new elite governed by stricter rules. The value of restricting Church membership to the families of those men who owned large herds of cattle had ceased to be apparent to the king, and many of these people, his own relations, had dispersed anyway. In the end, Khama knew it would be decades before the old core of the Church died away entirely, whatever Willoughby did.

---

54 The rebels moved to the Lepokole Hills, between the Shashi and Motloutse rivers, and then BSAC land after Khama's famed visit to England in 1895. Christians soon gravitated to a separate village under Mphoeng; later they requested their own missionary. K III A/5, Copy (W. C. Willoughby) Res. Com. to Asst. Com., Phalapye, 1895; LMS SA 52/2/B, Raditladi to R. Price, Phalapye, 2/11/1895, 54/1/A, W. C. Willoughby to Cousins, Phalapye, 23/2/1897, and 67/5, C. Reed to Cousins, Plumtree, 7/12/06; "A Letter from Messrs. Helm and Willoughby," *Supplement to the Chronicle of the LMS* (Dec. 1897), 6; W. C. Willoughby, "Review of Five Years," 12.

55 LMS SA 53/1/D, W. C. Willoughby to F. W. Thompson, Phalapye, 21/4/1896; W. C. Willoughby to LMS, Mafeking, 12/10/1896. A case of "immoral intercourse" between venerable Church members in 1898 also did the congregation "much harm," LMS SA 55/1/B, W. C. Willoughby to R. W. Thompson, Phalapye, 22/4/1898.

56 W. C. Willoughby, "Review of Five Years," 19.

57 One must assume that Willoughby understood wealth as the sum of a household's possessions, not as an individual's, because he excluded servants and MaSarwa from the ranks of the poor; see Iliffe, *The African Poor*, 8, 236. Secretary Wardlow Thompson had written Khama through Willoughby in July, remarking that "the loss of all the cattle" was a lesson from God, as too many cattle kept people back from "education," K III G/50, R. W. Thompson to Khama, 2/7/1896. WCW/17, Notes: Church Festival, Began 26 June [1897].

As we have seen, herding cattle was a ready trope for depictions of the Ngwato Church under God and his shepherds. For both the Church and the kingdom, herding helped order people's understanding of what belonging to these bodies meant. The word for the "mark of God," which meant "the sign left by baptism," was *lotshwao*; and the first and persisting meaning of *lotshwao* is the ear-brand or cutting used to identify one's cattle or goats. In the 1890s, the two meanings were not yet entirely separable: the mark of "God," or biblically speaking, of *kgosi e kgolo*; or mark of the king, *kgosi*, the largest cattle-owner in the land. People, like oxen, were gathered (*phuthegile*) into a congregation (*phuthego*) of the Ngwato Church. Rinderpest carried away substantial sections of the royal herds, but the king had another means of establishing rights in people; he not only gathered all strays by his own authority, he collected the *phuthego* of Church members.

Willoughby understood this, and so took oxen to mean Christians, producing a metaphor linking ox teeth to human literacy, and green grass to the Word. When examining a catechumen, Willoughby

> objected to proceed farther . . . as soon as I found that he could not read. "But," said the Deacons, "this man is a Christian even if he cannot read." "Yes," I replied. "I want to buy an ox, you bring me one. I look into its mouth and decide that I will not buy. But you tell me that it is an ox . . . [but] I see that it has no teeth, and wonder how long it will continue to be an ox."[58]

As the Church "bought" new enquirers—the unintended implication of Willoughby's poesy—literacy became the most important of its new rules, required increasingly within the catechumenate and hence for confirmation. In the 1860s, three months of schooling had sometimes been considered more than sufficient for confirmation, and Hepburn had allowed rote memorization of short texts to pass for literacy. Willoughby now fought against such habits, and as literacy came to guard the Church perimeter, illiteracy was left as a negative marker for the plebeian masses.[59] While Willoughby frequently excepted the infirm and poor-sighted from the requirement, and even some he judged incapable of literacy, overall his regime was astonishingly strict. In a "definite and public promotion" through three year-long classes, most "confessors" actually spent five, six, or even eight or more years in the catechumenate before the moment of their reception and confirmation, *go amogelwa*. In many cases the rigors of the bird season or the harvest led people to miss months of classes, and they might move up and back again several times, all the while subjected to incessant scrutiny and moral evaluation. Khama favored these measures because they limited the Church's growth and maintained its elite stature; Willoughby, because they helped to draw "a clear distinction between the members of the Church and those who are outside."[60]

Acts were as critical as faith in the reformed Church. Willoughby knew how to deal with activities that seemed explicitly "dirty," like "village frolics [that] mimick" obscenity; they would be banned outright, along with the exchange of cattle as

[58] WCW/QNP, W. C. Willoughby, "Five Years," 19; also, Parsons, "Khama III," 204.

[59] Head, *Serowe*, 29; LMS SA Reports, 1/?, H. Kitchingham for Griquatown, 26/12/1866; JR LMS/S 3 Notes on Catechumens (Willoughby).

[60] WCW/QNP, W. C. Willoughby, "Review of Five Years Work, 1893–8," 18.

bridewealth, which engendered lascivious "communal" rights over women.[61] Similarly Willoughby attacked puberty rituals, with their songs "reek[ing] with the miasma of sexual suggestion." More than any other previous missionary, Willoughby codified Tswana sexuality into the licit and illicit. Europeans had both religion and science for discursive explorations of sexuality, and Willoughby himself wrote an ethnographic essay touching on the "sexual suggestion" in Tswana puberty rites or *bogwera*; the only forum in which BaTswana were supposed to explore their own sexual practices was the aural venue of the deacons' meeting or formal "confession."[62]

Sins and Festivals of Induction

Beginning with a June 1897 Church "festival," Willoughby kept scrupulous records of the sins and attainments of Christians in a permanent volume, in the manner of Scottish Congregational Churches of the day. Although the record dwindled to nothing soon after his departure, seen alongside other sources it allows us to fathom the new dynamics by which people began to enter the reformed Church. Both the deacons and the missionary by turn examined catechumens and members; the missionary wrote.[63]

> Rra M—— son of N——, Malwelamotse regiment, unbaptised, catechumen for five years. Does not know alphabet. Never made the smallest effort to learn, and knows nothing.
> M—— daughter of R——, unbaptised . . . catechumen from 1884, fell away again but made a new start 1896. Widow with three children alive and four dead. Can read a few sentences in *Sepeleta* [the standard LMS primer]. . . . [1899:] Has gone back rather than made progress, this is on account of sickness. I have put her back another year and told her we will not insist on her learning to read. . . .

There were finer standards at work, as well. Candidates had to navigate a maze of prejudices, those of their families, the deacons, *and* the missionary, who could either "recommend" candidates or simply decide to receive them. Willoughby's formal notations sometimes sought to capture this world of subtlety.

---

[61] LMS SA, A. Jennings, Notes for *Bogadi: A Study of the Marriage Laws and Customs of the Bechuana Tribes of South Africa* (Tiger Kloof, LMS, 1933), 5: "On the side of the bridegroom's family, every male who contributes to the Bogadi is ipso facto, entitled to a share of the woman by sexual intercourse."

[62] Michel Foucault, *A History of Sexuality, Vol. I: An Introduction* (New York, 1990), 40–49 esp.; WCW/290, W. C. Willoughby, "The Upbuilding of the Body of Christ." For *bogwera*, see W. C. Willoughby, "Notes on the Initiations Ceremonies of the Becwana," *Journal of the Royal Anthropological Institute* 39 (1909), 228–45. Willoughby also aborted the sexual life of Ella Sharp (schoolteacher, 1900–1930) in 1903. Col. Panzera, living very far away from his wife and daughters, had been spending "every possible hour in [Sharp's] hut." Willoughby, of course, "suspected" nothing but thought it a poor spectacle for the BaTswana. Unfortunately Mrs. Willoughby, strolling by, "heard a rustle in the bedroom." Sharp called out that Panzera had left for his wagon, which was a lie, as he emerged from her hut a moment later. Willoughby, against his better judgment, refrained from reporting directly to the directors, but wrote a monstrously deft letter to Sharp's father, LMS Africa Personals, P/6, W. C. Willoughby to J. P. Sharp, 18/6/03.

[63] Excerpts are from JR LMS/S 3 Register: "Notes on Catechumens," transcribed by John and Olive Rutherford. See also Rutherford, "Willoughby," 64ff.

R—— son of T—— . . . was hindered from joining the church by the fact that he had been betrothed to a little girl and wanted to get out of it and marry a woman whom he loved, but his father objected and [the catechumen] *ultimately yielded.* Knowledge good. Recommend.

M—— son of M—— . . . unbaptised, catechumen, 1887. Can't read though he has tried. Fairly well acquainted with some of the chief incidents in the Gospel. Testimony clearer than any of the preceding concerning the duty of living without sin, etc. Hesitating on account of inability to read, *but finding deacons emphatic* in their testimony decided to recommend.

M—— son of K—— of Shoshong, can read very well, Church objected to him on account of his wives, but he put away some and kept one, *there was a discussion* about those that were put away and doubts about the bona fides of the business . . . after 15 years. . . . *Church raised questions* concerning his dabbling in native medicine . . . Decided to receive him on condition that he confesses his fault publicly at baptism.

Christians were not to patronize *dingaka*, but distinctions were drawn between "professionals" with integrity, herbalists, and witchdoctors who read pieces of bone. Yet who was which? Despite Willoughby's unremitting search for the truth, candidates came to him packaged in the perceptions of those around them. Such concerns were swept away only by good Christian parentage, which spared missionaries the pain of recognizing the work of culture-makers.

M—— son of M—— of Tebalala . . . has been helping his father teach the children of the village. Have met no catechumen so well up in knowledge of the scriptures. He is a credit to his father who has evidently spared no pains in teaching him. Recommend without hesitation.

K—— daughter of M——, baptised, father and mother both Christians. . . . Been living with Miss Young and teaching in elementary school for 18 months. Catechumen 1896. Can read well, testimony simple and clear, good knowledge of the N.T., recommend.[64]

Christians were expected to open every recess of their sinful lives to the observations of the deacons. Surely much of what they saw never made it to the missionary's book, but John Rutherford has enumerated the chief offenses that did, and that warranted suspension or expulsion.[65] Among the most common was drinking beer "to excess" (an occasional lapse seemingly demanding only censure) or worse, drinking any other alcohol. Equally common, however, were sins related to sexual deviance. They were:

1) "adultery," which did not immediately result in expulsion, contrary to what one might expect;
2) concubinage (*bonyatsi*), which embraced unsuccessfully camouflaged polygyny, and was variably punished;[66]
3) divorce or marriage undisclosed to the Church;

---

[64] *Ibid.*; my emphasis. There is some uncertainty as to punctuation in the source.

[65] The following quotes are taken from JR LMS/S 3, Registers: "Notes on Catechumens" and "Notes on Members." Emphasis is my own.

[66] See Nancy Rose Hunt, "Noise Over Camouflaged Polygyny: Colonial Morality Taxation and a Woman-Naming Crisis in Belgian Congo," *Journal of African History* 32, 3 (1991), 471–94.

4) women or girls becoming pregnant outside marriage;
5) failure by mothers (and, in a few cases, fathers) to bar "access" to their daughters, the proof being the resulting pregnancy;
6) men "allowing" wives to have congress with other men (the implication was that some men actively sought the oxen to be gained in a *kgotla* legal suit in this way);
7) abortion, which was sometimes fatal to the mother;
8) unilateral or mutual desertion.

In addition, the deacons and missionary forbade witchcraft, which included poisoning, but which might also lurk beneath the charge of "spiteful behaviour" brought against some members. It should be emphasized here that despite such codification, unseen webs of familiarity and reputation brought some Christians to the point of confirmation quickly, but mysteriously kept others returning to the catechumenate for as long as fourteen years in a row.

> [1899:] K—— R——, this is a case of most profound ignorance in spiritual matters yet the deacons gave a good account of her life. Surely there must be *something wrong in the methods pursued by the deacons.* . . . Told her to wait another year.
> [1901:] M—— son of M—— . . . [had] remained in the Church till 1893, then *his wife complained to the deacons about him* and though he [said] then that it was all untrue and [due to his resentment at her infidelity], he was expelled. . . .

The Church, meaning in effect the capital's confirmed Church members, voted on conditionally approved candidates. In the end, however, the missionary's decision was final:

> K—— son of S——, Malwelamotse regiment, unbaptised, catechumen 1889, can read and has several books, has never committed any sin in thought, word, and deed. . . . Told him it would be very wrong, we are not worthy of such companionship for we have all sinned and find our sins still clinging to us. . . . [He] lost all interest.

On Sunday morning of the 1897 festival, Willoughby lectured on the "privileges and duties of Church membership," and baptized forty-one adults "from heathenism." Each convert knelt in turn before the front of the seated congregation, and hence before Khama; the deacons, two from each of three constituent sections, sat at Khama's sides, personally witnessing the baptisms. The names of the new catechumens were promptly written in the register. "I became a catechumen" is often spoken as "I was written." The inscription was an important bit of metonymy for the introduction of *thuto* that followed, which entailed learning to read; joining the literate community of the kingdom was also entering the "book of life." In addition to the "writing," sixty-three of the membership's young children were baptized.[67]

Next, a scant eight catechumens were confirmed in full membership. They and other members were handed tickets that legitimated their admission to Commun-

---

[67]   *Ibid.*; UCCSA Papers, Baptismal Register 1, entries for 1897. Included among the forty-one adults was Semane, Setlhoko's daughter and Khama's future wife. Perhaps this is where they met. Included among the sixty-three children was Bontle, a daughter by Khama's current wife Sefhakwane, whom he soon divorced.

ion. Later, the reverse of each bore a ledger for the tithe, *phalalo*, signifying a new link to the money economy: indeed the requirement for this monthly Church contribution in GammaNgwato preceded the introduction of the colonial tax by two years. During monthly Communion, *Selalelo*, from 160 to 200 people would arrive in their "best" clothes and hand in their *phalalo*; during services, one or another member would rise and "confess" her personal interest in God.[68]

From their proxy signatures in the register to their approval of Communion tickets, deacons clearly still exercised a great deal of authority in determining who would be a Christian. They lived among their people; most of them held positions of authority outside the Church, and as Willoughby noted, they "sternly object to those who do not satisfy them by their life."[69] They reported to the Church on the status of the Christians in their districts, and some also reported to Khama as headmen in his *kgotla*. It was to them and their lay allies that Willoughby alluded when he remarked in print that the Ngwato "high-born" had hampered the freedom of the Church. Khama wrote to the LMS pointedly to contradict him.[70]

Khama, Willoughby, and the events of 1895 nonetheless set in motion a process in which the Church began to diverge from the larger social hierarchy. The process was slow, however, and a recurring method for attracting enquirers was to move Sunday services directly into the king's *kgotla*, as if to refresh the memories of enquirers. Ecclesiastic reforms could not proceed without political change. None of Willoughby's bureaucratic reforms would have made any difference had not Khama simultaneously undertaken far-reaching political changes in his administration, spurred by his own conflict with his adult son, Sekgoma.

Khama's Territorial Decentralization, 1898–1902

The administrative system that Khama's grandfather Kgari had refined and bequeathed to him was still in place in 1896. It had essentially developed from the domestic social order, and the power of the king was expressed in his and his brothers' supreme rights over cattle. When Khama's father Sekgoma incorporated large numbers of economically diverse groups of people in the nineteenth century, the royal prerogative was put under strain; cattle-owning men within subordinate groups often saw royal levies as theft. At the same time, the capital grew too crowded. The de facto expansion of the kingdom's borders under British auspices in 1885 and again in 1895, extended Khama's juridical authority to distant villagers and led diverse families to move to the capital town. Many Kalanga-speakers from the north, for instance, came to town in the 1880s.[71]

---

[68] *Selalelo* is from *go lala*, to rest for the night, the connection being with the Last Supper. WCW/17, W. C. Willoughby, "Notes: Church Festival, Began 26 June"; LMS SA Reports, 3/1, Phalapye, 1899 (H. Williams); UCCSA Papers, #C, example of card from 1927; WCW/374, W. C. Willoughby, "In Remembrance of Me," ca. 1896. The tax was introduced in 1899.

[69] WCW/742, W. C. Willoughby to "Harry," Phalapye, 3/6/1896.

[70] WCW/374, W. C. Willoughby, "In Remembrance of Me," ca. 1896; LMS SA 74/4, E. Lloyd to F.W. Hawkins, Shoshong, 4/4/12; K III G/50/21, Khama to Hawkins, Serowe, 10/3/13; G/50/36, W. C. Willoughby to Khama, Tiger Kloof, 7/7/14.

[71] Resentment of levies was certainly growing among conquered *bafaladi*; see Motswedi Dimpe, "Batswapong-Bangwato relations: The Politics of Subordination and Exploitation, 1895–1949" (unpaginated thesis, University of Botswana, 1986); and Mrs. J. D. Hepburn, *Jottings*, 45.

The solution reached in conjunction with the reform of the Church was to disperse non-"Ngwato" wards in the capital to the kingdom's periphery, "decentralizing" the state. The Rev. Willoughby and the LMS may have even encouraged such a move in 1895. After all, Phalapye's byways stank of refuse, and there were ever fewer fertile lands near the town; missionaries might well have assumed that peasants could live in the countryside. When Khama acted on these ideas in July 1898, and added to them, moving even the core of the capital town to a cattle post some forty miles west, the LMS nevertheless professed surprise. Merchants lost their shops, and the Society spent £6,000 in the transition. To make matters worse, Willoughby's son, Howard, was dying of tuberculosis at the time.[72]

It is not hard to see why Khama adopted the decentralizing plan, however. By dispersing BaKaa, BaBirwa, BaKalanga, and BaPhaleng to both preexisting and new villages, he populated his recognized domain and kept his judicial rights in an appeals process. At the same time, he handpicked loyal men, mostly royals, to be governors. Many of the minor *dikgosi* within the small diaspora were Christians, and they founded loci of Ngwato hegemony where there had been none before. The king then moved the capital to Serowe, the site of a long-abandoned Ngwato settlement.[73]

For years, Sekgoma, Khama's eldest son, had chafed under the rule of his cantankerous and austere father, who always managed to find fault with him. The policy of decentralization now appeared to threaten Sekgoma's inheritance. During the rainy season in 1898, Sekgoma reacted by trying to confiscate his aristocratic friends' cattle from a commoner division of the capital.[74] By hijacking cattle, he thought he could persuade their keepers to remain in town. Sekgoma clearly marked this act as an insult to Khama (reminiscent of Khama's insults to his own father) by then plowing—and on the Sabbath!—without awaiting his father's ceremonial word. Khama replied by burning down some of the homes of Sekgoma's followers. With the resident magistrate in tow, Khama legislated the effective end of the old system of royal ownership of the kingdoms's herds.[75] In subsequent de-

---

[72] See Parsons, "Khama III," 213-14, 220-21; LMS SA 53/1/C, Willoughby to Thompson, Serowe, 16/3/96; LMS SA Reports, 3/2, Serowe, 1902 (W. C. Willoughby, 1902); Rutherford, "Willoughby," 80–81; BNA H.C. 130/2 R.C. Mafeking to H.C. A. Milner, 5/5/1898; BNA S.1/12 A. Milner (H.C.) to R.C. Mafeking, 18/8/1898. Khama's own explanation for this and his related trouble with his son is in WCW/742, "Mafhoko a Sekgoma . . .", Phalapye, 2/9/00 (SeTswana).

[73] LMS SA 55/? W. C. Willoughby to LMS, Phalapye, 22/4/1898; BNA S.1/13, R.C. Mafeking to H.C., 20/12/1898. Khama wished in part to populate his land so Europeans would not deprive him of it; see Louis W. Truschel, "Political Survival in Colonial Botswana: The Preservation of Khama's State and the Growth of the Ngwato Monarchy," *Transafrican Journal of History* IV, 1 and 2 (1974), 71–93, 83 esp.; Neil Parsons, "Settlement in East-Central Botswana, ca. 1800--1920," 115--29 in *Settlement in Botswana* (Gaborone, 1980), 115; BNA S. 1/13, Res. Com. to High Com., Mafeking 20/12/1898; and Interview: The Rev. Johane Lenyebe, b. 1917, Serowe, May 1989.

[74] The legislation may actually have come as late as 1907; see next note. K III D/27, "Phalapye Khama's Town," 14/11/98, prob. by ass't to Res. Mag. (SeTswana); BNA S.1/13, A.C. (Ashburnham) to R.C. Mafeking, 14/11/1898. Like Sekgoma, aristocratic and royal BaNgwato lent cattle to commoners under the *mafisa* system; see BNA, H.C. 130/2, A.C. Phalapye to Res. Com., Phalapye, 18/7/1898, encl. in R.C. to High Com., Mafeking, 22/7/1898, and Khama to High Com., ?/6/1898.

[75] BNA S.1/13, Sekgoma Khama to R.C., Phalapye, ?/2/1899; A. Milner (H.C.) to R.C., 2/3/1899. By 1907 Khama claimed he had long since given all such cattle to their holders; K III B/10/Exhibit 3; and B/10/bound volume "Lephephe," redacted statement by Khama, 13/6/07 and 14/6/07; 1907 is thus the outside date by which time his reforms had been implemented, though they may have legitimized an existing state of affairs.

cades, commoners would own the cattle long left under their care, keep all the herds' offspring, and thereby lose the patronage of particular senior royal elites.

Cattle and Plows

More commoners might then also plow their household fields. Plows were known and valued from the 1890s onward in GammaNgwato; Khama himself introduced them to his people, as H. A. Bryden, a hunter, saw "hundreds of American ploughs lying near the [king's] residence, ready for distribution," after the capital had moved to Phalapye in 1890. Plows were common in GammaNgwato by 1911.[76] A plowing team required about forty waiting oxen. Often those men who had so many oxen could also afford to drill bore-hole wells. With a supply of perennial water, they eliminated the need for prolonged transhumance, and this allowed them to plow at the optimum moment.[77]

With the plow and their own cattle, wealthy households reduced the time required to turn and sow a given area of soil, and swelled their output of grain. They also could determine the order in which related households lacking a plow or enough oxen would plow after them, and increase *their* outputs. Such decisions were usually made either in line with patriarchal kin-relations or by contractual agreements.[78] As plowers accumulated wealth and power, others lost power, and propertyless men and women began to hire themselves out to others for the first time. The plow lessened women's labor in November and December, but at June's harvest women had to work harder, since fields were often plowed too large for their normal harvesting and threshing period to accommodate.

Overall, the plow, combined with Khama's cancelling of the royals' rights over cattle, moved wealth from royalty to commoner headmen and household-heads. Such men increased their spending power just as material goods proliferated and the pressure to spend mounted. They might then buy clothes for their families, or withhold them. They, and their wives, made up the bulk of the Church.

The king's strategy in relinquishing royal cattle, although applauded by missionaries and administrators, held drawbacks for him. A fair proportion of

---

[76] LMS SA 50/2, A. J. Wookey to R. W. Thompson, Lake Ngami, 13/7/1893; K III H/60/"1923" obituaries, H. A. Bryden, "Khama, Chief of the Bamangwato," also published in *The Field (The Country Gentleman's Newspaper)*, n.d.; Head, *Serowe, Village of the Rain-Wind*, 12, Mokgojwa Mathware, an Ngwato historian of ninety-six years in ca. 1975; Parsons, "Economic History of Khama's Country," 122–23. William Duggan, *An Economic Analysis of Southern African Agriculture* (New York, 1986), 104, has it that for a population of 34,886, there were 3,072 plows. This number compared favorably in both absolute and per capita terms with other Bechuanaland Protectorate kingdoms, but underestimates the population by basing its figures on tax receipts.

[77] Duggan, *An Economic Analysis*, 107, 115; these forces pressed more labor, not less, on men and especially women with very scant resources—no extended households or cattle—to rely on. They either lived as low-status dependents (like MaSarwa) or had to hire themselves out.

[78] Interviews: Ms. Kadimo Serema, Palapye, 17 Dec. 1988; Mr. Kereeditse Sesinye, b. approx. 1908, on the road to Ratholo, 20 April 1990; Mr. Tlotleng Pipedi, Lerala, 12 June 1990. We will see later that Christians sometimes plowed for one another outside family ties. Pnina Motzafi-Haller also documents these relationships, "Transformations," part 2, *passim* and 182, citing D. Curtis, "The Social Organization of Ploughing," *Botswana Notes and Records* 4 (1972), 62–80.

wealthy "pure Ngwato" families were drawn to Sekgoma, because the new cattle laws struck at their estates, and Sekgoma made a point of promising to replace cattle his father had taken from them.[79] Many of these people were old-guard Christians. The conflict created havoc in the Church, with Khama in constant attendance; loyalists wished to deny Sekgoma's men Communion. Sekgoma's inevitable exile from the capital was the last chapter in Phalapye's "decentralizing." Among the two thousand or so people who followed him away from the capital were three of seven Church deacons and fifty-nine of 480 Church members.[80]

After some years living north of the Makgadikgadi Pans in Nekati, Sekgoma's followers grew disenchanted with him and trickled back to Serowe. In the first decade of the 1900s, they fed into a stream of returning men and women, the descendants of most of the old rebels and royals whom Khama had exiled in the 1890s. In 1909 Serowe was "increasing every year with the various sections of the 'dispersion,' which are gradually . . . returning to the control" of the king. This trend has already been remarked in Chapter 2. By 1917 Khama and his son had finally reconciled, and the rest of Sekgoma's followers returned to Serowe in due course.[81] The returnees took the place of some of the dispersed wards.

In the midst of all this shifting about, a slight but perceptible transformation occurred, and the social and political life of the country would never be the same. When the dust settled on Khama's decentralizing policy, his regime had expanded far into the hinterland. Khama's reforms may possibly have been spurred by the rinderpest's sudden if temporary decimation of cattle holdings. Despite the cattle epizootic, cattle continued to embody male authority and wealth in the kingdom at large. At some point, however, the king recognized that the legitimacy of the link between his name and the kingdom's cattle had fallen below the level of his name's association with the distribution of *thuto*. As Church rules began to replace the intangible barriers of the 1880s, commoners who learned to read, understood scripture, and especially who married, stood a good chance of joining the Church. The great virtue of *thuto* was that while it meant so many things, touching the wider textual world as well as the fate of one's very soul, the authority of the king still mattered greatly in its provision.

All other aspects being equal, an institutionalized *thuto* quietly replaced the possession of cattle as the key emblem of the kingdom's power. This was a different thing from male power in general, in which cattle remained preeminent, and it is therefore all the more remarkable that (among other things) *thuto*

---

[79] Sekgoma already commanded a great deal of support, especially among his peers and in the commoner division that Khama had previously assigned to him. K III D/27 "Phalapye Khama's Town" (SeTswana); BNA, Ass't. Comm. 5/26, Correspondence concerning Sekgoma Khama: R.M. Daniel to (Ass't. R.C.) B. May, Francistown, 21/12/10, and Mahalapye, 22/5/11; WCW/742, "Mafhoko a Sekgoma. . .".

[80] WCW/810, W. C. Willoughby, "Notes Taken from my Letters to my Wife," 20/11/1897, 17/11/1897, and 2/12/1897; Parsons, "Khama III," 225, 377; K III B/10 "Lophephe," Exhibit 1 (28/4/07) and 2 (16/5/07); Arnold W. Hodson, *Trekking the Great Thirst* (Buluwayo, 1987), 193; and see Paul Landau, "Preacher, Chief and Prophetess: *Moruti* Seakgano in the Ngwato Kingdom," *Journal of Southern African Studies* 17, 1 (1991), 5–8.

[81] K III E/34/60, Khama to Sekgoma, Serowe, 15/12/17; LMS SA Reports 4/3, Serowe, for 1911 (A. Jennings, 1911); also, Reports 4/2, Serowe for 1909 (A. Jennings, 1910).

BLACK AND WHITE.

Frontispiece in A. J. Wookey, *First Steps in English for Becwana Scholars* (London, 1915[?]).

became a set of signs for the Ngwato state. Only a decade later, as part of their own acquisition of *thuto*, thousands of Ngwato schoolchildren would recite lessons in which commoners freely bought and sold cattle—as if such things has always been a commonplace.

Thuto Revisited

It now remains to return to the content of *thuto* during the time of its broader provision to the stratum of wealthy commoners who were now entering its domain.

The frontispiece of the missionary A. J. Wookey's compilation, *First Steps in English for Becwana Scholars*,[82] depicts an African matron in mission smock and scarf, holding a Tswana baby in one arm and a white baby in the other, captioned "Black and White." The image epitomizes the way missionaries coupled reminders of social inequality (the woman can only be read as a servant) with assertions of extrasocietal, incipient equality. *First Steps* employs many familiar objects in various grammatical circumstances besides the free selling of cattle. For example, dogs live in their own doghouses, a parody of domesticity amusing to BaTswana. Then, in a section ostensibly for Tswana children, hats return once again:

6. No, he has no hat.
7. But the girl has a new hat. . . .
10. But I will buy one today.
11. I will put it in a box.
12. Have you a box?[83]

In GammaNgwato boxed hats belonged to men, and only the wealthiest women, as everyone knew. The implication of status in such statements was patent. Yet it might be objected that these were mere grammatical and lexical forms, not intended to teach the signification of "cultural capital" or immanent political power. If forms they were, they sat among doctrinal truths; Wookey's *First Steps* continues:

1. God has made us, and the horse, and dog, and sheep.
2. And goat, and kid and lamb . . .
24. Can you make an ox?
25. No, we cannot make an ox.[84]

Similar to Wookey's text was J. Tom Brown's *Dilo tse di Chwanetseng go Itsiwe* (in English, *Things that Should be Known*). *Things* is a hodgepodge of material culture, from the tents of Orientals in the Bible to the value of owning one's own dog; next in the booklet we find the beauty of stars, which should be gazed at in wonder; then paper ("Today if a person wishes to send some words to friends of his/hers, s/he will write him/her a letter"); and immediately following that, an essay on *Bopelotshetlha*, "Covetousness." At once, though, we are back to material goods, with *diaparo*, clothing. Students and enquirers read in SeTswana:

> Long ago people did not dress as they dress today. The first clothing was the skins of the animals they killed. Even though there are many people of this country who still dress in animal skins, they are only servants who live [*agileng*] out in the wild like bushmen [*barwa*], and those who live on cattle posts far from home [i.e. boys].[85]

---

[82] A. J. Wookey, *First Steps in English for Becwana Scholars, Part 1* (London, 1915[?], 1st ed.).

[83] *Ibid.*, 3.

[84] *Ibid.*, 18–19.

[85] J. Tom Brown, *Dilo tse di Chwanetseng go Itsiwe* [Things that Should be Known] (London, n.d. [1920?]), 105. For servants, *batala* [sic]; probably *balala* or *balata* is meant.

The distinction established, next comes an evolutionary narrative:

Animals had skins which were their own clothing, but a person had to take for himself the necessary clothing in the country where he built. Some people pleased themselves with clothing from animal hides, but others realized that this apparel was not right for them, and then decided to make what they required. The clothing that they made was of thread, and wool [and cotton].[86]

When BaNgwato learned to read in Miss Ella Sharp's school (1900–1930), their texts were thus imbued with meaning, mixing medium and message, word and Word. Her students were also the missionaries' students; and her school "always" taught "Scripture truths." This was partly a conscious emulation of countryside English practice, and in fact the attachment of "Sunday school" to church architecture was a Nonconformist invention.[87] Christianity and education derived from the same source, go ruta, and their overlap lay on a single plane in the language and thought of the people. In a sense, Ngwato Christian practice harked back to early modern Europe or early New England. The separation between form and content apparent at least in nineteenth-century English pedagogy had been bypassed. The separation between reading and what was read was not automatic in GammaNgwato. From the very start, when baruti seemed drawn from the highest ranks of the BaNgwato, context became content.

The morpheme for "example" betrays itself in this regard. Sekao or sekai (from go kaya, to regard, point, or aim), is reflected in sekaelo (also glossed by Brown's Dictionary as "example"); deriving from the milieu of thuto, sekaelo means a homiletic or patterning lesson, a catechizing.[88] Dikaelo (the plural), meant "guidance-" and catechumen classes, and so the very word for "examples" came to embody the action of social transformation. Dikaelo often staged competitive choral events and placed themselves in the center of town society; from the turn of the century, one Sunday a month "the children from different schools march[ed] into the kgotla singing,"[89] followed by curious nonschooled children in their trail. Twenty years before such behavior would have been unthinkable: a thuto embracing the phenomenon of children parading into the kgotla! What perhaps stayed constant was the presence of adults, standing about wearing their most expensive hats.

During his dispute with his brothers, Mphoeng and Raditladi, Khama's desire to restrict thuto to an elitist dispensation had been apparent. As late as 1908, Lloyd noted that Khama "opposes universal education."[90] By 1921, however, this was no longer the case. An aged Khama called "the children of the town" to his kgotla

---

[86]   Ibid.

[87]   Quote: LMS SA 71/3 E. Sharp to R. W. Thompson, Serowe, 29/7/09; and see Dixon and Mathesias, *Victorian Architecture*, 230–31; and D. Lovegrove, "Idealism and Association," in Sheils and Wood, eds., *Voluntary Religion*, 307. Compare Hall, *World of Wonders*, Ch. 1.

[88]   Jack Goody, *The Domestication of the Savage Mind*, 104–106, suggests that literate culture (a problematic concept) entails the consciousness that morphemes may be discontinuously arranged, allowing for lexical "lists," i.e., "examples." However we label Tswana Christian culture, it is notable that dikaelo—and I think dikae also—were not abstractly "examples," but concrete patternings.

[89]   LMS SA Reports 3/1, Phalapye for 1898 (H. Williams); and Interviews: Mrs. Balatheo Moloi, Serowe, 17 Nov. 1988; Archbishop (Spiritual Healing Church) Israel Motswasele, Matsiloje, 17 Jan. 1989.

[90]   Lloyd added that Khama's death "will do the Church good," a feeling most missionaries shared, LMS SA 69/3, E. Lloyd to R. W. Thompson, Shoshong, 15/7/8.

(*dikaelo* having pioneered their way) "and asked them why so many did not attend school[.] They throw the blame on their parents, saying they kept them home to work, and would not provide them with clothes, etc."[91] *Thuto* required cash for clothing, fees of £1 per child per year, and servants to release children from labor, which not everyone had. But now Khama enjoined *all* his people to aspire to *thuto*, to buy what books and hats they could.

This expression of *thuto* as a universal ideal was an indication of the spreading of Ngwato identity. After 1910 or so, *thuto* was institutionalized by the Church within the precise borders of the kingdom. The Church assigned young men as *baruti* outside Serowe, subject to Khama's approval, as we shall see; and by 1906, the Church paid most of their paltry salaries with monies collected among its membership.[92] In such a milieu, "schooling" an elite drawn both from Khama's distant subjects as well as his capital town was a script for unity, even a nationalism of sorts. And as women revised the composition of the kingdom's schools and enquirers' classes, and so became Church members, the kingdom's incipient nationalism lost its old gender.

At the end of his life, King Khama wished *thuto* might be compulsory for all his citizens.[93] In February 1923, at a "Native" conference of all the major Ngwato Church congregations, he interrupted the proceedings and lectured for one of the last times in his life. His words merit some attention. After ascertaining that MaTswapong, BaKaa, and BaPhaleng from Shoshong, and BaKhurutshe were present and paying attention, he asked,

> Have you received [*baruti*]? . . . What have the missionaries taught you? They replied the Word and the Law of God. Then the [king] turned to the BaKhurutshe and asked them who taught them. And they replied, [King] Khama and *Moruti* Hepburn. The [king] said, since they are dead [*sic*], I wish to inform you that the Word of God is still living. The [king] continued questioning one village after another in this fashion . . . [saying] How have you treated your [*baruti*]? Have you ploughed a garden for them? or brought wood for them?[94]

Was not Khama's late message one aspect of the emerging "nationalism" of GammaNgwato, deriving from an infrastructure of well-clothed, literate women and men on whom all citizens might model themselves? One might see in the term *moruti* a cadre, a representative of this will toward a unified identity within the realm of the Word, an identity based in *thuto*. With a bit of license—but only a bit—let us return to the harangue:

> How have you treated your [cadres]? Have you ploughed a garden for them? or brought wood for them?. . . Drink, the sale of your daughters in marriage, and bigamy. What is it that has destroyed your girls in [the cadre's] school? it is just these three things. . . . [*Thuto*] is a work which

---

91   LMS SA 84/1, E. Sharp to F. H. Hawkins, Serowe, 11/4/21.

92   LMS SA 67/3, A. Jennings to W. Thompson, Serowe, 2/2/06.

93   TK A/2, Khama to J. T. Brown, Serowe, 27/1/23, Setswana; enclosed in N. Brown to Tshekedi Khama, 9/8/35.

94   LMS SA 85/2, Minutes [f]or the Annual Conference of the Mangwato Churches held at Serowe, [wrongly dated] May 3 to May 7 1923 [Feb. 3 to Feb. 7, 1923]. Khama died in the morning of 21 February 1923, LMS SA 85/1, Telegram, Lewis to LMS, 21/2/23.

will bring life to us, because it means more *thuto* and *thuto* is life. . . . I have seen you in the Conference and I will journey to you in company with your missionary and will visit you in your homes.[95]

The king did not live long enough to carry out such intimate intervention. But in his last extant piece of correspondence, Khama praised a subordinate Kalanga chief by saying

let us work hand in hand, mightily, for God. You know your fathers hastened to be BaNgwato. My word is, you know if you are a MoNgwato; and when you do the work of God [i.e., pay your teachers' salaries], you know yourself as a MoNgwato then.[96]

Thus in the end Khama treated *thuto* as an index of national identity. Its meanings were never divorced from its media, its texts and supervised recitations, and it held the practice of evangelism within itself. Nor did it lose its associations with seniority and status, but this made possessing *thuto* desirable. The very elements through which an elite, male, and royal coterie recreated their social prerogatives also made it attractive to a wider audience; political, economic, and ecclesiastical reforms gave that audience access to it.

---

[95] Ibid. Without a doubt in the original (lost) SeTswana, Khama's word given as "education" was *thuto*. My contextual translations are in brackets. Here I am influenced by Benedict Anderson's arguments in *Imagined Communities*.

[96] K III E/36/49, Khama to Ngwana oa Kgosi Mfhafshe, Serowe, 12/2/23. Khama stated this equivalence baldly precisely because the BakaNswazwi, Kalanga-speaking "BaPedi"-descended people (one of the more complex Ngwato identities!) had not made it implicit themselves. They had originally been taught from Dombodema's LMS station, as Terence Ranger reminds me.

4

Women, Beer, and the Making of a New Community

When a man is exiled for beer drinking, he is driven like an ox over the border.

Ratshosa Motswetla[1]

As the composition of the Church changed, the senior members of Serowe's congregation increasingly demanded the perquisites they felt were due to them. They took liberties with the Church's prohibitions on "concubinage," and some even abused their power over female catechumens. They behaved as if their positions in the Church were hereditary and unassailable. As one missionary reported, many men still sensed that Christianity was reserved for men whom "God will think of," meaning those who had at least a hundred cattle; otherwise a man was a "mere thing" (*selo hela*).[2]

As we might expect, such an attitude was met by confusion among the missionaries. Haydon Lewis replaced Jennings in 1915, and at Khama's and the Church deacons' request, the Rev. Cullen Reed served with him in Serowe. The two men were often at odds from the start, and wrote to complain about one another.[3] The internal affairs of the Church thus proceeded without intimate intervention. In 1916 Lewis noted (in typically hyperbolic prose) that "for the most part the Church membership represents mass, sheer weight, dead inertia."[4]

---

[1] Testimony before Sir Sidney Shippard, Resident Commissioner, Phalapye, 24/6/1895, in P.R.O. CO/417/141, Annexure A. Enclosures in Despatch No. 136.G 24/7/1895.

[2] LMS SA Reports, 5/?, Shoshong for 1913 (E. Lloyd, 1914).

[3] Although Lewis also weirdly wrote that they were "the two binary orbs, whose destiny it is to revolve about their common centre Serowe, [and] have managed to do so for two successive years," LMS SA Reports, 5/2, Serowe for 1916 (R. H. Lewis, 1917); LMS SA 77/2, C. Reed to F. W. Hawkins, Serowe 6/2/15.

[4] One suspects Khama wished two men to serve with unspecified briefs in order to divide the LMS's authority. LMS SA Reports 5/2, Serowe for 1916 (R. H. Lewis, 1917).

81

Feuds burst open within the deaconate. In 1917 some Church members sent Lewis an "anonymous" letter accusing several deacons of immoral practices, and eventually Lewis expelled ten prominent members, suspended the senior deacon, and deferred Communion for six months. New rules were applied to regulate wedding feasts, which too often included ostentatious exchanges of familial gifts, suggesting the transfer of bridewealth. The Rev. Brown, in Serowe in 1921, thought the Ngwato Church a hotbed of disgraceful immorality.[5]

At the same time, however, another, very different trend had long been visible in the composition of the Church's membership. Women had practically taken over the Church. They ran its primary schools, managed most of its pastoral duties, organized its festivals, staffed its evangelizing efforts, and filled its pews on Sunday. The voices of the conspiratory male core were drowned by those of the women as they sang their favorite hymns. In 1922 the ratio of women to men among Church members was exactly two to one.

The frustration of senior male elites, and the population of the Church by women, were aspects of the same set of social changes in GammaNgwato. For as *thuto* provided a new means for women to organize themselves in the public domain, the realm of the Word was undercutting the ability of men to do so. Sixty years before, men gathered in two institutions: for sober council, in the kgotla; and in beery fellowship, in one another's yards. The several wives of a senior man brewed beer (*bojalwa*) for a gathering of his peers and his juniors, and these men would celebrate together with this "token that life is going well."[6] *Bojalwa*, the flower of the harvest, connected and empowered men and women in profound ways. It provided a set of practices and a mode of discourse that joined motherhood and production to the constant reassemblage of the body politic. Yet from 1900 up to the 1930s, while the regendering of Christianity proceeded, the Ngwato kingship kept *bojalwa* illegal. Thus in tracing the gendered history of the Church, we must consider the meaning of beer, and the meaning of its prohibition.

Beer and Ngwato Society

Sorghum *bojalwa* is mild and nutritious. Men and women have to drink large amounts of it to fall into a pleasant stupor. In rural Botswana today, as before Khama's time, women ferment sorghum malt in quantity after a good harvest. Indeed, before wage labor and the ox-drawn plow changed things, the making of beer both symbolized and derived from the relations of production in the household. *Bojalwa* was a "dramatized" form of *bogobe*, the staple breadlike mash of sorghum.

Women produced and prepared both beer and grain from "their" fields, and served both to their families. In hoe-farming before the plow, Willoughby noted that although men helped out, "corn was the property of the *woman*." Because

---

5   Among Brown's complaints was that deacons demanded sexual favors from female catechumens; and on his return from furlough, Lewis expelled three more members. LMS SA 84/2, T. Brown to F. H. Hawkins, Claremont, 7/7/21; LMS SA 85/2, S. Ratshosa to J. C. Harris, Serowe, 15/5/23; 85/3 R. H. Lewis to F.H. Hawkins, Serowe, 24/8/23; LMS SA 6/1, Serowe for 1921 (R. H. Lewis, 1922).

6   Donald Curtis, "Cash Brewing in a Rural Economy," *Botswana Notes and Records* 5 (1973), 25. Melon rinds were used to make beer before the final harvest.

women controlled the produce of the field, the Rev. Williams allowed them to contribute a monthly basket of sorghum instead of money to the Church. Mothers-in-law and wives stored the produce of the homestead's fields in their grain bins.[7] Similarly, *bojalwa* was women's work: mothers and daughters made it around the *segotla*, or rear threshing floor, laid the moistened sorghum seeds out to germinate in the dark of their own *dintlo* ("houses," and also "wombs"), to be *apeile* ("cooked," fermented) later.[8] They served it in their own beer-pots. Women's offerance of beer, primarily to adult men but also to one another, gave everyone a chance to recognize (and benefit from) their labor through its wide range: hoeing, planting, reaping, threshing, winnowing, pounding, and cooking. Although women had to work hard, especially in the harvest season, the joyful and deliberate presentation of beer, the fragrant sign of the harvest, invested women with the prestige inhering in the act of voluntary giving.[9]

Even the nourishment of *dikgosi* and the king had to move through the benefaction of women. But if beer's production valorized women's power over distribution, it also physicalized senior men's dominance of social consumption. Beer tied the harvest to the circulation of gestures and pleasantries that underpinned the circulation of cattle and daughters. At the moment of beer *drinking*, women were atomized and peripatetic, retiring to the sideline when they drank at all.[10] As a social food, the consumption of beer connected different households, and men who would not eat together might still drink together. Men and women drank in work parties called to assist in harvesting or threshing, but men also drank at social functions, within the nexus of kinship, village life, or ethnic sameness, and for intangible friendship. In a different vocabulary: the *oikos* produced, but men drank for the *polis*.

King Khama prohibited all *bojalwa*-brewing and -drinking in 1872, along with any other consumption of alcoholic beverages; he renewed his prohibition upon resuming his reign in 1875.[11] Willoughby heard a story from Khama that others later used to explain the king's hatred for drink. In the second-hand retelling, a young and impressionable Khama witnessed a Boer trader swindle his father, Kgosi

---

[7]   Quote: WCW/706, W. C. Willoughby, "Cultivation & Food," undated notes, my emphasis. Women stored grain in their own or their mother's granaries; see Duggan, *Economic Analysis*, 82–84; oral traditions from Tswapong also recognize female ownership of the field, even when anachronistically reading male farming (with the ox-driven plow) back into the mid-nineteenth century; Interviews: Mr. Mathuba a Madikwe, b. 1901, Mmakgabo village, 24 May 1990, and 16 June 1990; LMS SA Reports, 2/4, Molepolole for 1894 (H. Williams, 5/2/1895).

[8]   Jean and John L. Comaroff, *Of Revelation and Revolution*, 136–37, and Jean Comaroff, *Body of Power*, 54–56.

[9]   This clearly fits Marx's idea of the laborer representing him/herself in work, but also Marcel Mauss's notion of the gift as a figuration of the self of the giver; see *The Gift*, trans. I. Cunnison (London, 1966), 55, and 58, discussing the "irrevocable link" in the gift of food; and Jean and John L. Comaroff, *Of Revelation and Revolution*, 183. Similar considerations lead Ivan Karp to consider beer-gatherings among the Iteso of Kenya as "Iteso social theory," Ivan Karp, "Beer Drinking and Social Experience in an African Society: An Essay in Formal Sociology," 83–119, in Ivan Karp and Charles Bird, eds., *Explorations in African Systems of Thought* (Bloomington, Ind., 1980), 83, 103.

[10]   I am not arguing that this duality produced no tensions in signification or action; later sections are devoted to discussing the elaboration of these tensions. Older, senior women did drink with men, although they sat to the side.

[11]   Dachs, *Papers of John Mackenzie*, 41 (J. Mackenzie, memo, Shoshong 30/12/1872).

Sekgoma, out of some ivory after plying him with brandy.[12] Khama was suppos-edly traumatized. The specter of a boy dragging home his drunken, penniless fa-ther held pathos for most Englishmen. It fit perfectly magic-lantern morality plays like *The Drink Fiend*, shown to adolescents throughout Britain. A look at an early transcription of Khama's story compels a different interpretation. First, as Khama insisted, he was already over forty years old at the time. Second, he derailed his father's trade, and himself excoriated the trader. At the end of the actual tale, Sekgoma sobers up and is silently grateful for his son's interference in his affairs, thenceforth "never touching liquor when he went on business."[13] The point of Khama's story was Khama's fitness to rule.

Why, then, did Khama dislike *bojalwa* so? Although the industrious Rev. Willoughby felt that beer drinks meant "time wasted . . . a serious drain in the community," he nonetheless wondered the same thing. Willoughby rejected the radical Evangelical condemnation of all drinking. Homemade beer and brandy were clearly not equivalent.[14] After Khama was forced to repeal his ban on beer-drinking in 1895, Willoughby demurred from the radical temperance advocated by Khama and the deacons of the Church.[15] Yet by 1902 Khama had brought him around, and Willoughby prohibited "beer-drinks," and later any beer, to Christians who wanted to remain in the Church. Turning a Biblical idiom to his purpose, Willoughby ar-gued at Communion that a person "cannot be a slave to Beer and a slave to Jesus at the same time."

The metaphor of servitude provides a clue to Khama's thinking. According to the king, "nearly all the political strife that disturbs the nation comes from these beer drinking parties."[16] Certainly beer lubricated and cloaked diverse conversations between men. Mackenzie recalled that Ngwato envoys would re-tire "ostensibly for the purpose of drinking beer, but in reality" to deliver dip-lomatic messages, and Lloyd also shared the view that the loquacity around "the beer pot" eventually led men to "mutter and whisper disloyal language."[17] All Khama's attacks on *bojalwa* were charged with political content: "Your [king], my people, has funny laws," he said sarcastically. "He refuses your children [*thuto*] . . . I have been dethroned and in my place [*bojalwa*] has been installed."[18]

---

[12] Chirenje, *History of Northern Botswana*, 243; W. C. Willoughby, "Khama: A Bantu Reformer," *International Review of Missions* (Jan. 1924), 74–76.

[13] WCW/742, Khama (in Willoughby's paraphrasing and hand), "Khama and the Dutchman's Brandy." The incident must have occurred after 1870.

[14] Khama expelled the traders Francis and Clark in 1887–1888 for selling liquor to BaNgwato, scolding them with the words, "You, the people of the Word of God!" Hepburn, *Twenty Years*, 147; BHP, Goold-Adams 22/3/1888; for traders' charters banning liquor, see K III C/14, Phalapye, 12/5/1890 (A. C. Clark) and 13/5/1890 (S. and W. Blackbeard). BaTswana did not distill liquor, and clearly Khama despised the extreme effect of brandy. Teetotalism was not popular among Congregationalists in late nineteenth-cen-tury England in any form, however; Lilian Shiman, *The Crusade Against Drink in Victorian England* (Lon-don, 1988), 62, 184. Quote: WCW/742, W. C. Willoughby, "Beer Drinking," n.d.

[15] LMS SA 53/1/C, W. C. Willoughby to R. W. Thompson, 16/3/1896, encl. Letter from Congregation of same date, signed by B. Kalaeakgosi, Deacons Mocwaedi Masarwa, Ntetwe Mpapatsi, Motswaledi Semetsabotlhoko, and evangelists Tshomakwe Tsimane and Lesiapetlo Moloko.

[16] WCW/742, W. C. Willoughby, "Beer Drinking."

[17] Mackenzie, *Ten Years*, 401; Edwin Lloyd, *Three Great African Chiefs* (London, 1895), 16–17.

[18] BHP, Box "Ntbks", Ntbk 3, from BNA, "Rec'ts and Accts., n.d.," Transcription of one of Khama's speeches by Gaopotlhake K. Sekgoma.

When Kgamane defied Khama and served *bojalwa* to Moremi of the BaTawana, Khama rightly inferred a subversion of his authority over political assembly and personally burned down his brother's house.

Recall that Khama had accused his Church opposition of drinking beer, *bojalwa*, as a shorthand for moral illegitimacy and political treason. In 1895 Raditladi and Mphoeng, the king's rebellious half-brothers, may indeed have drunk beer as "a way of talking" to Khama, in the words of one rebel. Moreover, during the resident commissioner's hearing on the matter, a servant, Phepheng, testified that he had thought that the law banning beer had been made for the high-born only; the family servant Bareki understood that "secret" drinking was acceptable.[19] If so, the law was aimed at those men who had the most wives or mistresses to brew for them, who occupied permanent positions in the *kgotla*, or who wished to attain greater political visibility—men who were most likely to cause Khama trouble.

Khama repealed his prohibition, partly to decrease the followings of his rebellious siblings as they went into exile. During the fifteen years of repeal, from 1896 to 1911, the Church's prohibition of *bojalwa* targeted many of the same people as Khama's had: prominent Christian families and young men. Abstention from beer continued to signify loyalty to the kingdom. In one typical case from 1913, some non-Christians asserted that Christians had been drinking beer. This obloquy from a "heathen" was tantamount to an accusation of subversion, although the accusers refused at the last minute to name the drinkers in *kgotla*. Khama knew the identities of the women who brewed, however, and several eventually confessed their guilt after days of meetings.[20] The male heads of their wards then split up the burden of the fine in cattle.

Roving beer gatherings menaced the ecclesiastical stabilization of *thuto* as the language of the *kgotla*, because the affiliation within beer-drinks was uncontrolled from above. Relying only on the cycle of the seasons and the whim of the hour, wherever beer was available, men might hold discussions hidden from the view of the state. At the same time, even in the transience of a bowl passed from man to man, beer-gatherings dangerously reflected the paradigm of the village *kgotla*. The behavior in *bojalwa*-drinking created and recreated the local *community*.[21] Men talked freely over beer and exchanged their views of local issues in local idioms: ethnicity, *badimo* (ancestors), or even, if dimly hinted, witchcraft. Indeed, many subordinate communities within the kingdom used *bojalwa*, the best possible concretization of

---

19   Kgamane: Hepburn, *Twenty Years*, 85. An aged Nkobele (the last surviving 1895 rebel) recalled forty years later, "the question of beer and the Church were not disconnected because Raditladi wanted to have a way of talking to his brother," TK Papers, K/75, "Evidence," with Mr. Fraenkel; and PRO 21/7/1895, 19, 26, courtesy Isaac Schapera.

20   *Report of the LMS*, Vol. 63 (Cape Town, 1914), 267.

21   See Eric Hobsbawm, *Primitive Rebels* [1959] (New York, 1965), Ch. 5, "The City Mob;" J. Gusfield, "Benevolent Repression: Popular Culture, Social Structure, and the Control of Drinking," in Barrows and Room, eds., *Drinking: Behavior and Belief in Modern History* (Berkeley, 1991), 399–424; and Paul Virilio, *Vitesse et Politique* (Paris, 1977), Ch. 1. Charles H. Ambler discusses the variable cultural constructions of drunken behavior in "Alcohol and Disorder in Precolonial Africa," *Working Papers in African Studies* No. 126 (Boston University, 1987), esp. 4–5. I agree with his doubts as to beer's nutritional value per unit of labor to produce it. The word *"kgotla"* has a colloquial use even today to describe any meeting of men put to a judicial or political purpose.

communal productivity and satisfaction, as an offering to placate village or household *badimo*.[22]

From the vantage point of the *"kgotla"* of the beer-gathering, the *kgotla* of the state and its insistent *thuto* appeared alien indeed. Prohibition therefore articulated the clash between two notions of political assembly. In the 1930s BaNgwato would recall that Khama had often come in disguise to a suspected beer-drink, extending his hand at the door to receive a bowl and then dashing it to the ground; the next day his agents arrested the drinkers. Khama was also memorialized in the 1930s in a praise-poem, as "the owl . . . [B]eware you don't mention him at night," because of his ability to detect enemy conspirators.[23] When translated in their idiomatic context, these two traditions describe aspects of the same mode of power.

In sum Khama and his Christian allies wished to disrupt the nexa of kin and community that expressed village autonomy. The beer-drink had once stood for more than this, as a microcosmic arena for symbolizing the social and productive relationships undergirding Tswana political authority. At the level of the state, the changing modes of power in the realm of the Word ended this metaphoric relationship, though it persisted as a constant possibility at the grassroots. From the king's point of view, beer-drinks became kernels of opposition to his regime, because the kingdom was replacing ethnicity with citizenship, *badimo* with *Modimo*, and as the main representative of *communitas*, man with woman.

The drive against beer captured many Christian women's ambitions and desires. Their campaigns ensured that the tropology of *bojalwa* would survive long after Khama's death. We now turn to the kingdom and Church in the 1920s, and to women's place within them, before returning to beer in this enfleshed context.

"The Lord is Among the Kings": A Transition

Sekgoma returned from his Nekati exile in 1922. While the Church continued its accelerating growth, Sekgoma's presence challenged the social and ecclesiastical prominence of Semane, the king's last wife, with her family and supporters. Missionaries suspected the king and his son were not as friendly as they seemed. Matters took a turn for the worse that year when the Church suspended Simon Ratshosa, Sekgoma's closest ally and son-in-law, and Khama fired him from the headship of the capital's private school.[24]

In this tangle of alliances, the old king still cast a deep shadow in the Church to his dying day. In early 1923 Lewis noted that some deacons

---

[22]   This was noted, for instance, by an agricultural officer in Botswana in 1982, J. Lesotlho, *"Badimo* in the Tswapong Hills: A Traditional Institution in Action," *Botswana Notes and Records* 15 (1982), 7–8. See also Chapter 8.

[23]   LMS SA 90/Gilbert, "Beer Drinking in Serowe and the Efforts of Chiefs and Temperance Societies to Check it," 1930; and Schapera, *Praise-Poems*, 205. To understand the immensity of the shift necessary for people to tolerate an attack on beer-drinking, see Audrey I. Richards, *Land, Labour and Diet in Northern Rhodesia* (Oxford, 1939), 76–82.

[24]   LMS SA 84/2, J. T. Brown to F. H. Hawkins, Claremont, 7/7/21; 84/2, R. H. Lewis to F. H. Hawkins, Serowe, 24/4/22.

[belonged] to the ruling caste, others to the tribes considered to be on the level of servants and tributaries. The first ready to bear secretly any words spoken by the second to the ears of the [king] . . . the second knowing all this, and maintaining a discreet silence upon all matters brought up for discussion, until they have heard the [others'] opinions.[25]

Khama died in February 1923, and Lewis exulted that "the heavy hand of the state" had been taken from Church affairs.[26] The new king, Sekgoma II, provided a Christian funeral for his father, and posted a guard on the grave for a year to foil any possible wickedness. He was "installed" by the Protectorate in April. Shortly afterwards a series of crises erupted that jeopardized the nexus of connections between Christian practice and authority in the kingdom. And yet, what is most striking is how quickly the nexus recovered.

First, the new king came across J. C. Harris's book, *Khama the Great African Chief*, prepared under loose LMS auspices. Khama had seen the book before his death and had laughed at its denigration of the Ratshosa family as a "brood" of scoundrels. Sekgoma was not amused to find in it such attacks on himself and his sister's family. He wrote to the LMS to condemn the "abuse and insult" of "your book," and Lewis was soon fretting that Sekgoma might bar him from the pulpit. In the Church itself, royal women expressed outrage, and they did so at the obsequious and elder core. Oratile Ratshosa and her allies vilified male Church members "wildly, madly," and Sekgoma was seen waving Harris's book about with "wild passion."[27] A dam had broken, and the Ngwato Church's earlier censures of Sekgoma were suddenly and forcefully remembered, now that Sekgoma was king for better or worse.

Next, Sekgoma himself accused Phethu Mphoeng, his brother Oteng Mphoeng, and the Raditladi brothers, Lebang and Kelethokile, of plotting to kill him. This broad tarring of the descendants of Mphoeng and Raditladi, Khama's brothers exiled after the 1895 dispute, shifted the balance of power in the new king's *kgotla* to the Ratshosa family. Unlike the Mphoengs and Raditladis, the Ratshosas were considered "commoners" because they were only very distant agnates of the king.[28] They were, however, sons of Ratshosa and Sekgoma's full sister Besi (or Bessie), making them Sekgoma's maternal nephews—always a close kinship link. Simon Ratshosa had then also married Sekgoma's daughter. In contrast, Phethu Mphoeng,

---

[25] LMS SA Reports, Serowe for 1923 (R. H. Lewis, 1924).

[26] LMS SA 85/1, R. H. Lewis to F. W. Hawkins, Serowe, 30/3/23; 85/2, Semane Khama to F. H. Hawkins, Serowe, 17/4/23, "Khama: How He Died," contains a day-by-day account of the state of the king's bowels.

[27] S II Papers, A/5, Sekgoma to LMS, B.P. 4/6/23; LMS SA 85/1, R. H. Lewis to F. W. Hawkins, Serowe, 20/1/23; Serowe, 30/3/23. The book, J. C. Harris's *Khama, the Great African Chief* (London, 1922), was later bowdlerized and re-released; LMS SA 85/2 E. Sharp to F. H. Hawkins, Serowe, 30/5/23.

[28] TK Papers, K/74, "Tshimologo ea Puo ea I, BooTshosa" [The Beginning of the First Testimony, the Ratshosas]. John had been Khama's secretary, and he and Simon had a third brother, Obeditse, an interpreter for the resident magistrate's office; LMS SA 85/1 E. Sharp to F. H. Hawkins, Serowe, 5/3/23; 85/3 R. H. Lewis to F. H. Hawkins, Serowe, 24/8/23; Hope Fountain 6/9/23; Minutes of the SAEC, Hope Fountain, Sept. 1923; Sillery, *Founding a Protectorate* (The Hague, 1965), 205. See Parsons, "Khama III," 425, and especially Michael Crowder, "The Succession Crisis over the Illness and Death of Kgosi Sekgoma II of the Bangwato, 1925," in Jack Parson, ed., *Succession to High Office in Botswana* (Athens, Ohio, 1990), 33–72.

Partial Genealogy of Ngwato Royals and Aristocrats

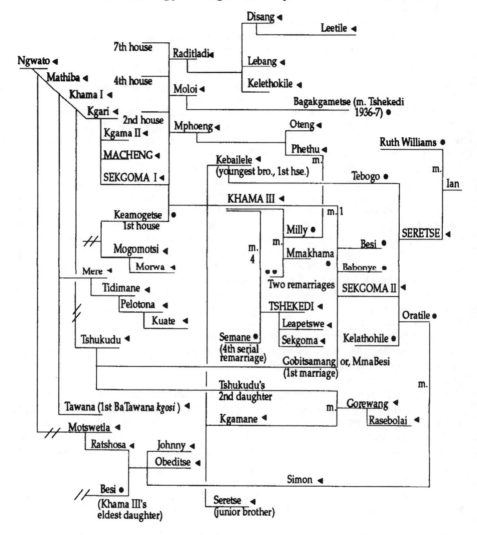

who had returned from his family's exile, was married to Milly Khama, a daughter from one of Khama's later, but defunct, marriages. Phethu had governed Mmadinare and its nearby villages for the king since 1904, and was an imperious and affluent man. His brother Oteng ran his own creamery and taught in Mmadinare's school.[29]

---

[29]   Sekgoma wrote that Phethu's power was "gigantic" and his rule "one of oppression" in Mmadinare, as he flogged Kalanga headmen in public, etc.; S II Papers, A/5, Sekgoma to Ellenberger, Serowe 16/1/24. Oteng too was a man of importance and owed several outstanding debts to merchants, i.e., K III F/39/25, J.J. Rouncivell to Khama, 18/2/14.

In the context of his attacks on the Church, Sekgoma claimed that Milly had purchased poison to kill him. This meant sorcery, always a dreadful accusation but especially insulting in this case because both Milly and Phethu were active Christians. As such, they stood in contrast to the Ratshosas, who had severed most of their ties with the LMS and with the Ngwato Church. Sekgoma now relied on them, and demanded that the Church expel Phethu. Christian headmen loyal to Sekgoma wrote the resident magistrate a telling letter:

> The word of God says: the Spirit of the Lord is among the Kings. It does not say among the people although God is for all. A Nation is a Nation by the King as the Church's only foundation is Jesus Christ.[30]

Such a comparison came not from the young followers of some messianic breakaway church, but from senior members in a staunch mission. A year later, in 1924, an LMS deputation came from London to try to mollify King Sekgoma II. By the time Secretary Hawkins reached Sekgoma, however, the king had begun to change his mind. Sekgoma showed the Rev. Lewis "six or seven verses of a poem" Simon Ratshosa had composed, intended to be taught to children of the "native school" under him. Sekgoma felt the poem to be insulting in a subtle way.[31] All royal BaNgwato were highly attuned to discussions of power and character in the form of *thuto*, even in a sort of makeshift hymn.

The perceived slight evidently woke the new king to the realities of Ngwato politics. The Ratshosas were factious allies, and without them he had little. He therefore set himself to the task of making peace with *thuto*. Lewis and Sekgoma thus agreed that Simon Ratshosa was "evil," Lewis jeering that Simon was posing as a "teacher and a prophet."[32] All blame for Sekgoma's past troubles with missionaries, traders, and former friends like Phethu Mphoeng was shifted onto the Ratshosas. Soon afterwards, John Ratshosa was dismissed as royal secretary, and Sekgoma announced that the Harris book spoke the truth. Clear of these impediments, Sekgoma began his own fitful negotiations for control over the Church, the most powerful institution in his kingdom. His task was not impossible, for certainly missionaries and most Christians wished to have the king safely ensconced in the Church, if not at its helm. Part of Sekgoma's effort was to reassert the prohibition of beer and liquor.

Regardless of his personal preferences, Sekgoma had always understood the test of citizenship behind prohibition. When left in charge during Khama's journey to London in 1895, Sekgoma unexpectedly pursued drinkers, earning him the praise-name "the elephant."[33] True, Khama associated his son with beer after Sekgoma's rebellion and exile, but this did not mean that Sekgoma allowed drinking. Rather, it reflects *bojalwa*'s use as a political trope. Khama wrote to the Rev. Tom Brown in 1911 that Sekgoma was "destroying my people," those BaNgwato with him in exile, "hampering [them] from knowing God," in part by allowing them to "drink beer as much as they want."[34] Khama wished Brown to convey these views person-

---

[30] S II Papers, B/1, my translation of "Sekgoma's Common Headman's words" of Serowe, 2/1/24. This is a section of a longer letter.

[31] LMS SA 86/2, Hawkins to Chirgwin, Tiger Kloof, 30/4/24.

[32] LMS SA 86/4, R. H. Lewis to Wilson, Fish Hoek, Cape, 14/10/24.

[33] Schapera, *Praise-Poems*, 216.

[34] Khama added bitterly, "the [Protectorate] government disturbs no one." K III E/36/83, Khama to J.T. Brown, Serowe, 22/8/11, SeTswana.

ally to Sekgoma. According to the Protectorate policeman in Nekati, however, Sekgoma's people did *not* make beer. Upon reconciling with his son, Khama wrote, "My child, I am glad you have talked to me about beer," as if to seal their reunion; and again at Khama's death in 1923, Sekgoma appeared "just as keen on the drink question as Khama." Little suggests he had ever been otherwise.[35]

It appeared that after a rough patch, Sekgoma was going to live up to his stated intention to "give his full support to all that Khama held to be essential." After all, Sekgoma's wife, Tebogo, taught alongside Semane in Sunday school.[36] In July 1924, Sekgoma invited himself to open a new Church in Lecheng, a village in Tswapong that was especially friendly to him. Sekgoma criticized the deacons for relying too much on the kingship's material favors, and said "he was not Khama, and would not do their work for them."[37] Immediately undercutting his disclaimer, he demanded that Christians keep their children in *sekole*, berated the deacons for absurdly crowding the preacher during services, and demanded a shilling from every Christian with which to pay school salaries.[38] Sekgoma was simultaneously issuing directives to *baruti* and even fining an entire village for leaving the Ngwato Church, as Chapter 7 discusses. In this way he began to walk about in Khama's shoes.

He would not have much chance to continue, for he soon fell ill. Khama's widow, Semane, unexpectedly became his nurse, and the Protectorate's medical officers converged on Sekgoma to determine his treatment. The Rev. Lewis gave Sekgoma a laxative. During his illness, his sister Babonye and his daughter Oratile vied with all comers for the succession. Babonye backed a malleable pretender, while Oratile simply backed herself. In Sekgoma's treatment, the Ratshosas (including Oratile) favored the biomedicine of the contemptuous white doctors, but nearly everyone else supported Sekgoma in asking for *dingaka* and herbalists, who did in fact come. The new king died on the 16th of November, 1925.[39]

Unfortunately for Christians, in his last hour Sekgoma was under European care. In the ensuing political fracas in Serowe, elite Ngwato women were again visible. Khama's elder daughters, Babonye and Mmakhama, led an attack on Semane, accusing her of poisoning Sekgoma for the benefit of her son Tshekedi, who would rule as regent. Semane fled to the Rev. Lewis's home, where cursing women cornered Lewis outside, and "pinched and pushed" him. Headmen and Church members joined in at least a verbal attack, and Lewis's and Semane's only

[35] BNA S.26/4, "Confidential Reports on Sekgoma Khama," O.C. Police, Nekati, to Res. Com. Mafeking, 23/3/15. According to one report Sekgoma punished drinkers by sending men off to the mines, fining them ten oxen, or beating them in the *kgotla*, LMS SA 90/Gilbert, "Beer Drinking," 1930; LMS SA Reports 6/3, Serowe, for 1924 (R. H. Lewis, 1925). First quote: K III E/34/60, Khama to Sekgoma Khama, Serowe, 15/12/17; second quote: LMS SA Photographs, B/4, "Letter Copied from Edith Smith, 1923"; see also LMS SA 84/2, J.T. Brown to Hawkins, Claremont, 7/7/21, and K III H/60/"1921" Sekgoma Khama to Khama, Francistown, 24/6/21, in which Sekgoma adjudicates a case having to do with beer, reporting that "Something has been done to their beer so [people] always go there—they even drink English beer in large quantities!"

[36] LMS SA 85/1, R. H. Lewis to F. H. Hawkins, Serowe, 30/3/23; WCW/193, *Report . . . 1924*, 17.

[37] LMS SA 86/3 R. H. Lewis to F. W. Hawkins, Serowe, 31/7/24.

[38] *Ibid.*

[39] Lewis moralized that a history of overindulgence killed Sekgoma, but diabetes was likely the culprit. Personal communication, Neil Parsons, 11/90; LMS SA 87/4, R. H. Lewis to Barradale, Serowe, 16/11/25; and Crowder, "The Illness and Death," 64–70.

active defenders were a *moruti* (the puritan Rev. Kalaeakgosi), a few other Christians, and the Ratshosas—who, having been purged by Sekgoma, wanted new allies.[40] The crisis fast abated, and the political logic of the Church reemerged. In January 1926, Tshekedi moved to position himself as an unopposed regent king, ruling for Sekgoma's son Seretse. His first policy decision was to demote the Ratshosas. He abolished a "Council of Twelve" convened by Simon Ratshosa and then forcibly took several MaSarwa servants from Oratile Ratshosa. Finally Tshekedi provoked all three Ratshosa brothers into defiance and tried to have them publicly flogged. Simon and John ran home in a frenzy, returned with rifles, and wounded Tshekedi. Their imprisonment and banishment followed.[41]

In the end, out of the struggle between the intermarried groups arrayed about the kingship in the 1920s, the Christian heirs of the "rebellious" cult of the Word (Mphoeng - Raditladi) came out ahead, and the central connections between Christianity and the kingship survived. The men and women of the anti-"tradition," antimonarchist (Ratshosa) faction lost. As a result, Semane regained her stature in town life and her son Tshekedi settled down to rule for twenty years. Upon his installation, Tshekedi was instantly received into the Church membership by the Rev. Lewis, despite his tutelage under an Anglican at Fort Hare college.[42]

Amidst these two bumpy dynastic transitions, the new prominence of aristocratic women—Oratile, Milly, Semane, Babonye, and Mmakhama, in particular—became apparent. Their coeducational schooling in *thuto* and the Ngwato Church helped to crystallize their visibility. Even after the Ratshosas were jailed, Sekgoma's sisters Babonye and Mmakhama continued to litigate with and harass Tshekedi, moving Lewis to refer opaquely to Babonye's "witchcraft."[43]

De-Gendering the *Kgotla*

Perhaps the new visibility of women in the 1920s was an illusion. Had women never before led public lives in GammaNgwato? In a way, the argument that women's sphere was "private," that men "held power" over women in precolonial Africa, owes a lot to the male perspective. As men are seen to have engaged in formal, jural discussions that have a bearing on the lives of others, men are assumed to be the dispensers of household produce. From this view, it follows that women also comprised wealth in and of themselves. As Claude Meillassoux remarks, in subsistence-production societies, the wealth that produces other wealth is not "gold, cloth, and ivory" (though it certainly became ivory for a time in

40   LMS SA 87/4, R. H. Lewis to Barradale, Serowe, 16/11/25; Lewis to Barradale, 20/11/25.

41   Tshekedi called all three Ratshosa brothers to the *kgotla* when he knew they were attending Babonye Khama's wedding. See Q.N. Parsons, "Shots for a Black Republic? Simon Ratshosa and Botswana Nationalism," *African Affairs* 73, 293 (1974), 456 (449–58); TK Papers, X/Hearing on Ratshosa case, 22/6/26; X/ Minutes of Res. Magistrate's court, for Ngwato district, 5/12/29; X/Translation, Oratile petition, to Res. Comm. of Bech. Prot., Mafeking 26/9/26. There was a lengthy trial. See also T. Mooko, "The Role of Women in Bangwato Politics" (B.A. thesis, University of Botswana, 1985), esp. 2–8; and Wylie, *A Little God*, 70ff., 90–96.

42   LMS SA 88/1, A. J. Haile to A. Jennings, Tiger Kloof 21/1/26; J. L. H. Burns and A. Sandilands, *One Hundred Years of Christianity Among the Bangwato* (Lobatsi, 1962).

43   LMS SA 88/2 R. H. Lewis to Barradale, Serowe, 20/4/26.

KOTLA AT SHOSHONG.

January, 1874. The smaller enclosure is "the king's cattle kraal." From Emil Holub, *Seven Years in South Africa, Vol. 1* (Boston, 1881), 374.

GammaNgwato). *Women* were the source of wealth, and their wombs were traded against the flow of cattle in *bogadi* ("bride-price"), in a routinized "abduction."[44] Clearly, however, Meillassoux's view centers society on "political" and public territory, in other words on the carved wooden stools of Ngwato counsellors seated in the *kgotla*. From a motile, decentered perspective, things look a bit different. One should ask how women associated with one another, how they allocated food within and between households, and how they influenced political activity. There is something circular about the notion that women lacked a "status" based on production.[45]

Even so, it seems apparent that the *kgotla* (and the beer-gathering too in a sense) was a recurring public space made for men—and more, that it defined aspects of the idea of maleness itself. In arguing this point, it must first be admitted that men's control over cattle in southern Africa is not a recent development. On the contrary, it is an old social feature, even if it is diluted among BaTswana today. Secondly, according to Jim Denbow and other archaeologists, regional settlements from as long ago as the twelfth century show the logistics of cattle-keeping: circles of kraals and concomitant grazing lands with their own satellite kraals, radiating from a central kraal, in a hierarchy of human-cattle settlements. The same spatial arrangement was reflected in the placement of *dikgotla* (court spaces and neighborhoods) in the Tswana town. It seems

---

[44] See Kuper, *Wives for Cattle*; and Jean and John L. Comaroff, *Of Revelation and Revolution*, 146 esp.

[45] Claude Meillassoux, *Maidens, Meal and Money* (Cambridge, 1981), 72, 77 esp.; see also his essential "'The Economy' in Agricultural Self-Sustaining Societies: A Preliminary Analysis," in David Seddon, ed., *Relations of Production: Marxist Approaches to Economic Anthropology* (London, 1978), 127–58. Also, John Wright, "Control of Women's Labour in the Zulu Kingdom," in J. B. Peires, ed., *Before and After Shaka: Papers in Nguni History* (Grahamstown, S.A., 1981), 82–99; Jeff Guy, "Analysing Precapitalist Societies in Southern Africa," *Journal of Southern African Studies* 10, 1 (1983), 39–54; and Margaret Kinsman, "'Beasts of Burden,' the Subordination of Southern Tswana Women, 1800–1840," in the same issue. See also Joan May's perspective in *Zimbabwean Women in Colonial and Customary Law* (Gweru, 1983), 34. Thanks to Gay Seidman for her critique here.

reasonable to surmise that the *kgotla* was and is an analogue kraal, an arena for cattle-holders. My oral source material supports this assessment, as does the general political language of BaTswana.[46] The *kgotla* was a male space.

It was a male space, that is, until the Church began making regular use of the *kgotla* after the turn of the century. While *thuto* collected mostly wives and youths, not husbands, in its own central and radially linked spaces, the Church also changed the gender of the *kgotla*.[47] The process was both occasional and constant. It was occasional in the sense of Christians' use of the physical place itself, and constant both in the displacement of the *"kgotla"* idea into the Church and in the ongoing use of prayers and pastoral language in actual *kgotla* meetings.

It is important to grasp the full importance of this transition. *Badimo*, male, patrilineal ancestors, had long been present in the cattle kraal and *kgotla*, buried under and watching over the perpetuation of the body politic. Women had a fuzzier expectation than did men of "surviving" into this realm, since they married into patrilineages; and evangelism played on their fears, as we will see later. Women therefore came to the prospect of "life everlasting" with greater fervency, deposited their eschatology into the *kgotla*, and challenged men to re-image their "collective," gendered continuity in terms other than *badimo*, if they could.[48]

"Let Us Begin the Work":
Being a Christian Woman in Serowe

Doing this was a kind of power. Its flavor in women's life in Church in the 1920s can be sampled by carefully reading both written and oral testimony. Surely it is significant, for instance, that *baruti* and Church members granted women ecclesiastical labels before missionaries did. Already in 1910 Jennings had discovered two "deaconesses" in the small congregation in Nekati. The Rev. Lloyd commented gladly in Shoshong that year that "[t]he women too are finding their feet, and are not so ready to be imposed upon . . . no longer will she be married to any man chosen by her father."[49] An interim level of membership was added to the Church,

---

[46] The so-called Central Cattle Pattern of southern Africa is typified by Mapungubwe. See Tim Maggs and Gerald Whitelaw, "A Review of Recent Archaeological Research on Food-Producing Communities in Southern Africa," *Journal of African History* 32, 1 (1991), esp. 20ff. Under certain grave circumstances, women may long have entered the *kgotla* as a rebuke to the king and his social order, but here the exception proves the rule; Schapera, *Rainmaking Rites*, 3ff.; Pauline Peters, "Gender, Development Cycles and Historical Processes: A Critique of Recent Research on Women in Botswana," *Journal of Southern African Studies* 10, 1 (1983), 100–122; and Leonard Ngcongco, "Tswana Political Tradition," in J. Holm and Patrick Molutsi, eds., *Democracy in Botswana* (Athens, OH, 1989).

[47] I am drawing on Joan Scott, "Gender: A Useful Category of Historical Analysis," in her *Gender and the Politics of History* (New York, 1988), esp. 43–45.

[48] It may be added that death in the Protestant sense depends on an acceptance of the frightening notion of individuated, unidirectional time, a concept with which Christian schooling saturated girls. See John Mbiti, *African Religions and Philosophy* (New York, 1969), 17–19, 235, and Jean and John L. Comaroff, *Of Revelation and Revolution*, 154. In some small villages, *badimo* have become, delightfully, angels.

[49] LMS SA 72/8, A. Jennings to Thompson, Durban, 20/10/10.; LMS SA Reports, 4/1, Shoshong for 1907 (E. Lloyd, 1908); 4/2, Serowe for 1909 (A. Jennings, 1910); 5/1, Serowe 1913 (A. Jennings, 1914); 4/4, Shoshong 1912–3 (E. Lloyd, 1913). I would suggest that increasing numbers of women enjoyed sexual relations before marriage rather than bucking parental authority to marry; see also Bozzoli, *Women of Phokeng*, Ch. 5.

Semane, Khama's last wife and Tshekedi's mother, ca. 1900. Unknown photographer. Reproduced courtesy of the Council for World Mission, London.

the "Holders-on," women whose polygynous husbands would not divorce them. When the Serowe members voted deaconesses into place in 1913, following Secretary Hawkin's instructions, they merely reflected the changed character of the Church.

"At one time," wrote Ella Sharp, "the women were all taught in one class in the Sunday School by Semane. But this last year [1914] we have had to divide them up into three classes. . . . "[50] By 1922, all female catechumens in Serowe would pass through the hands of deaconesses, starting from Sunday school, which was taught by women led by Semane.[51] Although deaconesses were never posted to a congregation by the Church, never alienated from their own village, and never paid or granted the title *moruti*, they were often nearly equivalent to *baruti* in function. As in other pastoral walks of life, men tried to reserve incorporative power and mobility to themselves.

Yet Semane taught, and even had the authority to permit others to teach.

Her yard was always full. The following day you would see those people who wanted to believe, raising their hands in the congregation. [In those days,] rain fell very much, not like these days now; life was very much better than it is today.[52]

After Sekgoma's death in 1925, Semane emerged in as powerful a position as ever, structuring the mentality of an expanded corps of deaconesses, and helping women conduct their own Church classes for other women. By one account, in 1934 Semane supervised no fewer than nineteen deaconesses.[53]

Women institutionalized their presence throughout the 1930s. Kadimo Serema recalls that schoolteachers in the 1930s still "made it a law" that their students, most of whom were girls, attend Church.[54] Balatheo Moloi, recalling the same period, said:

Some children were not going to school, but the students were all in the Church. The people in Church used to teach scripture to the children, and this prepared them to do better in school.[55]

Becoming a Christian was often a duty as well as a personal attainment, a set of learned behaviors as well as a catharsis. Another woman spoke to Bessie Head, recalling the 1940s,

It was compulsory for us, especially as schoolchildren, to participate in all Church activities—Bible class once a week and Sunday school every Sunday. We had prayers at home every evening—the old people were all caught up in this atmosphere [which was] very strict and we feared hell-fire. . . .[56]

Sunday school, recalls Bernice Sebina, often consisted of greetings and songs intoned in unison, a Bible story, and a verbal quiz.

[50] F. H. Hawkins, *Report to the Directors . . . Nov. 1912 to March 1913* (Cape Town, 1914), and quote, LMS SA Reports, 6/1, School Report for Serowe, 1914 (E. Sharp, 1915).

[51] R. H. Lewis, "General Drought," *Annual Reports of the LMS*, 1922.

[52] Interview: Mrs. Sethuhile Sebina, Serowe, 28 Feb. 1989.

[53] LMS SA 87/1 Minutes of the SADC, Serowe, 12/20/25; 94/Burns, J. Burns to Chirgwin, 16/10/33; WCW/383, Semane Khama, "*Tiro ya Basadi*," *Tiger Kloof Magazine* 16 (Dec. 1934).

[54] Interview: Ms. Kadimo Serema, Palapye, 17 Dec. 1988.

[55] Interview: Mrs. Balatheo Moloi, Serowe, 17 Nov. 1988.

[56] BHP, Box "Ntbks," Ntbk N3, 1974, Mrs. Matome, age forty-two [in 1970]. Mrs. Matome later left the Ngwato Church for another, so this colors her reminiscences somewhat; and see LMS SA Reports, 6/2 Serowe for 1922 (R. H. Lewis, 1923).

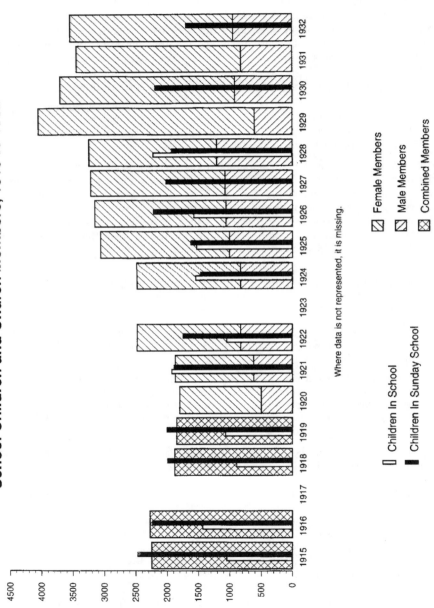

School Children and Church Members, 1915 to 1932

Where data is not represented, it is missing.

Children In School
Children In Sunday School

Female Members
Male Members
Combined Members

TABLE 4.1: THE NGWATO CHURCH, 1915 TO 1932

Year	Membership Male	Female	In School M	F	In Sun. School	Relevant events
1915	2,247		1,040		2,460	
1916	2,275		1,423		2,224	Expulsions and stagnation
1917	n.a.					
1918	1,879		881		1,982	Spanish Flu kills 15
1919	1,846		1,058		1,992	
1920	500	1,300	n.a.	n.a.		Drought begins
1921	619	1,251	638	1,277	1,876	Drought
1922	825	1,650	674	363	1,737	Bad drought, poverty, disease
1923	n.a.					Attack of *Q. Quelea* finches
1924	825[1]	1,650[1]	530	1,005	1,450	Sekgoma II's reign
1925	1,001	2,050	303	1,212	1,605	Tshekedi succeeds
1926	1,055	2,089	557	1,004	2,199	Drought
1927	1,068	2,137	n.a.	n.a.	2,000	
1928	1,200	2,031	597	1,606	1,908	
1929	599	3,432	n.a.	n.a.	n.a.	
1930	911	2,768	n.a.	n.a.	2,163	Rev. Burns purges roll
1931	812	2,605	n.a.	n.a.	n.a.	
1932	934	2,581	n.a.	n.a.	1,671	

[1]Repeated and so estimated or unreliable.

After the questions, we prayed. Then we left for the midday meal. Afterwards the senior children would go to Church, [and the younger] would stay home.[57]

The figures in Table 4.1 and their representation in Graph 4 reveal the dramatic expansion of women in the Church and with them, the youth they instructed.

Semane was not the only teacher. The shape of *thuto* demanded teaching from the start, when Khama had taught with the Rev. Price, and Christians viewed the designation "Christian" as pedagogical. *Mokereseti* meant someone confirmed in Church membership and participating in the spreading of the Word. *Bakereseti* led others in singing hymns, exhorted the faithful in prayers, and beseeched enquirers or even nonbelievers in evangelical revivals and campaigns. Again, such activity took place in village and town *dikgotla*. Although women hardly counted in the daily affairs of this forum, and had trouble presenting a case without male kin, on Sunday, Church women preached in the *kgotla* to both sexes. They soon began to view this occupation as a right, even in *dikgotla* outside their own neighborhoods, and even outside Serowe.[58] One elderly woman recalled,

---

57 Interview: Miss Bernice N. Sebina, Serowe, 4 Nov. 1988.

58 The Rev. Lewis reveals as much when he writes, during the Prince of Wales' visit to Serowe in 1925, that women would *not* be permitted in the *kgotla* on that occasion, LMS SA 87/3, R. H. Lewis to Barradale, 11/7/25. For the patriarchy of the *kgotla*, see Wylie, *A Little God*, Ch. 3 especially.

Children at the opening of the Sekgoma I Memorial Hospital, Serowe, November 1928. Photograph by A. M. Chirgwin. Reproduced courtesy of the Council for World Mission, London.

A Christian was respected because he/she was a believer. When you came, just entering the *kgotla* easily, it was like that, as we had warned them. . . . You would find them waiting, you just enter and open the Bible, they being gathered and quiet, and then you would say, "let us begin the work," and you started. . . . We did the work without discrimination in favor of Christians, [although] Christians were [justly] held to distinguish themselves from other people.[59]

These involved, and restrictive, connotations of Christianity account for the peculiarly low figure cited by Isaac Schapera as the percentage of Ngwato citizens who were Christians in the 1940s. His number, 7 percent, mainly counted those people who could take Communion (*Selalelo*) and were thus willing to call themselves Christians to a MoTswana census-taker.[60] Most Churchgoers hesitated at doing so, and the confirmed members who called themselves Bakeresete were making something of a statement.

> The main activity for women was the women's Bible-study groups. They took turns preaching to one another, reading from the Bible and so on. Women were as good as men in preaching—because they [we] too are people! A woman is a person herself, just like the missionary.[61]

Moruti Tshipa told me categorically that his parents were not Christians. But he continued (in English),

> I began to attend the Church long ago, in 1909, with my mothers, ah, my mother and my . . . old women in our village [(Tonota), who] used to go to Church, when I was still a little boy. [I thought your mother was not a Church member? —P.L.] She was not a Church member. She used to attend the Church. . . . The only ones who can take *Selalelo* are full members. [Enquirers] can only listen when the service is going on, then after that they go out. [They just choose to leave? —P.L.] Yes. . . . They do not have to be told. They know very well that "this is not our part to take."[62]

Similarly, Otaajang Kedikilwe, the aged daughter of a first-generation Christian, described herself in her Christian youth as a non-Christian. "At Nekati I had not yet entered the faith. . . . I only espoused the faith in 1930, while we were in Serowe," in other words, when she was confirmed.[63] Strict Christian parents sometimes kept their children from playing with unbaptized children, preparing for their future stature. As Ms. Gabotepele Ntsosa recalled of the same household:

> I grew up under Christians, I was not allowed to go out and play with the other kids. I was not allowed to . . . because [my grandfather] *Moruti* Seakgano did not want us to go astray, although we could go out and play with the other Christian children.[64]

True "Christianity" came later, as a result of personal decisions.

---

[59]   Interview: Ms. Maretha Masheto, Radisele, 18 April 1989.

[60]   Isaac Schapera, "Christianity and the Tswana," *Journal of the Royal Anthropological Institute* 83 (1958), 1–9; and Schapera, *Tribal Innovators*, in which he gives "under 20%," evidently realizing the misleading nature of his earlier figure, 129.

[61]   Quote, Interview: Mrs. Botsanyang Ramatsela, b. 1908, Serowe, 10 Nov. 1988; and also, the Rev. Johane Lenyebe, b. 1917, Serowe, May 1989.

[62]   Interview: The Rev. B. R. Tshipa, b. 1902, Serowe, 17 February 1989, English. "Mothers" was Tshipa's English for "boMme."

[63]   Interview: Mrs. Otaajang Kedikilwe, b. 1902, Sefhope, 20 May 1989.

[64]   Interview: Ms. Gabotepele Ntsosa, b. 1910, Serowe, 27 Feb. 1989.

Yes, [catechumens] were tested, yes, they were asked questions, not like Christianity today. The person tells the *moruti* what s/he came for, I came for such and such [a reason], do you know Jesus, this and that thing about God you must be asked, a question, an examination. The day you are received, you are termed a true believer. It was not like it is today, where you are received when you say, I love God. . . . [Did you read? —P.L.] Every day! I was only separated from my Bible by blindness.[65]

On the whole, women Church members distinguished themselves by fearlessly presenting a public face to the world, something many Ngwato women hesitated to do. Very occasionally, a woman might strive for even more. The following is drawn from my notes.[66]

Leah M. was enrolled as a catechumen in a deacon's *dikaelo* class in Lerala (a village in the Tswapong Hills) in 1935. She had three dreams. In the first dream she dreamed that Abraham spoke to her and ordered her to leave the village and go out into the world (*go tswa lehatshe*). Then shortly afterwards, she dreamed another dream in which a voice spoke to her, it could have been "Joseph," and told her to take ten bundles of grass (*dingata*). Nine of the bundles belonged to she knew not whom. The tenth one was her own. The nine fell down before her bundle in obeisance.

One would expect Leah M. to liken this adolescent dream to Genesis 37:5, since she mentions Joseph and something like sheaves of wheat; in Joseph's prophetic dream his sheaf stood upright while his brothers' bowed to his own. She disliked my analysis, perhaps because it implied a certain vindictiveness.[67] In any case, like Joseph's, her voyage to greater things had begun.

She saw the dream as meaning she should visit the people in the Church, which she did. They interpreted the dream to mean that she "should become a Christian," but she did nothing for two weeks. Finally she dreamt a third dream, in which a voice came to her and said, why haven't you joined the Church? So she became serious about it and discussed the matter with Lebogang, the *moruti*.

The only route out of the village to "the wider world," aside from marriage, was the Church. For Leah, higher education, *thuto*, meant moving in with relatives in Serowe.

She went out to Serowe, and enrolled in the Khama Memorial School. Her Bible school was "in Khama's Church in Serowe"—whereas in Lerala, she had merely taken a lesser Bible class (*thuto ya baibele*) after school. After some years of study, in 1942 she was formally received in the Church in Serowe. She says she then went on to study theology for five years, and is therefore more qualified than many *baruti* with official

[65]   Interview: Mrs. Otaajang Kedikilwe, b. 1902, Sefhope, 20 May 1989; this woman is Moruti Seakgano Ncaga's daughter; and Ms. Gabotepele Ntsosa, b. 1910, Serowe, 27 Feb. 1989, his granddaughter, who grew up with her in Seakgano's home.

[66]   Interview: Ms. Leah M., Lerala, 3 April 1990.

[67]   She herself wished to draw an analogy to Joseph's interpretation of the Pharaoh's dream, also about grain, which she explicitly knew as Genesis 41:1–32.

positions today—she says she can administer *Selalelo*—but is denied a position because of her age (she says) and, I would guess, her sex.

Is this just a nice story? Undeniably few women cared to carry *thuto* so far. Yet Leah M. based her ambitions in a new identity that Christian women had participated in building. Previously, the term *mosadi*, usually glossed as "woman," had been defined in relationship to men; it named a female who had left her father's household for that of another man. In the public domain, *mosadi* had lain flooded beneath other identities of ethnicity, status, and politics. In the 1910s and 1920s, elite women in the capital went some distance in transforming that identity. Stamped with the sacramental seal of the king's marriage ministers, elevated over ethnicity, and educated in *thuto*, *mosadi* took on a new centrality and colored the idea of the kingdom itself.

"Raising the Tone of Womanhood": The LMS Draws Gender

In the 1880s, the attention of LMS missionaries had paralleled that of the early Ngwato Church in seeing women as men's helpmeets. After the century's turn, the LMS began to pay more attention to Christian women and the negotiation of what women's affairs were to be. In 1905 Jennings sent the Society a photograph of his "annual Church meeting," proudly pointing out the "tea and buns—an innovation for the Man[g]wato."[68] Christian women were to schedule time for such plotted sociability, alongside choir and prayer groups, meetings, and Sunday school teaching class. Some of these groups sewed uniforms, and some bought Western finery. As women became more "public" to Ngwato men, they also materialized to missionaries, but largely as imperfect human beings in need of improvement.

And so the LMS wanted to do something about women. In 1905 the Rev. Tom Brown remarked:

> There is plenty of work to be done among the women in our missions, . . . which a missionary's wife cannot do owing to domestic duties. Surely, if we can raise the tone of womanhood of the Bechuana we shall be doing more for the next generation than anything else we can do. . . . [U]ntil we change the attitude of both men and women towards a purer womanhood we cannot hope for much growth in spiritual matters.[69]

Brown was motivated in some measure by the "Zezana Missions" of the LMS in India, which secluded women in carefully controlled homes.[70] The nature of Tswana society prevented that extreme, and Brown was necessarily vague. Apparently what was lacking were activities explicitly designed for women *by Europeans*. There was a need to begin at the threshold of life itself. "Lady missionaries who are trained nurses with a knowledge of midwifery would find great opportunity,"

---

68 LMS SA 66/1, A. Jennings to R. W. Thompson, Serowe, 12/3/05.

69 J. Tom Brown, in *The Chronicle of the LMS* XIV (1905), 47.

70 See, e.g., LMS, *Quarterly News of Women's Work* 1, 1 (1887), 5, and 1, 2 (1888), 8. This was far from unknown in Africa; see Nancy Rose Hunt, "Domesticity and Colonialism in Belgian Africa: Usumbura's *Foyer Social*, 1946–1960," *Signs: Journal of Women and Culture in Society* 15, 3 (1990), 447–74.

Secretary Hawkins suggested. "This means of approach to the native woman is one the importance of which cannot be exaggerated." Unintentionally, missionaries thus pointed to the vaginal canal as the way in to the psyches of women—this "open door," in another revealing simile.[71]

Regardless of the need for midwifery, nothing was done during World War I; after it, as wealthy Edwardian benefactors died off, the Society entered a new era of austerity. In 1920 the regional organ of the LMS (the SADC) lamented that what it defined, with specific content, as "women's work" occurred on only four southern African mission stations.[72] Public worship, confessions, and exhortations were not work, because they were not schooled, subdivided, and scheduled. The 1924 LMS Deputation pointed out further that, in a Church of 1,650 women and 825 men, "the dejected appearance of such a large proportion of women Christians [was] depressing." Their report took the view that it was the bearing and raising of children that immiserated women. A European midwife would somehow lessen their burden. Finally, in 1925, Miss Francis Gilbert was sent to Serowe.

Gilbert immediately began a small sewing class in Sharp's school, visited sick Christians, and offered to teach women how to raise their babies, something all anglophone Europeans in Africa in this period labelled "mothercraft."[73] Although the concept of an English maiden telling experienced, married Ngwato women how to bear and care for infants might seem grotesque, novelty and prestige attracted some eighty women to her childcare class. In a bitter irony, a Johannesburg doctor advised Gilbert not to marry because of her ill health, and she resigned in 1931. Miss Evelyn Haile came and took over "the work" in 1933.[74] The next year, Semane wrote,

> Sister Haile made up a group of women who have already gone to their homes [i.e. are married—*basadi*], to help and guide [*kaela*] them in how they must care for their children and in giving birth. The work is progressing . . . but not many come to it.[75]

---

[71]   LMS, *Report of Mrs. John May, Mr. Talbot E.B. Wilson, and Mr. F. H. Hawkins, Deputation to South and Central Africa, Jan.–July, 1924* (Strictly Private and Confidential), 2, quoting 1913 Report; and see Margaret Strobel's discussion in *European Women and the Second British Empire* (Bloomington, IN, 1991), 49–53. "Open door" is Evelyn Haile's precise phrase denoting midwifery, Evelyn Haile, "Beliefs in Bechuanaland," *Nursing Mirror and Midwives' Journal* (6 Oct. 1934), 14.

[72]   LMS SA 83/1 Minutes of the Annual SADC, Tiger Kloof 12–20/3/20. Serowe was one of the four. The SADC apparently took "women's work" to mean, inclusively, all of the following: Sunday school teaching, attendance of a Women's Bible Class, visitation of the sick (which certainly occurred in all mission stations), private prayer meetings, care of the Communion plate, and responsibility for women's infractions.

[73]   LMS, *Report of . . . 1924*, 25; LMS SA Reports, 6/4, Report on Women's Work in Serowe for 1926 (F. H. Gilbert, 1927); LMS SA 88/2 F. H. Gilbert to Barradale, Serowe 2/5/26; *Report of the LMS*, Vol. 136 (1930–31), 422. Gilbert had previously served for six years in India.

[74]   Gilbert's and Haile's duties were directly prefigured by the rise of women health care visiting and sanitary inspection in Britain. See Celia Davies, "The Health Visitor as Mother's Friend: A woman's place in public health, 1900–1914," *Social History of Medicine* 1, 1 (April 1988), 39–60. Gilbert had TB and acute eczema. LMS 93/Gilbert, F. H. Gilbert to Chirgwin, Leicester 4/11/31; 90/Gilbert, F. H. Gilbert to Barradale, Serowe 8/4/28.

[75]   WCW/383, "Tiro ya Basadi mo Serowe," 10; the English translation given in the magazine has "but they are not very keen on it."

The thrill of the new had worn off. Nevertheless, Haile is remembered fondly in Serowe even today.

> It is all a joy. I love evangelizing in the huts where I have previously nursed the mother and baby—and when all [i.e., the birth] is over, I hold a little dedication service for the baby. I am up against heathenism and superstition—and I often feel it where there are Christians.[76]

The first act of the parturient mother was to make a hat; "the mother will sew a little bonnet and dress that first day." It is clear from Haile's own descriptions that it was mainly the capital's elite who accepted her midwifery. While Christian mothers adopted some postpartum semiotics Haile deemed critical, like bodily washing and sewing, most of their birth routines were beyond her control.[77] We return to the subject of medicine and the Church next chapter.

In defining women, some LMS interventions tried to reverse previous gender roles. Teaching women to sew was difficult, because stitching clothing had been an activity of men.[78] Weaving cloth was a new technology and so promised more success, but King Khama himself, when asked in 1895 about women's "progress" as compared with men's, complained of women's lack of zeal in spinning and weaving. At the LMS College at Tiger Kloof in the northern Cape, boys were to learn how to construct houses, a practice begun by missionaries teaching carpentry on their stations. Lloyd found he could generate little interest in it, because house-building had long been a task allotted to women. These attempts to reverse gendered "village work" did not succeed.[79] Behind both failed and successful maneuvers lay the missionaries' desire to parse Christians' time according to an industrial ethic. They wished to isolate and create "leisure," and to regender work, on the one hand, and Church activities in the off-hours, on the other.

Their concern to make leisure paralleled many girls' real superannuation from basic agricultural labor in November through January, which increased their attendance in school.[80] This came about partly because Christian women of high birth or marriage could afford female servants, who helped in caring

---

[76] LMS SA 95/Haile, E. Haile to Hawkins, Serowe 4/6/33.

[77] Haile, "Beliefs in Bechuanaland," *Nursing Mirror and Midwives' Journal*; thanks to Nancy Hunt.

[78] The Rev. Williams' wife taught sewing; Headmistress Ella Sharp also taught girls crocheting. LMS SA Reports, 3/3, Shoshong for 1904 (H. Williams, 1905); Mgadla, "Education," 257 n54, R. Sekgoma, Serowe, 17/1/83. Tiger Kloof Missionary College taught girls "housewifery," including cleanliness and needlepoint, but the Rev. Willoughby recognized that tailoring was and would remain a male occupation; Willoughby, *Tiger Kloof,* 74.

[79] "King Khama Interviewed by a Lady in London; Christianity and Native Wives," *Christian World* (12 Sept. 1895), clipping in BHP, Box "Ntbks," Bk. 3; LMS SA 7/1, Rules for Pupils in the Tiger Kloof Native Institution (n.d., ca. 1905); *Chronicle of the LMS* XVI (1907), 143ff.; LMS SA 74/6, *Report on Education in the B.P.*, 1912. Willoughby's audacity as principle of Tiger Kloof's extended to teaching boys how to tend cattle. Deborah Gaitskell discusses "gender switches" in "Devout Domesticity? A Century of African Women's Christianity in South Africa," in Walker, ed., *Women and Gender in Southern Africa*, 251–72. Compare Elizabeth Schmidt, *Peasants, Traders and Wives: Shona Women in the History of Zimbabwe* (Portsmouth, NH, 1992), 129–33, for Zimbabwe.

[80] It is interesting in this regard that the Greek root of the word school, *scholē*, also signified leisure. Leisure nonetheless might not mean ease, or happy, familial activity, but rather the space for any "activity." Its invention and isolation were part of the demarcation of time; leisure implies nothing more than that work is a separable time and activity.

for children and cooking. More critically, however, women's exertions in the first half of the agricultural year were lightened after 1900 by the ox-drawn plow, which replaced the iron hoe. As we have seen, the plow allowed affluent household-heads to expand output, and shifted power and wealth from Ngwato royalty to commoner entrepreneurs, who were permitted to "own" their cattle. Because plows (and the new wheeled ox carts) required herding, inspanning, and leading oxen, male household heads, who controlled cattle, took to the fields themselves. They also sought to manage the disposal of their increased outputs of sorghum, millet, and maize. Decisions about how much grain was "surplus" and could be sold, how much was to be put in a *mosadi*'s mother's bin, and how much consumed, took place within the hedges and walls of the household; but any such decisions reflected the new positioning of men at the start of the productive cycle.[81]

When women needed to make beer, however, they took grain from their own stores, as they had always done.[82]

Tea Instead of Beer

In this context we must return to *bojalwa*, this time to review many women's desire *not* to make beer, to enter a Church that forbade it, and even to crusade for temperance. Having been outlawed, *bojalwa* survived as a political trope into the 1930s and beyond. Under Tshekedi, *bojalwa* was recriminalized. In 1937 Tshekedi accused Leetile Disang Raditladi of having intercourse with his wife, Bagakgametse, whom he subsequently divorced. In the resulting hearings, beer again emerged as a trope for loyalty. Here is a hostile exchange between Tshekedi and Leetile's aged father, Disang, whose own father Raditladi had been accused by Khama of beer-drinking forty-two years earlier.

> [Disang:] Khama had a strict law forbidding beer. Today beer is being used as freely [as] at Mokwena . . . where there is no prohibition. [Yet] *If I drink beer* I can be arrested. . . . To-day I am unwell. . . .
>
> [Tshekedi:] Disang stated that a man can be found guilty for beer-drinking *if it is so desired*. Beer-drinking is indulged in an excessive manner here. I am not afraid to tell the District Commissioner that the increase in its brewing is through him in his capacity as an official. . . . I could not

---

[81]   Belinda Bozzoli, "Marxism, Feminism and South African Studies," *Journal of Southern African Studies* 9, 2 (1983); but see her *Women of Phokeng*, as her answer to her own queries. Isaac Schapera, *Native Land Tenure in the Bechuanaland Protectorate* (Cape Town, 1943), 200, reports that 70 percent of a household's grain was kept from a man's mother-in-law and stored in his wife's bin (placing GammaNgwato in the statistical middle of Protectorate kingdoms), but there is no discussion of how men and women arrived at the percentage of this grain to be sold.

[82]   WCW/706, W. C. Willoughby, "Cultivation and Food;" Duggan, *An Economic Analysis*, 105–111; and see Samuel Broadbent, cited in Jean Comaroff, "Home-Made Hegemony," 14–15, along with her discussion. Except for Duggan, there is actually a dearth of work on the changing relations of production after the advent of the plow, but see also Norman Mahoney, "Contract and Neighborly Exchange among the Birwa of Botswana," *Journal of African Law* 21, 1 (1977), 55 and 62–63; and Marcia Wright, "Technology, Marriage, and Women's Work in the History of Maize-Growers in Mazabuka, Zambia: A Reconnaissance," *Journal of Southern African Studies* 10, 1 (1983), 81, 88.

prohibit it seeing that I had continuous cases against me [from the government to weaken] the powers exercised by the Chief.[83]

Tshekedi then sent out a regiment to smash all beer pots in Serowe, and redoubled his prohibition of stronger alcohol in the same period.[84] And beer-drinking, or at least its revelation, still served as an index of disloyalty much later. In 1950, during a dispute between Tshekedi and the young heir, Seretse Sekgoma, there was a three-day battle in Mahalapye—fought, according to one of Tshekedi's agents,

> between the Mahalapye women and the women leaving for Rametsana [Tshekedi's partisans]. The war started when Manyaphiri's wife tried to prevent the Rametsana women from drinking beer. Manyaphiri [the village governor] was present but did not stop the fight, [which] left some people wounded.[85]

The plow and wagon remade the agricultural cycle, to the detriment of women's relationship to production. The manufacture and presentation of beer no longer stood as a fair representation of their now-devalued labor; brewing had become more of a service than a celebration, and an illicit service at that. While women had to make *bogobe*, the porridge-like staple of daily survival, in abjuring beer they earned accolades for upholding Ngwato political identity, and indeed for good citizenship. In lieu of a beer-drink, they took tea together in Church groups.

As we have seen, the kingship aimed prohibition mostly at competitive men, not women. With temperance agitation, women thus allied themselves with the "state" against these men and helped define what that state was. In Christians' consciousness, abstinence was central both to the law of the realm and to "Christianity" itself.

> [During my confirmation] we were asked questions like "where was Jesus born," when, what is the essence of Christianity, what it means to be a Christian. I have forgotten some of the questions since it was long ago, [but] one was, "do you drink beer." So God help me because I do not drink . . . I do not even know the taste of it on the tongue. . . . Starting from long ago, when we became Christians, beer was utterly forbidden—you could not find it anywhere.[86]

> The Rev. Tebape told us that a Christian child must be obedient to his parents. But not only—everybody is your parent in the village . . . [and] drink—beer—is not right; beer-drinking is a very bad habit.[87]

83 TKP K/74, Hearing on Disang and Leetile Raditladi, May 1937, 16, 20 (English); my emphasis. For those unfamiliar with SeTswana but familiar with New York City, this passage might be read as if two old Orchard Street Jewish men were talking to one another; I often felt that Yiddish speech rhythms and idioms paralleled "formal" SeTswana. I hope this observation will not revive the Hamitic theory.

84 Mary Benson, *Tshekedi Khama* (London, 1960), 137; TKP, A/1, Tshekedi to R. W. Cruikshank, Rhodesian Temperance Alliance, Serowe, 4/5/38.

85 TKP, Box 52, "Manyaphiri" report to Tshekedi, Mahalapye [Oct. 1950]. Seretse dismissed prohibition as belonging to a bygone era, Interview: Mr. Oabona Nthobatsang, Serowe, 9 May 1989; but to this very day, Christians in GammaNgwato will grow either sheepish or defensive when asked if they make or drink *bojalwa*.

86 Interview: The Rev. Johane Lenyebe, b. 1917, Serowe, May 1989.

87 Interview: *Moruti* Modise Segaise (b. ca. 1910) with Mrs. Gasethata Segaise, Serowe, 20 Dec. 1988.

Temperance agitators in Serowe stirred conflict right within the household, a conflict perhaps related to other household negotiations on apportioning grain and its proceeds from sale. Christian women found guilty of brewing beer in 1913 confessed that their "heathen" husbands had ordered them to brew: they themselves had "agreed" to give up the practice.[88] In 1922 Andrew Kgasa, an ordained Tswana minister, wrote from Ngamiland that "Many women say that they do not drink [beer] but have to make it for their husbands. I fight strongly against that, . . . though not yet successful."[89] A woman's acceptance of prohibition often pitted her against her husband. As Miss Gilbert told her hygiene classes, temperance was not an easy ride. She appealed to women to "stand firm and refuse" to brew beer for their sons, husbands, and fathers, even though she understood that men now had "the whip in hand," and could withhold clothing and other commodities.[90]

After some delays, a formal Church temperance society was launched under the Rev. Lewis. He and Sekgoma II decried a disturbing trend whereby Ngwato men, including Christians, crossed the border to Francistown to drink.[91] He commenced what he called "Total Abstinence Propaganda," for the work of "Temperance . . . which has been done in the past solely by the [king]." In 1927 there were 130 temperance society members, all women, with white ribbons and pledge cards. This vanguard was led by Semane, whose presence served as a constant reminder (should one be needed) that temperance held the full endorsement of the kingship.[92] She and her daughter Bonyerile led 271 women in the Serowe Temperance Union in 1929. The work was divided amongst "women evangelists," each, like deaconesses and headmen, responsible for the women in her own *kgotla* neighborhood. Because more than half the Ngwato Church's membership resided outside Serowe by that year, it seemed necessary to extend the movement. Accordingly, at the end of 1929, the Serowe group decided to affiliate with the Transvaal chapter of the Women's Christian Temperance Union (WCTU) after a "stirring address" by one of their Johannesburg members.[93]

Conferences were organized and agendas compiled. Mrs. Evelyn Shaw, the wife of a Palapye shopkeeper, arranged for the construction of a community hall—built from bricks first used in the church at old Phalapye. This hall became a center of temperance work in New Palapye. As a railway town, Palapye saw plenty of

---

[88]   *Report of the LMS*, Vol. 63 (Cape Town, 1914), 267.

[89]   LMS SA Reports 6/1, Ngami District, 1922 (R. H. Lewis, 1923), containing an extract of Kgasa's letter.

[90]   LMS SA 91/Gilbert, "Beer Drinking," 1930.

[91]   LMS SA Reports, 5/3, Serowe for 1919 (R. H. Lewis, 1920); LMS SA 82/1, R. H. Lewis to F. H. Hawkins, Serowe, 3/2/19; LMS Reports 5/4, Serowe for 1919 (R. H. Lewis, 1920). The Tati mining company owned and operated Francistown; see Henderson Mpakati Tapela's excellent dissertation, "The Tati District of Botswana" (Ph.D. dissertation, University of Sussex, 1976), esp. 265–66.

[92]   LMS SA Reports, 7/1, Report of Women's Work in Serowe for 1927 (F. H. Gilbert, 1928). The Serowe Temperance Union dissolved in 1944; Evelyn Haile and Evelyn Shaw resigned, and Bonyerile Khama refused to meet with a full committee. The Rev. Griffiths opined that the problem was "Kingship versus Christianity," but a late resurgence of "LMS versus Ngwato elites" seems a better explanation, BNA/ Sandilands Papers, "Griffiths/King," Griffiths to Sandilands, Serowe 11/1/43.

[93]   For Francis Gilbert's efforts, Tshekedi gave her a motor car. LMS SA 91/Gilbert, "Beer Drinking," 1930; 91/Lewis, Lewis to Barradale, Serowe 21/5/28; 90/Burns, J. H. L. Burns to Barradale, Molepolole, 23/10/28. The South African Women's Christian Temperance Union was founded in 1889, and franchised in 1895. In 1910 the World's WCTU had 434,000 dues-payers; in Britain, as in GammaNgwato, its members were considered wealthy and well-connected. See Ian Tyrell, "Women's Temperance in International Perspective: The World's WCTU, 1880s–1920s, in Barrow and Room, eds., *Drinking*, 217–42.

men familiar with the drinking life on the Witwatersrand. In 1931 "A contingent of 41 people from Lech[eng], headed by Mrs. Samuel [Serema]," the wife of Lecheng's *moruti,* "walked 12 miles to be present" in Palapye.[94]

> I remember being carried by my father [*Moruti* Serema] on his shoulders to . . . Palapye, to town, to meet with people like Mrs. Shaw. She was a sort of *moruti*—she . . . came from London with her husband, who opened a business, and she chose to do Christian work. She worked with my father [and] formed a group called Temperance . . . with MmaBonyerile [i.e. Semane] in Serowe.[95]

Led by Semane Khama, local headmen, evangelists, women, and a number of missionaries came from Serowe; about two hundred people gathered in all. Semane gave an inspirational talk and the Lecheng group sang a specially written hymn.[96] In 1934, Semane's opinions on her branch of the WCTU, called the Women's Regiment (*Mophato*) of Beer (*Bojalwa*), appeared in the *Tiger Kloof Magazine*:

> Our wish is that people fear beer with their hearts, not just with their bodies; that they respect the law against beer, and the kingship[.] [O]ur helpers in the work are the women preachers I spoke of, and other women and deaconesses.[97]

Ngwato temperance categorically reviled *bojalwa*, the product of the hearth, alongside brandy, in a single attack. Temperance efforts therefore had little recourse to appeals to "custom" and "tradition." This was not the case in areas affected to a greater degree by the settlement of Europeans and their demand for labor. Dombodema, for instance, was a Rhodesian village closer both to the Tati territory gold mines, to Rhodesian Native Labor Association activity, and to Francistown.[98] There temperance dealt also with the encroaching forces of the market, as it threatened to disrupt the sexual status quo of the monogamous family constantly under Christian construction. In one gathering, for instance, a Mrs. Makeba read an "interesting" paper, concluding that girls should not work for unmarried European men in shops.[99] Although temperance in GammaNgwato carried less of an expressive burden than in Dombodema, the dislocations brought on by the wage labor economy did provoke the LMS in 1931 to seek a revival of discarded African customs, so long as they were not "antagonistic to the spirit of Christian faith."[100]

---

94 This was true even before 1936, when the price of gold was guaranteed internationally, moving the mines on the Rand to step up production and begin recruiting labor heavily from Francistown and other railway depots; and LMS SA 93/Shaw, Mrs. T. W. Shaw to Chirgwin, Palapye, 6/8/31.

95 Interview: Ms. Kadimo Serema, Palapye, 17 Dec. 1988.

96 LMS SA 93/Shaw, Mrs. T. W. Shaw to Chirgwin, Palapye, 6/8/31.

97 WCW/383, "Tiro ya Basadi mo Serowe," *Tiger Kloof Magazine* 16 (Dec. 1934), 10–12. My translation, not the adjacent English version.

98 See Alan Jeeves, "Migrant Labor and South African Expansion, 1920–1950," *South African Historical Journal* 18 (1986), 73–92; and Charles van Onselen, *Chibaro* (London, 1976), 104–109.

99 LMS SA 93/Sharp, E. Sharp, "First Conference held at Dombodema, 21–23 August, 1931, Association of Christian Temperance Native Women for God, Home and Every Land." See also Paul la Hausse, *Brewers, Beerhalls and Boycotts, A History of Liquor in South Africa* (Johannesburg, 1988), 42–47.

100 LMS SA 93/Sharp, Minutes of the SADC, 17/1/31; and see BNA, Sandilands Papers, Arthur Sandilands, *Sexual Morality, British and Bechuana* (Cape Town, 1951), in which Sandilands praises Tswana marriage for binding together families rather than just individuals, as the LMS had sought to engineer.

Had the LMS been left to their devices, away from the active will of elite Christian women and the kingship, perhaps the beer-drinking of yore might have returned as a quaint and harmless custom. For in fact, the experience of wage labor in South Africa, combined with *bojalwa*'s illegal status in Serowe, changed *bojalwa* itself, both in its composition and in the patterns of its use. In Serowe, *bojalwa* came to denote not only sorghum beer but an adulterated and potent brew called *kgadi*. Lumped as an evil with the old *bojalwa*, *kgadi* was sold to anyone who would violate Ngwato law. Men bought *kgadi* and brandy and *bojalwa jwa setswana* outside the rhythm of social and agricultural celebrations. Very early, C. C. Vialls of Palapye Station wrote to Khama that

> My boys are continually getting drunk. . . . [T]here are some native women here who make a living by making and selling beer, it is not what my boys get at their own homes, but these women have established themselves just for the purpose. . . . Trusting you will send out an injunction to these people here, which I am sure will have the desired effect. . . .[101]

Despite the technicality that railway land was not his own, Khama responded quickly, burning down their houses. These women had to be kept as the exception, not the rule, which they were fast becoming throughout the rest of southern Africa. Meanwhile, in GammaNgwato during the harvest, instead of offering beer to mobilize communal labor (*letsema*) as had once been common, good Christian women substituted cooked meat, *bogobe*, or simple reciprocality.[102] Thus, while the prohibition of beer discouraged its consumption, it also widened the distance between its consumption and the soil. *Bojalwa* came to mean any alcohol, any time.

As men bought stronger liquors, especially while outside the kingdom, they began to fight more often, as drinking in mine barracks accelerated new behaviors. Quarrelsomeness and ethnic divisions, not communality, became associated with "*bojalwa*." Violence may also have entered the home with new force; and it is noteworthy that both Khama and Tshekedi had been "especially strict" in forbidding beer to young men.[103] Some women hinted that violence gave them another reason for joining the Church; they drew an opposition between quarrelling and the essence of congregation (*phuthego*). Outright wife abuse was not tolerated among male catechumens.[104] One woman said:

---

[101] K III C/16/20, C. C. Vialls, Gen. Merchant, to Khama, Palapye Station, 17/12/02. For colonial-era beer-brewing as a female economy, see Helen Bradford, "We Are Now the Men: Women's Beer Protests in the Natal Countryside, 1929," in Belinda Bozzoli, ed., *Class, Community and Conflict: South African Perspectives* (Johannesburg, 1984), 292–323; and Charles Ambler, "Drunks, Brewers and Chiefs: Alcohol Regulation in Colonial Kenya, 1900–1939," in Barrows and Room, eds., *Drinking*, 166; and Marianna Adler, "From Symbolic Exchange to Commodity Consumption," 376–98 in the same volume.

[102] K III A/6/5, Notice from Col. Panzera, Assist. Commissioner; C/16/21, Khama to C.C. Vialls, Serowe 20/12/02; H/60/"1902–3", C. C. Vialls to Khama, 12/2/03; and Interview: The Rev. Phethu Sekgoma, b. 1922, Bobonong, 2 May 1989. Such communal labor is, like the planting season, referred to as *letsema*.

[103] TKP, A/1, Tshekedi to E.E. Warden, 1/4/35; Interview: The Rev. Phethu Sekgoma, b. 1922, Bobonong, 2 May 1989.

[104] See JR LMS/S 3 Register "Notes on Catechumens," 1901 for S. Cweni (Tshwene). Schapera, *Migrant Labor and Tribal Life*, mentions "bad manners" and "unpleasantness," 169, 185; and see J.B. Loudon, "Psychogenic Disorder and Social Conflict among the Zulu," in M. K. Opler, *Culture and Mental Health* (New York, 1959). Philip Bonner writes that migrancy "profoundly warped marital relations," bringing rampant adultery, in "Liquor, Prostitution and the Migration of BaSotho Women to the Rand, 1920–1945," in Walker, ed., *Women and Gender in Southern Africa*, 221–50.

[When you were converted] they asked you, "do you feel yourself becoming a Christian?" Meaning, that a person must love God and forgo the things of Satan. [In answering "What have you seen"—] we saw God. They asked whether you've parted with all the bad ways— such as, drinking beer and fighting. You must not drink *bojalwa*. You must not fight, or scold others . . . if you passed, you could then eat *Selalelo* [Communion].[105]

Such concerns were voiced only by implication. Another woman remarked,

[The *baruti*] pressed me to follow them, because I liked them and I liked their habits, so I became a Christian myself. It was the will of God to give me Christianity. [Christians] were protected from all bad habits, as they did not drink beer or fight with fists, and I was attracted by that. [In the old days they] were protected, the Spirit of God protected them because they did not drink beer or fight. . . . Nowadays . . . as soon as the deacon or evangelist gets out of Church, he . . . fights, drinks, or quarrels at home.[106]

Women's interest in Christianity has long dwarfed men's *throughout* southern Africa. Surely this fact must be discussed in the terms I have used here: Church participation was a means of self-protection and mobilization; it re-gendered, and encroached upon, the public, social sphere of human activity. Hence, in GammaNgwato, temperance crusades were simultaneously acts of feminine resistance and elite feminist aggression. While women fought for the right to brew beer in much of southern Africa, including in parts of GammaNgwato, Christian women struggled for the right not to brew. These women grasped the communal forum of the Church as they lost much of their control over production and distribution, and hammered at the besieged communality of their husbands, interweaving domestic and political struggle. In so doing they lent force to the king's Word and substance to the kingship itself.

Women, Citizenship, and the Church

Women and men entering the membership in the 1920s and 1930s maintained a clear appreciation of the Ngwato Church's relationship to Ngwato citizenship. Mass prayer meetings in the Serowe church transpired during the high commissioner's summary suspension of Tshekedi Khama in 1933.[107] Many Christians had been raised in the Church and saw it as an anchor of continuity.

I had believed in [the Church] just because Khama used to be a member—then, it was the only Church. I visited Mrs. Maemo Sesupo, and explained all my concerns. When we got to Deacon Taba's house together, Maema said, "this woman wants to talk with you." Maema said "it was high time I joined."[108]

---

[105] Interview: Mrs. Tsogang Serema, b. 1901, Palapye, 7 Dec. 1988.

[106] Interview: Ms. Oathokwa Samoele, b. 1918, Radisele, 18 Feb. 1989.

[107] Crowder, *Flogging of Phineas McIntosh*, 84.

[108] Interview: Mrs. Lebogang Bolokeng, b. 1920, Serowe, n.d.; not entirely verbatim.

I went to Church when it was still called *Lontone*. I went there because I was supposed to, with some other people so that I could also be made to believe in God. . . . [W]hen I was still young, I went, with mother and father, who were both members. . . . It is Khama who converted people; he was the one who went to London, and came back with missionaries, coming back here. Yes, he is the one who went to look for *thuto* there.[109]

Although the Word of God was open to individual interpretation, it carried a general syntax of behavior similar to that which Khama's moral and legalistic edicts announced. Self-described Christians may have composed a small minority of Ngwato adults, but they could act as GammaNgwato's exemplars for this precise reason. To reprise a very important point, two elderly Christians sum up:

[What is the difference after someone converts? —P.L.] The major difference of them, was that we were following Khama's law. [We] could not drink beer, or insult others. People no longer interested themselves in *dingaka*.[110]

The law [against *bojalwa*] was made because it was according to Khama's wishes, as he saw it was necessary. *Bojalwa* was there but people did not noisily drink; by Khama's law if you were found creating a disturbance or fighting, [you] were not doing right.[111]

Christian women absorbed and propagated these ideals. Wherever they were, there was the realm of the Word.

---

[109] Interview: Mrs. Setuhile Sebina, Serowe, 28 Feb. 1989. As in some other interviews, Khama's visit to England in 1895 for "protection" from rapacious settler colonies is elided with his communication of the Word of God.

[110] *Ibid.*

[111] Interview: The Rev. Phethu Sekgoma, b. 1922, Bobonong, 2 May 1989.

PART II

THE PERIPHERY OF
THE REALM OF THE WORD

Up to this point, we have been concerned with the three successive Ngwato capital towns, Shoshong (up to 1889), Phalapye (1890–1902), and Serowe (1902–present), and with Shoshong after it ceased to be the capital. Nonetheless, more than half the people in the Ngwato District of the Protectorate, at least nominally subject to the authority of the Ngwato kingdom, lived outside these towns. Most of them were of non-Ngwato ancestry and lived in smaller villages. Part II of this book discusses this hinterland and its incorporation into the Ngwato realm of the Word. As the kingdom sought to recreate its power among both Tswana and Kalanga people, it had to contend with the LMS's own contrasting efforts, with a local resistance often built from the evangelical language of the Church, and, most of all, with the daily negotiation of its hegemony within village society.

5

The Body of Christians: Medicine, Extraction, and Prayer

Now, if he prayed for a [sick] person, if it were someone he had already dealt with, he stretched over him/her, and when he had put his arms over the person he spoke thus!

Otaajang Kedikilwe, born 1902,
on her father, Moruti Seakgano[1]

In Chapter 1, we saw how Khama first approached Christianity as if it were a variation on the practice of *dingaka*, or priest-healers. The work of several scholars has shown that southern Africans generally assumed such a congruence between early missionaries and healers.[2] The expressions, activities, and indeed the presence of missionaries were fitted into this regional cultural grammar in order to be understood. Yet if meaning consists in the uses to which people and actions are put, the similarity to the *ngaka* is only the beginning of the story. From the moment the missionary John Mackenzie assumed the duties of priest-healer for Khama's cult of the Word, his practice separated him from that role. As missionaries' medicine diverged from the expectations that had encased it, so did the practices of ordinary Christians. What happened, this chapter argues, is that Ngwato Christians progressively embraced those elements of healing that missionaries rejected. Missionaries demanded, as part and parcel of their therapy, that existing communities relinquish their ontological hold on the health of individuals; and as this occurred in GammaNgwato, for a variety of reasons, Christians offered new communities of

---

[1]   Interview: Mrs. Otaajang Kedikilwe, b. 1902, Sefhope, 20 May 1989.

[2]   See Caroline F. Seeley, "The Reaction of the BaTswana to the Practice of Western Medicine" (M.Phil thesis, London School of Economics, 1973), 78, 88ff.; Thomas Tlou, "Khama III—Great Reformer and Innovator," *Botswana Notes and Records* 2 (1970), 99; in Tlou's phrase, to the rank and file, "*dingaka* and missionaries were species of the same genus."

support for the dispossessed. Taken as a whole, this two-part provision of Christian health care was a microcosm of the general fragmentation and reincorporation of GammaNgwato's communities into the regime of power given force by the Word. This process did not begin with the spread of independent "healing churches" in GammaNgwato in the 1950s, but rather started much earlier.

Congruence and Divergence Between Missionary and Priest-Healer

Missionaries to the BaNgwato after Mackenzie healed and provided therapy as a central part of their ministries. Each one dispensed medicines and tended to the sick. The Rev. Price charged for the service, although his wife thought he charged much less than "native Doctors." When missionaries honestly disavowed a knowledge of medicine, they were sometimes disbelieved. BaTswana persisted in seeing doctoring as intrinsic to the missionaries' position. From an early date, the LMS's proposed solution was to "send more medically-informed missionaries."[3] Meno, a Tawana royal, suffered acute pain from a fall; the Rev. Hepburn drugged him with opium. "My medicines worked *the potent charm* of procuring for him his first night's sleep, which was little less than miraculous in the eyes of Meno," he joked, putting the distance of irony between himself and *dingaka*, yet his words reveal his emulation of them. The BaTawana were fearful at the sight of Hepburn's medicines, and they asked him for potions to help their hearts understand the Bible and hymnbook—a common request that Livingstone twice refused.[4] In 1893 the Rev. Willoughby wrote, "Two of the Chief's daughters were sick, so I had to begin doctoring without loss of time, and I am glad to say they are quite well now. The consequence is that my patients are increasing in number." He opened his medicinal clinic for two hours each morning, at one point amputating someone's big toe with a pair of "tinman's shears." And yet Willoughby knew nothing about medicine. It was his patients who kept him at the work.[5]

Why did they do so? Essentially missionaries and *dingaka* were similar, and concerned themselves with the same sorts of problems. All across southern Africa, missionaries spoke about the mortality and decay of the body as manageable experiences, and in Tswana societies it was *dingaka* who engaged with the same universal problem. It is no wonder that Livingstone was commonly addressed simply as "Ngaka." Missionaries were not averse to herbal cures, and some of them consulted with *dingaka* to procure emetics or purgatives. In the nineteenth century and on into the early twentieth, both missionaries and *dingaka*

---

[3]   Long, *Diary of Elizabeth Lees Price*, 444. See Seeley, "The Reaction of the BaTswana," 40–70 esp.; and LMS SA 49/1/B, E. Lloyd to R. W. Thompson, Kanye 4/3/1892.

[4]   WCW/374, offprint, *Chronicle of the LMS*, Feb. 1878; David Livingstone, *Missionary Correspondence, 1841–1856* (London, 1961), Serowe, entry for 3 July 1842; and his *The Last Journals of David Livingstone, Vol. 1* (London, 1874), Ujiji, entry for 24 Feb. 1868.

[5]   LMS SA 50/2, W. C. Willoughby to W. Thompson, Serowe, 3/7/1893; LMS SA Reports 2/4, W. C. Willoughby, Phalapye, 1894 (20/3/1895); LMS SA 51/1/B, W. C. Willoughby to R. W. Thompson, Phalapye, 21/7/94: "I like the work, but it is a great tax on my time. I know little about it."

saw illnesses, in the words of one missionary, as "a chastisement" for lapses in behavior.[6] The missionary wanted his cure to beget a personal transformation, but such hopes were not always manifested in practice. The Rev. Lloyd wrote of a MoKgalagadi man, Modirwe, who was the "subject of religious impressions for some time, before he understood what was the matter with him." A Tswana Christian taught Modirwe the Gospel, and Lloyd quoted him with evident approval: "I know Modirwe was sick within but the Word of God will heal him."[7] When Africans pressed missionaries to doctor them, missionaries usually did so; when missionaries connected healing with salvation, people seemed to understand them. Missionaries spoke of "everlasting life"; in many southern Bantu languages the word for "life" seemed to signify "health." Their medical practices resonated with a SeTswana "family" of meanings, and local words and concepts lay close at hand for translations in both directions.[8]

Yet the work of translating is also altering. None doubted that southern Africans and missionaries chose very different "therapies" according to very dissimilar criteria. In the nineteenth century the highest priest-healers performed secretive rites of imitative magic and rectified symbolical hierarchies that seemed askew, so as to clarify the mimetic bridge between the natural and social worlds. Occasionally they tackled actual iniquities for the same purpose: ensuring rain and fertility for their communities while preparing the body politic to survive drought relatively intact. Not only royal *dingaka* but most others saw their duty as including both the patient and the social relationships around her. They performed prophylaxes like scratching medicines on interstitial, vulnerable areas of the body, placing special substances in house thresholds, and marking the edges of villages and fields to close boundaries against sorcery. Other healers divined using bits of cut animal bone, *ditaola*, with which they composed a microcosm of signs; by the same principles that rainmakers reordered the world, they sought to read it as it was. Other healers used a sort of group call-and-response as part therapy and part diagnosis. In both types of divination, *badimo*, ancestors, "spoke" through the devices at hand to make manifest the forces affecting the patient.[9] It would be difficult to sum up such a rich range of practices, but an important and unifying feature within them was an abiding concern with the *patient's community*. That is, of great moment were the hierarchical

---

[6]   LMS SA Reports 2/1, J. Hepburn, Shoshong 1886 (11/2/1887); Norman Etherington, "Missionary Doctors and African Healers in Mid-Victorian South Africa," *South African History Journal*, 19 (1987), 77–92, and Seeley, "The Reaction of the BaTswana," 78, 88 ff.

[7]   LMS SA Journals, 4/117, S.A. 1891–92, E. Lloyd, "Visit to Lake Ngami."

[8]   Wittgenstein refers to "family resemblances" in meaning, Ludwig Wittgenstein, *Philosophical Investigations*, 32.

[9]   Setiloane, *The Image of God*, 201; Harriet Ngubane, *Body and Mind in Zulu Medicine* (London, 1977), esp. 58; Jean Comaroff, *Body of Power, Spirit of Resistance*, 81–82; and her "Healing and Cultural Transition: The Tswana of Southern Africa," *Social Science and Medicine* 15 B (1981); Richard Werbner, "Making the Hidden Seen: Tswapong Divination," Ch. 1 in Richard Werbner, *Ritual Practices, Sacred Journeys* (Washington, 1989); for rain-herds, see Henry Callaway, *The Religious System of the Amazulu* [reprint] (Wynberg, Cape, 1970). In general, see Steven Feierman, "Struggles for Control: The Social Roots of Health and Healing in Modern Africa," *African Studies Review* 28, 2/3 (1985), 73–147; and see his "African Therapeutic Systems," *Social Science and Medicine* 13 B (1979), 277–84; and John M. Janzen, *Ngoma: Discourses of Healing in Southern and Central Africa* (Berkeley, 1992).

relationships defining the patient's social self, as epitomized by the will of ancestors—relationships of peers and friends, but also those of patriarchy, seniority, and descent.[10]

In short, although there was a cultural resonance between missionary and African healer, it hid fundamental differences. As the nineteenth century wore on,
missionaries separated their practices from those of *dingaka* as they followed earlier medical trends. Increasingly they accepted that natural science was the legitimate framework in which to understand health; that health was a commodity to be
distributed by institutions and experts; and most of all, that the body was the only
possible site in which to heal. If nineteenth- and early twentieth-century Protestant
missionaries did feel, in the memorable phrase quoted by Thomas Beidelman, that
sickness was "the sweat of Sin in Adam,"[11] such sin did not just cling to Adam, it
was *in* him. Sin lay on the inside, and had to be dealt with there.

Missionaries as Surgeons in Botswana

Medical doctors were scarce in nineteenth-century GammaNgwato. People patron-
ized local priest-healers for most complaints. Even after the turn of the century,
licensed doctors only intermittently impacted Ngwato health care. Few stayed long;
a resident physician, Dr. Black, died "suddenly" in 1914; a Dr. Mackenzie then took
a share of the work until 1919, after which much of it "again" fell on the Rev.
Lewis. When Dr. Worrall, who was employed by the Protectorate, died in 1924, the
district committee begged the LMS for a replacement; in the meantime, the Rev.
Lewis would "continue to offer medical assistance to the natives during the
interregnum as he has unofficially done for many past years, to the best of his
ability." Dr. Eleanor Shepheard arrived in 1928 but was gone by 1930 to "nurse her
knee." The railway doctor, Dr. Bachelor, was "a dud."[12] People interested in Western therapies most often had to come to reluctant missionaries or even to local
merchants. Such men operated with the uneasy feeling that their practices were
not wholly legitimate, an impression deepened by their dim awareness of the on-

---

[10]   I thus disagree with Schoffeleers, who depicts "traditional healing," being like all "healing," as locating illness in the individual ("Ritual Healing and Political Acquiescence: The Case of the Zionist Churches
in Southern Africa," *Africa* 60, 1 (1991)). Yet I do not see how my position offends his overall argument
(that healing entails a refusal to deal with the wider world), since the social units within which precolonial
sicknesses were referenced, were undoubtedly as small as the antipolitical communities of Zion-style
congregations. Neither group sought to combat larger, extra-societal forces. For case studies showing
how African healers need not focus on the individual, see John M. Janzen (with Louis Arkinstall), *The
Quest for Therapy: Medical Pluralism in Lower Zaire* (Berkeley, 1978), 93–9, 107–13; Seeley, "The Reaction of
Batswana," 39; Waite, "Public Health in Precolonial East-Central Africa," and Michael Taussig, "Reification
and the Consciousness of the Patient," *Social Science and Medicine* 14B, 1 (1980).

[11]   Beidelman, *Colonial Evangelism*, 109–10; see also Bruce Haley, *The Healthy Body in Victorian Culture*
(1978), 44ff. After 1800, external lesions provided, as Moscucci puts it, "the model for understanding the
anatomical changes wrought by diseases on the inner fabric of the body." Ornella Moscucci, *The Science of
Woman: Gynaecology and Gender in England, 1800–1929* (Cambridge, 1990), 109, in part citing S. Reiser,
Medicine and the Reign of Technology (Cambridge, 1978).

[12]   LMS SA 76/3 E. Sharp to F. H. Hawkins, Serowe, 18/5/14; 82/4, R. H. Lewis to F. H. Hawkins,
Serowe, 30/10/19; 86/3, A. Jennings to Ellenberger, Kuruman, 4/7/24; 91/Lewis, Lewis to Barradale,
Serowe, 9/2/28, and 21/5/28; 92/Tshekedi, Semane Khama to Dr. E. Shepheard, Serowe, 8/7/30 (type-
script).

going revolution in biomedicine after 1900. John Smith Moffat and Haydon Lewis had medical kits and a few months' training between them, but Lewis refrained from keeping records for such an "illegal" business.[13]

Factors other than the most pressing needs of BaTswana determined the medical focus of missionaries. Missionaries could not adequately distinguish syphilis from gonorrhea, but they did note the prevalence of venereal diseases north and south of the Molopo River. In 1922 the government's district meeting at Serowe surmised that "Probably very few individuals among the Serowe Natives escape Gonorrhea throughout life. Sterile and infertile marriages are very common."[14] Unfortunately missionaries had no effective treatment for venereal diseases. Nor, for that matter, did they understand the epidemiology of tuberculosis, typhoid, cholera, yaws, scurvy, kwashiorkor, or other major southern African illnesses. Their specific methods lagged behind contemporary advances in European medicine by twenty years.[15] For a long time, they limited themselves to distributing herbal potions, pills, and eye washes, and to removing sores, crushed limbs, and rotted teeth.

Even potions and pills imposed unfamiliar habits on BaTswana. The Western use of medicine demanded obedience to norms dislocated from the social milieu; BaTswana were asked to adhere to regimens. Much of the time they preferred to bolt all in one drought. What was truly revolutionary, however, was the missionary emphasis on surgery, present from the start of the LMS's activity in southern Africa. Surgery manipulated Africans' bodies, and by absenting patients from their own treatment, left them with little room for rebellion. Of the twenty-one types of medical instruments known to have been in David Livingstone's possession, most were surgical, and ten were cutting tools.[16] For Tswana patients from Livingstone's time up through the 1930s, what best marked missionary medicine was its passion for cutting.

The most common type of surgery practiced by missionaries was dentistry. BaTswana may have practiced a bit of dentistry before the advent of Europeans, but it had been an uncommon therapy. Missionaries greatly expanded it. The Revs. Mackenzie and Price pulled teeth, and presumably Hepburn did too; Willoughby "averaged" one or more teeth pulled per day in Phalapye. While BaNgwato, even Christians, went to *dingaka* for many complaints, they sought out missionaries to have their teeth pulled.[17] Toothache was a major draw in the Rev. Lewis's practice

---

[13]   R. H. Lewis, "Medicine at Molepolole," *Chronicle of the LMS* XV (1906), 41; LMS SA 6/4 Serowe for 1925/6 (R. H. Lewis).

[14]   LMS SA 75/3, F. H. Hawkins to R. W. Thompson, Tiger Kloof, 22/3/13; see Chapter 6 for an extension of this discussion; and BNA DCS 2/5 Serowe, Annual Report 1921–22 (1922); also, LMS SA 91/Lewis, Lewis to Barradale, Serowe, 21/5/28.

[15]   Thabo Fako, "Historical Processes and African Health Systems: The Case of Botswana" (Ph.D. dissertation, University of Wisconsin, 1984), 276, 390. Lister had developed antisepsis in 1864, and Pasteur and Koch bacteriology in the 1870s. Norman Goodall, in his sympathetic *History of the London Missionary Society* (Oxford, 1954) roundly scolds the Society for its inadequacy in the medical field in Africa, 512. Western advances did have an effect even in the Rev. Hepburn's time, as he ordered and received vaccines from Francistown; K III A/2/11, G. Main to J. Hepburn, 13/7/1887; Hepburn, *Twenty Years*, 52.

[16]   Seeley, "Reaction of the Batswana," 80.

[17]   Seeley, "Reaction of the Batswana," 49, and Caroline [Seeley] Dennis, "The Role of *Dingaka tsa SeTswana* from the 19th C. to the Present," *Botswana Notes and Records* 10 (1980), 56; LMS SA Reports 2/4, Palapye, 1894 (W. C. Willoughby, 20/3/1895); Interview: Mrs. Barophi Ratshosa, b. 1918, Serowe, 9 Nov. 1988, English.

in the BaKwena's capital town, where he doctored 400 to 500 people per month, the numbers rising in winter to "an average" of 580 people per month. This represented a fair proportion of the adults living there.[18]

It is tempting to fashion a sociocultural explanation for dental surgery, but it must first be noted that southern Africans' physical need for dentistry may well have increased as they ate refined sugars. Sidney Mintz points out that every society with a "nonsugar tradition" has quickly taken to sucrose after being introduced to it, and southern African polities were no exception.[19] Tswana tea-drinkers took sugar from early in the century, and today half-kilo bags of white sucrose and Coca Cola cans of liquid sugar are ubiquitous in village hearth and canteen. The generally decreasing quality of many southern Africans' diets also probably contributed to tooth decay.

Thus one finds in 1907, among the Ndebele mission stations in Rhodesia, that Shishu, a "Native Teacher," managed to have the entire community at Insiza build a "veritable mission station" for his use. Instead of payment, the builders received only a promise that the missionary, the Rev. Rees, "would come soon, and take all their bad teeth out, and would bring medicine to cure their diseases."[20] Southern Rhodesian towns near the railway line had been involved longer and more closely than Bechuanaland in the economy of wages and commodities, including sugar. The Rev. Helm of Inyati yanked so many teeth that he hurt his right elbow. Fortunately,

> I feel it only when I use the arm in driving [and] tooth pulling . . . I have had to pull a tooth with my left hand, people come from a long distance and it is hard to send them away unrelieved.[21]

In Molepolole in 1905, the Rev. Lewis described his practice, which he pursued into the 1910s and 1920s in Serowe: BaTswana sat waiting in a row while he moved from one to the other, using a forceps to extract teeth without anaesthetic. Other patients and onlookers "convulsed with laughter."[22] An increase in dental caries does not fully explain this phenomenon.

Modes of Conversion: Pulling Teeth and Cutting

Dentistry evolved in England from the practice of barber-surgeons. Barbering in turn developed in the context of the growing urban early-modern emphasis on public appearance, and barber-surgeons institutionalized the treatment of hair, skin, nails, and teeth as one package. In the eighteenth century, barbers' parlors became gathering places for men, especially of the laboring class, as they remain up to the present day. The work of early barbers often became an

---

[18]   R. H. Lewis, "Medicine at Molepolole," and LMS SA Reports 3/3, Molepolole for 1904 (R. H. Lewis, 1905); 6/4 Serowe, for 1926, R. H. Lewis.

[19]   Sidney Mintz, *Sweetness and Power: The Place of Sugar in Modern History* (New York, 1985), 15 esp.

[20]   LMS SA 68/4, B. Rees to R. W. Thompson, Inyati, 26/9/07.

[21]   LMS SA 69/1 R. Helm to R. W. Thompson, Inyati, 28/5/8.

[22]   Interview: Mrs. Barophi Ratshosa, b. 1918, Serowe, 9 Nov. 1988, English; R. H. Lewis, "Medicine at Molepolole," and LMS SA Reports 3/3, Molepolole for 1904 (R. H. Lewis, 1905); 6/4 Serowe, for 1926, R. H. Lewis. Some of the bystanders around the missionary-dentist were undoubtedly kin of the patients.

arena for spectators and passersby. Barbers trimmed beards, removed moles, and drew teeth. In London barbers were situated in the less reputable districts, not only to accommodate their excruciating and public procedures but also because they treated stigmatized conditions like syphilitic epidermal eruptions, the so-called "pox."[23]

By the early 1800s, many of the unkind images pertaining to dentistry had long been sketched. Dentists' own assumptions were changing, however. For decades barber-surgeons had assumed that tooth rot was a result of an internal process, manifesting itself in the excretion of poisons and slime on the teeth. In medicalized dental thinking in the nineteenth century, however, the teeth lost this implicit unity with the body and assumed a new fragility to attack from the outside. This development clearly owed much to the barber-surgeon's earlier appropriation of the teeth as an external site for therapy, along with hair and nails. The most recent scholar of the tooth, however, borrowing from Foucault's work, sees a more sudden "invention" of the mouth. In either case, by the 1890s teeth were seen to decay because of a separable "chemico-parasitic process." The mouth, which housed the teeth in a space newly conceptualized and scrutinized, if not invented, moved away from the body as an "external" portal to the person's now vulnerable (as opposed to culpable) interior.[24]

Thus the production of the mouth-and-teeth as a site in which to give shape to illness, to *image* "dental pain," was a part of a certain process. While pain is clearly present in all societies, its localization is a product of the history of how it is normally handled. To some extent, the same might be said of any sensation. Yet pain is a special case, as Elaine Scarry has sought to show; because it takes no immediate object, because one does not "experience-as-pain" *this* or *that*, pain is difficult to verbalize to another person except in what she calls its "presentness." As a result its *re*presentation is often appropriated from the pained by others. Thus Wittgenstein discusses pain because it offers him a *sine qua non*: if it can be shown that such an internal experience exists only insofar as it is communicated, then much the same can be said of less intimate expressions. Were no one to have ever uttered a cry or exclaimed their hurt—making pain an interpersonal event and calling for certain responses—then it is impossible to say what pain would "mean."[25]

To return to the main lines of the argument, from the point of view of the Tswana patient, missionaries wished to invent a new meaning for a pain grouped vaguely about the mouth and teeth. As part of their therapy, they pushed the sensible effects of "tooth decay" firmly towards the tooth; in other words, as tooth-pulling alleviated pain, it brought into existence the very sort of pain it erased. In Wittgenstein's terms, missionary dentistry among BaTswana forced into being a new *Sprachenspiel* because something new and effective was being *done*. As part of this speech-game, BaTswana briefly accepted another "speaking" of pain before their own, and indeed it is almost too appropriate that in pulling teeth missionar-

[23] Margaret Pelling, "Appearance and Reality: Barber-surgeons, the Body and Disease," in A. L. Beier and Roger Finley, eds., *London 1500–1700* (London, 1986), 82–112.

[24] Sarah Nettleton, *Power, Pain and Dentistry* (Philadelphia, 1992), 9, and Ch. 3 *passim*; and Idem, "Protecting a Vulnerable Margin: Towards and Analysis of How the Mouth Came to be Separated from the Body," *Sociology of Health and Illness* 10, 2 (June 1988), 156–69.

[25] Elaine Scarry, *The Body in Pain: The Making and Unmaking of the World* (Oxford, 1985), Introduction, and 9; Wittgenstein, *Philosophical Investigations*, 103–104 esp.

ies physically occupied the source of speech. The therapy itself enacted the implication that "folk" remedies (those of "oral" cultures) were mute before the vigor of direct intervention.[26] Proper treatment went straight to the heart of the matter, the thing itself, the tooth, set in the gums and the cavity of the mouth.

For a long time, surgery and dentistry proceeded in this straightforward manner in GammaNgwato. Besides missionaries, general merchants also sometimes practiced medicine on the side, including, for example, the entrepreneur C. C. Vialls and Samuel Blackbeard, a general merchant and teetotaller friend of Khama's.[27] Blackbeard's son recalls,

> Dad befriended John [Smith] Moffat, who was the Magistrate, [and] used to get advice on how to treat different ailments . . . he even taught Dad how to do minor surgery and one of the big things was how to be able to extract teeth. So he presented my Dad with a complete set of forceps and also . . . surgical instruments.[28]

On one memorable occasion a man had come to Blackbeard with his leg crushed by an ox wagon; Blackbeard performed a full amputation using the flap procedure, quite successfully, in his "consulting room on the side of his shop."

> [I]f the doctor is fortunate enough to be a missionary, it gives him a chance of spreading the gospel at the same time as healing . . . now Dad was always consulted [by] the Rev. Lewis, and when there wasn't any doctor available, the two of them would very often consult and do their best. Many a child with [severe] burns [from having] fallen in the fire. . . . Dad seemed to have a knack with these people. And so he was greatly respected. . . . He was a butcher and a barber![29]

Two medical guides survived in possession of the LMS congregation in Serowe, where Lewis, Blackbeard, and others practiced. Blackbeard relied on *Dr. Chase's Last and Complete Recipe Book and Household Physician* (1884), and the Rev. Lewis almost certainly consulted Frank Rossiter's *The Practical Guide to Health* (1913) in the 1920s. Both books moralized illness and tied it to group or class proclivities. In Blackbeard's *Dr. Chase* text, in which he pasted housekeeping tips and poems exhorting temperance, the field of phrenology finds a large place.[30] In general, Chase follows the pattern set by Nicholas Culpeper's classic, *The Complete Herbal*, reprinted throughout the nineteenth century. Among its remedies, wounds are to be infused "with the smoke of wool," rabies requires vapor baths, and eating a raw onion clears the blood. Lewis's *Practical Guide* of 1913 shows the great medical advances made in the closing years of the century. Still, illness is subtly moralized. Lousiness is "acquired," for instance, "by contagion from the filthy, on steam-cars, and in cheap boarding houses." Typhoid is darkly adduced as "not a disease to be treated

---

[26]   See David Kunzle, "The Art of Pulling Teeth in the Seventeenth and Nineteenth Centuries: From Public Martyrdom to Private Nightmare and Political Struggle?" in Michael Feher, ed., *Zone 5: Fragments for a History of the Human Body, Part Three* (New York, 1989).

[27]   TK A/1, C.C. Vialls to Tshekedi, Serowe, 7/2/36.

[28]   Interview: Mr. Dennis Blackbeard, b. 1918, Serowe, 7 Nov. 1988, English.

[29]   *Ibid.*

[30]   Frank M. Rossiter, M.D., *The Practical Guide to Health* [1908] (Nashville, Tx., 1913), found among UCCSA Papers, Serowe; and *Dr. Chase's Last and Complete Recipe Book and Household Physician* (London, 1884), 83, 131, 136.

by medicine," and epilepsy is said to be caused by mental weakness or parental alcoholism.[31] The dominant message of *The Practical Guide* is that the body is a machine, a twentieth-century phase of Foucault's "docile-utile" body.[32] In its digressions, the ear is a "mechanism," digestion is "a living manufacturing plant" with a "receiving room," "sorting room," and "door-keepers"; the heart is a "force pump," etc.[33] Siegfried Giedion writes of this period that "the animate being was considered simply the sum of its parts, assembled like those of a machine. Organic processes were regarded as purely physico-chemical in nature, as if an organism were a kind of chemical plant."[34] As with a machine or an industrial site, some bad components (like teeth) were subject to removal. Moreover, the "parts" themselves are personified as proletarian laborers. Close-fitting garments "stifle millions of body-workers;" caffeine "robs every little nerve worker . . . [and] is poison to the little builders." Tobacco "makes the little workers very sick. The stomach workers try to make it go out again . . ." etc. The body was a happy factory. If the *ngaka* concerned himself with the patient's community, here the relevant community was placed within the body itself.[35]

This man-machine was not entirely a secular entity. Wellness required the grace of God. Hence *The Practical Guide*'s body is a "living temple," a form constructed by the "Master Architect."[36] Such a synthesis was a bit old-fashioned, but the language alerts us to a deeper parallelism between medical trends and Nonconformist evangelical thought.[37] Surgery and dentistry relocated pain (as opposed to wellness) in somatic dysfunctions, and "cured" it—surely pulling teeth did "work"! Missionaries also tried to place sin (as opposed to wellness) in the individual. Any*body* might seek to be healed apart from the interests and restrictions defining his/her local community. Even more, in the missionaries' eyes, healing *had* to occur in isolation from the precolonial interpersonal mesh that *dingaka* took as determining who was and who was not well. The wellness of BaNgwato could not express the

---

[31] Rossiter, *The Practical Guide to Health*, table of contents, and 480. In South Africa at the time, non-whites riding in third-class cars were subjected to delousing; Shula Marks and Neil Andersson, "Typhus and Social Control: South Africa 1917–1950," in Roy Macleod and Milton Lewis, eds., *Disease, Medicine and Empire* (New York, 1988), 271.

[32] "The human body was entering a machinery of power that explores it, breaks it down and rearranges it. A 'political anatomy,' which was also a 'mechanics of power,' was being born; it defined how one may have a hold over others' bodies. . . . Thus discipline produces subjected and practiced bodies, 'docile' bodies." Michel Foucault, *Discipline and Punish, The Birth of the Prison*, trans. A. Sheridan (New York, 1979), 138. Foucault is writing of the eighteenth century; see also A. Vartanian, "Man-Machine from the Greeks to the Computer," in P. Weiner, ed., *Dictionary of the History of Ideas*, III (New York, 1973), 131–46.

[33] *Ibid.*, and 33.

[34] Siegfried Giedion, *Mechanization Takes Command* (New York, 1975), 718.

[35] I realize that this reads like a peculiar involution of the tropes discussed by Catherine Gallagher in "The Body and the Social Body from Malthus to Mayhew," in C. Gallagher and T. Laqueur, eds., *The Making of the Modern Body: Sexuality and Society in the 19th Century* (Berkeley, 1987).

[36] Rossiter, *Practical Guide*, 17, 225; my emphasis. Chapter 17's topics tellingly proceed: "Healing Power and Forgiveness of Sins—Christ's Manifestation of—Heart Compared to Engine or Force-Pump." *The Living Temple* was Rossiter's first book.

[37] The parallel middle-class rise of biomedicine and Nonconformism in the late nineteenth century did not result in an intellectual alliance. See Mort, *Dangerous Sexualities*, 175; B. Hilton, *The Age of Atonement* (Oxford, 1980), 19–22; and especially Jeane Peters, *The Medical Profession in Mid-Victorian London* (Berkeley, 1978), 195–97, arguing that the social ascent of the medical doctor was part and parcel of the rise of the middle class after 1880.

rightness of societal relationships held together with the threads of pagan ritual and superstition. If health had to be conceived in reference to others, then the others would be Europeans and God, not fellow villagers.

Missionaries' attitudes were ragged at the edges and oscillated depending on the situation. "The BaNgwato" were an undifferentiated body, a sinning tribe in themselves. Still, pathology lay apart from "the BaNgwato's" internal discourse of wellness and transpired inside the MoNgwato's body.[38] If missionaries oscillated between these two models, it is also true that the movement from the first model to the second was itself a sort of cutting, one that expresses much of what missionaries had come to GammaNgwato to do.[39]

The "science" of medicine and the linked practices of surgery and dentistry also reinforced missionaries' (and merchants') sense of superiority: they were the operators and observers; they exerted power over BaTswana. Most importantly, their conception of health required them to separate and extract BaTswana from the social nexus within which the Tswana conception of health resided. Surgery divided relationships into parts. As pain was removed from the arena of human intercourse and placed here or there in the scope of biological removals, the individual was also lifted from his or her *social* matrix. Men such as Lewis and Willoughby saw in this severance a distinct encouragement of conversion. Becoming a Christian was, after all, a lonesome act; the convert had to get rid of interior occlusions blocking the Light from the true self.

Decline of Missionary Medicine

We may recall the conflicts over Sekgoma II's deathbed therapy, and the opposing medical coalitions, European and *ngaka*, that formed at the time. Certainly many BaTswana were strongly out of sympathy with Western medicine as a whole in the 1920s. The attitude of the Protectorate government, as it increased its quotidian presence, did nothing to change this. At the October 1929 opening of the ironically named Sekgoma I Memorial Hospital in Serowe, the speech given by the high commissioner[40] reflected his own irritation. His remarks were entitled "God, Christ and Healing."

> It has taken the white races hundreds of years to acquire the knowledge which they possess to-day and which they wish to give the more backward races. But it frequently happens that the people like the Bamangwato . . . prefer to consult their own doctors believing that because they are sick they have been bewitched[,] and they frequently resist progress and civilization. . . . It is just as stupid to refuse to go to Hospital because a friend died there as it would be to refuse to go to bed because most people die in their beds.[41]

---

[38] Jean and John L. Comaroff, *Of Revelation and Revolution*, 90, aptly compare English visions of Africa with those of the insides of a body.

[39] This accorded with the biomedical propensity to view society as "an aggregation of self-contained individuals." Vaughan, "Directions in the Social History of Medicine."

[40] It is not clear whether this "high commissioner" was Leopold Amery, who would have been bitter over the 1929 Labour defeat of the Conservative Party, or Charles Rey, the new *resident* commissioner.

[41] LMS SA 91/Jennings, High Commissioner's Speech at Serowe. 6/10/29.

The high commissioner coupled this comparison with a warning that BaNgwato might become displaced by more active people, just like "the Masarwa are today." His attitude only pushed patients away from the hospital's Kafkaesque presence. For many complaints, people continued to visit *dingaka* and family herbalists. If they were very ill, most Christians were no less resolved to use any therapy at their disposal. Missionary dispensaries continued as a significant third recourse, until hospitals and clinics (including the later LMS hospital in Sefhare, just south of Tswapong) and a lack of financing eventually eroded their practices. Still Evelyn Haile, the missionary nurse and "mothercare" worker in Serowe, could in the 1930s pose and answer a conundrum in one breath: "Natives do not quite understand my position, and come to me instead of the government dispensary, where they have to pay."[42]

Medical performances were acted out in an operating theater only briefly. Pliers, scalpels, and forceps were instruments designed to concentrate force, but that force soon dissipated: no determined colonial presence stood behind them. Europeans never forced BaNgwato to accept medical treatments, and BaNgwato helped shape those they did accept. The viability of the Ngwato kingdom hampered the Protectorate from elaborating the ideology and personnel for medical coercion, even had they so wished. Such measures as the removal of populations from tsetse fly areas in Tanganyika, or the humiliating anti-yaws campaign in Nigeria, were not possible here.

Therefore, when BaTswana played the missionary *Sprachenspiel* of individual wellness, they did so for only a short while. Family and friends, as well as Christians, waited to receive them after they left the missionary surgery. The effect of a medicinal regimen or an open-mouthed ordeal might be indelible, the experience transforming, but home was where the heart was.

Christian Women and Prayer for the Ill

In times of sickness and stress, Christians turned to each other. Outside Serowe, in smaller villages lacking both doctors and missionaries, Christian support was given side by side with the efforts of *dingaka*. For the few Christians who staunchly refused to seek the advice of any *ngaka* but the local herbalist, the prayers of their community were central. Before the revolution brought by antibiotics, prayer was often as effective as surgery, and better than half the nostrums in mission dispensaries. Prayer for the ill was a critical feature of congregational life.

> If a person was sick, s/he was prayed for. Prayers would be voiced by any Christian in church. Or a deacon. They would pray right beside the sick bed. They would keep on praying for a few days, perhaps three days; they kept coming, perhaps one at a time or in small groups.[43]

---

[42] Interview: Mrs. Ogaletse Phiri, Serowe, 3 Nov. 1988; LMS SA 95/Haile, E. Haile to F. H. Hawkins, Serowe, 4/6/33.

[43] Interview: Mrs. Botsanyang Ramatsela, b. 1908, Serowe, 10 Nov. 1988.

When Jesus Christ went with people he healed the ill. No, [it wasn't necessarily] that sick people were the ones converting. When one heard that a person was sick, one went to pray for him. We did not yet pray for the sick in the fashion of some Churches [today].[44]

[Did Christians pray for the sick in Tonota? —P. L.] Yes. It is so, even now. . . . [P]eople pray for someone who is a Christian, who is a member of the Church. If there are people who are very near your place, if you know that he is sick, even if you know that he is not a member of your Church, nor a Church-goer, well, [perhaps a bit more rarely but still] you go to him or her, to pray for him or her. Even the deacons do this . . . it is their job to do that because they are *Moruti's* helpers—they are the people who go about in the village to pray for those who are sick . . . They believe that the prayer works, [at least,] most of them believe that the prayer is worthwhile.[45]

Sick enquirers and prospective catechumens might receive such visits, which placed a net of concern beneath them, validating their condition within a group they might wish to join upon recovering. Even more, congregations were concerned with the health and welfare of their members, and an important pastoral duty of deacons and deaconesses was to visit ailing Christians.[46] The patient's family was assured some tangible assistance if the condition worsened, and if he or she approached death, there was the comfort of knowing the Church would provide a proper burial. These were aspects of healing.

Few Christians felt that prayer erased illnesses, but they had no reason to doubt its broad benefits for a convalescent's health. Almost no one thought in terms of the biomedical paradigms in which finer distinctions were required. Christian women were not concerned to cut and separate.[47] Illness was a matter of a person's situation in her environment as a whole, not the interplay of conflicting elements within her body or the breakdown of one or more of her "parts." Prayerful visits reinvented the idiom of Tswana medicine, by working on the boundaries and connections between the patient and her changeful human milieu. The body of the congregation, rather than the patient's corporeal limits, became a relevant field in which both to heal and to valorize the experience of being sick. While missionaries slowly accepted their own illegitimacy as healers, then, Christian Ngwato citizens rebuilt their interpersonal understanding of health, working on the relationships enmeshing sick people as part of the healing process.

Baruti as Healers

Overall, missionaries and *dingaka* had very little contact with one another in GammaNgwato. A certain fluidity in the construction of therapeutic roles none-

---

44   Interview: Mrs. Obolokile Sekga, b. approx. 1903, Serowe, 12 Nov. 1988.

45   Interview: The Rev. B.R. Tshipa, b. 1902, Serowe, 17 February 1989, English.

46   Here as elsewhere I am struck by the similarity of Deborah Gaitskell's findings for Christian women in Johannesburg. See her "Devout Domesticity? A Century of African Women's Christianity in South Africa," in Walker, ed., *Women and Gender in South Africa*, 256.

47   A Lutheran colloquium in 1967 drew this conclusion: "African medicine is closer to the concepts of Christian healing than orthodox Western medicine in that it accepts the "wholeness" of the individual, the indivisible interdependence between body and soul, between matter and spirit," Lutheran Theological College (Mapumulo, Natal, South Africa), *The Report of the Umpumulo Consultation on the Healing Ministry of the Church* (Typescript, 19–27/9/67), 63.

theless persisted. As *dingaka* fell in prestige and limited their practices to private consultations, most descended to a common level of herbalists. At the same time, the LMS's interest in amateur missionary medicine occasionally resulted in the training of even evangelists (*baruti*) in medicine, and Tiger Kloof's Bible school gave all its African student evangelists a "course" in medicine and a "Health Booklet."[48] People also extended their apprehensions about the *ngaka* to the *moruti*, sensing that all such special talents might harm as well as heal. Moreover, many *baruti* came from lineages that had produced *dingaka*, and some even reflected the particular prominence of their *ngaka* ancestors.[49] Kuate Pelotona, one of the very first *baruti* in GammaNgwato, was the son of Pelotona Tidimane, Sekgoma I's chief *ngaka*. The Rev. Tebape's maternal grandfather, to whom he was very close, was the major Nswazwi *ngaka*; Tebape's own father, who carried this *ngaka*'s medicine bag, also became an herbalist. According to the Rev. Lekalake Maphakela, an early and prominent minister, his father Maphakela served the BaKwena as the chief Kwena *ngaka ya kgosing* in the time of Kgosi Sechele's youth. There are more recent examples.[50] Even more intriguing, some evidence suggests that at least a few Ngwato-Church *baruti* were renowned, as *dingaka* had been, for their ability to heal sick people through their own ministrations.

Moruti Seakgano Ncaga, for instance, who was born into the second generation of Ngwato Christians in about 1865, healed through prayer in the 1920s.[51] According to Seakgano's daughter, Otaajang (born about 1901), when people fell ill, Seakgano

> went to pray for them. . . . [He] was a seeker of the gravely ill, whom God listened to, and he awakened people through prayer. Yes, deacons were perhaps there as well, praying. Now, if he prayed for a person, if it were someone he had already dealt with, he stretched over him/her, and when he had put his arms over the person he spoke thus! he called God like so! he just called God, he prayed, prayed, and later the person breathed if he/she was one who had been so ordered, because of God, he/she breathed. . . . [Seakgano] was given prayer by God.[52]

Many people prayed for the sick, but the most respected man, and the congregation's mediator with the Holy Spirit, naturally had the greatest chance to render effective prayers. This man was *ipso facto* the *moruti*, although sometimes

---

[48] LMS SA Reports, 4/2, Tiger Kloof for 1909 (W. C. Willoughby, 1910).

[49] [Q.] N. Parsons, "Independency and Ethiopianism among the Tswana in the Late 19th and Early 20th Centuries," *Collected Seminar Papers on the Societies of Southern Africa in the 19th and 20th Centuries*, I (London, 1971), esp. 68 n48. And Interview: Ms. Oathokwa Samoele, b. 1918, Radisele, 18 Feb. 1989: "I was afraid of him! He was a *moruti*," and Interview: Mrs. Otaajang Kedikilwe, b. 1902, Sefhope, 20 May 1989. *Go boifa* is "to fear," a word often used of *baruti*.

[50] Interview: The Rev. Harsh Ramolefhe, Gaborone, 15 June 1989, English; Mrs. Ogaletse Phiri, Serowe, 3 Nov. 1988; Mr. Samuel Malete, Lerala, 25 May 1990; and esp. Mr. Jenamo Tebape, Serowe, 24 Nov. 1988, English; and ZKM, Register of Pupils . . ., No. 138; WCW/804 [Confessions], L. Maphakela, 1–3. It may have been Maphakela Snr. whom Livingstone typecast as the "Rain Doctor" in his oft-cited "dialogue," the most complete original of which is in I. Schapera, ed., *Livingstone's Private Journals, 1851–1853* (Cape Town, 1960), 239–43.

[51] See Landau, "Preacher, Chief and Prophetess," 3 and *passim*.

[52] Interview: Mrs. Otaajang Kedikilwe, b. 1902, Sefhope, 20 May 1989.

another prominent deacon or a deaconess aspired to lead and focus prayers. As Selo Mafoko, once an informal *moruti* or senior deacon, recalls,

> If I wished to place my hands on a person, I did so; if I wanted only to pray, then I just prayed. If in my own feelings the Spirit perhaps grew near and told me to move closer to the sick person, then [I] put my hands on him/her; no fault there. . . . When a sick person came, I would take my Bible here; I faced him/her just as I might see that you are ill now; in the Bible this verse here would inspire me [*mphe*], and I could draw on it. I prayed from it and drew on it. . . . When you are really praying, you choke a bit, feeling it in your upper chest like *this*. You don't just pray, as in, "here, I'll just take these verses and read them." You *pray* directly facing the sick person.[53]

What could missionaries do about such practices? They scarcely wished to diminish the stature of Church *baruti*, and they could not determine the shape that stature took. Even in the 1930s their own attitudes might verge toward those held by Ngwato Christians. The Rev. Burns wrote in a private letter to his sister in 1938:

> [Because of drought] on Thursday of last week meetings for prayers for rain were started. We met at 6:30 a.m. each day. . . . At the Chief's [Tshekedi's] call people came in from their fields, some of them from a distance of 25 miles. Yesterday [Saturday] morning the leader of the service was Seakgano, an old Evangelist, a very fine fellow. His prayer at the service was most striking, like that of a child pleading with his father for something he needs desperately. . . . At four in the afternoon [it started to rain, becoming] blasts and sheets—a glorious rain. At Church this morning, everybody was happy.[54]

The production of rain was an integral part of health among BaTswana. As we have seen, one leaned on community well-being in asking for rain and expected rain when confident about the general good will. In their prayers for rain, *baruti* such as Seakgano sought wellness for others in a domain extending far beyond the body.

It might be argued that a pragmatism has been imputed to the prayers of Christians that really only grew later on, after numerous independent Churches had challenged the dominance of the Ngwato Church. The problem, however, is defining "pragmatism" in a way that is meaningful to the expressions of Ngwato Christians of the time. In the case of a sickbed vigil, Christians' prayers always had "practical significance,"[55] because people gauged a convalescent's improvement on flexible grounds, including his or her feelings. It is also true, however, that people *today* distinguish between the healing practices of the small "water Church" (*tsa metse*) congregations and the prayer of the Ngwato Church. (The huge growth in the 1950s of these Churches is touched upon in Chapters 8 and 9.) The Rev. Jani Tebape's son, a businessman fluent in English, told me that some ministers said

---

[53]   Interview: Mr. Selo Mafoko, b. 1900, Lerala, 11 April 1990.

[54]   BNA Burns Papers, Microfiche 1334B, J. Burns to Millie Simpson, Serowe 23/1/38. See my article, "When Rain Falls: Rainmaking and Community in a Tswana Village, ca. 1870 to Recent Times," *International Journal of African Historical Studies*, 26, 1 (1993), 1–29; and Isaac Schapera, *Rainmaking Rites of Tswana Tribes* (Cambridge, 1971), 29–31.

[55]   *The Concise Oxford English Dictionary*, 6th ed. (Oxford, 1976), 868, gives this as one definition of pragmatic.

they could heal people who were sick, but the London [Mission] never. It maintained [that] it was only God or Jesus Christ who could heal. . . . naturally if a person was sick [the Rev. Tebape] would pray for them, but he did not have that ability to [make them] recover.[56]

Similarly, an elderly deaconess of the Ngwato Church remarked,

No, our converts were not sick. We were in Church—it was a congregation . . . When one heard that a person was sick, one went to pray for her. Even if they were not a yet a friend. It was not considered healing people.[57]

At the same time, *most* older Christians did not bother to distinguish between healing and praying, unless I suggested it. For them, one prayed for the ill because it was good and useful to do so. The consciousness of younger or more educated Christians today has arisen from the juxtaposition of "water Churches," so-called because they made healing with water and ashes their *raison d'être*, and the Ngwato Church, which never did so. Many Ngwato men reached adulthood in the 1930s and 1940s, the start of intensified mine recruiting and broadened labor migrancy, and they brought influences from "Zion" healing churches on the Rand back home to their Ngwato congregations. The habits of distinguishing "water" healing from orthodoxy developed in the 1940s and 1950s in GammaNgwato, and so most of the aging generation of Christians who joined the Church before that time never shared in it.

Reintegration

Perhaps more important than anachronistic considerations of pragmatism is the signal truth that most *baruti* healed by integrating people into the larger gathering of Ngwato Christians. As the Rev. Tumedisho put it, the main functions of a pastor were to "settle disputes, visit the sick, and comfort orphans."[58] Most of the time, *baruti* joined ranks with their congregations in order to pray, for group prayer was most effective. *Baruti* dealt with troubled or sick people as members of the Christian *community*. Even as missionaries decisively rejected the crucial integrative function of precolonial *dingaka*, the *baruti* did not.

When young men abandoned their villages in the 1930s to go to work on the Witwatersrand mines, they left behind their wives and mothers, many of whom had children or parents to care for.[59] The Church stayed in the hands of these vil-

---

56   Interview: Mr. Jenamo Tebape, Serowe, 24 Nov. 1988, English.

57   Interview: Mrs. Obolokile Sekga, b. approx. 1903, Serowe, 12 Nov. 1988.

58   WCW/804 [Confessions,] Tiger Kloof Ordinations Examinations, 1910–16, Tumedisho Maruapula, 9.

59   Isaac Schapera, *Migrant Labour and Tribal Life* (Oxford, 1947), 118ff., etc.; this reflected trends set in motion after the doubling of the price of gold in 1932–1933. Jonathan Crush, Alan Jeeves, and David Yudelman, *South Africa's Labor Empire: A History of Black Migrancy to the Gold Mines* (Boulder, Colo., 1991), Table A.3, 232–33, presents the most considered statistics to date on mining figures. GammaNgwato probably supplied something like one-quarter of Bechuanaland's migrants to the mines and white farms, judging also from *Report on the Census of the Bechuanaland Protectorate, 1964* (Bulawayo, S.R., 1965), Tables VII and VIII (which, however, contains an obvious error in the Ngwato column). This leads to the estimate that over 2,500 men were absent from GammaNgwato during part or all of 1936, around 5,000 in 1940, dropping to less than 3,000 again in 1944 before slowly rising again to a peak of about 9,000 in 1966. Although the censuses of 1921 and 1936 were terribly inaccurate, it is safe to say that the 1940 figure corresponds to at least one in five able adult men in GammaNgwato—an appreciable number.

lagers, fixed as always in the life of the town. Women met to sing hymns and discuss "what to teach our daughters"; they visited for days beside each other's sickbeds, and prayed together on Sundays.[60] And many waited for men who would not return to them. After a decade of absence, some migrants could not or would not face their families and kin. Perhaps trouble in their village or ward had spurred their departure in the first place; perhaps they had since neglected their homes. They looked for other places to settle and live. Ironically, it was the Ngwato Church that prepared the way for their return in the late 1940s. In an unfamiliar town, or a railway or border settlement where a man knew few souls, the Ngwato Church congregation still allowed anyone, as a principle, to join their ranks.

Steven M. is typical of the laborers who sought the embrace of the Church in an alien place. He was born in 1917, grew up in Sefhare, and was baptized by Christian parents. In 1936 he left his father's cattlepost for Johannesburg, and worked on the Rand gold mines, where a fellow miner taught him to read using a hymnbook and Bible. He came home for only brief periods. Much later he moved to Mahalapye, then Serowe, and then Palapye, losing close contact with his family. After settling in Palapye, he was "attacked by a disease." Stories like his, below, were not uncommon after 1935.

> This [disease] made me think about Church especially while I was sleeping. When I awoke mornings, I would feel cross with everyone and not have the patience to listen to them. Now, when I was so afflicted I went to Church. [He joined youths in Sunday school in Serowe.] I just wanted to believe in God, but no one was telling me the truth. In 1948 I came to Palapye from Serowe. Upon arriving, the affliction returned. I went to Church again, and spoke to several of the Church people. Some of them told me, I must stay, and one day I would see a white horse . . . [Did you see such a thing? —P. L.] No, I saw nothing. I realized [the woman who said this] did not have the Light.[61]
>
> One day the *moruti* was preaching and I was just listening without understanding what he was teaching. When he finished, I [followed him and] began to question him. According to him, I had to join the Church to hear the Word of God. Then he said, okay, I will give you a card [not verbatim: that will prove to everyone] you are a member of the Church. From there I started getting better, up to today. I was taught [*rutwa*] as soon as I entered the Church.

Steven subsequently married, and in 1989 he was working as a tailor in Palapye. I asked him directly, "Did Church members visit you before, when you were sick?"

> Extremely so! They each of them went to visit me to see what it was that troubled me. They prayed very much . . . if you were quite ill, they took three days, . . . coming from their own homes to stay from dawn till dusk. [Now many people go to the healing churches,] but I know that prayer is what helps.[62]

---

[60]   Quote, Interview: Mrs. Setuhile Sebina, Serowe, 28 Feb. 1989; and Mrs. Botsanyang Ramatsela, b. 1908, Serowe, 10 Nov. 1988. These Church-groups are known as *manyanos* throughout most of South Africa (but not GammaNgwato). See Mia Brandel-Syrier, *Black Women in Search of God* (London, 1962); and Gaitskell, "Devout Domesticity."

[61]   Interview: Mr. Steven M., b. 1917, Palapye, 19 Dec. 1988. The white horse probably derived from the Book of Revelation.

[62]   *Ibid.*

Despite my impact on this narrative, it still belongs in essence to the teller, in its ambiguities as much as its usefulness as a paradigm, for subtle negotiations ruled the life of a Christian outsider. Steven M. resented some current upstarts in the congregation, and the woman who foretold the coming of "a white horse" was perhaps involved in his more recent troubles, in which he was accused of trying to make himself into a *moruti* by praying for rain with people stuck at their cattleposts outside Palapye.[63]

The Somatic and the Incorporative

Nineteenth-century missionary medicine treated the body as the sole arena for the interrogation of impure forces. As this view matured "scientifically," it saw in the body an assemblage of possibly faulty components. The patient always contained his or her own health, however, echoing the evangelical demand that the individual conquer his or her inner demons and make a personal commitment to Christ. After 1920 biomedicine in GammaNgwato continued to ignore most industrial vectors for illness, limitations in arable and pasture land, and the commoditization of cattle, which impoverished many households.[64] It also ignored the travail of laboring on white-owned farms, on distant mines, and eating the newly monotonous so-called "Tswana" diet of sugar, fat, field-grown sorghum, and store-bought maize. Illness was seen as a somatic phenomenon, and Africans were to achieve health by allowing themselves to be extracted and clarified as individuals: a paradoxical prescription at best.

Yet if one wishes to argue that the individuation of health became a way to introduce people to Christianity, as so many missionaries felt, how is it that women and *baruti* in Ngwato Church congregations, by integrating people into a caring community, also attracted people to the Church? Are not these contrary motions, extraction and integration?

While these notions surely stood in tension with one another, they also lay in series. Missionaries embraced many bodily tropes that alienated BaTswana as often as not: cleanliness, clothedness, individuality, and the body as mechanism. Nevertheless, their first duty and the mark of their success or failure was to populate the Ngwato Church. "Extraction" was a mode of conversion only if it led to Church participation, "integration" in a congregation of Ngwato Christians. Although it is difficult to quantify, the medicalized version of these two stages did map one of many paths to the Church.

Both Christianity and colonialism reduced the seeming scale of the preexisting Tswana community—of the household, *kgotla,* and town—in the larger scheme of things. The path out from the community and into the kingdom and the world at large often followed the motion of conversion, the movement into the realm of the Word. Within life as it was lived, however, the local congregation became an arena

---

[63]   *Ibid.* Steven's standing evidently then suffered, and it is perhaps poignant that he recalls being frustrated as a child by having to stay out at his father's cattlepost instead of learning to read in school.

[64]   See L. Cliffe and R. Moorsom, "Rural Class Formation and Ecological Collapse in Botswana," *Review of African Political Economy* 15–16 (July 1980), 35–52, which states a rather dire case. For the transference of TB to South Africa's rural reserves, see Randall Packard, *White Plague, Black Labor: Tuberculosis and the Political Economy of Health and Disease in South Africa* (Berkeley, 1989).

where vectors of ill-health could be managed and where one's efforts to live well were given meaning. Missionaries operated within a disintegrative paradigm, whereas *baruti* and other Christians shouldered the integrative functions that the southern African conception of health had always demanded.

As we shall see in the following chapters, however, it was more often the *baruti* than the missionaries who supervised the entire process of what might be called conversion. *Baruti* mediated the Word of the Church for sick or afflicted persons and also paraphrased their affliction as a point of imbalance in a network of relationships. Church members with their Christian visits and deacons with their wary reports contextualized people's illnesses and stabilized the integrity of the congregation. In effect, the *moruti* stood halfway between two visions of "bodies": the individualized healing of missionaries, traders, and Western doctors, who isolated and drew metaphors from within the bodies of their patients; and the incorporative activity of Christian women, who built a body of support around individuals. Through his office, two discourses became a single concourse.

6

The Way, the Truth, and the Light: How Christians Spread the Word

> The baruti *would tell the people that, "If you do not believe in Jesus Christ you are like people left back. Because Jesus is the Way and the Truth and the Light."*
>
> Mr. Maatlametlo Mokobi[1]

From the very first, Africans tried to convert other Africans to their newly found faith. BaTswana evangelized not merely as intermediaries or agents of missionaries, but with a vigorous appropriation of those aspects of missionary teachings they grasped as most meaningful. Missionaries themselves recognized the importance of *baruti*, Tswana men who evangelized and taught. David Livingstone left evangelists in his wake, confident that they could best carry on "the work," and John Mackenzie trained four students in Shoshong even before the "Moffat Institution" moved to the Cape in 1878.[2] Always, African Christians translated the sermons of Europeans. Many a small outstation, a day school and congregation, began and finished each day under the care of local deacons and a *moruti*, who rarely encountered a European missionary. It seems reasonable to argue that since BaTswana evangelized more converts than did missionaries, they were more important in spreading Christianity than missionaries. And this judgment scarcely considers the central role played by informal lay evangelism, which, as has already been seen, became critical to people's self-definition as Christians throughout GammaNgwato.

---

[1]   Interview: Moruti Maatlametlo Mokobi, b. 1901, Mahalapye, 20 Jan. 1989.

[2]   LMS SA Personals 2/2, R. Price to J. Mackenzie, Shoshong, 29/7/1875; Mgadla, "Education," 95–97. The Moffat Institution thus became "Kuruman" (after Kudumane). The names of the four initial students were Ramotshane, Diphukwe, Matsane, and Khukwe; LMS Committee Minutes 1, 19/6/1879.

It must come as some surprise, then, to note that relatively little attention has been paid to the critical role of southern African agency in the spreading of the Word under mission Churches. Lamin Sanneh has pioneered with his treatment of West African Christianity as an integral part of the broad band of Christianity's historical flow; he accuses scholarly works of constructing "African Christianity" as Other, like missionaries themselves did, in part by overemphasizing the missionaries's own roles.[3] One sees a similar myopia even in recent scholarship in southern African studies, with a few prominent exceptions.[4] The most important and theoretically sophisticated contribution to our current understanding of southern African missions, for example, contains virtually nothing on African evangelists. Although simple imperialist aims are no longer automatically attributed to missionaries, the historiography of religion in Africa still views them as the truly active force behind mission Christianity. Africans are thus prefigured in an essentially reactive posture with regard to missionaries' messages and expectations.[5]

Southern African Christians therefore have not been credited with the same autonomy and influence in the domain of everyday religious life granted to Europeans. Thus the break between mission Churches and "independent" Churches shorn of white ministers takes on importance as a dramatic empowerment. As I noted in the Introduction, there has been an intense effort to explore how such Churches arose.[6] Yet the only scholar who attempted to find a generalized reason for "independency" conceived in this way largely failed; and the best specialized study associates the rise of the "Zion" healing churches of southern Africa with a spirit of defiance, despite their political acquiescence.[7] The problem in southern

---

[3]   Lamin Sanneh, *West African Christianity: The Religious Impact* (Maryknoll, NY, 1983), 243, and Ch. 9. Sanneh's argument is vitiated slightly by his apparent argument that Christianity was in a sense already present in "traditional African religions."

[4]   Deborah Gaitskell's work is the major current exception here. Some of it is listed in the bibliography, and her book is forthcoming. Other partial exceptions in English are B. A. Pauw, *Religion in a Tswana Chiefdom*, and Gabriel Setiloane, *The Image of God among the Sotho-Tswana*. See also Norman Etherington, *Preachers, Peasants and Prophets in Southeast Africa, 1835–1880* (London, 1978), esp. 150–54. J. Mutero Chirenje sees African evangelism as "ambivalent" and a prelude to Independency, *A History of Northern Botswana*, 203 esp.

[5]   Jean and John L. Comaroff, *Of Revelation and Revolution*, I (Chicago, 1991), 176–77, discuss missionaries' reliance on African carriage only. Richard Grey follows Lamin Sanneh's arguments in *Black Christians, White Missionaries* (New Haven, 1990), that Christianity has been incorrectly identified with missionaries, 80–81, and see 67. The same problem is felt even in Jean and John L. Comaroff's interesting article, "Christianity and Colonialism in South Africa," *American Ethnologist* 13 (1986), 1–22, written to question the notion of a workable political alliance between missionaries and the colonial state, as it is for one object of their criticism, Anthony Dachs' "Missionary Imperialism: The Case of Bechuanaland," *Journal of African History* 13 (1972), 647–58, and Dach's perspective in editing the *Papers of John Mackenzie* (Johannesburg, 1975). John Mbiti, *African Religions*, 229, despite his totalizing views, sees Christianity as a joint effort between missionaries and African converts.

[6]   Much of this work, of course, is very significant, beginning with Bengt Sundkler, *Bantu Prophets in South Africa* [1948] (London, 1961).

[7]   David Barrett, *Schism and Renewal in Africa* (Nairobi, 1968); and Jean Comaroff, *Body of Power, Spirit of Resistance* (Chicago, 1985). Comaroff's position on resistance has met with a somewhat intimidated academic silence, with a few exceptions, e.g., Richard Werbner, "The Political Economy of Bricolage," *Journal of Southern African Studies* 13, 1 (1986), 151–56; and J. P. Kiernan's review in *Africa* 57, 1 (1987), 131–32. See also Terrence Ranger's review essay, "Religious Movements and Politics in Sub-Saharan Africa," *African Studies Review* 29, 2 (1986), 1–71, in which he relates Zion Christians' disagreement to scholars' view of them, and recently, Matthew Schoffeleers' attempt to face the issue in "Ritual Healing and Political Acquiescence: The Case of the Zionist Churches in Southern Africa," *Africa* 60, 1 (1991).

African studies may be that the paradigm behind the search listens well only to the dialogue between colonialist and indigene, but misses other social expressions of power.

How important were the breakaways by African ministers to rank-and-file mission-Church members? There may be several different answers,[8] but in any case the necessary information is not yet available. It would be unwise to claim that the particular situation in GammaNgwato was typical of Africa. The prominence of the *Ngwato* Church, in which (to simplify) an allegiance to the Word was superimposed over kingship, remains an extreme. Missionaries in other parts of Africa exerted more, and in some cases much more, programmatic and even coercive power— a power representing the vanguard of larger colonial intervention. Nevertheless, analyses that underestimate African agency in mission Churches end up with serious flaws. They evince a sneaking regret that southern Africa failed to reject at once all those aspects of missionary teachings tagged as hegemonic by scholars. Only awkwardly can such studies depict the contentment of practicing mission Church members without seeming to denigrate African consciousness. And it grows difficult to unravel "conversions."[9] The Ngwato Church warns us to reject a blanket application of the misleading idea that Africans can only make Christianity their own when they have moved towards resistance or revolution.

The *Baruti* as Recognized by the London Missionary Society

From the start the LMS lost the ability to define the vernacular conception of what a *moruti* was. Congregations applied the term to many learned male Church members, especially deacons, as a recognition of prestige. Like other active senior members, all *baruti* led prayers, evangelized nonbelievers, and exhorted the membership. Moreover, even the *baruti* who were trained in the Moffat Institution established by John Mackenzie at Kuruman (or Kudumane) frequently went their own way. An 1893 review lists No. 1, Diphukwe (one of four *baruti* Mackenzie and Price trained in Shoshong): moved from Lake Ngami to Shoshong, then to Mashupa, finally dismissed for drink, and later emerging as a leader in a separatist Church outside GammaNgwato.[10] No. 2, Pule, from the Vaal, then at Shoshong, was dismissed for "immorality." No. 13, Basii of Taung, then of Motito, quarrelled and was dismissed, etc. Nothing prevented these men from continuing to preach the Word. Moreover, No. 15, Maphanyane of Shoshong, "was never employed by the [LMS's Bechunanaland District Committee, the BDC]—but is still doing something among his people." Others as well were "not employed" or were "self-supporting." That the Ngwato kingdom is lightly represented in the list attests to the even

---

[8]   Adam Kuper suggests an answer of "not very," in "The Magician and the Missionary" (1st pub. 1979), Ch. 11 in his *South Africa and the Anthropologist* (New York, 1987).

[9]   The Comaroffs avoid discussing the reasons BaTswana had for welcoming Christianity, and argue for the inutility of the term "conversion," *Of Revelation and Revolution*, 244–51.

[10]   LMS SA 50/1, R. Price to R. W. Thompson, 10/1/1893; Q. N. Parsons, "Independency and Ethiopianism among the Tswana in the Late 19th and Early 20th Centuries" in University of London Institute of Comparative Studies, *Collected Seminar Papers on the Societies of Southern Africa in the 19th and 20th Centuries*, I (London, 1971), 63, for Diphukwe after the LMS.

smaller degree of the LMS's formal control over the training of *baruti* there.[11] There was no shortage of *baruti* in the kingdom, however; according to Ella Sharp, there were 93 in 1870, 80 "evangelists" in 1900, and, if one includes primary school teachers, there were 320 *baruti* in 1925.[12]

For *baruti* who hoped to be officially recognized and perhaps paid some minimal salary by the Ngwato Church, the most important training ground was their own local congregation, so long as it was regularly overseen by a missionary. Nevertheless it is also true that *baruti* had to look to the LMS directly if they aspired to positions of the highest status. They might then attend the Moffat Institution or, after 1907, the LMS College, "Tiger Kloof," near Vryburg. In Tiger Kloof, candidates found a rigorous program with its own interior Bible school, under Headmaster William C. Willoughby, whom the reader by now knows as a strict disciplinarian.[13]

The careers of three ordained *baruti*, one named Baruti Kaleakgosi Sehularo, one Monyeki Mashabe, and the last Tumedisho Maruapula, illustrate the sort of trajectory available to men desiring to become "full," or ordained *baruti*. Their careers argue that no matter how fervently the LMS preached the importance of separating congregational authority from the power of the Ngwato state, its actual practices conflated the two in the realm of the Word.

Baruti Kaleakgosi was born in 1873 in Shoshong, of elevated commoner ancestry. His first name reveals the sympathy of his parents; his surname (his father's name) means "confidant of the king."[14] Baruti belonged to Sekgoma II's age regiment (*mophato*) and grew up close to the prince, maintaining his friendship while he taught at Miss Sharp's school. After Baruti married, Sekgoma raised a collection to pay for his admission to Tiger Kloof with the first Bible class. This apparently irritated Khama. At any rate, the Rev. Albert Jennings briefly recalled Baruti to Serowe to discuss his "alleged shiftiness and lying," and then complained to the BDC about Baruti again in 1908, causing his name to be withdrawn from the Bible school. It was a very discouraged man who left GammaNgwato to join Sekgoma II in exile. In 1910 Willoughby accused Jennings, and by implication Khama, of sabotaging Baruti's career with spurious accusations. Willoughby's own notations for Baruti after his eventual return to Tiger Kloof in 1911 refer to him as "reliable" and as a "keen-thinker"—dramatic praise from the headmaster.[15] Baruti rose to the top of his class. In 1913 the LMS prepared for his ordination, and he humbly asked Khama to permit him to rejoin Sekgoma in exile as his resident minister. With a rhetorical gesture of disgust, Khama gave his written consent. Sadly, during Baruti's last year at Tiger Kloof, his wife died in childbirth. Although Baruti's grades there-

[11]   LMS SA 50/1, R. Price to R. W. Thompson, 10/1/1893.

[12]   Although the published *Report of the LMS* lists only eighteen *baruti* for 1881, Vol. 87, "Shoshong." Sharp's definition was broader than that of the LMS *Reports*, but one could certainly defend a far broader definition than hers, based on general salutation and community usage, LMS SA 92/Sharp, n.d. (1930).

[13]   Interview: Mr. L. G. Baruti, b. 1902, Baruti ward, Serowe, 8 Nov. 1988, English; and see J. Rutherford, "William C. Willoughby."

[14]   *Kala ya kgosi*. Interview: Mr. L. G. Baruti, b. 1902, Baruti ward, Serowe, 8 Nov. 1988, English; ZKM, LMS Register of Pupils in Tiger Kloof from 1904, No. 91.

[15]   WCW/476, G. Cousins, W. Dower and Sir C. J. Tarring, *Strictly Private and Confidential Report on Visit to the South African Missions of the Society, Nov. 1910–April 1911* (London, 1911), 113–14; ZKM, LMS Reg. of Pupils in Tiger Kloof from 1904, No. 91.

after declined, he finished school and became the second MoNgwato to be ordained a minister under LMS auspices.[16]

Baruti's career shows that Khama's favor was never to be discounted, not even by the brightest students of the decade. Monyeki Mashabe's fortunes reinforce the point. The son of a Serowe deacon of commoner and distantly Kalanga extraction, Monyeki served as the schoolmaster in Shoshong before attending Tiger Kloof in both 1907 and then later in 1916–1920. He recieved poor to middling marks. Worse, he left under false pretences to visit his just-widowed mother. For this offense Rev. Willoughby brought him before the LMS's "South African Executive Committee," which was meeting in Tiger Kloof in 1916. Monyeki defended himself, saying that "he understood that the matter would be put before the [LMS but that] he also had his fathers, meaning the Bamangwato." Before long Monyeki had confessed his error and accepted a reprimand before his fellow students.[17] Tiger Kloof's stone walls enclosed an ideological order that substituted loyalty to the LMS for what it called "tribal" identity. Yet such identities were quickly resumed later, especially in GammaNgwato; thus, despite Monyeki's poor record, the Rev. Lewis requested him for the Serowe district after his ordination in 1923. That request certainly came from King Khama; after all, Monyeki was a MoNgwato.[18]

We are fortunate to have a source that allows us to peer into the process of accomodation at the heart of the LMS's training of *baruti* who would either become ordained as ministers or else approach this level. A set of Tiger Kloof's ordination examinations from the 1910s and 1920s survives, in which the thoughts of the early *baruti* trained by the LMS are displayed in the form of personal histories. Candidates had to answer a set of broad questions about how they came to Christianity. The resulting "confession" was a key element in their personal "production of truth," creating an "intrinsic modification" in their self-image.[19] The power to interpret and validate the confession as part of "conversion" of course remained outside the confession itself. "A great change came into me after I was converted, hatred, evil deeds and desires left me and I . . . left off drunkenness and fighting, I have now new thoughts which are . . . to avoid evil manners," wrote Lanie Tiko, who had been a young tough in the Orange Free State. Yet Willoughby could and did suspend Lanie later for making unseemly jokes in the presence of women.[20]

Despite these constraints, or perhaps because of them, the confession was a creative act. Roger Khukwe told his mentors that while he had still been "in darkness," his friends used to say that "there was no God anywhere, but that it was only the wisdom of the White people." Some of them even went so far as to claim

---

16   K III D/31/57, Khama to Baruti Kaleakgosi, Serowe, 1/6/13. With Tumedisho Maruapula slightly ahead of him, Baruti K. was ordained in Serowe in 1915. LMS SA Reports, Tiger Kloof for 1913, Appendix O; Tiger Kloof for 1914: Tiger Kloof Bible Students' Exam; Report of Theological Tutor S. G. Organe.

17   ZKM, LMS Register of Pupils in Tiger Kloof from 1904, No. 24; LMS SA Reports 4/1 Shoshong for 1907, E. Lloyd; 79/2, SAEC, Tiger Kloof 23-9/11/16; 80/2 Minutes of SAEC, Hope Fountain 23/3/17; Reports, Tiger Kloof Examination Reports, 1916; 82/1 Minutes of the SAEC, Tiger Kloof 3/19.

18   LMS SA 82/4 SAEC, Tiger Kloof 6–12/11/19; 84/5 SAEC, Serowe, 20/7/22; ZKM, LMS Register of Pupils in Tiger Kloof.

19   Michel Foucault, *The History of Sexuality,* I [1978] (New York, 1990), 58, 61. Willoughby felt that "publicity" counted for much in the profession of faith in order to accomplish "a break" with the past; WCW/290, W. C. Willoughby, uncorrected proof of "The Upbuilding of the Body of Christ."

20   WCW/804 [Confessions], Tiger Kloof Ordinations Examinations, 1910–16, Lanie Tiko 1, 5.

that "the whites had killed a child of their own nation, and now they have come to
. . . say that we killed Jesus."[21]

Tumedisho Maruapula was another Bible student. He was born in Shoshong,
then the Ngwato capital, and grew up in its Talaote ward under strict parents.[22]
After leaving the cattle post of his youth, he helped out at home by plowing and
transporting grain by ox wagon, which suggests that his family had some wealth.
He then entered Ella Sharp's school, and struggled to "leave those things which
my parents favored and respected." In this he was aided by his mother's family, in
which several uncles were prominent early Church members; one of them, Deacon
Lencwe, had guided him to the Church beginning with a gift of the *Sepeleta*, the
LMS lesson book, while Tumedisho still tended his father's cattle. Tumedisho's
parents allowed him to read the Bible, and his other relatives proved no hindrance.
They would themselves feel the influence of Christian thought and practice even
though few were members of the Church: "My brothers do not drink any beer and
among all my people superstitious beliefs and the use of medicines to fumigate
property and [sorghum] have all now come to an end." For Tumedisho, it was his
uncle Lencwe's "good deeds and manners" that, far more than any "words," taught
Tumedisho about Christ. Like all *baruti*, Tumedisho had then to wait until he married before he could become a ministerial candidate.[23]

The rest of Tumedisho's Tiger Kloof confession is a rather formulaic exposition
of Low Church Protestant doctrine. Tumedisho may have felt cowed because
Willoughby had had differences with him, thinking him "conceited" and "weak-
minded." At one point an inquiry met over Tumedisho's imputation that witchcraft had taken place in the College; another time he was suspected of keeping a
Serowe mistress.[24] Still, in line with both the ideal of an active laity and the meaning of "being a Christian" in GammaNgwato, Tumedisho saw "The Duty of Church
Members" as first and foremost "to teach the other people the word of God."
Willoughby noted with pride, "Ask twenty male catechumens why they want to
join the church [i.e., the LMS], and fifteen of them will answer, 'That I may go forth
as a preacher.'"[25] Like many candidates, Tumedisho mentioned healing as a central
feature of Christ's ministry. Lastly, he reflected Willoughby's conflicted attempts to
denigrate the power of Khama (and other Tswana rulers) in matters of religion.
Khama opposed Tiger Kloof as an institutional threat to Ngwato patriotism, and
continued a loose boycott of the school for the first eight or nine years of its existence. The very first question of the ordination procedure asked for a promise of
ultimate loyalty to the principles and methods of the LMS, but Tumedisho went
further, writing, "Kings and rulers have no right in the church."[26] Later in his ca-

---

[21]   WCW/804 [Confessions], Roger Khukwe, 4.

[22]   The next section thus derives from WCW/804 [Confessions], Tiger Kloof Ordination Examinations,
1910-16, Tumedisho Maruapula, 1-11.

[23]   LMS SA 87/4, SAEC Tiger Kloof, 3/9/25; and Interview: The Rev. Harsh Ramolefhe, Gaborone, 15
June 1989, English, who discusses his own family's desire hastily to arrange a marriage for this purpose.

[24]   LMS SA 75/5, SAEC, Tiger Kloof 16/10/13; and ZKM, LMS Register, No. 59. Of course, Willoughby
also praised Joseph M. as "excellent" and of good nature; while Tumedisho had a distinguished and
selfless career, M. impregnated several students and resigned his position as Sekgoma Khama's teacher in
disgrace.

[25]   W. C. Willoughby, *Tiger Kloof: The L.M.S.'s Native Institution in South Africa* (London, 1912), 39.

[26]   LMS SA SAEC Serowe, 19/7/18, Appendix 2.

reer, however, Willoughby and Khama both acted to impress the opposite upon him, as we shall see.

Upon his ordination in 1915 Tumedisho joined a select group; the LMS ordained only nineteen men in all their southern African stations up to 1930, and the pace and number of ordinations decreased for many years thereafter. There would hardly have been nineteen had not *baruti* complained loudly to the LMS.[27] In 1907 at the first meeting of the LMS "Native Advisory Council," delegates criticized the attending missionaries for sluggishness in training "Native Ministers." Missionaries were shocked to hear BaTswana shout the refrain, "Re a lo nyatsa!" which means something like "We despise you!"[28] They continued: "Open the gate. When will you teach a MoTswana to be a [full] *moruti*? When will he give Communion and baptize people?" The LMS still moved slowly, but thenceforth allowed "junior *baruti*" to baptize and offer Communion in consultation with their regional missionary.[29]

In fact *baruti* did these things anyway, away from the prying gaze of missionaries and the Bechuanaland District Committee, as was well known.[30] The LMS was powerless to stop them. To begin with, the influence of the BDC was much diminished by its inability, given its priorities, to pay *baruti* more than a pittance. Upon Moruti Peter Gaeonale's retirement after twenty-five years of service, he was awarded a mere £10. The Ngwato Church, not the LMS, paid most of its fifty or so school teachers at the turn of the century, out of a budget of £80 or £90. Ordained *baruti* still received only £50 per year in 1922. Apart from "school" *baruti* and full ministers lay the nebulous corps of informal *baruti*, and the BDC's inability to tell who exactly these men were boded ill for the possibility of remuneration. In 1912, after many requests, the BDC put aside £100 for the education of the children of "100 to 200 recognized Native Evangelists," yet the Rev. James Burns, for instance, counted only thirteen evangelists in GammaNgwato in 1930.[31] The LMS subsequently made a virtue of necessity and began to insist that deacons raise more funds for *baruti*'s salaries.[32]

In each main "outstation", explained Rev. Jennings in 1912,

> there resides an Evangelist paid by the home church at Serowe, who in the absence of the missionary [99 percent of the time] controls the whole of the church activities of the district. He administers Communion and baptizes children of church members—suspends those guilty of gross errors in conduct and reports to the missionary. . . .[33]

---

[27]   Goodall, *History of the LMS*, 282; LMS SA 74/5, R. H. Lewis to F. H. Hawkins, Molepolole, n.d. (1912?). Anglican and Wesleyan societies ordained far more frequently and the LMS paid close attention to *baruti*'s disgruntlement in consequence.

[28]   LMS SA 68/3, BDC Minutes, Kanye, 21/2/07, which translates the shouts as "We are disappointed in you."

[29]   WCW/374, "Mahoko a Phuthego ba LMS," Kanye, 1907. Ngwato *baruti* remained largely silent.

[30]   LMS SA Reports 3/1, Report of Phalapye Mission Outstations, 1900 (H. Williams).

[31]   LMS SA Reports 3/1, Phalapye, for 1899 (H. Williams); LMS SA 74/4 SADC, Tiger Kloof, 10/6/12; 78/1 SADC Minutes, 20/3/16; 84/4 SAEC, Tiger Kloof 10/3/22; 94/Burns, J. Burns to Chirgwin, Serowe, 23/5/32; Interviews: Ms. Kadimo Serema, Palapye, 30 Nov. 1988 and 17 Dec. 1988.

[32]   LMS SA 93/Sharp SAEC, Serowe, 17/1/31; Interview: Mrs. Tsogang Serema, b. 1901, Palapye, 7 Dec. 1988, who recalls one pound sterling as her late husband's yearly salary as a *moruti*. We will see in Chapter 8 that village congregations also assisted their *baruti* economically.

[33]   LMS SA, 1912, A. Jennings to LMS. Exact reference misplaced.

Most of these men upheld the visible side of the LMS's work admirably, as far as missionaries could tell. The Rev. Williams' judgment on Moruti Peter Morwetsi's household tells us something of what missionaries expected from *baruti*:

> [Peter's] household is without exception the best regulated of any I have seen among our Native Teachers, whilst his house and lolwapa [enclosing yard] are just what I would wish every native teacher's house to be—a pattern to all the neighbors of neatness and durability.[34]

But equally important, surely, was the fact that *baruti* were responsible for introducing the citizens of GammaNgwato to the gospel. Outside the largest congregations, it was often the presence of a small church building and a *moruti* that initiated people's association with the Ngwato Church. If the *moruti* lived at some distance from a very small village, he might walk to it once a week or schedule a regional service.[35] Most *baruti*, preferred such "higher" labors to school-teaching, according to J. T. Brown. The Rev. Lewis remarked in 1930,

> They are good fellows most of them, and are doing a great work for their people, but their work brings fuller responsibility, and needs to be constantly reinforced by the stronger thinking and deeper spiritual sense and wider outlook of the European missionary.[36]

Wider outlook or not, the fact was that missionaries rarely set eyes on most *baruti*, neither those paid directly by the LMS or the Ngwato Church nor, certainly, the majority of the others.[37] *Baruti* in GammaNgwato owed more to the leadership and structure of the Ngwato kingdom than they did to the LMS.

The *Baruti* as Citizens of the Ngwato Kingdom

There is ample evidence that Khama controlled the appointment and dismissal of the major *baruti* in GammaNgwato, both directly and indirectly, through the nominal agency of his missionary and the BDC. Thereafter, he relied on *baruti* for key services. The king barred any *baruti* tied to societies other than the LMS from teaching or, often, even entering his country. One Sencho was arrested at the border and sentenced to an immediate caning after travelling freely through Ngwaketse country preaching for his independent church. Khama had the resident magistrate jail a travelling Ndebele who supposedly claimed he was "a god"; and he preemptively forbade an independent Rolong *moruti* from entering Serowe.[38] Tshekedi scarcely modified this stance, expelling independent preachers and prophets, and outlaw-

---

[34]   *Sic* throughout. LMS SA Reports 3/1, Palapye Mission Outstations for 1900 (H. Williams).

[35]   Interviews: Mrs. Obolokile Sekga, b. approx. 1903, Serowe, 12 Nov. 1988; Mr. Koowetse Molebalwa, b. 1905, Lerala, 16 June 1990; Mr. Selo Mafoko, b. 1900, Lerala, 12 April 1990.

[36]   LMS SA 91/Lewis, R. H. Lewis to Chirgwin, Kanye, 26/2/30.

[37]   A similar situation probably obtained elsewhere in southern Africa; see Pauw, *Religion in a Tswana Chiefdom*, 62, 146 ff.

[38]   The first instance could have been a misunderstanding of the man's advocacy of the Mwali cult, LMS SA Reports 4/2, Shoshong, for 1908 (E. Lloyd); Chirenje, *History of Northern Botswana*, 218 (for Sencho); K III Papers, Khama to Samuel Moroka (full citation misplaced); Interviews: Mrs. Boikanyo Motlhagodi, with Ditaolo Motlhagodi, Lerala, 17 May 1990, and 1 June 1990.

ing "Zion" adherents hailing from South Africa. Chapter 7 treats this history of repression and colonial complicity in more depth.

Secondly, Khama repeatedly forbade the BDC to place non-Ngwato *baruti*, especially men with whom he was not familiar, within the borders of his kingdom.[39] He feared their possible disloyalty and recalled how several such men had supported his brothers Raditladi and Mphoeng, and then his son Sekgoma, when they broke from his rule. Thirdly, it appears that Khama's ability to determine the installation and dismissal of *baruti* was accepted by everyone in the kingdom, even his missionaries. For instance, in 1897 Ratshosa tried for some reason to get rid of Moruti Pule, Hepburn's old assistant, a tired widower who obediently left for his home village. The Rev. Willoughby was outraged when he heard that the order had not originated with Khama—thus demonstrating the currency of the expectation that Khama could issue such orders. We have seen how Baruti Kaleakgosi had to solicit Khama's acceptance of his plans to teach among Sekgoma Khama's following at Nekati. Similarly, Khama specially requested and received Peter Morwetsi for Makomi, a recently centralized Kalanga village near Mmadinare of about 700 people, with 39 Church members and 152 students.[40]

The authority of the Ngwato capital over the Kalanga villages around Francistown required immediate reinforcement after the kingdom's border was extended northward in 1895. The BaNgwato had no previous claim over this large and populous region (called BoKalaka in SeNgwato). From Tonota in the south to Selolwane in the north, Kalanga-speakers, BaKhurutshe, and the BakaNswazwi lived in a multitude of fragmented settlements.[41] *Baruti* there became correspondingly important agents of the Ngwato king, and decisions about them were made with care. For instance, at one point, Khama ordered Moruti Moses Holonga to take the place of the BakaNswazwi's unpopular *moruti*, Motiki. Moses would then relinquish his position among the BaKhurutshe to the Bible student Tumedisho Maruapula. Subsequent developments delayed these plans. In July 1914, Willoughby—who at the time was telling his students at Tiger Kloof that Tswana kings had no business in Church affairs—wrote directly to Khama about the matter. He warned that the Khurutshe *kgosi*, Rawe, was embracing Anglicanism, thereby threatening to "undermine your power as chief." Willoughby suggested that Tumedisho "go up at once and settle among the people" at Tonota to prevent this, and remain with them and Moses after his approaching ordination.[42] The king followed this suggestion, even though he was pleased neither with Tumedisho nor with Tiger Kloof. Tumedisho supported Willoughby's efforts to attract other BaNgwato there as secondary school students, and Khama wrote to him, "We did

---

39   LMS SA 67/4, A. Jennings to R. W. Thompson, Serowe, 3/5/06; and Parsons, "Khama III," 204.

40   WCW/QNP, "Additional Docs.," W. C. Willoughby to Mrs. Willoughby, Palapye, 24/9/1897; LMS SA Reports 4/1, Serowe, for 1906 (A. Jennings); K III D/31/57, Khama to B. Kaleakgosi, Serowe, 1/6/13.

41   BNA S.413/9, Bakalaka: Bamangwato Reserve. Need for Medical . . . etc., R. M. Nettleton to Medical Officer, Mafeking, 26/11/34. Nettleton listed Kalanga "sub areas," groups of small villages all "saturated with native superstition and the native doctor," as Mathangwane, Sebina's, Nswazwi's, Tutume, Nkanke, Maitengwe, in a roughly even division of 18,760 people computed by hut tax returns and so underestimated.

42   LMS SA Reports 5/1, Serowe, for 1913 (A. Jennings); quote, K III Papers G/50/36, W. C. Willoughby to Khama, Tiger Kloof, 7/7/14, my emphasis. BaNgwato sometimes wrote the name Moses "Mosisi" or "Musisi."

not know that you were for the Whites." In the end, however, Tumedisho was an important Ngwato citizen who, in serving the Ngwato Church among the BaKhurutshe, was expected to serve the kingdom.[43]

The haphazard nature of the northeastern Ngwato borders with South African capitalist farmers and ranchers, and with the Tati Mining Company, unsettled local villages and their congregations.[44] When a rival Khurutshe chief's people were squeezed out of the Tati area into Tonota in 1920, Moses felt he was being eclipsed by the now-Reverend Tumedisho's ministry, especially after resident BaKalanga began leaving Moses for newly founded villages. Moses complained that Tumedisho was taking over his work, and Moses was "afraid" because he was not sure that Khama, his "father and mother" and his "master," knew about the situation. "I should move when my father tells me to do so," he wrote, implicitly asking to follow his congregation wherever they went.[45] Such a loyal man was needed, but not in Tonota. Khama therefore placed Moses at Nswazwi village.

Baruti did more than move about like pawns. They were also involved willy-nilly in matters of state. As literate men trained in the *thuto* of the kingship, *baruti* might prove indispensible for diplomatic reportage. In early 1901 Moruti Peter Gaeonale was on his way to Kuruman, travelling up through Cape Province, and stopped at Thaba Nchu, the Rolong capital forty miles from Bloemfontein. At Thaba Nchu the British had garrisoned 1,700 troops in 1900, before walking into Christian de Wet's ambush at the end of March. They also set up concentration camps for African refugees, in which the level of mortality resembled that in the more famous camps for Boers.[46] Here is Gaeonale's politico-religious report to Khama from Thaba Nchu about the condust of the South African war there:

> The BaRolong are delaying me with cases and . . . I am refusing them, but they force disputes onto me with strength; I've not seen Father's [*Rre*] people, and this will delay me, as I have yet to go to Kudumane [Kuruman]. Insofar as I am able, I speak night and day; everybody contradicts me, even the white police, and there are hard words and I don't have the power to judge them, so I almost lose my temper. I will sneak away once I have seen the *baruti* . . . they themselves trouble us by their sins [*bosilo*, filth], as do the Boers; while the BaTswana sin greatly! the Boers are killing people in the street. The English declare their laws, the BaTswana transgress them,

[43]   K III D/30/82, Khama to T. Maruapula, Serowe, 6/7/12; and see D/31/14, Khama to W. C. Willoughby, Serowe, 23/11/12. Tumedisho annoyed Khama with his minority defense of the Rev. Jennings in 1914, LMS SA 76/3 W. C. Willoughby to F. H. Hawkins, Tiger Kloof, 25/6/14; after which Khama still kept in touch, however.

[44]   In 1907 it was found that the British South Africa Company's survey of the "Tuli Block" land had illegally taken thousands of morgen from GammaNgwato; Parsons, "Khama II," 384. Other discrepancies followed. See Julie Croston, "An Economic and Social History of the Freehold Land Tenure District of Bechuanaland Protectorate (Botswana), 1903–1966" (Ph.D. dissertation, Boston University, 1993). Land sales escalated in the white-owned areas up to the early 1920s, and Khama exerted informal control over who received occupation certificates, Interview: Mr. Dennis Blackbeard, b. 1918, Serowe, 7 Nov. 1988, English.

[45]   K III H/59/1921, Sekgoma II to Khama, 16/7/1921, enclosing Mosisi to Sekgoma, pers. comm.

[46]   E. M. G. Belfield, *The Boer War* (London, 1975), 142; and Peter Warwick, *Black People and the South African War, 1899–1902* (Johannesburg, 1983), 152–57. Mostly children died of pneumonia, and fatalites were heaviest in November–December 1901. In nearby Boer camps, deaths approached 350/1000 in October 1901.

and they die—so it goes, Phuti [praise-name for Ngwato king]. I am P. Gaeonale, let God help them.⁴⁷

The quote is not self-explanatory—I do not know who Father is—and that is itself important. The written evidence for *baruti*'s foreign political duties, as for their far more critical domestic issuance of *thuto*, relies on uneven patches of text dispersed through the kingship's correspondence (most of which dealt with finance and trade). In reading it, one often has the sense of dropping in on a conversation already in progress. Written letters were introduced into existing networks of authority in GammNgwato, and they were penned and read in now-forgotten contexts of interpersonal communication. Many referred conversationally to nonliterate communiqués, and some even required simultaneous transmission in oral and literate modes.⁴⁸ When traders and evangelists carried letters back and forth for the king, they often added a whole latticework of explanation; *baruti*'s letters are our only traces of these complex modes of contact.

As nodes of oral and literate expression, *baruti* guarded and reconstructed religio-political loyalty and represented GammaNgwato as a kingdom. In 1916 we find King Khama writing to his governor in Bobonong, Modisaotsile (whom we will meet again); Solomon is Solomon Kebothilwe, a *moruti* in Selolwane, then under Modisaotsile's authority.

> I disdain your opinion [*mafoko*] that Solomon teaches [*ruta*] well and that you have no trouble with him. When Solomon left here and I placed him there, many people doubted him, you included. Now, if those whom he teaches and who stay with him doubt him, how can he do well? . . . you say you are alone in standing by him. You should not have hidden anything [from me].⁴⁹

One gathers that Khama was concerned about Selolwane, and well he might have been; a missionary had only visited the village for the very first time six years earlier, and it hung precariously on the margin of the kingdom.⁵⁰ Solomon's sin apparently had been to split up the local school under another and junior *moruti*, Seitlhano.⁵¹ Solomon learned his lesson, and invoked the idea of regional unity when he wrote to Khama a few years later to complain about the activities of the Ngwato hut-tax collector. Keeditse Kgosietsile performed this duty and was himself a major Ngwato presence in the Kalanga region.⁵² According to Solomon, Keeditse was driving people to

---

⁴⁷ K III C/16, P. Gaeonale to Khama, Thaba Nchu, 14/3/01. This passage was very hard to read, as Gaeonale was a Kalanga-speaker native to GammaNgwato and wrote in a peculiar SeTswana-ized Kalanga idiolect. (The most noted African account of the South African War is Solomon Plaatje, *The Boer War Diaries of Sol Plaatje*, ed. John L. Comaroff (Cape Town, 1973).

⁴⁸ Isabel Hofmeyr subtly shows this interdigitation of the oral and written for the chiefdoms and bureacracies in the Transvaal in the 1920s, and I am indebted to her thinking here. See her *"We Spend Our Years as a Tale That is Told": Oral Historical Narrative in a South African Chiefdom* (Portsmouth, NH, 1993). See also Roger Chartier's discussion, "Texts, Printing, Readings," in Lynn Hunt, ed., *The New Cultural History* (Berkeley, 1989), 156–59 esp.

⁴⁹ K III E/33/64, Khama to Modisaotsile, Serowe, 12/12/16.

⁵⁰ LMS SA 78/2, C. Reed to F. H. Hawkins, Selolwane, 27/5/16.

⁵¹ Seitlhano had evidently complained of this earlier; again one is reminded that *baruti* must often have spoken with Ngwato representatives or sent verbal messages to missionaries, and the written record preserves only a part of the kingship's dialogue with them.

⁵² S II A/2 Keeditse Kgosietsile to Sekgoma, Shashe, 10/6/23.

relocate from Selolwane to various other villages. He expressly contrasts these sense-less dispersals of people to the homogenizing role of his own congregation:

> Keeditse is scattering people . . . he is not gathering them in, but instead, taking off the roof of the house [church] since he is scattering the chiefdoms. [Previously] there were many peoples present because thay were gathered by the Church.[53]

By now we are growing familar with this opposition between scattering and gathering. In this case, Solomon responded two days later to what was clearly an immediate susequent request from Khama. He reported by post on the exact location of the Ngwato border, with distances given in walking time. At the end Solomon touted his own status:

> I am your eyes, King . . . if the [Protectorate's representative] has not seen to the border properly, he then checks it when I inform them that I am inspecting Mongwato's [the king's] boundary, then they wake up first thing and accompany me. . . . I am the child of your servant, [signed] Solomon Kebothilwe.[54]

Finally, the kingdom's relationship with its *baruti* was also juridical. In 1916 Khama dealt with Moruti Noke Modisakgosi's assertion that he was having trouble making certain intractable persons attend "Church and School." Noke then dispatched the offenders to Serowe for punishment in the central *kgotla*. Thus early on it was considered reasonable to force *thuto* on certain groups, using *baruti* for the purpose, although in this case it is true that Khama asked Noke to deal with the issue in his own village of Ratholo.[55] Other *baruti* asked for Khama's direct intervention on potentially explosive Church matters. Moruti Seakgano Ncaga begged several times for the king to send a representative to adjudicate a thorny divorce case, complaining that "it pains me that your decision will not be heard; it hurts me that you have not acceded to your small servant's request." He also referred a sensitive sorcery case between ethnic groups in Shoshong to Khama's *kgotla*, with his own recommendation as to the verdict.[56]

Hence through the interwoven channels of oral message and written letter, a literati of sorts was put in service of GammaNgwato's administration. Dispersed among the larger citizenry, such men bound the Ngwato kingdom to the capital. Their services continued in muted form into the 1930s and beyond. In the midst of several internal and external conflicts besetting the weakening kingdom in the late 1930s, Tshekedi took time, as one woman remembers, to call upon men:

> to sacrifice, to leave their homes and take up as *baruti*. . . . my father was one of those men who left his country [i.e., his region of GammaNgwato] and his home and began a ministry, in Lecheng. . . . he was not the only untrained *moruti*.[57]

[53]   K III H/29, S. Kebothilwe to Khama, Selolwane, 23/10/22, "ethnicities" is *merafe*; and LMS SA 78/2, C. Reed to F. H. Hawkins, Selolwane, 27/5/16.

[54]   K III H/59, Solomon Kebothilwe to Khama, Selolwane, 25/10/22. This was not the first administrative use Khama made of Solomon; earlier he had had him turn down the applications of two black South African entrepreneurs to open shops near the railway line, K III E/32, Khama to S. Kebothilwe, n.d.

[55]   K III E/33/25, Khama to N. Modisakgosi, Serowe, 24/11/16.

[56]   K III H/59, S. Ncaga to Khama, Shoshong, 15/7/22.

[57]   Interview: Ms. Kadimo Serema, Palapye, 30 Nov. 1988.

These men carried the banner of the realm of the Word, and indeed they formed a bulwark against the disintegration of the Ngwato state. Their children ensured the survival of *thuto* long after the monarchy ended.[58]

"You are a MoNgwato but I am Kgosi!"
Ngwato Evangelism and the BaTawana

Baruti also attempted to extend the hegemony of Ngwato *thuto* beyond the borders of the kingdom. This effort was directed toward Ngamiland, in the northwest corner of Botswana. There, the BaTawana had built a complex and stratified polity, entirely independent of Khama's authority as recognized by the Protectorate. They were also, nonetheless, genealogical juniors to the BaNgwato, and King Khama wished to reassert that relationship by subordinating Tawana Christians to the Ngwato Church.

In 1878 the Rev. James Hepburn journeyed to Ngamiland and established a Christian mission among the BaTawana. Hepburn preached on the Creation and Fall, the Covenant with Abraham, and the Ten Commandments, "clearly indicating the path of duty toward God and toward man," the Death and Resurrection, judgment at death, and the "law of marriage." Without apparent incongruity or pause, he included the "duties of a chief toward his people" and how Kgosi Moremi of the BaTawana in particular should "conduct the affairs of the town; how to form his council," and so on.

We should not disbelieve Hepburn that some people were deeply moved, not by Hepburn's administrative directives but by the concept of literacy. Hepburn read, "Thou shalt rise up before the hoary head, and honor the face of the old man, and fear thy God! I am the Lord" (Lev. 19:32), "a great man times" to one particular "old man," who pointed at the text with yearning, saying, "What am I to do? My eyes are too old."[59] Nonetheless, the provision of *thuto* as an explicit program interpreted by *baruti* sent by Khama ("if any matter perplexes you, you may rely upon them," said Hepburn) was just as central to the Ngwato endeavor as was literacy or doctrine. Hepburn did not hesitate to call for an end to Tawana "slave-dealing" in this connection. The BaTawana subordinated previously autonomous populations and based their economy upon them to a greater degree than the BaNgwato. The issue would arise again, but Hepburn discussed it in terms of larger reforms somehow dictated and encoded in *thuto*.[60]

---

[58] Many of their children and grandchildren are Botswana's leading politicians, academics, businesspeople and lawyers today.

[59] *Chronicle of the LMS,* Feb. 1878, 37, 56–57.

[60] *Ibid.,* March 1878, 58. There is no room here for a discussion of Tawana exploitation of "MaSarwa" and other groups as servants and cattleherds, but see Wilmsen, *Land Filled with Flies,* who argues that the "Sarwa" ethnicity was formed out of an economy of domination. See also Thomas Tlou, "Servility and Political Control: Batlhanka among the BaTawana in Northwestern Botswana, ca. 1750–1906," in Suzanne Miers and Igor Kopytoff, eds., *Slavery in Africa* (Madison, 1977), 367–90; Suzanne Miers and Michael Crowder, "The Politics of Slavery in Bechuanaland: Power Struggles and the Plight of the Basarwa in the Bamangwato Reserve, 1926–1940," Ch. 5, in Suzanne Miers and Richard Roberts, eds., *The End of Slavery in Africa* (Madison, 1988).

One of the elderly wives of Moremi's father demanded to be taught separately next to Hepburn's wife's wagon, which Hepburn insisted was "sacred from intrusion." At being refused, the old woman hit the missionary in the face with his own spelling book. Hepburn threatened to withdraw from Ngamiland at this "insult to the Directors" and, more important, "to the great Chief Khame, whose teacher I was, and," Hepburn added significantly, "who had sent Mokgwati to accompany me as his representative." He secured an apology, and leaving his evangelists Diphukwe and Khukwe with the BaTawana, he returned to GammaNgwato.[61]

Khukwe's son later recalled their family's early days in Ngamiland as hard; the BaTawana "were detestable" as they mocked Khukwe and said that Europeans "had been driven by poverty from their homes, and have come to us in big wagons saying they bring us a God."[62] These were salad days, nevertheless. In 1882 fresh Ngwato *baruti* arrived in Ngamiland, carrying not only books but also "coffee, tea, sugar, candles, soap," impressive clothing, and other goods to further inform the meaning of *thuto*.[63] Then, late that year, Lobengula's terrifying Ndebele attacked the BaTawana. Although the Ndebele refrained from assaulting the Ngwato kingdom, during their siege of the BaTawana, they took care to stamp out the signs of Ngwato hegemony, the new *thuto*. In addition to taking over 30,000 cattle, they removed every school book and Bible in possession of the small royalist Church, very likely turning the books into bodily ornaments. The year before, the Jesuit Father Depelchin had seen other "Protestant" Bibles set into the warriors' head plumes (yet another way to bear the signs of *thuto*). The attack seriously dampened the Christian fervor of the BaTawana.[64]

In 1886, at the start of the "unstable" portion of his tenure already recounted in Chapter 2, Hepburn turned again to Ngamiland. Eight years after his first trip, he found a diminished and isolated group of Tawana Christians. The king, Moremi, had lapsed into "heathenism" and was less pleasant than he had been before. Referring to Hepburn's moderate espousal of the rights of servants, *batlhanka* ("slaves"), Moremi replied

> that he knew all the Scriptures from end to end; fulminating fiery vengeance against the Matebele, and uttering his wicked defiance against God, who, do what He would, should never prevent them from killing Masarwa and Makoba [river people] for ever.[65]

---

[61] Hepburn, *Twenty Years*, 181–82; cited by Parsons, "Khama III," 237. The BaTawana had broken off from the BaNgwato in the eighteenth century and were therefore their genealogical juniors; Tlou, *History of Ngamiland*, 38–40.

[62] WCW/804 [Confessions], Roger Khukwe Mogodi, 7.

[63] Rhodesian National Archives, "Phalapye, March 23, 1894," marked "[29]" and "handwriting of W. C. Willoughby, apparently copied from ms. by Tiro," courtesy Isaac Schapera (my trans.), 2. Khukwe was appointed in 1878 but his position was terminated soon after; he continued anyway from January 1881, along with Diphukwe, who soon left. Khukwe was reappointed in 1890 at £40 per year. Parsons, "Khama III," 206; LMS Committee Minutes 1, 20/1/1881; LMS SA 47/1/B, BDC Minutes 4/3/189.

[64] Tlou, *History of Ngamiland*, 80; WCW/374, *Report of the LMS*, Vol. 93 (1886–87), J. Hepburn, 189–90; *Chronicle of the LMS* (Feb. 1887), 73. See Tlou, "The Batawana of Northwestern Botswana and Christian Missionaries, 1877–1906," *Transafrican Journal of History* 3, 1–2 (1973), 112–20; and Depelchin and Croonenbergh, *Journey to Gubulawayo* (Bulawayo, 1979), 199, as cited by Leroy Vail and Landeg White, *Power and the Praise Poem: Southern African Voices in History* (Charlottesville, 1991), 97.

[65] *Chronicle of the LMS*, Feb. 1887, 77.

"Has no one about here got a book?" Hepburn said. He made one last attempt to rejuvenate the Spirit among the Tawana royalty. Sharing in the Ndebele's semiotic, the missionary likened the Bible to a "powerful charm," and dramatically produced Moremi's own Bible, which a fellow missionary had recovered from Lobengula and the Ndebele. His meaning was not lost on Moremi, and his response was immediate: he sprang back in alarm, and asked, "Am I not *Kgosi*?" Suddenly turning on Hepburn's assistant (not Mokgwati but a new man, Mopaleng), he shouted, "You are a MoNgwato, but I am *Kgosi*, do you hear!" Hepburn then perceived that his life was in danger and left the next day. "Who can say what I left behind?" he wondered emptily.[66]

For one thing, he again left Khukwe Mogodi behind. Khukwe stayed in Ngamiland until 1905. Except for the fact that the Ngwato Church (not the LMS) paid his salary, for most of the time the ties between him and Khama's missionaries remained in a minor key. Moremi's mother was a practicing Christian, and a discreet and quiescent congregation did not bother the *kgosi*.[67] In 1892, Moremi died and was suceeded by Sekgoma Letsholathebe; that same year the LMS finally sent the BaTawana a European missionary of their own, A. J. Wookey, whose presence expanded the congregation and distanced it from Khama. He was conducted to Ngamiland by Lloyd, who found that Christianity had spread mainly among peoples outside the capital. Besides Khukwe, the other full-time LMS *moruti* was Somolekae, who proselytized with complete autonomy in the backwaters of BaSubiya and BaYei settlements.[68] After three years, the Rev. Wookey retired from the Lake with malarial fever. Nonetheless some contacts between the BaTawana and the Ngwato Church remained. A surviving letter from Khukwe to Willoughby in Serowe reads as if it were one of many, and reports on the state of the eighty-nine-member Tawana Church and a sub-mission to the BaSubiya.[69]

As Khukwe and the congregation aged, Khukwe grew dissatisfied with his situation and tried once more to deploy Khama's assertion of hegemony over all *thuto*. After rumors began circulating in GammaNgwato that Khukwe had quarrelled with Kgosi Sekgoma Letsholathebe, Khama wrote Khukwe to argue against the legitimacy of the Tawana *kgosi*. Complaints and counter-accusations led Khukwe to invoke his own authority as *moruti* over Letsholathebe, who held the status of catechumen. Stunned by this breach of boundaries, Letsholathebe withdrew at once from the Church.

The Tawana *kgosi* next advised the Rev. Jennings by post that Khukwe had interfered in "the affairs of the kingdom." The Serowe congregation outfitted Jennings with a wagon and supplies for the six-week journey to Ngamiland, and two members accompanied him, prepared to mix with Christian friends

---

[66] WCW/374, *Report of the LMS*, Vol. 93 (1886–87), J. Hepburn, 189–90; LMS SA Reports 2/1, Shoshong for 1886 (J. Hepburn); *Chronicle of the LMS*, Feb. 1887, 81.

[67] LMS SA 58/?, W. C. Willoughby to LMS, Palapye, 5/6/01; LMS SA Journals 4/117, A. J. Wookey, 27/2/1892.

[68] J. T. Brown wrote a book of inspirational character about Somolekae, entitled *The Apostle of the Marshes: The Story of Shomolekae* (London, 1925).

[69] LMS SA P/6 Khukhwe Mogodi to W. C. Willoughby, Tsao, 2/10/03, SeTswana. See also D. M. Shamukuni, "The BaSubiya," *Botswana Notes and Records*, 4 (1972), 161–84.

"Village leader, Christian, with wife and child, in a village northeast in Ngamiland near the Chobe and Zambesi rivers. This man died soon after—probably he was poisoned by an enemy." Photograph and text by Arthur Sandilands, ca. 1930. Reproduced courtesy of the Council for World Mission, London.

and relatives and listen.[70] Letsholathebe's accusations covered a lot of ground, but essentially focussed on Khukwe's ill-temper and his usurpation of Letsholathebe's ritual prerogatives. One unerring shot in his salvo accused Moruti Khukwe of demanding to be paid for medical services with "a man"—a slave. Of this "Church members . . . complained greatly, [remarking that Khukwe] was in the habit of preaching that slavery was not right." Jennings

---

[70]   LMS SA Reports 3/3, "Report of the Visit of A. E. Jennings to Lake Ngami and District, April to August 1905."

withdrew from intricate deliberations and considered merely whether Khukwe's flock had abandoned him. That much was clear; their feelings were "vehement." Jennings agreed to Khukwe's removal and left the BaTawana after marrying, as was then his habit, dozens of couples at once.[71]

Christ drew all people into His kingdom, extending far beyond Ngamiland. But the Ngwato kingdom was also greater than the BaTawana's. The following year, the LMS and the Protectorate government combined their energies with Khama's, and deposed the factious Sekgoma Letsholathebe. It seemed that *baruti*'s words had teeth. Letsholathebe's nephew Mathiba commenced to rule, and Khukwe's replacement, Gaorakgwe, was later reported to be "doing well."[72] Eleven years later, in late 1915, the Rev. Cullen Reed was appointed to supervise the BaTawana from the distance of Serowe. He was able to describe GammaNgwato in good faith as "split into two sections[,] the BaK[h]ama & the BaTawana, each under its own chief." Like Hepburn, he visted Ngamiland with a Ngwato deacon, yoking together the geographic and ideological trajectory of *thuto*.[73]

After Reed's untimely death, the tension between various configurations of Christianity, its expansive and institutional sides, was once again felt in the Tawana Church. Although Kgosi Mathiba repeated the longstanding Tswana request for a white missionary, it was the Rev. Andrew Kgasa who moved to Ngamiland. Kgasa was a "cautious and careful man, with a conscience which would not retreat even if it meant a loss of friendship with people."[74] He too found his position difficult. After a Christian prophet arose among the riparian BaSubiya and stole many of them away from the LMS, he begged for more personnel from his senior missionary in GammNgwato. Like some *baruti*, Kgasa called the directors "*Bagolo*," Great Ones. "I am crying," he wrote. "The *Bagolo* do not pay any notice."[75]

To be accepted as an authority of any kind, the Rev. Kgasa had to position himself among the Tawana masters of the land in Maun, the Tawana town. The "Makoba [BaYei] and Mampukushu [HaMbukushu] are of a lower race. We are working among these people; our fathers started to work among them first, and they left it to us to carry on the work," Kgasa reported. Historic relations of servitude were transformed into those of instruction; *thuto* engendered this contradiction in all it touched. To Kgasa, such hierarchy only pointed all the more to the

---

[71] *Ibid.*; and J. Mutero Chirenje, "Chief Sekgoma Letsholathebe II: Rebel or 20th Century Tswana Nationalist?" *Botswana Notes and Records* 3 (1971), 64–69.

[72] LMS SA Reports 4/1, Serowe, for 1906 (A. Jennings).

[73] LMS SA 77/5, C. Reed to F. H. Hawkins, Serowe, 18/11/15, 13/12/15. Cullen Reed and a Ngwato deacon only once visited the BaTawana. The old man was intrepid, and set out by canoe to investigate the each riparian village in Somolekae's pastorate. It was then that he died of some tropical fever.

[74] LMS SA 79/1, C. Reed to F. H. Hawkins, Mababi Flat, 20/7/16; quote, Reports 6/4, Ngami for 1926 (R. H. Lewis); WCW/804, Ordination Examinations, Tiger Kloof, A. J. M. Kgasa. For Kgasa's dealings with the local "prophet" Samoxate, and the BaHerero, see Parsons, "Independency and Ethiopianism."

[75] LMS SA 89/1, A. Sandilands to F. H. Hawkins, Serowe, 8/1/27, enclosing correspondence especially from A. Kgasa to R. H. Lewis and others; Letters Nos. 1, 2, 6; LMS SA 89/2, Minutes of the SAEC, Hope Fountain 27-28/3/27. The LMS paid Kgasa £60 Sterling per year, ten pounds more than the going rate for ordained BaTswana, but Ngamiland's distance from the Cape made bought goods much more costly. The fact that Kgasa's wife died suddenly in Ngamiland added to his disquiet.

A missionary (probably Albert Jennings) and two *baruti* outspanned by their wagon while "intinerating," 1920s. Reproduced courtesy of the Council for World Mission, London.

necessity for a white missionary.[76] Kgasa stood firm against "custom," beer, *bogwera* initiation, and Tawana ancestral practices, all violations of Ngwato/LMS law; but without a white missionary, such laws were always in danger of seeming more Ngwato than not. With Khama's death in 1923, the fragile hold of the regime of the Word broke, and Kgasa and his lone Ngwato assistant living three weeks away could no longer cope. Kgosi Mathiba returned from Khama's funeral in Serowe and decided that he might thenceforth run "his" Church as he wished. In 1925 Kgasa quit, describing his entire tenure as a failure. At that time little, perhaps nothing, separated "members" from adherents in Maun. Christian Tawana masters refused to allow their Subiya and Yei servants to undergo Christian marriages, "for they say that will set them [the servants] free from slavery." Deacons held Communion as they pleased in the small marsh congregations outside the capital, many of which had fractured into "diffuse bodies." As the Rev. Arthur Sandilands, who took over the station, would comment, Maun deacons and deaconesses, mostly men and their wives, acted like "'chiefs' or 'headmen' of the church, in the tribal sense." Khama's death had stripped away the authority that supposedly belonged to the LMS. Left behind was a Church that quickly returned to the relations of power proper to Ngamiland.[77]

Our purpose in considering the Tawana Church stops here. The Rev. Sandilands began procedures drawn from his understanding of the Ngwato Church in Serowe, moving to institutionalize a defined Church elite. By 1929 the membership increased from 209 to 389 and, tellingly, the catechumenate from 176 to 1015. Sandilands nonetheless always felt a certain unease in Maun, viewing it as an "unsatisfactory" station. *Thuto* never found its center in Ngamiland, and life in the outskirt villages reflected this hollow. In 1936 the following was reported from the village of Kabamokoni in Ngamiland:

> [T]he people call the Christian faith boloi [witchcraft] or something that kills people that are not in it. . . . [W]e saw a young woman called Keatlhocwe who said: "I was married by a man who took my catechumen ticket and went and threw it into the river among the hippos, thinking I was going to bewitch him . . . but after that my husband fell sick and died."[78]

Evangelism as Itineration

Ngwato Church evangelists gathered for Christ while at the same time extending the hegemony of the kingdom. Overall it mattered little in this respect whether the

---

[76] LMS SA 83/3, Minutes of South African Executive Committee, Tiger Kloof, 5/8/20, A. Kgasa's report. I do not know how "lower race" was given in SeTswana. For the Herero, see Horst Drechsler, *Let Us Die Fighting* (London, 1980), 132, 154–56, 172 ff.; Kirsten Alnaes, "Living with the Past: The Songs of the Herero in Botswana," *Africa* 59, 3 (1989), 270 (267–99); and LMS SA Reports, Ngamiland for 1920 (A. Kgasa, 5/7/20). For Kgasa, ZKM, LMS TK Register 1904, No. 103, "Andrew M. Kgasa"; LMS SA 89/1, A. Sandilands to F. H. Hawkins, Serowe, 8/1/27, Letters Nos. 6, 7 and 9 cited.

[77] *Ibid.*, Letters Nos. 10, 14, 18, 21, 23, 24. Last two quotes: BNA, Sandilands Papers, A. Sandilands, "Annual Report for Maun, 1927," and "Annual Report for Maun, 1928"; LMS SA 92/Sandilands, A. Sandilands to Barradale, Maun 28/6/28.

[78] LMS SA 7/1, Ngami, for 1927 (A. Sandilands); LMS SA 93/Sandilands, A. Sandilands to Hawkins, Maun 27/3/31. Quote: BNA, Sandilands Papers, "Africa Calling!", Isaac B. Sekgwa, Jan. 1936.

evangelists were European or Tswana; both worked in the service of the realm of the Word. Before communities had their own *baruti* stationed with them, missionaries' itinerations, or circuits of travel, were essentially evangelistic. Thus the Revs. Mackenzie, Hepburn, Lloyd, and Willoughby all preached to unconverted BaTswana. Because before about 1910 Khama distrusted the zeal of the Church deacons, as we have seen, most of the formal evangelism out from the capital town was led by missionaries. Willoughby, for example, toured the Tswapong and Tshweneng Hills by donkey wagon in 1896, the very area of Raditladi's contentious evangelism in 1895.

Willoughby's account of his 1896 tour is revealing. First of all, Bessie Khama, Khama's eldest child, accompanied Willoughby (and A. J. Wookey) as their royal passport.[79] Secondly, the missionaries viewed their journey through a haze of romantic imagery, of "roughing it" under wet blankets, spurning the grace of local villagers who would have supplied food and lodgings. Although Willoughby sampled the *frisson* of potatoes boiling in a three-legged pot, it was his own pot, and tins of salmon and jam lay by its side. We recall that the Rev. Hepburn refused to teach the BaTawana beside his wife's wagon.[80] The domestic material of the tented wagons had to be kept from the more involved environment of evangelism itself. In later years, the Rev. Burns simply slept in his automobile when "camped" outside a village. Whether evangelical peers like Bessie Khama ate with her own people is not reported.[81] Thirdly, upon reaching each village, the evangelists met with the *kgosi* and freely entered his *kgotla* to preach to the people. Villagers gathered to hear them both as a matter of courtesy and out of obedience to the known will of their king, Khama. Their encounter with Willoughby's party at GooMoremi in the Tswapong Hills illustrates the relations of power within this program.

> Nobody knew us at Moremi's, and they doubted us and were not willing that we should outspan [note the biblical phrasing], though they feared to oppose us strongly lest we should be telling the truth. . . . Bessie & I went down to the village and chatted with Chief & people in *kgotla*: he soon believed that I was myself [and, of course, that Bessie was their king's daughter] and tried to atone for his coldness by making coffee. Not very nice, probably not very clean pot, but we drank a beakerfull. Wagon arrived after sunset. Sunday 30 Aug. Service morning & evening in the *Kgotla*.[82]

---

[79]   On later trips to Maun, for instance, a Christian royal came along to facilitate the use of private wells and, if necessary, "obtain the assistance" of people living along the route. LMS SA Reports 7/1, Serowe for 1927 (R. H. Lewis); 89/1 E. Sharp to Hawkins, Serowe, 28/2/27.

[80]   BNA Burns Papers, Micro 1334B, Burns to Millie Burns, Serowe, 24/7/38; Burns to McVicker, Serowe, 11/10/39. For the English roots of the Boys Brigade and Girls Guides, see Allen Warren, "'Mothers for Empire?' The Girl Guides Association in Britain, 1909–39," in J. A. Mangan, ed., *Making Imperial Mentalities: Socialization and British Imperialism* (New York, 1990), 96–109.

[81] This colonial self-positioning, as outsider (i.e., "camper") as opposed to indigene, had become so common by the 1930s that its symbology floated free from its referents. Rev. J. H. L. Burns thus used the khaki shorts of the colonial hunter to outfit his Serowe "Boys Brigade," a Tswana incarnation of Baden-Powell's Boy Scouts. Bestowing the "Camper's Badge" on BaTswana was just too bizarre, however, and even Burns declined to do so. But his reasoning went no deeper than this: Tswana boys "do not use tents."

[82]   *Sic* throughout. WCW/734, W. C. Willoughby, "Notes of Tour in Cwenin and Cwapon Hills, August 19th to Sept. 1st, 1896," 6–7.

Here we see the standard reliance on Ngwato prestige, and the inability of the people to refuse missionaries and evangelists entrance to the *kgotla* even if they wished to.

Khama himself sometimes accompanied missionaries on short itinerations, as he did with Edwin Lloyd in February 1909, Khama "in the character of a zealous missionary." The king encouraged people to school their children and reiterated his authority: "I thought, perhaps, you did not know me. So I came to let you see me. Here I am. I am Khama, your [king]!"[83] In 1910, the Rev. Lloyd visited Maunatlala and held services in the *kgotla*; he was given a hearty welcome and Christians and non-Christians alike brought gifts of meal and pumpkins. At this time, Khama still owned a *lesotla* nearby, a field tilled, sown, and harvested for him as tribute by local people; beyond that, Khama or a representative sometimes travelled through the region and collected enough grain to fill the outgoing wagon. It seems safe to say that as the villagers had rarely seen a missionary, they gave Lloyd harvest gifts largely in response to his evident association with the Ngwato capital.[84]

On itinerations, missionaries or ordained *baruti* baptized members' children, married couples vetted by the local congregation, and, in a village such as Ratholo with a respected *moruti* in charge, received new members into the Church on the *moruti*'s advice. By 1910 the larger villages in Tswapong, in Kalanga areas, and around Serowe and Shoshong had *baruti*, and often their own sub-outstations.[85] Less is known about their work, but its scope rivalled the missionaries'. Regional *baruti* increasingly mounted their own itinerations and revivals, and occupied nearby *dikgotla* with their congregations on days set aside for the purpose by local headmen and *dikgosi*. After these "revivals," a lone literate person was sometimes left in charge of a rudimentary "school" to teach the Bible as *thuto*.[86] As early as 1892 the Rev. Lloyd found Christians in a small village twenty miles north of Lehuhutu in the Kalahari. They owed their faith to "a Christian named Moshweu, who regularly holds services for the people, and induced a few to become inquirers."[87]

Because of the political centrality of the town, Ngwato evangelism almost intrinsically directed itself toward settled villages and therefore ignored low-status cattle-herding MaSarwa as well as surviving hunter-gatherers in the Kalahari. Some missionaries hardly viewed MaSarwa, also called Barwa (sing. Morwa) as persons. In one extraordinary communication, the Rev. Lewis asked Kgosi Sebele of the BaKwena to procure for him "a true Morwa woman" for his "observations . . . [of] steatopygracal

[83] LMS SA Reports, 4/2 Shoshong for 1909 (E. Lloyd).

[84] Mackenzie, *Ten Years North of the Orange River*, 366; Interviews: Mrs. Boikanyo Motlhagodi, with Ditaolo Motlhagodi, Lerala, 17 May 1990; Mr. Bonnetswe K. Dialwa, b. 1923, Lerala, 2 May 1990; Mr. Kereeditse Sesinye, b. approx. 1908, on the road to Ratholo, 20 April 1990; Mr. Lekgaritha Mokakapadi and wife, 19 May 1990, Moremi village; Diana Wylie, *A Little God*, 51; LMS SA 72/7, E. Lloyd to Thompson, Shoshong, 17/8/10.

[85] LMS SA Reports 4/3, Shoshong, for 1911–12 (E. Lloyd), and LMS SA 74/3, E. Lloyd to F. H. Hawkins, Shoshong, 11/1/12. The earliest outstation villages were Ratholo, under Moruti Noke Modisaokgosi, with twelve outstations; Sefhare, Tlhabala, Moijabana, Mogonono, and Makomi (Motsomi), and in BoKalaka Nswazwi, Nkange, and Magapatona also had Ngwato-paid *baruti* by 1902. I suspect this list is incomplete. See Parsons, "Khama III," 250–54.

[86] Interviews: The Rev. B. R. Tshipa, b. 1902, Serowe, 17 February 1989, English; Miss Dichetiso Balang, b. 1908, Serowe, 3 Nov. 1988.

[87] LMS SA Journals, 4/17, S.A. 1891–92, letter, 2/ or 27/2/1892. Cf. R. W. Ambler, "From Ranters to Chapel Builders," in Sheils and Wood, eds., *Voluntary Religion*, 319–37.

[*sic*] tendencies." Later, Lewis informed the Rev. Willoughby that a "specimen" had been "confined." His fixation on these women's bodies sat easily with his simultaneous concern for Tswana women and the Church issues affecting them; in one breath he wrote, "The names of the three Barwa girls which [*sic*] will be represented are Barari, Bagwapa & Bakuti. Returning to the Church question . . ."[88] Only decades later in the 1930s did the LMS make some effort to evangelize these people, and only after being accused of using MaSarwa "slaves" to tend LMS-owned cattle. The LMS's regional committee then launched defensive efforts to convert these cattleherds and foragers, many of whom were *batlhanka*, servants "owned" by about a hundred elite Ngwato households.[89] As one deacon recalls,

> We tried to teach them [MaSarwa], and they had a school built for them;
> but when rain fell, they just moved on, they left the school to go eat
> wild fruits in the desert. They did not have churches. They foiled us; we
> rode donkeys . . . and when they saw us they were afraid.[90]

How fluid were the barriers between MaSarwa *batlhanka* and gatherer-hunter "bushmen"? It is difficult to know, but at least for Ngwato Christians, the question was irrelevant. "MaSarwa" grazed cattle and lived, like cattle, in the veldt. They were a perenially scattered people, and the *phuthego* (congregation) was too opposed to their apparent lifeways; they "did not have churches."[91]

Evangelism as a Church Campaign

As Khama's wariness over the free distribution of *thuto* diminished with two decades of relative political quiet, the 1920s saw a new form of evangelism arise that soon dwarfed itinerations in importance. It was the Church-run evangelizing campaign—in SeTswana, *Tsosoloso*, Revival or Awakening.

It appears that the first construction of a campaign came from the Kuruman station, which conceived the idea after the flight of the region's peasantry from the onslaught of European settlement. Indeed the idea of "converting" held different ramifications south of Kuruman, where Christian Boers had expropriated land and

---

[88] ZKM Sm/49, R. H. Lewis to W. C. Willoughby, Molepolole, 9/10/07; Lewis to Willoughby (postcard), Molepolole, 15/11/07. I do not know where the girls were "represented." See Stephen J. Gould, "The Hottentot Venus," Ch. 19 in *The Flamingo's Smile: Reflections in Natural History* (New York, 1985), on *steatopygia* and the "Hottentot" labia minora. In 1932 a Protectorate official, S. Langton, was disciplined for taking pictures of MaSarwa's labias, Rey, *Monarch of All I Survey*, 252 n15.

[89] The charge stemmed from testimony by Simon Ratshosa after his exile for attempting to murder King Tshekedi Khama; motivated by other concerns, Resident Commissioner Rey "investigated" the institution of *bolata* (servitude) in GammaNgwato in 1931. Servants were not determined to be outright slaves, but their status became an issue with the liberal South African and British press. See Miers and Crowder, "The Politics of Slavery in Bechuanaland," 185–89, 192.

[90] Interview: Mr. Radikabari R. Thedi, b. 1903, Palapye, 19 Dec. 1988.

[91] As perceived at least by the BaNgwato; I interpret Tshekedi's remarks in this source as implying that MaSarwa were long seen as belonging to the land like fauna. LMS, *The MaSarwa (Bushmen): Report of an Inquiry by the SADC* (Cape Town, 1935). Edwin Wilmsen argues that indigenes were only drawn into unequal relationships with BaTswana this century. He summarizes the argument of his book (*Land Filled With Flies*) in "The Real Bushman is the Male One: Labour and Power in the Creation of Ethnicity," *Botswana Notes and Records* 22 (1990), 21–35.

uprooted Sotho-Tswana polities. The Church at Kuruman had to chase down their "once fellow citizens" to preach to them. Some villagers refused to pray with Moruti Maphakela Lekalake in 1912, who said that "the object and aim of the missionaries [was] to help people live better lives: [but] Chief Seneo stood up," and told the gathering that the nearby BaTlharo, having become Church people, had "suffered greatly from being such."[92]

This misfired campaign was only a preliminary. The first great Kuruman campaign occurred in 1926. Intended to reach the families of farm laborers who had been indentured on European-owned land after the Langeberg Rebellion of 1897, it was a revival in the sense that many of the people targeted were already Christians of one sort or another. Most significantly, the "Native Church" rather than the missionaries orchestrated and ran the project, and preached in both SeTswana and Dutch. Boers were "glad to hear services in their own language," which might have embraced SeTswana, since they happily attended those services as well. Over 500 new catechumens signed registers at Oliphants Hoek, where an ox was slaughtered "by an enthusiastic deacon."[93]

The Ngwato Church then began its own campaign toward the end of the Rev. Haydon Lewis's tenure in Serowe. Like Lloyd, Lewis sometimes itinerated with Khama at his side, allowing "a unique opportunity to urge the claims of Christ among a very large number of people."[94] Lewis also observed the Kuruman campaign in 1926 through his association with the LMS's district committee. That year he decreased Willoughby's three-year catechumenate promotion to a more manageable two-year class, and attracted seventy-seven "converts" in July. With Lewis's help, after the sorghum harvest of the following year, the Church's Serowe deacons mounted an evangelistic campaign right in town. It met with unprecedented success: 619 people confessed their faith, and 505 of them were new converts who then enrolled in the catechumenate. Never before had such a thing happened.[95]

What was more, a strange emotionalism emerged in the proceedings.

> One of the most memorable services was held on the Sunday morning when the Church itself was very full, and in the vestibule the people were standing as closely together as they could. Unfortunately at the close of the service a large [from here on the passage is crossed out] number of younger girls were seized with a form of hysteria, and what had been a very quiet and solemn service ended amid much tumult owing to the noise made by the women affected.[96]

---

[92] LMS SA 75/4, M. Lekalake, "Journey to the Kalahari Desert," by "my native helper," encl. in J. T. Brown to F. H. Hawkins, Kuruman, 7/5/12.

[93] LMS SA 86/2, Minutes of SADC, Tiger Kloof 25/4–1/5/24; 88/2, A. Jennings, "Fishing in Muddy Waters—The Kuruman Evangelical Campaign," 7/6/26. For the Langeberg Rebellion, see Kevin Shillington, *The Colonization of the Southern Tswana, 1870–1900* (Johannesburg, 1985), 240ff. Kuruman's mission was itself used as a prison in 1897.

[94] LMS Candidates Papers, 2nd series, Box 22, R. H. Lewis; and LMS SA Reports [box no. mislaid], Serowe for 1917 (R. H. Lewis). Lewis was in GammaNgwato from 1914 to 1928.

[95] LMS SA 88/1, Miss Gilbert to Barradale, Serowe, 8/2/26; 89/3, R. H. Lewis, "The Visit of the Native Advisory Council of the SADC to Serowe," 3–10/8/27.

[96] LMS SA 89/3, R. H. Lewis, "The Visit of the Native Advisory Council of the SADC to Serowe," 3–10/8/27. Lewis said he had not seen such an "outpouring" for many years, so this was not the first time.

Lewis lamely attributed the emotionalism to the "exceptional" visit of the Native Advisory Council of the district committee.[97] Undeterred, he encouraged the Church to prepare an even larger campaign for 1928. It too would be held in August, when the greatest number of people had returned to winnow, pound grain, and socialize in their villages.

Beginning on August 23, 1928, the Church set out to evangelize among eighteen villages in the Tswapong Hills.

> Our forces were composed of a strong contingent of Women Evangelists (in the care of the oldest really active member of the Church, Macosa a Deaconess . . .) along with 15 young men of the most devoted and earnest type.[98]

Lewis's mission automobile would arrive first, and he would arrange to sell the skins of the oxen that the Serowe Church members slaughtered to sustain themselves. Lewis's self-narrative reached for a more exalted explanation, however. Using the martial metaphors then current, Lewis wrote that the evangelists decided "to concentrate all our forces upon [Maunatlala] for three days, and then to divide forces, and attack the range of Hills from both the North and South." Thereupon, "[a]t each village our advent had been anticipated and camps for the women and the men had been made so as to admit of the maximum of privacy."

> On arriving at a Village, the first thing we did after getting settled down and arranging for the proper care of the cattle, was to have a meeting for prayer and preparation in the . . . Kgotla. Then in the evening, meetings were held in the various parts of the Village simultaneously. . . .[T]he women [would hold] their special service for the women of the village, which was always a very important item in each case.[99]

At one village, 115 people signed the register, and at the final stop in Lecheng, another 51. In total, 614 new names were collected. The missionary closed out each stop with a "straight talk" with local congregational leaders.

Shortly after this campaign, the LMS decided to shift Lewis to another station. Church women supposedly wept. On his departure, he estimated that 10,000 people met for worship any given Sunday morning, and that 50,000 people loyal to the LMS lived in GammaNgwato, "most of whom sometime . . . attend services."[100] James H. L.

---

[97] Missionaries referred to "orderly and quiet yet joyful" services, etc., compounding oxymorons. See Jean and John L. Comaroff's discussion in *Of Revelation and Revolution,* 239, and Interview: Moruti Maatlametlo Mokobi, b. 1901, Mahalapye 20 Jan. 1989, who recalls that Europeans discouraged too much emotion; LMS SA 89/3, E. Sharp to Barradale, Serowe 20/8/27.

[98] LMS SA 91/Lewis, "A Plenteous Harvest," in R. H. Lewis to Barradale, Serowe, 10/9/28, 1; hereafter "Harvest."

[99] "Harvest," 2, and 2–3.

[100] LMS SA 91/Jennings, A. Jennings to Barradale, Vryburg, 17/10/28; 91/Lewis, R. H. Lewis to Barradale, Serowe, 13/2/29; 92/Molete, Molete to Barradale, Serowe, 22/11/28.

Tshekedi Khama begged the LMS to allow Lewis to stay, but the LMS was unmoved. Resident Commissioner Charles Rey was pressing for Lewis's transfer because the missionary had opposed his efforts to limit Ngwato juridical authority. The "astounded" Church questioned the legality of Lewis's treatment, and an anonymous telegram from "Church and Tribe" startled the Society, reading, "If you remove Lewis kindly remove all your missionaries from Ba[mang]wato mission." The LMS stood firm, and Tshekedi soon backed down, wiring briefly that he would accept whomever the LMS chose. LMS SA 92/Serowe [Anon.] to Barradale, telegram, 29/12/28.

Burns, a Scotsman who had taught at Tiger Kloof, arrived as Lewis's replacement in April 1929. Burns held a far narrower view of what constituted a Christian, and wondered aloud how Lewis had arrived at his estimates. He also discovered that preparations for a second campaign had been moving ahead without him. Moruti Kelethokile Raditladi (ordained the following year) led the Church into the Shoshong hinterland, leaving the missionary in Serowe. "Without excitement or fuss," said Burns cautiously, the campaign signed up 760 people to the south and east of Serowe. Burns viewed the campaigns with deep ambivalence, however, and their days were numbered. His first action was to purge the rolls of the Church.[101]

A glance back at Graph 4.1 reminds us that by 1929 and 1930, the Church was essentially a female institution. It was three or four times as large as any other LMS Church in southern Africa. The evangelism of the late 1920s again attracted mainly women from among the unconverted.[102] By what means did it do so?

Birthing and Gathering: Two Discourses of Evangelism

The Rev. Lewis's portrayal of the 1928 campaign to the Tswapong Hills is basically an outsider's view, as his remark that women evangelists held "their own special service for the women" suggests. Much of the thematic content of the campaigns of the 1920s and 1930s was hidden not only from missionaries, but from all men.[103] Although difficult, it is important to try to approach the actual language of these meetings, to examine the interplay of gender and status in the encounter between the hinterland and royal women from the capital.

> We used to go to villages outside Serowe [in the 1920s and 1930s]. We went to spread the Word of God. We taught people about Jesus and God. And people understood, and they converted [*sokologa*], they turned about [*sokologile*] toward God.[104]

Women from Serowe, including royals like Semane and Bonyerile, her daughter, preached against drinking and brazenly equated local *badimo* (ancestors) with the "idols" of the Old Testament. Their messages assaulted local coherence and autonomy.

> Now, when we arrived in a village we would divide up, with *baruti* going to a different ward from the one we went to by lorry, and some of us going to another village/ward [*motse*]. We did not preach with the *baruti* even though they would come to where we were [later] to convert people there. We wrote them into the book of believers. We would report to the *baruti* when we reached a certain number. . . . We stopped

[101] LMS SA 90/Burns, J. H. L. Burns to Barradale, Molepolole, 23/10/28; Burns to F. H. Hawkins, Serowe, 1/10/29; Burns to Barradale, Serowe, 21/5/29; Burns to Hawkins, Serowe, 1/10/29; Burns to Chirgwin, Serowe, 28/10/29, 20/3/30. Burns's notion of an adherent was a registered enquirer. A conservative minister, his main impression after reading *Mein Kampf* was that Hitler was "an able man intellectually." BNA Burns Papers, Micro 1334 B, J. H. L. Burns to Millie, Serowe, 20/11/38 and 11/12/38.

[102] Judging from the gender of names in UCCSA Papers, Baptism Register for Serowe Parish, 1928–1950; although the majority of those who signed the *catechumen* register (now lost) did not reach the point of being confirmed and baptized; and *Reports of the LMS*, Vol. 79 (1929).

[103] Interview: Moruti Maatlametlo Mokobi, b. 1901, Mahalapye 20 Jan. 1989.

[104] Interview: Miss Dichetiso Balang, b. 1908, Serowe, 3 Nov. 1988.

in small hamlets/wards [*metsinyana*], while perhaps the *baruti* would
stop in the largest.[105]

What did they say to non-Christian women? One woman evangelist recalls:

> Women used to preach on their own, not with *baruti*! They spoke so as
> to encourage other women in Christianity; on the mightiness of God
> and . . . there was no difference between their words and the words of
> the *moruti*. Women seemed better than men, because when they taught
> as women . . . they converted people. For instance, [we] taught about the
> birth of Jesus and thus touched our feelings, we women; when [we]
> talked about the womb. Now, all we women are joined together in
> certain troubles of faith which make us think we can speak—Yes—just
> as well or better than men [to one another].[106]

Other women also recalled that the birth of Jesus was an important topic, both in
preaching and in examination questions; in contrast, the crucifixion and ascension
were hardly mentioned.[107] One woman explained,

> Who can help you other than God? . . . I mean, life on earth will never
> lack difficulties. Problems, for instance, like not being able to give birth
> well, a long time ago; then afterward, God heard our [my] needs.[108]

What problems were these, "about the womb," that made the story of a divine
birth poignant to women? Certainly women have worried about infertility and complications in giving birth from time immemorial (see Isaiah 54.1–4). For Tswana
women, however, and for great numbers of African women even today, childbearing
was of paramount importance. Syphilis and gonorrhea both struck at this central
concern. Now, one of Christ's main features to enquirers was his own miraculous
birth. As a healer, perhaps He might occasion new miracles among barren women.

> We taught the new confessors; we taught about the Bible and the birth
> of Christ. And about how when Jesus Christ went with people, he
> healed the sick.[109]

At the time that the Church planned its conversion campaigns, the Rev. Lewis
estimated that 75 percent of the Ngwato population had some form of venereal
disease. While this number was undoubtedly too high, and while such dicussions
may have encoded attacks on promiscuity, the problem was still real.[110] Unlike gon-

---

105   *Ibid.*

106   Interview: Ms. Oathokwa Samoele, b. 1918, Radisele, 18 Feb. 1989.

107   For instance, Interview: Mrs. Maatlametlo Mokobi, b. 1910, Mahalapye 14 Jan. 1989.

108   Interview: Mrs. Peter Mazebe Sebina, b. 1905, Serowe, 2 Dec. 1988; she added, "Today we have four
children, there might have been seven, but three passed away."

109   Interview: Mrs. Obolokile Sekga, b. approx. 1903, Serowe, 12 Nov. 1988.

110   LMS SA 91/Lewis, R. H. Lewis to Barradale, Serowe, 9/2/28 and 21/5/28. Work in the 1950s suggested that much of this "syphilis" was endemic syphilis and yaws, which declined over the first half of
the twentieth century and was largely replaced by the more intractable venereal syphilis; Vaughan, *Cur-
ing their Ills*, 137–38, citing, *inter alia*, A. M. Merriweather, "Endemic Syphilis—"Dichuchwa"—in the
Bechuanaland Protectorate," *Central African Journal of Medicine* 5 (1959), 181–85. For gonnorhea, see M.
Belsey, "The Epidemiology of Infertility: A Review of . . . Sub-Saharan Africa," *Bulletin of the World Health
Organization* 54 (1976), 319–41. Warnings about venereal diseases encoded Victorian morals in Britain;
Mort, *Dangerous Sexualities*, 156, 190.

orrhea, syphilis does not cause infertility, but it does lead to a syndrome now known as Pelvic Inflammatory Disease, which can cause ectopic pregnancies and prevent births. Livingstone remarked on venereal diseases among the BaKgatla in the 1840s, and syphilis was in Shoshong as early as 1885. Lewis was exposed to the medical complaints of a great many people, and other missionaries believed as he did. When Tiger Kloof retained a physician to write "advice" pamphlets translated into SeTswana, the first one, which was a great success, warned against the menace of venereal diseases. It was distributed to each LMS station in 1912.[111]

In the last chapter, we saw how women in congregations visited with one another and offered people a community in which to get well. An evangelical campaign was often the first such visit for barren women. It entailed a report of the miraculous birth of a great Healer. For many nonliterate listeners, its telling did not invoke perceptions of remote antiquity, as biblical events do in the West. Christ was born not so long ago, and His ability to heal sterility was vital evidence of his creation. Birth against the odds was His own ontology.

Ngwato Church evangelists also attracted converts by stirring their fears. This was the case in Ratholo in 1928, when more than a hundred girls rushed to the catechumen's register. Two now-elderly women, some of the only Tswapong people I could find who recalled the coming of evangelists from Serowe in 1928, remembered the campaign as having been led by Bonyerile, King Khama's daughter. Among other things, Bonyerile preached that locusts were coming and would bite unconverted people on the face. "We were frightened . . . it was not like [the preaching of] today!"[112] Many young people signed the enrolment register and then spread the warning to the cattle posts, whence others also left to sign the register. MmaWini, one of these women, gestured a "sign of Jesus," a cross, on her forehead to show me where the locusts would have bitten: "Right here." This was also a reference to baptism, which is said to leave the "mark of God."[113]

The text from which the Ngwato evangelists must have preached is Revelations 9:4, in which locusts destroy "not the grass on the earth . . . nor even a single tree," but only sting "people who lack the mark [*lotshwao*] of God on their foreheads and them alone."[114] Only those who were baptized would, in the prevailing interpretation, be protected on the place of baptism from this epitome of antisocial, "natural" force. Rev. 9:4 provided an especially apt image, in that the general phenomenon of a locust attack was personalized to the individual. She could protect

---

[111] The doctor was J. M. Mackenzie; Willoughby, *Tiger Kloof*, 114. See also Schapera, *Migrant Labour and Tribal Life*, 174–75; Livingstone in Seeley, "The Reaction of the Batswana," 81; LMS SA 75/3, F. H. Hawkins to R. W. Thompson, Tiger Kloof 22/3/13; BNA DCS 2/5 Serowe, Annual Report 1921–22 (1922); and *The South African Journal of Medicine* VI, 24 (1932), 805; and Barbara Brown, "Facing 'The Black Peril': The Politics of Population Control in South Africa," *Journal of Southern African Studies* 13, 3 (April, 1987), 268. Khama sought a doctor to treat a relation of his for syphilis in 1912, K III D/30/60, Khama to Phethu Mphoeng, Serowe, 11/5/12.

[112] This is utterly plausible, even though Lewis does not mention Bonyerile as one of the "Woman Evangelists" in the evangelists' party. Interview: Ms. Selebogo Mogame and MmaWini (Ms. Fetang), Lerala, 22 April 1990; in addition, Mrs. Miriam (MmaKgalemang) Tshinye, Lerala, 2 May 1990.

[113] Interview: Mr. Selo Mafoko, b. 1900, Lerala, 12 April 1990.

[114] As found in *Bibela e e Boitshepo* [1908] (Goodwood, South Africa, 1986), the Bible of the LMS in Southern Africa.

herself apart from other rites of ecological control that were always communal, and always performed by senior men.[115]

Moreover, the word *lotshwao* comes from the cutting of the ears of one's cattle or goats in a herd, to identify them, as already noted. If the greatest Shepherd was Christ, it was not lost on the people of Tswapong that the largest cattle-owner had been King Khama and was now his son Tshekedi, whose sister Bonyerile stood preaching before them. The proprietary senses of *lotshwao* connoted a "bringing together" under one allegiance. But unlike the "gathering" of the body politic by cattle-owners, the domain of *thuto* offered the trope to Christian women. Women evangelists further elaborated "gathering" as the Ngwato Church's gestalt by drawing on the abundant pastoralist imagery of the Bible. Miss Dichetiso Balang, a evangelist in the 1928 campaign, recalled:

> I had prepared lessons [*thuto*] which I myself took; I opened the Bible and [read] the words [*mafoko*] I had prepared to convert people. I distributed hymns which were about, for instance, searching for lost cattle. Think of Jesus, he saves the left-back ones! . . . I myself forget [how it goes] about finding strays. I'm not sure but it was Hymn 316. Luke chapter 15 the start of verse 11 [the prodigal son], about the child who was lost and then returns . . . and the hymn of "Lost Cattle, Think!" To save the lost ones, because the nation of the MoNgwato had gone astray not knowing it . . . but we called them to God, we converted them to know God. When they were lost, in blackest darkness![116]

Here a familiar array of images confronts us. Miss Balang pairs Luke 15:11–32 with Hymn 316; this is the story of the prodigal son, which ends, "your younger brother had died, but now he is alive; he had gotten lost [*latlhegile*], but now is found." Hymn 316, written down by the Rev. John Mackenzie, opens:

> Consider the stray cattle,
> Think about the dead,
> And don't let them fall to destruction;
> Cry for those-separating-themselves-to-do-evil [*baikepi*],
> And those-who-cannot-keep-up [*batenegi*],
> Show them their Saviour
> . . . Jesus saves the lost.[117]

Lost in darkness, they looked to the path leading toward the central kraal and *kgotla* in the kingdom of God, which was represented in the trusteeship of the kingdom of the BaNgwato.

The granddaughter of an early *moruti* recalls of him,

> I only know that some words in the Bible he said were, "Pride comes before a fall [*timelo*]." These are the words that he liked to say and to preach, which he emphasized to the people. That if you are proud, there is a *timelo*.[118]

---

[115] On locusts, see Ken Wilson, "Science, Authority and Ecology," unpub. paper, Nuffield College, Oxford, 10/3/90, 10; Interview: Mrs. Moswamasimo Molebalwa, Lerala, 27 March 1990.

[116] Interview: Miss Dichetiso Balang, b. 1908, Serowe, 3 Nov. 1988. I refer to Ditechiso Balang as Miss, because that was her preference.

[117] *Bibela e e Boitshepo;* and J. Mackenzie, "*Batla Matimela,*" Hymn No. 316, *Dihela,* 288–89. My trans.

[118] Interview: Ms. Gabotepele Ntsosa, b. 1910, Serowe, 27 Feb. 1989.

Timelo is a fascinating choice with which to denote "a fall," since it means "a getting lost," sharing its root with *matimela*, which means stray cattle. The flatness of the wide pasturage had replaced the verticality of a fall, and desocialization was the retraction of grace. As the 1930s and 1940s progressed, the wilderness of the veldt increasingly came to mean the disconnected life of Johannesburg and Francistown, mine labor, the abusiveness of white farmers, debts to merchants, and for many, the new loneliness of an abandoned old age. In the midst of all this, Ngwato rule persisted, and *baruti* and women emerged as *de facto* gatherers in rural villages.

In other words, not only *baruti*, but all Church members, and especially women, helped construct the realm of the Word. In their hands the Church sought to counter *timelo*, to bring stray cattle to the fold.[119] Women's evangelical messages were fraught with the tension of inequality; they touched on the capital's relations with a subordinated periphery, and indeed represented Christians as a herd or a flock. Even from within this framework, however, some among them alluded to a new strength, and whispered: are we not also now the cattle-owners?

---

[119] For a truly extended word play on this metaphoric mother lode, see the Rev. Jennings' conversation with Kuruman *baruti* during the 1932 drought (*Report of the LMS*, Vol. 137 [1931–32], 87), in Landau, "The Making of Christianity," 374.

7

Interference in Matters of Belief: Rape, Closed Spaces, and Colonial Complicity

The non-Christian section of the tribe has always been left free from interference in matters of belief. . . . There is no reason why Christians should not enjoy the same freedom.[1]
Athlone, high commissioner for South Africa, 1927

The Chief does not object to any religion. He refuses to have two.[2]
Keeditse Kgosietsile, Ngwato official, 1927

If *baruti*'s embodiment of the ideals of the Ngwato state made them invaluable to the kingdom, it also made them dangerous. In the realm of the Word, any "religious" factionalism on their part instantly became a "political" threat of high order. When Moruti Morwa revealed his partisanship for Sekgoma, Khama's wayward son, in 1899, he preached from Romans 1:16, saying, "there is no one who can stop me, Morwa, from preaching on the Evangelists . . . if I have sinned, I can be judged by the congregation but not by non-believers in a *kgotla*." His shocked regiment shouted, "take it all back!"[3] Morwa's position tore at the fabric of Ngwato authority.

If "religious" threats were political, "political" threats were also religious. This chapter examines the language and the historical terrain of three rebellions in the Ngwato kingdom. They reveal the efforts of the kingship to place citizenship over and above other particular identities, force *thuto* on unwilling subjects, and coerce outward signs of "conversion." The kingdom secured the cooperation of the

---

1   BNA S.218/5, Judgement delivered by H.C. (conveyed 2/27).

2   BNA S.34/5, Notes of a meeting held at Serowe, 7/1/27.

3   WCW/742, B. Kaleakgosi to W. C. Willoughby, Palapye, 22/11/1899, SeTswana.

Bechuanaland Protectorate in its efforts, emptying British ecumenical principles of their substance. In the following examination of the construction of power *in extremis*, the nature of the state alliances producing the Ngwato realm of the Word are starkly seen.

Several published works have given the three rebellions of the 1920s ethnic names, implying that preexisting groups were asserting a natural independence: BaKhurutshe, BaBirwa, and BakaNswazwi.[4] In fact this is a weak mode of explanation. The initial assertiveness of some Birwa and Khurutshe people, and of the Nswazwi chiefship (which had had a cohesive political identity for a long time) was connected to the marginalization of these ethnicities, all of which lay between recognized kingdoms or "districts" and were subject to larger, predatory economies. Nonetheless, those BaKhurutshe and BaBirwa who confronted the kingdom effectively abjured their ethnicities and had good reasons for doing so. The sale of some "Birwa" land to the British South Africa Company (BSAC) and then to white South African ranchers provoked a Birwa chief, Malema, pointedly to reject any notion of ethnic unity. Similarly, under the territorial rule of the Tati mining company, the BaKhurutshe living at Tonota lost their Khurutshe coherence.

The Voluntary Movement of Khurutshe People

Oral traditions link the early history of Khurutshe "ethnicity" to the Transvaal MaTebele. The Khurutshe chiefly lineage grew out of a faction of the BaHurutshe (the senior Tswana ethnicity), which had received aid from MaTebele mercenaries. The same traditions tie the BaKhurutshe to the BaNgwato; the Ngwato *kgosi* Mathiba was initiated in a *bogwera* with the Khurutshe heir sometime in the late eighteenth century.[5] The BaKhurutshe took to the north, where they soon split into smaller groups, sometimes even households. Some fell under tributary protection of the still tiny Ngwato regime of Kgari, the father of Sekgoma I. One section settled permanently with the BaNgwato to form the basis of the capital town's Khurutshe ward, one section spread over the Tswapong Hills, and one group crossed into what is now Zimbabwe, eventually to be ruled by the Ndebele. After thirty years, these BaKhurutshe hamstrung the Ndebele cattle under their care and fled to the confluence of the Shashi and Ramokgwebama rivers. There they pleaded with Khama's father Sekgoma I for protection. Sekgoma I is said to have replied, around 1864, "Tell Kgosi Sekoko to bring the

[4] Diana Wylie, *A Little God: The Twilight of Patriarchy in a Southern African Chiefdom* (Middletown, Conn., 1991), 150, 155, 157, for instance, first follows Chirenje and others in treating the rebelling groups as "the Birwa" or "the Khurutshe," although in the end ethnicity is said to be a "tool for making and denying political claims," and Christian sects the "fora" for those claims; see also Fred Morton and Jeff Ramsay, eds., *The Birth of Botswana: A History of the Bechuanaland Protectorate from 1910 to 1966* (Gaborone, 1987), 66–67, 74. Less credibly, Ramsay sees the rebelling groups as protonationalist, because they attacked the rights of Tswana kings and chiefs, and drew on modern resources like legal representation and the press. The best narrative of Malema's BaBirwa's rebellion is Parsons, "Khama III," 383–98; Parsons also touches on the BaKhurutshe of Tonota, 265, 381–82.

[5] Isaac Schapera, *Handbook of Tswana Law and Custom* [1938] (London, 1955), 304, 313. Madisakwane was the Khurutshe heir.

morafe home." Sekoko's son, Rawe, succeeded Sekoko under King Khama's rule, while he and his people were living with other BaKhurutshe in the capital at Shoshong.[6]

In 1866, a German discovered gold along the small Tati River between the Shashi and Ramokgwebama rivers. A syndicate formed and acquired a prospecting concession under Protectorate jurisdiction, but better finds on the Witwatersrand drew interest away from the Tati, and the "Company" was poorly capitalized. The British reaffirmed the Company's control over the Tati area in 1893 in such a way as almost to guarantee future abuses.[7] Bent on turning a profit, the Tati Company approached Rawe and asked him to move his people back to the confluence, where Rawe had maintained cattle posts. Kgosi Rawe would then collect rent and taxes not only from his own people, but also from the various Kalanga groups around him. Moreover, he was charged with supplying 10 percent of the region's adult men for the low-yield, low-pay Tati mines in Francistown. Problems between Kgosi Rawe and the Company developed almost as soon as he and his people arrived in Selepeng, his new village. In addition Rawe stirred ethnic resentment in pushing Kalanga adolescents to fulfil the bulk of the labor levy for the "filthy and demoralizing" mines.[8]

The Rev. A. J. Gould of the LMS began work in Selepeng in November 1898, also ministering to nearby peoples. His mission had no institutional link to the Ngwato Church, nor even to the LMS's Bechuanaland District Committee. Gould noted that many BaKalanga seemingly acknowledged "the Chief of the BaKhurutshe as their head," and so he began in Selepeng with high hopes. Tumedi, a local Khurutshe evangelist whom the Rev. Hepburn had trained, appeared to be "a very exemplary man." Ten "senior deacons" assisted Gould, even though the congregation only comprised forty-nine persons. Perhaps it worried him that roughly half the male members were thus known as *baruti*, and that most of his Church members had come from the Ngwato capital. Still, around this core, over 500 "adherents" would congregate on some Sundays, and the congregation grew.

As the months and years passed, the Rev. Gould's enthusiasm waned. His reports speak of "retrogression" and dissipation, and his ill temper began to frighten and irritate his deacons. Kalanga people were disenchanted with Rawe, married polygynously, and dropped away from the Selepeng ministry. Gould also fought with Moruti Tumedi, who was a more popular man. When Tumedi left the LMS and took a second wife, he formed the "Khurutshe Free Church" in opposition to

---

[6]   BNA BNB 9890, History of the Bakhurutse (the Phofu group) and the Bakalanga of Botswana—Oral Tradition (Institute of Adult Education), collected by D. M. Malikongwa and C. C. Ford, Sept. 1979 (including quote); other traditions echo Malikongwa's sketch, albeit from various subjective positions; Isaac Schapera, "The Early History of the Khurutshe," *Botswana Notes and Records* 2 (1970), 1–5; Mackenzie, *Ten Years*, 293–97.

[7]   Isaac Schapera, "Report and Recommendations Submitted to the Bechuanaland Protectorate Administration on the Native Land Problem in the Tati District, 1943," [reprinted in] *Botswana Notes and Records* 3 (1971), 223.

[8]   LMS SA 69/1 C. Reed to R. W. Thompson, Dombodema, 10/2/08; I. Schapera, "Report . . . Tati District," 224–25; Henderson M. Tapela, "The Tati District of Botswana" (Ph.D. dissertation, University of Sussex, 1976), 62–63, quote 71–72.

Gould. Around this time, Gould observed of the people around him that they seemed to view him as a "wizard."[9]

BaKhurutshe continued to join Kgosi Rawe's settlement even as his relationship with the Tati Company deteriorated.[10] Although King Khama had given permission to BaKhurutshe to leave the kingdom for Selepeng with their cattle and possessions, as late as 1902 a Ngwato governor attempted to extort cash for the privilege. A *kgotla* case in January 1903 whitewashed their shoddy treatment and underlined their low status in the nexus of Ngwato and Protectorate politics.[11] As they came to Selepeng, the social life there grew more anxious. Anger toward Gould swelled to the point where he had to leave. Even then, Rawe noticed that those who joined up with a fresh LMS congregation (and refused to touch beer) seemed to disrespect his authority. And despite his strategic polygynous relationship with Khama's daughter Babonye (or because of it), Rawe's dealings with BaNgwato were not warm.[12] He wished to have nothing to do with the Ngwato Church, and so the Rev. Cullen Reed found Selepeng's women "particularly unruly, even insolent." The instability of Rawe's reign was reflected in the turbulence of Khurutshe ecclesiastic shifts. Beyond Moruti Tumedi's "Free Church," Rawe and some Christians probably collaborated with nearby BaKalanga in cultic ceremonies for Mwali, the Kalanga high God. In 1908 Tumedi took his ten or twelve Church members into the Anglican faith, possibly aided by a Xhosa chaplain on the emerging Anglican "Railway Mission."[13]

Perhaps life was still tolerable in these years because of some unusually wet and productive agricultural seasons around Selepeng. Unhappily, the insolvent Tati Company had used the time to negotiate a new arrangement with the Protectorate government. Under this agreement, the BaKhurutshe would have to move in 1908, this time to a small piece of land "rented" from the company. Remarking that his situation made "everyone feel like a fugitive," Rawe led his people to the appointed territory, a "waterless" and narrow strip to the

9   LMS SA Reports, 3/1, Selepeng for 1899, 1900; 3/2, Selepeng for 1901, 1902, and 1903 (A.J. Gould); LMS SA 62/2, C. Reed to LMS, Plumtree, 17/9/03. Tumedi's first wife had gone blind, and his taking of a second may well have been an act of kindness to her. See also, Parsons, "Independency and Ethiopianism," 63; and Parsons, "Khama III," 265. "Wizard," LMS SA 3/2, Selepeng for 1903 (A.J. Gould).

10   Interview: Mrs. Tsogang Serema, b. 1901, Palapye, 7 Dec. 1988.

11   K III A/5/36, Acting A.C. (Nettleton) to Khama, Palapye, 1/10/02; A/5/37, Khama to A.C. Palapye, Palapye, 1/11/02; A/5 F. Edleston for Acting A.C. Palapye to Khama, Palapye, 16/6/12; A/6/7, A/6/8, Mojewa's [and others'] testimony, Serowe, 14/1/03 and Francistown, 9/4/03. The governor at Mmadinare, Mongwe, apparently extorted £5 sterling from six men in return for securing Serowe's permission for their departure, which he never did.

12   BNA S.178/1 A. J. Gould to Col. Panzera, Selepeng, 13/9/04. Khama III Papers H/60/"1904-5," [Unsigned] to Mma Semana Setlhoko, 10/10/14 (?). See Nancy Rose Hunt, "Noise Over Camouflaged Polygyny, Colonial Morality Taxation and a Woman-Naming Crisis in Belgian Congo," *Journal of African History* 32, 3 (1991), 471–94.

13   Richard Werbner links the BaKhurutshe to the Ramokgwebama Mwali shrine in "Regional Cult of the God Above," in Werbner, *Ritual Passage, Sacred Journey* (Washington, D.C., 1989), 245–99, and Moyo J. Mtutuki draws on interviews to report a 1911 joint prayer meeting with adepts, in "The Mwali Cult in Northern Botswana (Some Oral Traditions), c. 1893-1976)" (B.A. thesis University of Botswana, Lesotho, and Swaziland, 1976), 16; and BNA S.178/1, A. Gould to Col. Panzera, Selepeng, 13/9/04; LMS SA 66/ 4, C. Reed to R. W. Thompson, Dombodema, 26/12/05; 76/4, Reed to Thompson, Plumtree, 20/4/06; 66/ 2, A. Jennings to Thompson, Serowe, 7/4/05; 68/4 C. Reed to R. W. Thompson, Plumtree, 30/9/07.

north of Selepeng. They lost nearly all their old grazing land, and the normal space between village household and agricultural fields collapsed. At the same time, Rawe was charged with the unpopular duty of collecting the new hut tax in the area.[14]

From this point on Rawe's actions seem increasingly haphazard, as he cast about for ways to rebuild his alliances and survive as *kgosi*. Requesting a new LMS missionary, he tried to extend his domain in a Ngwato-style Church, with Khurutshe *baruti* at the Kalanga outstations. This effort failing, he apparently joined the Anglicans with Tumedi, believing that he could then be married to several women and so cement his alliances. To his chagrin, the LMS Christians under him defected to the rival authority of a kinsman.[15] In 1910 the rains came so late that the sorghum harvest shrank to nothing and people had to rely on their smaller plantings of millet. At the same time, the Tati Company abandoned its profitless mining operation and began selling off its land to white farmers, who charged BaKhurutshe with impoundment fees for stray cattle. Rawe only looked again to the LMS for a *moruti*, trying to heal useless rifts, and perhaps seeking ritual assistance to make rain.[16]

Then in 1912 and 1913 a great drought came, the worst since 1862.[17] As Richard Werbner has argued, the conjunction of this drought with the severe spatial limitations of the Tati Company's "tribal territory" proved too much for Rawe. As his people began to scatter in order to survive, he asked Khama if he might move them across the Shashi River, leaving a rump village under another kinsman amongst the scattered Kalanga settlements.[18]

Khama asked the government to ascertain whether the BaKhurutshe were prepared to abide by his laws, and whether they would pay their hut tax through him.[19] He and Rawe, with their senior headmen, then came to terms; their written agreement, signed on the 4th of July, specified that the incoming BaKhurutshe acknowledge Khama as their king, drink no beer, and obey all his laws, "some of which" (*e e mengwe*) are here recorded. This must have been a key provision, since BaNgwato later insisted—and Khama's letters imply—that both parties had agreed that Anglicanism be abandoned in favor of the Ngwato Church. That Rawe never denied this alerts us again to the hesitant way literate people began to integrate

---

[14] Richard Werbner, "Land and Chiefship in the Tati Concession," *Botswana Notes and Records* 2 (1970), 10 (6–13).

[15] Interview: The Rev. B. R. Tshipa, b. 1902, Serowe, 17 February 1989, English; LMS SA 87/1, R. H. Lewis to F. H. Hawkins, Serowe, 19/3/25; 69/1 C. Reed to Thompson, Plumtree, 25/2/08; Reed to Thompson, Hope Fountain, 13/4/08; 69/3, Report by Mr. Wm. Carleton to Matebeleland District Committee [hereafter MDC] on Selepeng District, n.d. (1908); 71/1 Reed to Thompson, Plumtree, 6/2/09; 84/4 R. H. Lewis to Andrew Reed, Serowe, 5/6/22. According to the Rev. Tshipa, some LMS members resettled Selepeng under Mpotokwane Maunya, before Rawe came to Tonota in 1913. The details are unclear (i.e., when did Babonye leave Rawe and return to Serowe?), but I believe Wylie, *A Little God*, 157, is incorrect in having Rawe convert to Anglicanism in 1904.

[16] LMS SA 72/5 A. Jennings to R. W. Thompson, Serowe, 6/1/10; C. Reed to Thompson, Plumtree, 7/3/10; S.34/5 Asst. Comm. (Daniel), Francistown to G.S., Francistown, 15/5/13; Interviews: The Rev. B. R. Tshipa, b. 1902, Serowe, 17 Feb. 1989 and 22 Feb. 1989, English.

[17] LMS SA Reports 4/4, Shoshong for 1912 (E. Lloyd); 5/1, Serowe for 1913 (A. Jennings), and Shoshong for 1913 (E. Lloyd); LMS SA 76/2, E. Sharp to F.H. Hawkins, Serowe 19/1/14.

[18] Werbner, "Land and Chiefship," 11–13.

[19] BNA S.34/5 Capt. Hannay to A.C. (Daniel) Francistown, Palapye, 25/5/13.

texts with other modes of communication. "It wasn't written down" was not a relevant legal point.

What is recorded is Rawe's desire to establish an Anglican church and school; Khama put him off until he had discussed the matter with Major Rowland Daniel, Francistown's senior official. The answer was no.[20] Khama's decision was his standard one. For instance, he effectively duplicated it for Chief Samuel Maherero's refugee OvaHerero only a few years later. Most refugee Herero Christians moved to Mahalapye southward on the rail line in 1922, in part as herders of royal cattle, and Tshekedi sent a Ngwato ward there to supervise them years later. Few of them became devoted Ngwato Church people, but neither did they import any Moravian priest.[21]

Kgosi Rawe's BaKhurutshe would prove less tractable. Approximately 2,600 men, women, and children, with over 8,000 cattle and 10,000 sheep and goats, settled in Tonota.[22] Rawe claimed he had incomplete control even over his relatively few subjects. "About the making of beer, we will abstain from making it. But I dare say that if any of my people be found with beer I must not be found guilty, for somebody may [be] making it without being allowed."[23] Soon enough Khama began to chastise him for letting his people drink beer and entice nearby Ngwato citizens to do the same. "Do you go with them [to drink], where you let them hold you by the ears? They say you drink beer yourself. . . . Mark my words: *Bojalwa* is prohibited here in my country." 1913 and 1914 were still drought years, "starving times" for Rawe's people, which exacerbated the problems of their immigration. Khama was unrelenting, reminding Rawe in 1915 that "when you came to this country we spoke of *thuto* and of beer."[24] The LMS gave the Ngwato king complete support. The Rev. Willoughby advised the king on how to bar the Anglican "railway mission" from his country, and he conspired secretly to intercept and ward off the Rhodesian bishop at the border.

[20]   Rowland Mortimer Daniel was assistant resident magistrate in Serowe from 1904; assistant (resident) commissioner for the Northern Protectorate, based in Francistown, from 1908; acting resident commissioner from 1926 to January 1928; and resident commissioner of the Bechuanaland Protectorate in 1928; see Crowder's list in Rey, *Monarch of all I Survey*, 237–38 n7. BNA S.34/5 Hannay to A.C. Francistown, Serowe, 26/6/13; Acting A.C. to Asst. R.C., Francistown, 1/7/13; LMS SA Reports, Serowe, for 1913; BNA S.34/5 A.C. (Daniel) to Acting R.C., Francistown 7/7/13; and K III D/31/74, Khama to Rauwe Sekoko, Serowe, 22/7/13.

[21]   LMS SA 75/1, J. T. Brown to R. W. Thompson, Kuruman, 24/1/13; Reports, Serowe for 1914-5 (R. H. Lewis), and Serowe for 1918 (R. H. Lewis), incl. quote; B. B. Kebonang, "The History of the Herero in Mahalapye, Central District, 1922-84," *Botswana Notes and Records* 21 (1989), 43–52; see n19, n21 esp.; Reports, Ngami for 1921 (R. H. Lewis). See my "Making of Christianity," 390–91, which describes the mode by which Khama and Maherero inducted over 200 people directly into the Church.

[22]   BNA S.34/5 Hannay to A.C. Francistown, Serowe, 26/6/13. Although Assistant Commissioner Daniel would remark that Rawe ruled upwards of 8,000 people, his estimate was derived from hut-tax receipts and so included thousands of BaKalanga of uncertain loyalty.

[23]   Quote: BNA S.34/5 Rawe to Res. Mag., 29/5/13; S.601/12, R.M. Serowe to G.S., Serowe, 30/5/24; S.218/5, Interpreter to R.M., Serowe, 13/6/31; K III E/33/34, Khama to Rauwe Sekoko, Serowe, 14/3/16; E/33/15, Khama to Rauwe Sekoko, Serowe, 3/2/16.

[24]   With reference to "holding ears," it is not clear whether Khama here means "conspire with you," with would be interesting. This would normally be given as "to bite your ear," *go loma tsebe*. The king might simply have wished to compare Rawe to a small child being led about, K III E/32/42, Khama to Rawe, 27/11/14; F/46/24, J. Haskins to Khama, 23/1/14; second quote, K III Papers E/33/97, Khama to Rauwe [*sic*] Sekoko, Serowe, 16/12/15.

On Willoughby's advice, Khama placed Moruti Tumedisho Maruapula at Tonota, to superintend the behavior of Khurutshe's people and report back to Serowe.[25]

Rawe died in 1918, and his brother Nkobelele, backed by Khama, took over in Tonota.[26] It may have been no more than the 1920 arrival of about ten nominally "LMS" households under Rawe's relative Molefhe that, in reaction, rejuvenated Anglicanism in 1922.[27] Relations with Serowe soured when the king heard that the teachings of the Church of England had entered Tonota. Khama soon burned down Molefhe's followers' rondavels and threatened Kgosi Nkobelele with the same treatment, coupling his warning with accusations of *bojalwa* drinking, as usual. "Gather [your people] and ask them if they are not looking for trouble [*kgang*], in my country with two *thutos*. The sole *thuto* that we began with is that of the LMS. I shall never agree to another."[28]

In April of that year, a Francistown merchant reported to Khama that Kgosi Nkobelele had asked him to buy various materials for building a church. (Such merchant intelligence was not at all unusual: it made sense to stay in the king's good graces.)[29] After further investigation, Khama ordered one of his representatives in Tonota to call the BaKhurutshe together and notify them of his awareness of their insolence. Kgosi Nkobelele then tried an evasion, explaining that although he himself had favored a tent, Tumedi had assured him a solid structure was acceptable because it would be a school, not a church [*kereke*]. The Ngwato man jeered at the distinction, noting that the "house of schooling [*thuto*] is the foundation of a church," and attempted to send Nkobelele to Serowe to report directly to King Khama.[30] No word of this episode seems to have reached the British.

Upon succeeding his father, King Sekgoma II continued to harass Nkobelele's BaKhurutshe for "drinking beer," and in 1924 he sent a Church party to Tonota to investigate. The Rev. Baruti Kaleakgosi and two junior *baruti* (Molepane and Kgoarego) met up with the Rev. Tumedisho Maruapula in Tonota and confronted the Anglicans, who denied building a church but admitted travelling to Francistown to worship there. The exchange between these men was later recalled as heroic: Molepane told the Anglicans they had been sent to "castrate" the followers of the Church of England. He received the retort, "You have not the power to castrate the H.[oly] S.[pirit]."[31]

[25]   K III G/50/34, W. C. Willoughby to Khama, 26/5/14; G/50/36, W. C. Willoughby to Khama, Tiger Kloof 7/7/14; R.M. Francistown to G.S., Francistown 22/4/27. LMS Reports, Serowe for 1913 (A. Jennings, 1914); LMS SA 75/6, Khama to F.H. Hawkins, Serowe 23/12/13; 76/3, W. C. Willoughby to F.H. Hawkins, Tiger Kloof 8/4/14. See also Rev. R. Lieta's idiosyncratic essay, "The Origin of the Anglican Church in Botswana," University of Botswana, *Religion in Botswana Project*, 3 (1984), 32–50.

[26]   Wylie's passage on these admittedly foggy events appears to be inaccurate, *A Little God*, 158; I have seen no mention of a Ramosenyi succeeding Rawe outside of Schapera, *Praise-Poems of Tswana Chiefs*, 241; see BNA S.34/5 Asst. R.M. Serowe to Acting G.S., Serowe 11/6/18. Of course, one hesitates to contradict Schapera without excellent evidence.

[27]   Parsons, "Khama III," 381–82 for Molefhe's and Tumedi's complex movements.

[28]   BNA S.601/12, R.M. Serowe to G.S., Serowe, 30/5/24; K III E/33/83, Khama to Kgosi Nkobelele Sekoko, Serowe, 10/2/19; E/36/44 Khama to Nkobelele Sekoko, Serowe, 8/1/22.

[29]   K III F/43/23, E. J. Phillips to Khama, Francistown, 22/4/22; see Croston, "An Economic and Social History of Freehold Land," 246.

[30]   K III H/59, M. Mokatane to Khama, Tonota, 23/10/22; and 3/11/22.

[31]   BNA S.34/5, Extract from "Bell's Report," dated 6/3/26. The sole source here is three BaKhurutshe who ran away from Serowe to report to the Anglican Bishop at Francistown, and so would be hostile to Kaleakgosi and Tumedisho.

Sekgoma then fined Nkobelele and a handful of senior men twelve head of cattle. Three animals were the punishment for beer-drinking; the other nine were for introducing Anglicanism into the Ngwato kingdom.[32] In September 1925 rumors circulated that Sekgoma intended to move the people of Tonota by force to Serowe. The king complained to sympathetic officials like Police Capt. H. D. Hannay that "Rawe's people" were drunken scofflaws, and Hannay added his official stamp. The only firm charge was that the Anglicans had refused invitations to Serowe and lagged in hut tax receipts. Few were surprised, however, when Serowe's *kgotla* unanimously resolved to move the "rebellious" BaKhurutshe to Khurutshe ward in Serowe, and Sekgoma got ready to make his case before the Protectorate government.[33]

It is worth pausing to note that, in contrast to the cattle- and people-gathering BaNgwato, Rawe's "BaKhurutshe" never attained enough coherence to embrace any sort of congregational hierarchy, nor to attract British support. In weakness as in strength, political and religious resilience depended on each other.

The Forced Movement of the Tonota Anglicans

Sekgoma's death in 1925 suspended these issues, but Tshekedi took them up again upon his succession. With the Ratshosa brothers safely in prison and in exile, the young Tshekedi fast made friends with the Ngwato Church and formed a close relationship with the Rev. Haydon Lewis. In mid-September 1926, Tshekedi ordered several residents of Tonota to come to Serowe. They refused and sought shelter at the local police camp, until B.P. Police Sergeant Lord received orders to "tell" them to obey Tshekedi, which they apparently did.

One of the Anglicans so ordered, Maifhala, then wrote several letters of protest to the South African press, and one letter to the Anglican priest, Peter Sekgoma,[34] asking the priest to seek help for his "seventy-nine" co-religionists in Tonota. Sadly for them, Father Peter's loyalties lay with his close cousin Tshekedi, and he merely forwarded Maifhala's letter to Serowe, appending a note of his own blaming Nkobelele for allowing renegades to attend Anglican mass![35] It may have been these letters that landed in the lap of Rowland Daniel, the then acting resident commissioner. Daniel now realized that "in the year 1925, the Bakhurutsh[e] who believed in the Church of England were prosecuted." This gave him pause. "It is difficult to believe," he pondered, that Sekgoma II "punished them for mere belief in a certain religious creed. ... [T]he subject of this matter is verging upon very delicate

[32]   BNA S.34/5, H.C. (Athlone) to Dominions Office (L.S. Amery), Cape Town, 9/2/27. There were other complications to this conflict as well; BNA DCS 9/1 Sekgoma Papers, R.M. to A.C., Francistown, 5/5/24 and A.C.to G.S., Francistown 4/6/24.

[33]   BNA S.34/5 Acting R.M. (Hannay) to G.S., Serowe 19/9/25.

[34]   Peter was the son of Mokhutshwane Sekgoma, who fled from Khama with his half-brothers Raditladi and Mphoeng and his full brother Seeletso, to live in exile near Francistown. Peter had nonetheless been raised with Tshekedi in Serowe, Interview: The Rev. Father Haskins Sekgoma, b. 1903, Serowe, 31 May 1989, English.

[35]   BNA S.34/5, Peter Sekgoma to Tskekedi, Francistown, 2/10/26, in translation; M. Morapedi to Bishop of Kimberley, Tonota, 30/6/26.

ground."[36] Kgosi Nkobelele, who had chosen sides and wisely allied himself with the kingdom, advised Tshekedi from Tonota that all Anglican BaKhurutshe had best be evacuated as soon as possible. Daniel, himself an Anglican, wondered what was the "real" offense that had led to the crisis. Such a tough nut was best dealt with by letting it drop. If only the Anglicans were not such tireless agitators. The *Cape Times* of 12th October, 1926, carried the story of alleged religious persecution, and Maifhala claimed that Ngwato officials had flogged Anglicans in Serowe.

It must be remembered that most administrative officials in Serowe were Anglicans. As if responding to imperial protocol, Tshekedi promptly reframed the problem as one of disobedience to property laws. Khama had stipulated, said Tshekedi, that Anglican services might be held on the Tati side of the Shashi, but "he would not allow a church to be built [on the Ngwato side] as he considered the [LMS] sufficient." Anglicanism already claimed several members of the Ngwato royal family, descendants of Mphoeng's followers who seceded in 1895.[37] Besides Peter Sekgoma, the Anglican Father Haskins Sekgoma was one of them. Named after a local white merchant, Haskins attended a Francistown school and secretly ministered to Tonota's Anglicans in the late 1920s. In those days, "I must come by night—you understand me—and then, run up in back [of houses of BaKhurutshe]," he said. "We [sometimes] took the whole day in Tonota, we tried to hide ourselves."[38]

Although Tshekedi had "no intention" of interfering with religious practices *per se*, said a congenial Serowe Magistrate's report, "those who did not belong to the [LMS] need not stay at Shashi but could worship in the Tati [area] or otherwise they should come to Serowe." In fact BaKhurutshe did cross the Shashi River specifically to hold services on the farm of Mr. James Haskins (Rev. Haskins' namesake), a farm bought from the Tati Company; and to buy beer from Kalanga beer-sellers unofficially licensed by the same Company. Beer was the red flag.[39] The Anglicans were presented with a stark choice: behave or move to Serowe for closer surveillance.

By December, these matters had reached the British high commissioner, the earl of Athlone.[40] He wrote to Jules Ellenberger, resident commissioner for the Protectorate, and ordered the agreement on *thuto* between Rawe and Khama rendered null and void since it constituted "interference with free exercise of religion."[41]

---

[36]   BNA S.34/5, Acting R.C. (Daniel) to R.M. Serowe, Mafeking 16/9/26; Lieta, "Origin of the Anglican Church," 40.

[37]   Head, *Serowe: Village of the Rain Wind*, 34–36, interview with William Duiker, Anglican Archdeacon of Botswana; S II A/DB/8, Tshekedi to "Father," Serowe, 4/10/26, English. Despite his position, Peter himself had held services including the BaKhurutshe in Francistown, Interview: The Rev. Father Haskins Sekgoma, b. 1903, Serowe, 31 May 1989, English.

[38]   Interview: The Rev. Father Haskins Sekgoma, b. 1903, Serowe, 31 May 1989, English. Haskins Sekgoma also noted that he himself was not really that frightened, because "I am of the royal family."

[39]   BNA S.34/5, R.M. Serowe to G.S., Serowe, 13/9/26; A.C. to R.M., Francistown, 9/11/26.

[40]   The earl of Athlone, grandson of Victoria, and high commissioner of South Africa from 1923 to 1930. Athlone had responsibility for the High Commission territories, Swaziland, Basutoland, and Bechuanaland.

[41]   Lieta, "Origin of the Anglican Church," 41, citing H.C. to R.C., Cape Town, n.d. Jules Ellenberger, born 1871, was the resident commissioner of the Bechuanaland Protectorate from 1924 to 1927, but as such actually lived in Mafikeng (spelled Mafeking by the British) in the Northern Cape. He reported to the high commissioner. Jules Ellenberger's father was a famous Paris Evangelical Missionary Society missionary to the BaSotho, and Jules's wife was none other than M. Casalis's daughter, so he was no stranger to southern African kings' dealings with missions. See Rey, *Monarch of All I Survey*, 237 n5; and F. H. Hawkins, *Through Lands That Were Dark* (London, 1914), 57.

Ellenberger then suggested that someone lecture Tshekedi on the principle of religious freedom as it was applied under British law. According to Athlone, however, what Ellenberger himself actually did was to tell Tshekedi to "inform these recalcitrants that they must return to their homes. [I]f they did not obey this order [they would be] compulsorily removed to Serowe."[42] It was up to Ellenberger's subaltern, Rowland Daniel, to rescue the high commissioner's judgement in a well-attended *kgotla* in Serowe on 7th January 1927. Each and every subject of His Majesty the King, Daniel said, was "at liberty to worship God according to his own views."[43] Tshekedi's counsellors reacted badly to Daniel, and "all pointed out that it was going to hit very hard at the Chief's authority." One man summarized the dilemma he and his fellow headmen felt in reference to Athlone's guarantees of freedom "in England and elsewhere."

> We natives are not like the people in England who know the difference between a Chief [i.e., authority] and a religion [probably *thuto*]. We do not know. We take religion and the Chief to be the same thing. . . . You must admit that you have made an opening for us to scatter [*phatlalala*].[44]

Daniel was being told that his orders would be fought. His solution was to recommend again that Maifhala and Tumedi be dealt with on the basis of insubordination only, not admitting religion into the matter at all. By now these injunctions were undeniably cynical. Keeditse even then reiterated, "Religion belongs to the Chiefship."[45]

Never one to avoid unpleasantness, Tshekedi would not rest, and appealed the magistrate's injunction in the *kgotla*, requesting an interview with the high commissioner.[46] On the 1st of February, Tshekedi achieved his end and stood beside Athlone in the Government House in Cape Town; with them was Edmund Clifford, the imperial secretary and British representative to South Africa, and Jules Ellenberger. Tshekedi openly described his complaint as revolving around the Ngwato requirement that Rawe's people stop worshipping in the Anglican faith. Ellenberger persisted: why had Tshekedi ordered these people to Serowe? Was it to prevent their maintaining an Anglican congregation at Tonota? Clearly it was. Tshekedi pointed out that the BaKhurutshe themselves lay riven by denominational quarrels. "I had to stop them," he said. The gathered men then spoke as follows:

> High Commissioner: You want them to stay in Serowe.
> Tshekedi: Yes. If they come to Serowe they must leave their denomination.
> [A break is taken and refreshments are served.]
> High Commissioner [resuming]: No mention should be made of religious beliefs. Their punishment should be for disobeying the Chief's orders. . . .

---

42   BNA S.34/5, Athlone to L. S. Amery, Cape Town, 9/2/27.

43   BNA S.218/4, Judgment delivered by H.C.

44   BNA S.34/5 Notes of a meeting held in Serowe, 7/1/27, with the Asst. Res. Comm. English.

45   BNA S.34/5, Notes of a meeting held at Serowe, 7/1/27; Daniel to R.M. Serowe, Mafeking, 9/11/26; Report of 25th October; R.C. (Ellenberger) to Asst. R.C. Francistown, Mafeking 3/1/27; Asst. R.C. (Daniel) to R.C., Francistown 10/1/27; LMS SA 89/1, R. H. Lewis to F. H. Hawkins, Serowe, 6/1/27.

46   BNA S.34/5, R.M. (Daniel) to G.S., Francistown, 13/1/27.

Imperial Secretary: [Can you] suggest any way of dealing with these people [which would not touch their faith]?
Tshekedi: I have no suggestion.[47]

The high commissioner and the imperial secretary thus chose to support Tshekedi, even though Tshekedi himself made no attempt to conceal his reasoning.

Upon returning home, Tshekedi dispatched a regiment of men to conduct the offending BaKhurutshe by wagon from Tonota to Serowe. When a bystander expressed concern to B.P. Police Lieutenant Poole over the prospect of people undergoing a long journey in chains, as one source had it, Poole replied, "You talk too much." The trip to Serowe would last three or four days. According to later protests, during the night members of the regiment attempted to rape women tied down to the wagonbed.[48] One Khurutshe prisoner, Ranthaka Sekoko, later managed to send a telegram to the high commissioner asking if the treatment of the Anglicans was "with your approval." Ellenberger stood by to reassure Athlone that the whole matter was tribal. Tshekedi was "enforcing his tribal law"; the removal had "nothing to do with any religious matter."[49]

This exchange must be considered extraordinary, since the two men had only two weeks ago questioned Tshekedi to his face. Now they professed a different understanding. The logic of "Indirect Rule" in the Protectorate was so overweening that it compelled them to beg the question of what *would* constitute a religious dispute. Intra-African issues were discrete, "tribal," and impenetrable to colonial analysis. The power to translate was also the power to refrain from translating: it did not matter that Tshekedi had spoken in English.[50]

Mere attempts to keep up appearances followed. Ellenberger wrote the Serowe magistrate of a rumor that disturbed him. He worried that BaKhurutshe had been "tied up with reins before being placed on wagons: please [ascertain] from Mr. Poole [of the Bechuanaland Police] what actually took place. . . ." Lieutenant Poole then reported as follows. After refusing the regiment's ("Headman" Nkate's) orders to "go to the wagons which were to carry them to Serowe," the miscreants were ordered seized. Further assaults and violence were prevented by the police. Nkate then had them fastened with reins "to keep them quiet." The magistrate was relieved that the reins had not been put on before people were placed in the wagons. Such was the extent of the inquiry.[51]

Once in Serowe, Anglican BaKhurutshe continued to press their case until finally the local clergy of the Church of England mounted a protest. The bishop of

---

[47]   BNA S.34/5, Notes of Interview between Tshekedi and the High Commissioner, Cape Town, 1/2/27.

[48]   Interview: The Rev. B.R. Tshipa, b. 1902, Serowe, 17 February 1989, English. The MaKobamotse *mophato*, officially under Kgamane Sekgoma's son Kaelo, was formed in 1894; Schapera, *Handbook of Tswana Law and Custom*, 313; BNA S.34/5, Bishop of Kimberley to H.C., 20/1/28.

[49]   BNA S.34/5, R.C. (Ellenberger) to H.C. (Athlone), 23/2/27. There may have been a bit of squeamishness about coming down too hard on Tshekedi for forcibly consolidating his people, given British policy in Nyasaland and Northern Rhodesia at the time, which attempted to do the same on a grand scale; John McCracken, "Colonialism, Capitalism and Ecological Crisis in Malawi: A Reassessment," in David Anderson and Richard Grove, eds., *Conservation in Africa* (Cambridge, 1987), 67.

[50]   This accords with what Edward Said calls a "textual" attitude, *Orientalism* (New York, 1979), 94–95.

[51]   BNA S.34/5, Lieut. Poole to R.M. Serowe, Palapye Road, 7/3/27; R.M. to G.S., Serowe, 11/3/27.

Kimberley challenged Ellenberger's assertion that the BaKhurutshe were using religion as a "screen." A screen for what precisely? he asked.[52] The resident commissioner adopted a new tactic. His interpretation of Athlone's December judgement was as follows: "No one could interfere with these people in their worshipping of God according to their own lights *in their own houses*," but no unwanted church could be erected (or any minister stationed) in the Ngwato District. Here was clear jurisprudence. As Tshekedi had previously hinted, the issue was really about property.[53]

Under this rubric came further British guarantees of religious freedom, calling for more lectures to Tshekedi. At last responding purely in the terms favored by colonial discourse, Tshekedi forewarned his resident magistrate that "the whole affair is not a religious movement, but an attempt to obtain independence."[54] The Anglicans now had to cease worshipping *even in the privacy* of their abodes, since, keeping to the letter of Ellenberger's interpretation of the high commissioner's ruling, the houses they then occupied were not "their own homes." "I am informed that Maifhale and his followers hold prayer meeting daily," Tshekedi noted curtly; now this was illegal. In order to pray in private, the Anglicans would all have to construct new rondavels in Khurutshe ward. British guarantees pertained only to these imaginary spaces.[55]

The Anglicans refused to build new houses, and asked the administration to allow them at least to move to a different part of Serowe. Nowhere can the misleading nature of "Khurutshe" ethnicity be more clearly seen than in this plea to build "away from their own people,"[56] outside the old Khurutshe ward of Serowe. Tshekedi knew well that Protectorate officials viewed the Tonota Anglicans foremost as BaKhurutshe. So were they individual troublemakers, or another "tribe"? Like Sekgoma II before him, Tshekedi used ethnicity to demonstrate that BaKhurutshe *per se* might accept his rule, and even argued that while some of those brought to Serowe had not been Anglicans, the bishop at Francistown had made "one group of them." Lumping this group with other BaKhurutshe, with in fact the loyal, Ngwato Church-going, and wealthy BaKhurutshe of Serowe,[57] re-inked the administration's opaque view of the matter. The offenders were rebelling, untenably, even *within* their own tribe; they were not behaving to type! Thus Tshekedi's hand was freed.

---

52   BNA S.34/5, Bishop of Kimberley to R.C., (received) 30/3/27.

53   BNA S.34/5, R.M. Francistown to G.S., Francistown, (received) 19/3/27; Bishop of S. Rhodesia to R.C., Salisbury, 7/3/27; R.C. to H.C., 2/3/27, quote, italics in the original. Tshekedi suggested that if he wished, the Bishop of Kimberley might keep to an integrated congregation of BaTswana and Europeans, in the European Church. This clever move threatened to expose the hypocrisy of the high commissioner's principles, and Athlone overruled the idea directly. BNA S.34/5, Tshekedi to R.M. Serowe, Serowe, 21/4/27.

54   BNA S.34/5 Report on Bishop of Kimberley's arrival at Serowe, 11/6/27; Quote, Wylie, *A Little God*, 158–59, citing Tshekedi to R.M. Serowe, 16/9/27, DO 9/7/11141; BNA S.34/5 R.C. (Ellenberger) to R.M. Serowe, Mafeking, 1/6/27; H.C. (Athone) to R.M. Serowe, Cape Town, 12/5/27, and Leita, "Origin of the Anglican Church," 42.

55   BNA S.34/5, R.M. (Nettleton) Francistown to G.S., Serowe, 5/7/27, 24/8/27, 23/9/27.

56   BNA S.34/5, Res. Mag. Nettleton to G.S. Mafeking, Serowe, 14/11/28.

57   Interview: Headman Mokgobelela, Serowe, 14 Feb. 1989; and BNA S.34/5 Tshekedi to R.M., Serowe, 16/9/27. Molefhe Tselawa, who had fomented trouble after Nkobelele's succession, was one non-Anglican whom events allied to the other dissidents.

As for Raletamo, Maifhale, Tumedi, and other leading Anglicans, they resisted. They had complained to the bishop of Kimberley of hunger, and in fact Serowe BaKhurutshe—BaNgwato, really—had nothing to gain by feeding distant kin whom Tshekedi had labelled as rebellious.

It was years before the Anglicans still residing in Serowe began slowly to build homes, having first worked enough slack in their captivity that Tshekedi complained they stayed at their Tonota cattleposts at will.[58] Although the MaTshetshe (Ma-Church), as they were known, presented their case *en masse* several times in the Ngwato *kgotla*, it was only in 1934 that Tshekedi allowed them finally and officially to return to Tonota. The aging Rev. Baruti Kaleakgosi settled in Tonota and supervised a congregation of over a hundred members; those Anglicans who wished to continue their dissent crossed the Shashi River to pray. At the end of his reign, when Tshekedi relaxed the national exclusivity of the Ngwato Church, the MaTshetshe ceremoniously recrossed the Shashi into GammaNgwato singing "Onward Christian Soldiers."[59]

Diana Wylie has written that the relationship between the Ngwato kingdom and Tonota BaKhurutshe demonstrated the "power of ordinary people to evade the directives of the Ngwato state,"[60] and perhaps this is so. Still a very odd thing had happened. The earl of Athlone—as English royalty, a representative of the Established Church, and a relative of its titular leader, King George V—had conspired with British officials, and a southern African "chief," to prevent Africans from praying to God under the conventions of his own true faith.[61] Why had such a thing happened?

In the Protectorate, the Church of England, as the colonial Church, in a sense surrounded the Ngwato Church and subordinated it. The British Crown's relationship to the Church of England paralleled the Ngwato king's oft-termed "tribal" relationship to the Ngwato Church. One hierarchy enfolded its smaller simile. For Tshekedi this was significant. He hardly opposed Anglicanism on liturgical or abstractly theological grounds, having been educated by Anglicans himself. Yet it was unacceptable that groups of clear subordinates adopt the faith of a Church that could and did portray itself as superior to the Ngwato Church. Their prayer was then the language of sedition, far worse than the muttered gripes of a beer party.[62] Anglicanism short-circuited the unitary spiritual and material authority of the kingdom, and with it the premise of Indirect Rule.

---

[58]   BNA S.34/5 R.M. (Nettleton) to G.S., Serowe 24/8/27, 20/2/28, 11/4/29; S.218/7, Tshekedi to R.M, Serowe 25/7/33; TK Papers, A/1 R.M. (Nettleton) Serowe to Edirilwe Seretse, Serowe 7/9/28; and see Michael Crowder, "Tshekedi Khama and Opposition to the British Administration of the Bechuanaland Protectorate, 1926–1936," *Journal of African History* 26 (1985), 193–214.

[59]   BNA S.218/7, R.C. (Rey) to H.C. (Stanley), 28/7/33; R.M. (Nettleton) to Asst. R.C., Serowe 4/7/34; LMS SA 99/Burns, A. Burns to J.T. Brown, Serowe 4/5/36; SADC, Inyati, 2/9/36; Head, *Serowe*, 36.

[60]   Wylie, *A Little God*, 160.

[61]   As the bishop of Kimberley wrote, "these people had been ordered to give up their religion by Khama, Sekgoma and Tshekedi. The native London Missionary exhorted them to forsake the English Church. . . ." BNA S.34/5, Bishop of Kimberley to H.C., 26/1/28.

[62]   Interview: The Rev. Father Haskins Sekgoma, b. 1903, Serowe, 31 May 1989, English: [How did you preach to people outside the Anglican Church? –P. L.] "I told them that the other Churches, they are not a proper Church—[with priests] with proper Christian training. Here [i.e., in the Ngwato Church] people are not trained about God."

Gaofetoge, a Ngwato headman, supposedly put the issue to the Tonota Anglicans in this way: "You must have been misled by someone because you think you belong to the Church of England, [the English] King's church. You must know we are also under the same flag. You will never have your church."[63]

Malema's BaBirwa

Rawe's BaKhurutshe were not the only people to provoke the kingship into a display of realpolitik. A group of BaBirwa did the same in 1920 and 1921. In considering their tale, we must first note the vagueness of the term "Birwa" itself.[64] What is known is that a *kgosi*, Malema, held himself as the *primus inter pares* among six villages; one his own, and five under headmen (Mateema, Pitso, Sebatani, Setsumalo, and Thutwa), comprising little more than a thousand people in all. In 1895 Ngwato boundaries were amended by the "railway grant" of ostensibly Ngwato land to the British South Africa Company. This grant, which was sold off in lots as the Tuli Block to white ranchers, included the area where Malema's BaBirwa lived. When Khama claimed in 1895 that he had previously "given" rights of residence to the BaBirwa in the area, he did so only to legitimize his repudiation of those rights. There is little reason to dispute Modisanyane Bobeng's observation that "the question of Malema being a subject of . . . Khama never came to the fore until 1920."[65]

Other self-called BaBirwa had fallen more clearly under Ngwato rule. From 1903 Khama consolidated Birwa hamlets into what became Bobonong and a few other villages; in 1910 he shifted different Tuli Block BaBirwa north to a "reserve" established by the BSAC. In 1916 Khama relocated the last of the BaBirwa from the Motloutse River to Bobonong. Bobonong's Ngwato governor, from 1906, was Khama's son-in-law and nephew Modisaotsile, whose domain grew with every importation of people.[66]

In 1920, white Tuli farmers began a fencing program, and the BSAC complained to Khama in the king's discourse: the "reserve" BaBirwa, and particularly Malema's people, were drunkards.[67] Khama ordered them to relocate inside GammaNgwato by 30th November, a very difficult order in view of the fact that it was only conveyed on the 4th of the month, after many BaBirwa had already plowed. With at least the tacit acceptance of the local B.P. police, Governor Modisaotsile arranged to take Malema's people to Bobonong. Malema supposedly complained, "We are not cattle that can be moved at a few days' notice to stand in the rain," but in fact there was little rain to be had, as an uneven three-year drought had begun, and in any case Khama was determined to proceed immediately.[68]

---

[63] BNA S.34/5, Extract from "Bell's Report," dated 6/3/26.

[64] It is of putatively Kalanga extraction; Schapera, *Ethnic Origins*, 76.

[65] Modisanyane Bobeng, "The Bangwato–Babirwa Conflict in the Late 19th and Early Twentieth Centuries" (B.A. thesis, University of BoLeSwa, 1976), 12. Neil Parsons feels otherwise ("Khama III," 391–93).

[66] K III D/29/60, Khama to Modisaotsile Mokomane, Serowe 22/5/11, and Morton and Ramsay, *The Birth of Botswana*, 66; Bobeng, "The Bangwato–Babirwa Conflict," 14, 27.

[67] They were also smuggling cattle over the border for illegal sale in South Africa. Wylie, *A Little God*, 150.

[68] K III H/59/"Tuli Letters;" BNA S.21/1/1 Sir Herbert Sloley, Special Commissioner, to Imperial Sec., Cape Town 29/4/22. I am glossing *moemelakgosi*, "king's representative," as "governor."

When Governor Modisaotsile set about forming a regiment of men to force Birwa people off Tuli territory, he went to Madikwe, the *kgosi* of those BaBirwa relocated in 1916; Madikwe raised a force of 200 men to be led by Oduetse Gamanwe, a twenty-seven-year old local man. Oduetse arrived with scores of wagons for the removal. Subsequent reports differ as to what happened next, but it is apparent that the BaBirwa of the six villages under Malema did not wish to go to Bobonong and refused to make things easy for Oduetse's regiment.[69] Oduetse's men probably looted and torched people's houses. Kgosi Malema was in the Transvaal on a visit to purchase medicine for his son, and returned to find his village in ruins; he was then beaten and tied up. Nevertheless, Modisaotsile wrote Khama that the transfer had proceeded well, adding, "God helped me."[70]

Rape as a Mode of Conversion

Malema surprised the administration and hired a white attorney to represent his interests, even though some of his allied *dikgosi* objected to pledging their cattle as payment. The lawyer, Emmanuel Gluckmann, claimed that women had been routinely assaulted during the six-day journey to Bobnonong. The context was similar to that of the mistreatment of the Tonota Anglicans while they were in transit. In both cases, as people were expelled from the organized and human space of the village and into the wild veldt, they were subjected to dehumanizing treatment. Women were attacked as a signal that the protective control of fathers and sons had been broken.[71]

Once in Bobonong, however, the rebellious BaBirwa were subjected to what appears to have been *systematic* oppression of a different kind.[72] Men and women were separated and quartered in the Church graveyard, where, deprived of the grain staple *bogobe*, they were forced to subsist on wild roots and other veldt food. The men were made to plow for Modisaotsile, and some were tortured; one was made to stand in the sun for a week. Two men were bound to posts and tormented with fire, possibly by Modisaotsile's son. In early 1921, Malema and some of his followers fled back to the Tuli Block. Modisaotsile's men went after him, flattened

---

[69] BNA S.21/1/1 Statement by Modisaotsile, Serowe, 27/1/22. It is not apparent whether Oduetse was a Mmirwa or MoNgwato. For the main source here, see E. Gluckmann, "The Tragedy of the Ababirwas," in six parts in *The Rand Daily Mail*, Johannesburg, 10, 11, 12, 13, 14, and 16/5/22; (hereafter *RDM* with date). *RDM*, 10/5/22, claimed thirty-two wagons arrived; other reports, twenty-three. In any case, with over a thousand people to move, many would have had to walk; BNA S.21/1/1 Madikwe's testimony, 27/1/22.

[70] BNA S.21/1/1 Modisaotsile to Khama, Bobonong 10/1/21 (translated); RDM, 10/5/22. Parsons, "Khama III," has the most complete summary of these events, 393–94.

[71] See Susan Brownmiller, *Against Our Will: Men, Women and Rape* (New York, 1975). Thanks to Gay Seidman.

[72] Wylie, *A Little God*, 149–55, and Parsons, "Khama III," 393–94, address the implications of Malema's hiring of Gluckmann, a Johannesburg attorney and the father of anthropologist Max Gluckmann. My discussion here will focus only on the issues salient to this chapter. On the rapes, Morton and Ramsay only remark generally that "many BaBirwa complained of mistreatment," in *The Birth of Botswana*, 66–67. Wylie writes of "unspeakable outrages" (p. 152) including rape occurring during the removal, but she is unclear on the situation in Bobonong.

and burned the remaining houses, and flogged Malema before he escaped to the Transvaal.[73]

We are concerned with the treatment of the Tuli Block BaBirwa who remained in Bobonong. Their regimen of punishment perplexed later inquiries, for it was administered, "curiously enough, for not attending Church."[74] For instance, not only Koma, the son of Mateema, one of Malema's six co-headmen, said he was beaten, but Koma's wife and "another woman" were also physically abused. They "were not in Church during the hour of service and were struck for neglecting their religious duties."[75] Oduetse, the regimental leader, raped three middle-aged wives of prominent Birwa men, two months *after* the move to Bobonong, and also beat another woman ("Papi's wife")—for not attending Church.[76] Mokhadi, the wife of Talona, testified that two Birwa "*kgotla* police" came with sjamboks and ejected an elderly visitor from her hut. They then raped her, "not a robust woman," in front of two of her friends. When investigators asked her why they had done this thing, she said, "It was because we did not go to Church." The two "policemen" were under Modisaotsile's command. He had "sent [them] round to see that people did not absent themselves from Church," and this appears to have been a regular duty both before and long after the rapes.[77]

A fair number of other assaults from Bobonong Birwa men on other Birwa women were reported, but motive was not mentioned. Refusal to attend Church was the only rationale stated to, as opposed to intuited by, Europeans.[78] The most egregious offender was Oduetse Gamanwe, who, in "sober" state, had deliberately led the attacks where the women were quartered, that is, first in the local graveyard, and later in the yard of the Bobonong Church.[79]

These basic facts of the matter were not easily ascertained. Malema, who eventually returned to GammaNgwato and was conducted to Serowe, attempted to present his case under Gluckmann's counsel in early 1922, after long delays. When another Birwa client tried to raise the subject of the rapes at the *kgotla*, Johnny Ratshosa, the hearing's interpreter, refused to translate his words and threatened him with arrest. Rape as a topic was "unfit" for Europeans to hear. Gluckmann was not in attendance, having been banned from participating in proceedings that were "in no way" to be considered a trial.[80]

---

[73] Nettleton's report, and Khama, contested this, claiming that Malema's people were fed, *RDM*, 10/5/22, 11/5/22; BNA S.21/1/1, E. Gluckmann to Leslie Blackwell, Cape Town, 12/4/22; BNA S.21/1/1 Malema Makhuru's testimony: Notes of Evidence, 11/4/22, and Parsons, "Khama III," 396.

[74] BNA S.21/1/1, E. Gluckmann to Leslie Blackwell, Cape Town, 12/4/22.

[75] BNA S.21/1/1 Sir H. Sloley, Special Commissioner, to Imperial Sec., Cape Town, 29/4/22, 13.

[76] BNA S.21/1/1 Malema Makhuru's testimony: Notes of Evidence, 11/4/22.

[77] Interview: The Rev. Phethu Sekgoma, b. 1922, Bobonong, 2 May 1989.

[78] Bobeng, "Bangwato–Babirwa Conflict," 27 ff.; BNA S.21/1/1 G.E. Nettleton to G.S., Mafeking 15/5/22.

[79] Bobeng, "Bangwato—Babirwa Conflict," 14.

[80] BNA S.21/1/1, E. Gluckmann to Khama, Palapye Road 17/4/22; *RDM* 14/5/22. According to the Rev. Lewis, Khama told the complaining BaBirwa that their lawyer was merely "an insignificant Jew." Gluckmann later responded by labeling Khama "pharoah." Parsons points out that Khama's angst at Gluckmann's involvement may have been due to Gluckmann's connections with South Africa, representing the spectre of incorporation, "Khama III," 396. *RDM*, 13/5/22; 14/5/22. The inquiry was on 13 April 1922.

In any case, the inquiries focused on the initial ride to Bobonong and only on isolated incidents during the following year. It was far less rewarding to consider the big picture, the sustained abuse of men and women held captive during a serious drought.[81] The two resulting reports were efforts at damage control. According to B.P. Police Captain Nettleton, there was no plan behind the crimes; Nettleton also questioned the reticence of women to name their assailants freely and quickly to the proper authority—Modisaotsile, the top Ngwato official in Bobonong. Such obtuseness infuses his entire report. On women's separation from men, perhaps this was simply according to "general principles," as they were "prisoners." The statement that women were "laid out in rows" before being raped Nettleton called an "exaggeration."[82]

Ethnicity again befuddled observers. Police Captain Hannay asserted that Malema's captors could not possibly have also been "Mabirwas, [since] it is contrary to native law or custom for members of the same clan" to beat up their headmen.[83] For Nettleton, the old Africa hand, however, rape was "not unknown in native villages," and given "the strained feeling between the Mabirwa of Malema and the Mabirwa of Modisa[otsile], it [sic] assumed the aspect of rape." The total number of women *reported* raped appears to have been twelve, and included Malema's wife, his son's wife, and his own daughter.[84]

Because Gluckmann argued in the print media that women "both mature and immature" had been raped, Sir Herbert Sloley, a one-man commission from the Basutoland Protectorate, countered that "native women" of fifteen were best considered mature. Sloley investigated claims of high mortality rates among the captive BaBirwa and revealed twenty-five deaths per 1,000 people in the fourteen months from December 1920 to January 1922, mainly of the young and elderly. Sloley felt this was due to the natural stress of moving.[85] He also repeated the Ngwato refrain that the BaBirwa were "fully accustomed to drink."

There was precious little hand-wringing over the rapes. High Commissioner Arthur Frederick, H.R.H. the prince of Connaught, wrote to Resident Commissioner J. C. MacGregor that Nettleton, "whose judgment seems to have been at fault, has retired from the Service." This was premature. Three days later Nettleton wrote his report and sent it to the government secretary, and he would return as Serowe's magistrate (soon district commissioner, or D.C.) in the 1930s.[86] On the Tswana side, the Sloley report recommended Modisaotsile's dismissal, but Khama refused, telling the administration that were he to remove Modisaotsile, "the Machwapong [MaTswapong], the Mabirwa at Phakwe, and some Bamangwato dissatisfied at [the] prohibition [of beer]" would rise against the governors he had placed over them.[87]

[81] "Great scarcity" was reported for Bobonong in 1922, with most people away foraging for veldt food; LMS/SA 85/2, Minutes of Mangwato Conference of Churches Held at Serowe, 3/[2]/23–7/[2]/23.

[82] BNA S.21/1/1, G.E. Nettleton, B.P. Police, to G.S., 15/5/22.

[83] BNA S.21/1/1, Capt. Hannay to G.S., 19/4/22; LMS SA, Serowe annual report, 1922 (R. H. Lewis).

[84] BNA S.21/1/1, G.E. Nettleton, BP Police, to G.S., 15/5/22.

[85] BNA S.21/1/1 Malema Makhuru's testimony: Notes of Evidence, 11/4/22; *RDM*, 10/5/22 ("no consideration being given to tender years"); and Bobeng, "Bangwato—Babirwa Conflict," 14.

[86] BNA S.21/1/1, H.C. to R.C., Cape Town, 12/5/22.

[87] BNA S.21/1/1, R.C. to H.C., 20/6/22; Khama wrote on 15th June, 1922.

In June 1922, the acting resident commissioner directed Serowe's magistrate that while no further steps would be taken against Modisaotsile's men arrested for destroying Birwa property, eight "Bangwato" men should be arrested "on charges of having raped certain Mabirwa women."[88] The high commissioner capitulated to Khama on all other points, and dropped Modisaotsile's dismissal. In a last bid to escape Ngwato rule, after Khama's death, Kgosi Malema wrote to the resident commissioner, "You are the only senior judge. I pray for freedom to kneel under you Sir. . . ." The administration would have none of it. Far better was King Sekgoma II's reassuring description of a "Native Custom which pertains to all of the Bamangwato."[89]

What BaNgwato Wanted from the BaBirwa: Acquiescence in the Realm of the Word

As we have seen, a central idea among Tswana-speaking peoples was and is that the human community is not so much led as it is gathered (*phuthegilwe*), in a place where it can live in a sturdily built space (*agile*, live, from *go aga*, to build). The converse, being scattered (*phatlaletswe*), connotes subservience, want, crisis, and inhumanity. Khama's argument, rejected by Malema, was that he himself had gathered and thus manufactured an identity for the BaBirwa. As Khama had put it,

They were living scattered throughout my country. A few were here in Serowe, some were in what is now the Tuli Block, which was then part of my country. They were living more like bushmen than anything else and had been so living for a generation past. I collected them and made a tribe [or *morafe*: polity] out of them.[90]

No missionary had ever visited the BaBirwa when Khama appointed Modisaotsile to Bobonong in 1906. Modisaotsile, however, had been a Christian and staunch Ngwato Church member back in Serowe. Soon a small congregation formed in Bobonong, among a people Jennings typified in 1909 for their "absence of clothes." Their *moruti*, Molebedi, did not have an easy time; under his care a mere ten Church members were "greatly troubled by internal dissension." In 1912 another appointed *moruti*, Sephote, was withdrawn after "political" disputes with Modisaotsile. And there was no church building for another eight years.[91] The reason behind these lapses was that Modisaotsile merged rulership with the notion of *moruti*. The governor and his wife, one of Khama's daughters, held the pivotal roles in the perpetuation of Bobonong's dull orthodoxy from the start. No *moruti* could take his place. As Phethu Sekgoma, an old Bobonong man, relates:

Really in Bobonong our first *moruti* that I know well myself, was our father, Modisaotsile, and Mmakhama [his wife] who collected us into this village. They were living here. It is she who established this church, that sister of

88   K III H/60/"Jan.–June 1922" E. A. Merivale Drury to Khama, 20/6/22.

89   S II A/5, Chief Malema Makhura to Res. Comm. J. C. MacGregor, 26/4/23; second ref. lost.

90   BNA S.21/1/1, Khama's statement cited, Serowe, 17/1/22.

91   LMS SA 4/2, Serowe for 1909 (A. Jennings); and LMS SA Reports 4/4, Shoshong 1912–13 (E. Lloyd). The Rev. Seodubeng Lesotho was briefly stationed in Bobonong before his untimely death in 1923. LMS/SA 85/2, Minutes of Mangwato Conference of Churches Held at Serowe, 3/[2]/23–7/[2]/23.

Sekgoma [II who was] married by Modisaotsile, it is both of them who built the church of Bobonong and made it grow.[92]

The Ngwato kingship desired just this sort of fealty, and so tolerated Modisaotsile. The best example of fealty's expression comes from a witness to an unrelated commission, a person who wished to praise Tshekedi Khama's rule over diverse people through Ngwato governors. His testimony offers a tableau of images of acquiescence.

I belong to the Bobirwa clan which lives in the Bobonong area [Madikwe's people]. It can be stated that Tshekedi is not the first Chief to rule us; we were under Chiefs who ruled us long ago. . . . Our people came from the areas in which [the MaTebele] lived and came to the Bamangwato. . . . These people have also left the Transvaal as a result of the way in which they were treated there and came back to their home, the Bamangwato Reserve. We came and lived in the country of the Bamangwato in our own kgotlas [sic] which are widespread.[93]

The speaker establishes that his forebears willingly relinquished a part of their fractured autonomy to come "home," and did so in their own interest. There is no contradiction between their history and accommodating the BaNgwato.

Out of his kindness in 1916 Khama sent out a representative of his to bring our villages together. . . . The message Chief Khama sent us was this: that we should come together so as to receive education [thuto] and the word of God in the schools because our villages were spread far and wide, and the man round whom we were gathered was Modisaotsile [a play on Modisaotsile's name, which means "the herder has arrived"]. We were taught and were also reminded that we should build a church, the house of God. We built a church [in 1920] which still stands as an example of our having received the word of God, and in building that church we were assisted by Chief Khama. It was out of his kindness that Chief Khama collected us together and built us into a clan [probably: morafe]. I feel sure that the Bamangwato Administration is always prepared to listen to the grievances of its people.[94]

The speaker lauds the gathering of BaBirwa into a stable society (a congregation, a polity) capable of receiving the benefits of thuto. In 1921 all BaBirwa, like all BaKhurutshe, had to make room for their new identity. The space of the church (newly built in Bobonong) physicalized this gathering under the pastoral care of the Ngwato king. Amid the dark side of this incorporation in Bobonong, one can see the influence of Modisaotsile.[95] When married Birwa women refused the identity offered under the realm of the Word, Modisaotsile had them raped. Rape illustrated the vulnerability of

---

[92]   Interview: The Rev. Phethu Sekgoma, b. 1922, Bobonong, 2 May 1989.

[93]   BNA S.78/4/2, Commission of Inquiry: Mswazi and Makalaka: Palapye, March, 1945, 157: Phofuetsile Selelo's testimony.

[94]   Ibid. In 1920 Lewis remarked that he left the opening of the new Bobonong church to Khama alone; LMS SA 83/2 R. H. Lewis to F.H. Hawkins, Serowe, 12/4/20.

[95]   Even if BaNgwato managed the mistreatment in Bobonong and Ngwato men committed most of the rapes (which is less than clear), BaBirwa at least looked on without a murmur. Gluckmann notes that some of Malema's people did avoid abuse by staying with relatives, RDM, 10/5/22. But given Modisaotsile's known autocratic temper, his presence during the first round of sexual violence, and women's fear of reporting anything to him, surely he okayed much of the treatment of Malema's BaBirwa. Wylie, A Little God, 156 n56, notes that many BaBirwa outside Bobonong still feel distaste for Modisaotsile's name.

their ungathered sex. Yet rape failed as a strategy, since it mocked the life of the Church and made the Church's promised effect on gender not a promise but a threat.

The Constructed Space of the Local Church

Modisaotsile tried to force women into a church; the kingship closely monitored the construction of churches. What defined this space? Phethu Sekgoma, the Bobonong man quoted above, recalled that Modisaotsile,

> if something came up between him and the community, he would say something in connection with it in Church. You know churches were built by Khama, the LMS was introduced by Khama, and it was his. . . . [On Sundays] everybody would come to Church, believers and also plain people. [Why? —P. L.] First of all, they were forced, the chief wanted each and every person to attend; Church was compulsory then . . . whether or not you wanted to go. Bobonong was small, but people sometimes left the village or hid in their houses.[96]

A bit of unpleasantness creeps in with this last phrase. Modisaotsile's Bobonong intensified the usual relationships that defined the physical space of the church from the start. As we have seen, in each of his successive capitals Khama won physical control over his main church building, as plaques and then cornerstones signified.[97] Outside the capital, other church spaces related to the capital's like village chiefships were supposed to relate to the kingship. But a church was not the *kgotla*. It squared the circle; it represented power as moving in one direction, from outside beyond the pulpit, as it were, through the *moruti* as mediator, widening unevenly and flowing back among the seated congregation. In contrast, the *kgotla* configured power as a relational force radiating into and then out from a center to the town and kingdom, reflected and modified by its subjects, the men whose station enabled the *kgotla*'s use and gave it meaning.

In smaller villages, the church building itself was either a mud-and-thatch structure or a brick or concrete building with a galvanized corrugated iron roof, glinting in the sun. Church services were often hot and uncomfortable. Going to services on a Sunday or, especially, a holiday, meant walling perhaps hundreds of people into a humid, closed room in which temperatures could soar above 120° F. Those of us who are used to commuter trains, elevators, mines, and meeting halls must grasp that Church services were the only occasions where BaTswana in villages enclosed themselves in tight spaces. If you sang together, stood side by side, and listened to one another pray with heads bowed, you had already begun to put a common identity ahead of antagonistic ones.

Outside the capital, Khama routinely paid for and personally opened new church buildings himself: in Shoshong, Ratholo, Sefhare, and other villages. Whether

---

96   Interview: The Rev. Phethu Sekgoma, b. 1922, Bobonong, 2 May 1989. Here I have not capitalized "church" (*kereke*, or *ntlo ya thuto*) so as to distinguish it from the institution, the Ngwato Church.

97   The cornerstone of the Serowe church, laid in 1915, attributes its construction to "the Bamangwato Church and Tribe," and a plaque to the left of the pulpit bears Khama's likeness and name. Khama delayed its opening a month in the hope that his son Sekgoma would attend and thus recognize his authority, S II A/2, Ratshosa to Sekgoma Khama, Serowe, 28/4/15.

he, or Sekgoma II or Tshekedi after him, elected to pay for a church building signified whether he wished to permit it.[98] In 1918 the Rev. Lewis reported the opening
of a church at one of the largest outstations of the Church, Maunatlala, at which
Khama physically described his own relationship to the building through the local
kgotla. "A most elaborate series of triumphal arches led from the [Maunatlala] chief's
Kgotla to the door of the New Church." School children sang for the assembled
guests in the *kgotla,* after which King Khama, the Rev. Lewis, and "local notables"
led a procession from the *kgotla* all the way to the doors of the church.[99] This expressed the Ngwato ideal, an unbroken parallel of authority moving from the kingship through the local *kgotla* and church. God Himself stood beside the king, hidden beyond the chancel wall.

The BakaNswazwi Build a Church

And so this physical space also gave rise to its own vocabulary of rebellion. The
BakaNswazwi, a chiefship of Pedi or Venda lineage and Kalanga connections, first asked
Khama for *baruti* in 1901. In around 1921 Moruti Moses Holonga began to serve in
Nswazwi village. Chief John Madawo Nswazwi, whom Khama had boosted to power,
then decided to built a church, which he opened in May 1922.[100] It seated 250 people,
and the BakaNswazwi paid for it themselves, raising £400 sterling for the purpose and
contributing their labor. Chief Nswazwi refused to place the Khama name on the cornerstone, substituting his own instead. That same year, the crops failed for a second
season, and famine struck in 1923.[101] At the same time, the BaNgwato pushed back
Nswazwi farmlands by expanding their cattle's grazing areas in the same vicinity. Ignoring the king's initiation of the plowing season, the BakaNswazwi plowed with the
first rains to maximize what they had during the drought.[102]

After Khama's death in 1923, King Sekgoma II encouraged Moruti Moses to
report on BakaNswazwi behavior. Moses and Keeditse, the tax collector, both found
the BakaNswazwi wanting. The Rev. Lewis had come to offer communion, it seems,
and Nswazwi headmen had been rude to him. Chief Nswazwi assumed the right
to recognize *baruti* in his village and accused persons who travelled to Serowe of
disloyalty. In general, as Moses put it, he and his men "acted like the English."[103]
The church building became a focus, as Sekgoma instructed Keeditse in 1925:

---

[98]   K III C/16 H. Williams to Khama, Shoshong, 12/12/04; LMS SA Reports 4/1 Shoshong for 1906 (H.
Williams); Sekgoma and Tshekedi kept a firm hand on the construction of churches, as we have seen; see
BNA DCS 1/20, Tshekedi to R.M. Serowe, Serowe, 24/3/31; DCS 20/1-6, Proposed Program for the Open-
ing of the Palapye Church, 3/12/41.

[99]   LMS Reports 5/3, Serowe for 1918 (R. H. Lewis).

[100]   LMS SA 71/4, A. Jennings to R. W. Thompson, Serowe 23/10/09; LMS SA Reports 4/2, Serowe for
1909 (A. Jennings); K III H/59/1921, Sekgoma II to Khama, 16/7/1921, enclosing Mosisi to Sekgoma,
pers. comm. See Mbako D.K. Mongwa, "The Struggle between BakaNswazwi under John Madawo
Nswazwi and the Bangwato under Tshekedi Khama, 1926–1932" (B.A. thesis, University of Botswana,
1977); and Schapera, *Ethnic Origins,* 57. I use "chief" rather than *kgosi,* since the Nswazwi term is *"she."*

[101]   Tapela, "The Tati District," 145; Mongwa, "The Struggle between BakaNswazwi," 35; Interview: Mrs.
Botsanyang Ramatsela, b. 1908, Serowe, 10 Nov. 1988; LMS SA Reports, Serowe for 1922 (R. H. Lewis).

[102]   BHP, Ntbk 3, Interview: Makatsela Modikwa, eighty years old in 1974.

[103]   S II A/2, M. Holonga to Sekgoma II, Shashe River, 9/8/23; K. Kgosietsile to Sekgoma, Tutume, 19/10/23.

about the house of *thuto* you shall tell them that Moruti Mosisi [Moses Holonga] must open it up so that it can be entered by the many. It was not build for nothing. . . . Let Mosisi open it up and not hold out for some supposed chief whom I do not know [i.e., do not like].[104]

The specifics of the issue are lost in the oral exchanges that must have paralleled these few texts; but significantly, King Sekgoma also demanded that future *baruti* in Nswazwi village be BaNgwato from Serowe.[105] For the present, he made do with Moses Holonga and tried to assume charge of the church in the nexus of recognized local authority, Ngwato centrality, and *thuto*. No matter that he had not built it.

When Sekgoma II died that same year, Tshekedi took over and refused to hear Nswazwi's ecclesiastic complaints in 1929 because they arrived via a letter handed to the missionary, the Rev. Burns, and not through Tshekedi's unambiguous subordinate, Moruti Moses. The channel was part of the message, and Burns "agreed" with Tshekedi's refusal.[106] Moses then personally carried the BakaNswazwi's message, which asked for "an ordained *moruti* able to marry people." Tshekedi's response commented that the request "was no small bit of work," and added (with underlining in the original SeTswana letter, giving the effect of shouting),

> The congregation [*phuthego*] of this land of the BaNgwato—there is absolutely no division between it and the nation [*morafe*]: they are all my people. I command Church congregants [*baphuthegi*] just like I do the nation. And the *baruti* of the LMS, I work with them in all their duties.[107]

After several episodes of Nswazwi recalcitrance before Ngwato levies and fees, Chief John Madawo Nzswazwi found himself in the Serowe *kgotla*. Although in 1929 it was felt that kingship could "no longer play the rude game of burning houses and compulsion," Chief Nswazwi was abused mightily as a "a dog, a cow, a cat," and as a MoTswapong (servant) who knew only "how to roast nuts and commit adultery." His crime was betraying *thuto*. "They want progress and yet indulge in inprogressive [sic] habits [like polygamy]," his Ngwato accusers said.[108] The *kgotla* delivered a long judgment concerned with Chief Nswazwi's various transgressions, especially his crucial refusals to pay the hut tax through Keeditse, but conspicuous among his offenses was that

> Mfhafsha [the deliberate SeNgwato corruption of Nswazwi] has been causing troubling about a church which he has built at sites suitable to himself

104 K III E/36/54, Sekgoma II to Keeditse, Serowe, 20/9/25.

105 BNA S.77/8, Inquiry into Nswazwi, 30/6/30, 1–2/7/30, 40ff., quoting Sekgoma II.

106 BNA S.77/8, Inquiry into Nswazwi, 45ff.

107 He concludes, "[I]f there is something to be said . . . raise the subject at the large meeting [of all congregations] here in Serowe." N. Parsons/M. Crowder holdings, Ballinger Papers, University of the Witswatersrand, Box 11: A 3.1.2, Tshekedi to J. Nswaze [sic], Serowe 25/6/29; thanks to Neil Parsons. For the Moanaphuti petition (in TK Papers, I/65, Edirilwe Seretse to Res. Mag., Serowe 29/6/31), an omnibus of grievances including some from Nswazwi, see Wylie, *A Little God*, 72.

108 BNA S.98/3, Edirilwe Seretse to R.C.; S.77/5, R.M to R.C., Serowe 24/3/30; S.77/5, Nswazwi to H.C., 27/11/29; R.M. Serowe (Nettleton) to McFarlane, Francistown 18/3/30; S.77/8, Inquiry into Nswazwi, 30/6/30, 1–2/7/30. Last quote: sic to original, Wylie, *A Little God*, 166; BNA S.77/5, Mswaze to Tshekedi, Francistown 16/11/29; Tshekedi to R.M. Serowe, Serowe, 22/11/29.

without consulting the Chief Khama. . . . He has endeavoured to procure ministers without consulting Khama. . . .[109]

Keeditse adduced as clear evidence that Chief Nswazwi wanted "to rule himself" the fact that he placed "his own name" on the foundation stone of the church. As a result, Nswazwi was forced to live in Serowe, while ten BaNgwato, headed by a new governor, Rasebolai, moved north to live with the BakaNswazi.

Although the BakaNswazwi never dispensed with the Ngwato Church *per se*, they persisted in rejecting Ngwato tax collectors and *baruti*, leading to John Madawo Nswazwi's imprisonment. He returned in 1945, this time in a merchant's flatbed truck driven at ceremonial pace, singing a hymn, "Lead us, Heavenly Father."[110] The discourse of the Church could indeed cut both ways. When Governor Rasebolai and a white policeman arrived to arrest Nswazwi again, interrupting a prayer meeting, they were beaten. A large Ngwato force finally assaulted the village, and in 1947, the BakaNswazwi left GammaNgwato for Southern Rhodesia.[111]

The way the kingdom constructed its authority pressed "religious issues," *ipso facto*, into the fabric of Indirect Rule as practiced in the Protectorate. In this way, Indirect Rule became the third component of the mode of power in GammaNgwato I have been calling the realm of the Word, a realm whose charter, although contested at every step, was set by the citizens and kings of GammaNgwato. The Protectorate government was not the "real" power; overall, Ngwato administration, the Church hierarchy, and colonial intervention reinforced one another. Their various strands were occasionally difficult to disentangle.

Few participants in the struggles depicted here found the division between the secular and the religious to be useful. At the root of each struggle lay a problem of identity. The struggle over BaKhurutshe's personal prayers was a conflict over which private identities they might hold. The rape of Birwa women was an attempt to violate and break open the limitations of their patrilineal Birwa-ness. Debates over who might build or pay for a church were debates about who possessed a sacred space in which new identities might be formed. Colonial Indirect Rule shared in these concerns. British officials especially denigrated the distinction between the sacred and profane; when it did arise, at the urgent prompting of subjects of the realm who wished to secularize their submission to the Ngwato kingdom, the administration of the Protectorate acted to erase it.

Yet not all citizens of the realm strove for independence. Most villages outside Serowe negotiated forms of authority workable for their small communities. The attraction of Christianity was sustainable among local configurations of gender, seniority, ethnicity, and ritual prominence. Chapter 8 treats these issues and focuses especially on Lerala, a village in the Tswapong Hills.

---

[109] BNA S.77/5, R.M. Serowe to R.C., telegram, Serowe, 24/3/30; S.77/6, Edirilwe's judgment, 15/3/30, [sic] throughout.

[110] BNA S.78/4/1, Acting Dist. Comm. to G.S., Serowe 26/7/43; K. T. Motsete to Grando, Cape Town, 13/2/45; S.78/4/2, Commission of Inquiry: Mswazi's and Makalaka, Palapye 3/45, 116, 129.

[111] Ramsay gives the high figure of 2,000 men for the advancing Ngwato regiment, *Birth of Botswana*, 80. Terence Ranger continues the story of the factious BakaNswazwi in his forthcoming book on the Matobo Hills.

8

The Masters of the Cattle Are Absent: Citizenship, Identity, and Power in the Village

Here in Lerala we wait, poised and alert
The milkers of the loaned-cattle, you tempted them,
The masters of the cattle are absent.
The milk of their possessions is not distributed.
                    Part of a praise-song from Lerala[1]

This chapter explores the way that the Christianity of the Ngwato Church, and the ideologies of the realm of the Word, entered and grew in villages outside the capital town. What sorts of people converted at which times, and why? What position in the village did Christians hold? Who opposed them? To answer such questions is to investigate changes in the balance among ethnic identities, between *dikgosi* and commoners, and between men and women; and even between *badimo*, people's deceased parents and grandparents, and the living.

These are worthwhile questions for two important reasons. For Western scholars, their answers lie in undiscovered country. Neither missionaries, colonial officials, nor "masters of the cattle" (in this case BaNgwato) had more than a fleeting place in most small villages within larger southern African polities. Certainly Tswana villagers were affected by royal and colonial policies, but little is known about life *within* the "myriad small, local Christian communities" of the mission-connected Churches.[2] Secondly, as was suggested in Chapter 6, the majority of people touched

---

1   Part of a reflexive praise song (*Leboka*) by Mokakapadi Ramosoka, pictured on the cover of this book; recorded Lerala 8/5/90. "Mono Lerala re thanyegile, bagami ba mafisa le ba lekile [unclear], beng ba dikgomo ga ba fa [possibly: ga ba a fa, "have not given"]. Kana mafshi a dilo tse ga a kgaoga."

2   In Richard Gray's words, in *Black Christians, White Missionaries* (New Haven, 1990), 66.

by the teaching of the Word lived in this milieu. This is so not merely in southern Africa, but in Africa generally. The memories of these people must be sought out. It is here that we are likely to bring new meaning to discussions not only of religion and politics, but of colonial-era ideological change in general. Thus I focus mainly on one village, Lerala of the Tswapong Hills; but within contexts arising from Lerala, indications also emerge about other villages in the kingdom, and perhaps more generally about small communities touched by Christianity and colonialism.

Lerala in the Nineteenth Century: Some Initial Referents

There are only a few uncontested points in Lerala's history from which to start. Modern Lerala is a village of over 2,000 people. It lies near the base of the southeastern foothills of the Tswapong Hill range in eastern Botswana. Before about 1940, the resident population of Lerala was, as one old man put it to me, "less than the number of children in primary school in the village today,"[3] probably under 500 people. The chiefships of most Tswapong villages, including Lerala's, identify themselves as "Pedi," an ethnic label derived from their elite, patrilineal migratory history. No Pedi MaTswapong disagree that "their" Pedi ancestors migrated in ancient times (certainly before 1800) from unnamed Pedi chiefdoms and perhaps ultimately from Venda territory in the "East," a cardinal direction in their symbolic geography.[4]

The present geographical position of Lerala is the last of a series of villages. Repeatedly resettling in search of secure, watered sites, and collecting a retinue along the way, the kin of Moroka I defined his heirs as Lerala's *dikgosi*. The name *moroka* means "rainmaker," bringer of fertility, which harks back to the preoccupation of his agriculturalist people. In the nineteenth century, Lerala moved along a southerly vector, mingling and breaking with other Tswapong villages. By 1860 it lay beside the Tlhakana River. It is said that the name "Lerala" derives, appropriately, from *go ralala*, to pass through. People of different descent and affiliation also came to Tswapong: in the eighteenth century, BaBirwa arrived; and in the nineteenth century, BaKhurutshe, BaKaa, and some BaSeleka came from the south. In Lerala, the BaKhurutshe now constitute a large ward.[5]

---

[3] Interview: The Rev. Tshinamo Molebalwa, Lerala, 28 March 1990. According to the Government of Botswana censuses, before 1946 Lerala probably had fewer than 1,000 inhabitants; in 1964 Lerala had 2,967 inhabitants, although this appears to take nonresidents into account, because in 1971, only ca. 1,500 people lived in Lerala; over 5,000 BaTswana living elsewhere claimed Lerala as their home village. Government of Botswana, *Report on the Census of the Bechuanaland Protectorate, 1964* (Bulawayo, 1964), and Neil Parsons, personal communication, 7/12/90.

[4] Interviews: Mr. Lekgaritha Mokakapadi and wife, 19 May 1990, Moremi village; Mr. Makwesa Leso, Lerala, 20 June 1990; with notebook, from father, ca. 1986; Mr. Mathuba a Madikwe, b. 1901, Mmakgabo village, 24 May 1990, and 16 June 1990; Mr. Molaodi Thakeng, b. 1901, Lerala, 12 June 1990; Mr. Sebele Gaborone, b. 1903, Lerala, 11 June 1990; Mr. Sematlho Pipedi, b. 1914, Lerala, 13 June 1990. And Isaac Schapera, *Ethnic Origins of Tswana Tribes* (London, 1952), 77–78, who oversimplifies by calling Lerala "Gananwa"; Sillery, *Founding a Protectorate* (Oxford, 1952), 185–187, whose dates are questionable.

[5] Interviews: Mr. Koowetse Molebalwa, b. 1905, Lerala, 9 April 1990 and 16 June 1990; Kgosi Mokakapadi (II) a Ramosoka, b. 1907, Lerala, 28 March 1990; Mr. Sematlho Pipedi, b. 1914, Lerala, 13 June 1990; Mrs. Miriam (MmaKgalemang) Tshinye, Lerala, 2 May 1990.

In 1895 the South African Republic's last conquests of its hinterland drove a forgotten senior section of Lerala's chiefship out of the Transvaal and back into the Tswapong Hills.[6] The return of this *kgosi*, Dialwa Mokakapadi, posed problems in Lerala. With his presence unacknowledged, it would be difficult to establish the congruence of propriety from the living to the natural world that was so necessary for peace and fertility. For a time Dialwa lived on the outskirts of the village, but eventually the ruling *kgosi*, Magosi Mpeo, convinced him to build within it. Magosi refused to step down for his senior "brother," and Magosi had the implied support of the Ngwato kingdom. A partnership of sorts then evolved between the two men, which cooled the residual friction between them. Its modus operandi invoked Dialwa's ability as Magosi's senior to preside over rainmaking and other operations concerning the ancestors, while Magosi retained judicial supremacy.

Among other rainmaking duties, Dialwa visited the defunct Gananwa chiefship across the border in the Transvaal, where he had grown up before its destruction by Paul Kruger's men. The BaGananwa were famous for rain, and Dialwa symbolically "took rain" from them in seasonal trips until around 1910.[7] When he re-crossed the Limpopo from the east to the west, just as the Tswapong BaPedi's ancestors had over a century before, he brought rain for all Tswapong villages. The relationship between Dialwa and Magosi, and the ostensible linkages between Dialwa's ritual activities, the other Pedi Tswapong villages, and the Transvaal, were fragile. While they lasted, they proposed a notion of community utterly alien to the incorporative modes of the Ngwato kingdom: one based on the fertility and promise of Pedi ancestral unity, looking away from the kingdom of the Word, its *thuto*, and its catch-all regional population of "MaTswapong."

Community and Direction in Lerala

Before looking at how Christians entered the *kgosi*'s *kgotla*, it is necessary to ad-dress Tswapong usage. After all, if you attempt to ask questions today in Lerala about "belief" or "faith,"[8] your interlocutors may very well refer only to Christian-ity in their answers, and not at all to the ancestors. Ancestor practices are part of *ngwao* or "nature," the way the world operates. Although in many situation *ngwao* is *mokgwa wa rona*, our "custom," it is not "belief," having no written form or insti-tutionalized format. *Ngwao* today conveys the flavor of common sense under fire, and perhaps false; but not *tumelo* (a belief or a faith), and so not a religion.

The correct name for the ancestors is *badimo* in Tswapong as elsewhere among BaTswana, as the reader by now knows. Respected and senior old people in

---

6   We can assume this from traditions placing Dialwa's departure during Paul Kruger's war on Mmalebogo of the BaGananwa, which dwells clearly in elite males' memory. Many people eluded the Boers' siege; see Colin Rae, *Malaboch or Notes from my Diary on the Boer Campaign of 1894* (Cape Town, 1898), esp. 170, 180; British War Office, Transvaal Dept. of Native Affairs, *The Native Tribes of the Transvaal* (1905), 115; Interviews: Mr. Lekgaritha Mokakapadi and wife, 19 May 1990, Moremi village; Kgosi Mokakapadi (II) a Ramosoka, b. 1907, Lerala, 28 March 1990.

7   I discuss and analyze his movements and techniques in "When Rain Falls."

8   For example, Please tell me about how you believed when you were still a young man? ("Le ntlhalosetse kafa le neng le dumela ka teng e ne e re le setse le lekolwane?") or, Long ago, what belief did your parents hold? ("Bogologolo batsadi ba lona ba ne ba na le tumelo efe?")

Tswapong shy away from the word, however, and prefer to say "them," "those people," or perhaps *makolojwane*, "the elderly." "Old man" and "old woman" are terms of respect. (This caused Khama some embarrassment when he addressed Queen Victoria).[9] In contrast, old men of Lerala often call one another "little boy," *mosimane*, with gentle mocking smiles. Avoiding the word *badimo* is the respectful thing to do, but when spoken, it suggests an undifferentiated, ectocorporeal presence. In Tswapong, there was always a close association between the continuity of community, seniority, and the ancestors.[10] The powers ancestors had had as senior patriarchs they still possessed in their new state, without power's mechanisms being sensible in lived experience.

A peculiar feature of Pedi Tswapong people's views on the *badimo*, however, is their apparent mobility. Although graves are places of *badimo*, they do not usually reside in the cattle kraal, as was once the case for most BaTswana. Instead, they travel through the wooded mountains of the Tswapong range, and especially they come from "BoPedi" in the Transvaal during important moments in village life, when they are fed and feted. GooMoremi, the senior Pedi Tswapong village, was "settled by" its ancestor Mapulana, and many Tswapong dwellers privilege Mapulana as a Pedi ur-ancestor. In general, *badimo* traverse and watch over the brambles and streams of the Tswapong Hills. Satisfying the supposed needs of *badimo* therefore re-enacted a two-sided paradigm: it expressed people's mobile history and it tied the health of the community to the ecology of the wider landscape in which they moved. In short, "rain" in Tswapong travelled with the ancestors.[11]

The expectation of rain affirmed the reinforcement of the village hierarchy as right and proper.[12] The most ancient means of securing it lay with the living Pedi senior, and as we have seen, at the turn of the century specifically with Dialwa. Disturbances among senior men and *badimo*, on the other hand, clogged the avenues of fertility, withered the crops, and dried up the rain before it fell. Because political disruption had contributed to the "scattering" of Lerala in the mid-nineteenth century, which required foraging techniques otherwise needed for surviving famine, there is a logic here. And indeed a general dry period coincided with Dialwa's arrival in Lerala from the Transvaal, caused much hunger, and spurred the *dikgosi* Magosi and Dialwa to bury their dynastic quarrel in a cooperative project.

---

[9]   Rutherford, "Willoughby," 72. A common expression of surprise among the old in Tswapong is also "Thakaa!" which is an abbreviated part of a saying no longer much used, meaning, "Come, let us gather the elders!" i.e., this is too much for us, we are but boys. I have heard a ninety-year old man use this expression: his elders would only be *badimo*. "Old" here also means "great" (-*golo*, like -*kolo*- in *makolojwane*).

[10]   Willoughby, *Soul of the Bantu*, 330; Mackenzie, *Ten Years*, 394. It is not clear to me, as some have argued, that *badimo* were *never* individually invoked in rituals. Certain ancestors appeared in dreams, *dikgosi* visited individual graves to make rain, and I myself heard men utter the names of ancestors in a *mophaso* healing ritual. Seeley, "Reaction of Batswana," 39, for *go phatsa*, and H. O. Monnig, *The Pedi* (Pretoria, 1967), 58, for *go phasa*.

[11]   Interview: Senior women singing, 19 May 1990, GooMoremi (in which jolly senior women and men shouted about BoPedi and the "visitors from the east"); cf. Steven Feierman, *The Shambaa Kingdom* (Madison, 1974), 87–88; Packard, *Chiefship and Cosmology*, 6; Feierman, *Peasant Intellectuals*, 69, 79, and Ch. 2, *passim*; and see Landau, "When Rain Falls."

[12]   Interviews: MmaRramatebele (Mrs. Mapula Ramosoka), b. ca 1908, Lerala, 2 May 1990; Ms. Sekibi Ramosoka, and MmaRramatebele, Lerala, 7 May 1990; The Rev. Tshinamo Molebalwa, Lerala, 28 March 1990; Kiyaga-Mulindwa, *Tswapong Historical Texts*, II, 45; Schapera, *Rainmaking Rites*, 22, 98, 113, 120.

While they sought to bring rain and fertility to Tswapong, however, Christianity crept through the Hills—not from the east, but from the west.[13]

Hymns and Harmony: The Vanguard

Lewatle Selato, the elder son of one of Lerala's first baruti, remarked to me, "The yards of nonbelievers were just people singing 'Ooeeeeeh.' They did not sing these songs of God . . . not those of Church, just their own singing."[14] In one sense, hymns were not people's own expressions; they were placed in Tswana mouths by missionaries. A successful rendition required discipline, conformity, repetition; "harmony" was the highest praise. Yet the idea that hymns were a cultural imposition does not sit well with their profound integration with community life throughout southern Africa.[15] As we have seen, the words in the hymns emerged from the charged environment of missionaries and their early converts, and sometimes owed more to the latter. Moreover, Ngwato Church members occasionally performed hymns of their own design, disturbing missionaries's expectations.[16]

Most of all, the great popularity of the LMS hymnbook can be explained in terms of its use. The meaning of the hymns cannot be separated from the total situation of their performance. Hymns travelled from village to village independently of missionaries, and often ahead of them, as a disembodied vanguard of Christianity. The hymn had two presences: one as a text, and the second as snippets or lead phrases overheard and repeated. These two forms reinforced and promulgated one another. In villages not yet visited by a missionary, the Rev. Lloyd found that "the people, generally, have a few books, and are able to read them. Everywhere the Hymn and Tune Book are to be seen, and I found the people trying their best to sing them."[17] The Rev. Reed realized that the most isolated communities learned hymns by using melody as a mnemonic aid.[18] Such communities' Churchgoers were very often illiterate, but music let them store the bulk of what knowledge of Christian doctrines they had. The Bible and hymnbook often travelled in tandem. A Lerala deacon remarked, "[W]hen I was a schoolboy I used to read my Bible in and out, and I used to sing, sometimes [I spent] the whole day singing."[19]

Tswana deacons and evangelists posted the hymns for many services, and they were sure to choose the ones known by such popular repetition. Still hymns were

---

[13]   Quote, WCW/734, W. C. Willoughby, "Notes of Tour in Cwenin[g] & Cwapon[g] Hills, Aug. 19th to Sept. 1st 1896," 14; S. E. Nicholson, "The Historical Climatology of Africa," in T. M. Wigley, ed., *Climate and History* (Cambridge, 1981), 263–64. Also, LMS SA 53/1/C, A. J. Wookey to LMS, Phalapye, 18/9/1896; and W. C. Willoughby to LMS, Mafeking, 12/10/1896.

[14]   Interview: Mr. Lewatle Selato, Lerala, 5 April 1990.

[15]   Setiloane, *Image of God*, 156.

[16]   Tunes were taken from Ira Sankey's *Sacred Songs and Solos* and similar compendiums of the time, like *Bristol* and *The Congregational Hymnbook*. LMS SA 84/5, "Leader of the Yellow Regiment," 23/7/22, in R. H. Lewis, "Khama salutes his Missionaries."

[17]   LMS SA 71/3, E. Lloyd to R. W. Thompson, Shoshong 19/7/09. Of course, very few indeed could read the musical notation.

[18]   LMS SA 80/3, C. Reed to Lenwood, Okavango River, 4/9/17.

[19]   Interview: Mr. Koowetse Molebalwa, b. 1905, Lerala, 16 June 1990.

just as personal as other elements of Christian practice, and could be carried far from Sunday services and day schools.[20] An old man told me,

> I [caught] all the hymns that were sung in the church, and these hymns remained in my memory, so that when I was a boy, who [was] able to look after—sheep and goats, I used to sing these hymns, yes, singing without knowing what I am singing about. . . but there was something very nice in these hymns. . . . I used to sing aloud even when I am alone!—in the veldt. These hymns remained with me for a long time, so that when I became a schoolboy, I went to Church *knowing* these hymns.[21]

Perhaps most importantly, women sang hymns, and lifted this form of public utterance to the level of an art. Some women mastered hundreds of hymns by heart, and were known for it. "From the Church I only want *thuto* and to be taught to sing," was how one Christian put things.[22] Hymns were a form of *mafoko*, like the *Lefoko* (the Word) itself: weighty language, spoken by persons of stature. Even more than for other modes of Christian expression, women captured these words and spoke them. Non-Christian women left the speaking of public words in the *kgotla* (and to the *badimo*) to senior men, but Church members and enquirers owned their own hymnbooks and with them they directly addressed God. It is perhaps through the raised voices of women that the Word was first heard in Lerala.

It is true that *thuto* came from outside the Hills, from the Ngwato capital in the west; but at the same time, villagers took up *thuto* and reworked it within the social life of the village. Itinerant *baruti* moved through the Hills from the Rev. Hepburn's time; it was the evangelism of Raditladi and Mphoeng in Tswapong that led to their exile. The Rev. Willoughby next journeyed through the Tswapong Hills in 1896, to prepare the way for permanent substations. By that time, hymns and other texts, at least in secondary, oral form, had spread ahead of the planned evangelism of the Church's *baruti*. Thus Willoughby repeatedly encountered apparent Christians, and had to determine what to do about them. In GooMoremi, Willoughby learned that "People always have Service here on Sunday, though there are only two catechumens here who seem to have no connection with any of our own people." By recognizing them, Willoughby established that very connection. Elsewhere, at GooTau, he found "no services here usually—only two people who can read and one doubtful sort of Christian." Too bad for him (or her). Such distinctions were dicey, and whomsoever Willoughby and his Ngwato *baruti* acknowledged as a "believer" in the village underwent a change in status, a change that had then to be worked out on a day-to-day basis with their fellow villagers.[23]

---

[20] According to Tshekedi, Khama himself used to sing Hymn 128 when he was astride his mount. Part of it is: "The kings of this earth / Let them remain in fear; / And fear him who is / The King of the Heavens. . . ." Tshekedi had part of the hymn engraved on Khama's memorial at his resting place; LMS SA 95/Haile, A. Jennings to Chirgwin, 15/6/32; Robert Moffat, Hymn 128, *Dihela*, 113.

[21] Interview: The Rev. B. R. Tshipa, b. 1902, Serowe, 17 February 1989, English.

[22] Interview: Ms. Maretha Masheto, Radisele 18 April 1989; and MmaTebo (Rachel) Mathare, Lerala, 2 April 1990, and others.

[23] WCW/734, W. C. Willoughby, "Notes of Tour in Cwenin[g] and Cwapon[g] Hills, Aug. 19th to Sept. 1st, 1896," 6–7 esp.

Thuto in Lerala

Shortly after Willoughby's tour in 1896, he dispatched Noke Modisakgosi to Ratholo and another moruti to Sefhare to the south, in Tshweneng.[24] Around this same time, the first Christians appeared in Lerala, drawn from the small Khurutshe ward. It is unclear whether they followed Noke's lead, or if their emergence preceded him. The Ngwato seat was then at Phalapye, in the west of the Hills. In 1898 Khama began to decentralize Phalapye and with it his juridical authority, as we saw in Chapter 3, and in consequence *thuto* became more important to his power. Within a few years, Ratholo and Maunatlala (a Birwa village) had the most substantial Christian communities in Tswapong.[25]

Moruti Noke of Ratholo earned the praise of several missionaries. Noke's classes attracted a trickle of enquirers from about the Hills. They convened in opposition to the Pedi perpetuation of regional community, based as it was in the idiom of *badimo*. Previous to Noke's ministry, elite expressions of Pedi historical identity were embodied in increasingly illegal yearly agricultural cults and the generational rites of initiation—*go rupa*, as Tswapong men called both of them. Such ceremonies continued across the Limpopo in Mmalebogo's village after the Z.A.R. conquest in 1894, and probably in GooMoremi as well.[26] These rituals, much like Dialwa's rain-gathering in local consciousness, reconstructed a community antagonistic to the essence of the *kingdom*, which was reproduced through the teaching of *thuto*.

At first, the intrusion of *thuto* into Tswapong would have been tenuous. With only a handful of young catechumens, *baruti* like Noke could not afford to offend parents, who might simply withdraw their children from school and Church.[27] Ministries such as Noke's soon received a boost from the king, however. 1901 fell in a period of mild drought, and in that year there was some sort of perceived resurgence of non-Christian ritual activity in Tswapong. This is known because Willoughby made notes entitled "Worshipping the Daft," about "people claiming to be Priests of the Gods" in various parts of the Hills. According to the missionary,

> People gathered round their daft "priest" or priestess[,] offered sacrifices, made beer, carried on their feasts and drinking bouts with dances far into the night. The animals offered to the gods were killed and eaten by the worshippers present.[28]

Although Willoughby thought he was describing some anomalous movement, his odd understanding of abnormalcy (the "daft") warns us that it may have been an annual set of rites. The "outbreak" most likely indicated a chain of periodic

---

[24] Parsons, "Khama III," 249–51.

[25] LMS SA Reports 4/4, A. Jennings, Serowe for 1911–12.

[26] Although Schapera, *Tribal Innovators*, 120, relates that Khama banned the *bogwera*, there is no reason to doubt testimony that it quietly continued in some places outside the capital through the end of the nineteenth century; Interviews: Mr. Molaodi Thakeng, b. 1901, Lerala, 12 June 1990; Mr. Sematlho Pipedi, b. 1914, Lerala, 22 June 1990; and Noel Roberts, "The Bagananoa or Ma-Laboch," *South African Journal of Science* 12 (1915), 241–56. Thanks to Dick Werbner for referring this source to me.

[27] As was the case in Magapatona in 1923; LMS SA 85/2, Minutes of Annual Conference of Mangwato Churches held at Serowe, 3/[2]–7/[2]/23, 6.

[28] WCW/770, W. C. Willoughby, "Worshipping the Daft," ms.

agricultural and rain-making rituals rooted in ancestor propitiation, and linked to Dialwa's activities, which I found were still recalled in the oral traditions of lineages rival to the chiefship's.

Here we may remark the contrast in 1901 between the situation in Lerala and the Ngwato capital. In Lerala, an alliance of non-Christians and *dikgosi* had sought to restore fertility to a Pedi-bound ancestral community. For the Ngwato kingship, 1901 was a year of Church reforms, territorial expansion, and disturbances as British troops were quartered in Phalapye for the duration of the South African War. The Ngwato kingdom was increasing its presence in its hinterland by dispatching or recognizing *baruti*; Willoughby had fifty men in a training class for making and delivering sermons.[29] What sharpened the contrast between the hegemonic center at Phalapye and Lerala's ethnic constructions, however, was the fundamental commonality between them: both the royal and village *kgotla* interwove what others might call political and religious power.

In this unquiet time, it was Christians in Tswapong who provided the kingship with a new source of knowledge about regional practices and a greater reason to put a stop to them. Willoughby mentions that several Church members were "afflicted" by the "daft" rites: this is what most likely commended the situation to Khama's attention. Hence a major factor in the Ngwato understanding of the "outbreak" was the unresolved connection between new adherents of the Church and those trusting in *badimo*. After several "ominous warnings," Khama sent out a regiment with matches to burn down the farmland homes of all transgressors. "Khama says you are sinning yourselves for want of work," the *mophato*-leader was to announce, "and so he wishes you to build new houses for yourselves."[30] This put Tswapong on notice. Five years after Willoughby's groping itineration, force moved through the Hills.

In the next few years Ratholo's and Sefhare's congregations expanded and seeded other hamlets nearby. Samuel Maremane, a MoSeleka briefly educated in Tiger Kloof as a regular student, assisted Moruti Noke in Ratholo, and then Moruti Mosinyane at Sefhare, for two years each. By 1905, Ratholo had its own church building, Sefhare was growing, and Samuel was living in Lerala.

In Lerala, Samuel Maremane supervised a small congregation and taught reading and Scripture to catechumens; his minimal salary was paid by the Serowe congregation.[31] In his classes perhaps twenty or thirty young people learned to read LMS primers and sing hymns together. As they moved to higher levels, they assisted in teaching their juniors. Just as Khama followed his training in *thuto* in the 1860s with a short stint of formal teaching, so there was a

---

[29]   *Ibid.*, and Parsons, "Khama III," 249, citing Willoughby to LMS, 27/8/01.

[30]   Parsons, "Khama III," 249, citing Willoughby to LMS, 27/8/01. Merchants were not a source of information here, since their shops were confined to the railway line. Tswapong people had to travel to Palapye Station to trade produce for the few items they needed. Interview: Mrs. Moswamasimo Molebalwa, Lerala, 27 March 1990.

[31]   Interviews: MmaMotlamma (Ms. Gasewame), Lerala, 17 June 1990; Mr. Samuel Malete, Lerala, 25 May 1990; Ms. Selebogo Mogame and MmaWini (Ms. Fetang), Lerala, 22 April 1990, and Mr. Selo Mafoko, b. 1900, Lerala, 11 April 1990; Hepburn, *Twenty Years in Khama's Country*, 245; WCW/734, "Notes of Tour;" LMS SA 66/3, A. Jennings to R. W. Thompson, 8/9/05; ZKM, LMS Tiger Kloof Register, "Samuel Maremane"; Kiyaga-Mulindwa, *Tswapong Historical Texts*, II, 5.

rough cycle of learning in Lerala: those with five years of instruction moved from receiver to giver of *thuto*.[32]

What did the new teaching mean in Lerala in the 1910s? Many old men and women in Lerala today cannot read, indicating that the early classes were not inclusive. Mathuba, a respected senior man, is illiterate. And yet he also bears the imprint of the written word; here is how he dismissed the notion that Mokakapadi I, Dialwa's father, had ruled as *kgosi*:

> Absolutely no one can show that Mokakapadi in fact ruled. He is not there in the tax register. They [people in Dialwa's lineage] were always talking their talk, but the deciding proof which shows that Mokakapadi never ruled is that there is no such name in the tax-book, a copy of which exists.[33]

Mathuba's argument is empirically dubious, since the *lekgetlho* or hut tax did not begin until 1899, but it is all the more rhetorically intriguing for being so. The inscription of a name legitimates its bearer, as writing also is *thuto*, the teachings that flowed from the Ngwato capital alongside the Ngwato hut-tax collector. The trend of his argument can be found in many of Lerala's traditions that feature appeals to Khama to settle disputes and sanction the rule of this or that *kgosi*. Another man remarked that the chiefship of Molebatsi was the first of Lerala to be "written" at the Ngwato capital. Such a "writing" of the person echoes the inscription of catechumens' names in the Church register.[34] When I asked senior Pedi men about Tswapong's relationship with the BaNgwato, most of them denied that Ngwato arms ever subdued Tswapong, but said the BaNgwato had "conquered" the Hills with *thuto*. Should they forget this conquest, they need only visit the literate adolescent government officials posted in many of their villages, who today outrank them. Indeed, as illiterate men retell their traditions, invoking Khama's legitimations of local authority, their own words must not taste so sweet.[35]

Lerala's Christians

The earliest enquirers in Moruti Samuel's classes in *thuto*, and indeed the earliest members of the Lerala congregation that preceded Samuel, came from the large Khurutshe household called, as a *kgotla*, Moatshe. The core lineage, Madoko/Matsutsubane, has oral traditions that tell of a history of occasional strife with the BaPedi calmed by appeals to "Khama" for adjudication. As Motsatsi Nakedi, now deceased, remarked, "We lived peaceably with our neighbors mainly because we were all under one power of the BaNgwato."[36] The first male Christians in Lerala were Nakedi, the father of Motsatsi; Sisaphoko, Motsatsi's brother; Mogame,

[32] Interview: Mr. Selo Mafoko, b. 1900, Lerala, 12 April 1990; cf. WCW/374, "Mahoko a Phuthego," 7.

[33] Interview: Mr. Mathuba a Madikwe, b. 1901, Mmakgabo village, 24 May 1990.

[34] Of course, Christ also pointed to the authority of the "written" Word, i.e., Matthew 4: 5–11.

[35] Kiyaga-Mulindwa, *Tswapong Historical Texts*, I, 110 (Leso Maifala); and Interviews: Mr. Koowetse Molebalwa, b. 1905, Lerala, 9 April 1990, and 16 June 1990; Mr. Lewatle Selato, Lerala, 5 April 1990; Mr. Selo Mafoko, b. 1900, Lerala, 11 April 1990; Mr. Sematlho Pipedi, b. 1914, Lerala, 13 June 1990.

[36] Kiyaga-Mulindwa, *Tswapong Historical Texts*, II, 49–50, quote 51, Motsatsi Nakedi; and *Ibid*, 5–7, group interview.

Motsamaye, Maemo, and Tlhalefang, all of them close Khurutshe kin. Along with them came wives often of other descent. Mogame's wife Gafalefhi was an important Church member, and surely so were others whose backgrounds are now forgotten by androcentric lineage stories. Nakedi and Mogame were old men by the 1920s, and Mogame supervised the congregation as a senior deacon until he became infirm in the 1930s. He led village prayers, blessed food and perhaps beer at Christmas, and sanctified the harvest. His children, and his father's brother's daughter, son, and son's wife also became Christians.[37]

Pedi men, both royals and commoners, also married Khurutshe women.[38] The current *kgosi*'s mother and aunt are both BaKhurutshe by birth. Although in certain situations such identities still come to the fore, they were secondary to their gender. Now, however, some wives had a new identity as Christians. Like them, the Pedi commoners of the oldest standing in the village never laid claim to a corporate history, because they are—by definition—subordinate homesteads thrown together under the ruling Pedi descent group. After a while, their *kgotla* also had Christians. For them as for Khurutshe women and men, the supraethnicity of the Church had great appeal beside their normal allegiance to the Pedi *kgosi*.

There was a limit to how far the realm of the Word could penetrate Lerala. The aristocratic monopoly on ritual was still premised on a Pedi ancestral community centered in the Transvaal. However, events in Lerala breached this limit. Magosi's brother, Ramosoka, took the chiefship away from him, and in the 1910s absorbed Magosi's estate. He stopped Dialwa's activities, spatially centralized the village around his own household, and left Dialwa's sons with the headmanship of a reduced *kgotla*, which was then entitled Monneng, "Place of the younger brother."[39] The *coup* and Ramosoka's rupture of the Pedi ancestral tie opened Lerala to the regime of the Word. The separation between the judicial and ritual spheres pioneered by Magosi and Dialwa persisted, however, because in order to uphold his own authority, Ramosoka accepted Christians as *his* ritual experts while continuing to be the juridical *kgosi*.

Interestingly, Dialwa's senior lineal descendant says that Ramosoka was Khama's "boy."

> Now Ramosoka told Magosi, "Get off my *kgotla* stool; I am your senior." Thereby they made war. And it was then that Khama gave Magosi the throne. So Ramosoka worked digging wells for Khama, he was Khama's "boy" [English, and repeated several times]. . . . Ramosoka, as he was accustomed to knowing Khama, as Khama's hired "boy," . . . then [felt he could fight] with Magosi. He killed Magosi with Tswana

---

[37] Interviews Mrs. Setuhile Sebina, Serowe, 28 Feb. 1989; Mrs. Boikanyo Motlhagodi, with Ditaolo Motlhagodi, Lerala, 17 May 1990, and 1 June 1990; Mr. Joel Tlhalefang, Lerala, 29 May 1990; Mr. Lewatle Selato, Lerala, 5 April 1990; MmaMotlamma (Ms. Gasewame), Lerala, 17 June 1990; Mr. Samuel Malete, Lerala, 25 May 1990, Mr. Selo Mafoko, b. 1900, Lerala, 11 April 1990; Kgosi Shaw Moroka, Lerala, 24 April 1990; Rev. Steven Nkgetsi, Lerala, 10 May 1990, and especially Ms. Selebogo Mogame, Lerala, 18 April 1990.

[38] Interview: Mrs. Miriam (MmaKgalemang) Tshinye, Lerala, 2 May 1990, for instance, was afraid to attend certain Pedi rituals for fear of being "smelled out."

[39] Interviews: Mr. Bonnetswe K. Dialwa, b. 1923, Lerala, 15 May 1990; Mr. Koolebile Kerekang Dialwa, Lerala, 25 June 1990; Mr. Makwesa Leso, Lerala, 20 June 1990.

methods, with medicine—Hey, you are causing me trouble, child! [directed to P.L.][40]

Regardless of the way Ramosoka came to rule the village, from his perspective—as the person ostensibly responsible for ensuring social harmony and rain—something was very wrong. A severe drought began in Tswapong and indeed affected the Protectorate and the Transvaal. As a possible remedy, Ramosoka had little at his disposal apart from the dangerously senior and probably hostile Dialwa, shorn of his ally Magosi, whom Ramosoka had deposed. Nonetheless, at first, Ramosoka resisted the only pressing alternative, which was to open his *kgotla* fully to Lerala's Christians; to do so would be to bow not only to the kingdom, but also to the village of Ratholo, which had the senior congregation in Tswapong.[41]

Ramosoka's recalcitrance appears in a letter Moruti Samuel wrote to Khama. Evidently Ramosoka had allied himself to the Boer farmers of the Tuli block, who wished to prevent their Lerala workers from attending "school." Some of these farmers, cattle-ranchers mostly, were far closer to Khama than anyone in Lerala. Therefore Samuel wrote plaintively to the king, "I put myself in the hands of the king and the Church."[42] Many BaKhurutshe in Lerala migrated to the Tuli Block to work for abysmal wages, often two Rand per month with mealie sacks as rations and a place to build a rondavel. Some even indentured themselves to farms to pay their hut-tax arrears. Among BaNgwato, this only confirmed their prejudices toward "MaTswapong," whose men, as one MoNgwato remarked, were all lowly workers on Boer farms.[43] But Ramosoka evidently saw an advantage in supporting whites' attack on *thuto*, which, in elevating men and women to a larger citizenship, also threatened his own authority in Lerala.

Drought would not let up. Green grass wilted and crisped on the brick-colored ground, melon fields were barren and hard, and the winter of 1913/14 had no rain. In this second year of crop failure, Ramosoka's resolve weakened. He adopted the Christian rain-prayers sanctioned by the Church (and by the kingdom), and thereby accepted Christianity into his *kgotla* in the process. Although Ramosoka himself never joined the Church, from that time on the Lerala *kgotla* would seem to belong to authorities external to Lerala, whether that of the Ngwato kingdom or of independent Botswana.[44]

---

[40] Interview: Mr. Bonnetswe K. Dialwa, b. 1923, Lerala, 15 May 1990. "Boy" is of course the ubiquitous *colonial* term for African men in positions of service. "Tswana methods" is *polanenyane*, diminutive of English, "plan."

[41] JR LMS/S 3 Register: "Notes on Members." Ratholo district included Lerala and six other villages.

[42] K III H/59/"loose papers," S. Maremane to Khama, Lerala 29/8/12.

[43] Interviews: Mr. Ditaolo Motlhagodi with Mrs. Boikanyo Motlhagodi, Lerala, 15 May 1990; Mrs. Boikanyo Motlhagodi, with Ditaolo Motlhagodi, Lerala, 17 May 1990; Sillery, *Founding a Protectorate*, 240; and Dimpe, "Batswapong-Bangwato Relations." See also M. Massey, "A Case of Colonial Collaboration: The Hut Tax and Migrant Labour," *Botswana Notes and Records* 10 (1978), 95–98. For Ngwato sentiment, K III H/59/"1923", Manyaphiri Ikitseng to Khama, Sefhala 14/1/23.

[44] LMS SA Reports, 4/4, Shoshong for 1912 (E. Lloyd); 5/1, Serowe for 1913 (A. Jennings), and Shoshong for 1913 (E. Lloyd), in which the drought is called "the worst in thirty years"; LMS SA 76/2, E. Sharp to F. H. Hawkins, Serowe, 19/1/14; and Interviews: Mr. Joel Tlhalefang, Lerala, 29 May 1990; Mr. Koowetse Molebalwa, b. 1905, Lerala, 9 April 1990; MmaMotlamma (Ms. Gasewame), Lerala, 17 June 1990; Kgosi Shaw Moroka, Lerala, 24 April 1990; and especially Mr. Sebele Gaborone, b. 1903, Lerala, 11 June 1990.

The Expansion of Lerala's Congregation

When the first Pedi commoners from Matalaganye ward (the nonchiefly "Pedi" ward) wished to join Lerala's catechumenate, their means of approach lay through the existing members of the congregation. No missionary was present to intervene. Even so, to an extent the same was true everywhere; the Rev. Andrew Kgasa thus wrote the Rev. Lewis that older Christians in Maun were not happy when he signed up catechumens on his own authority: they wished enquirers to "go round from one Christian to another as they used to do."[45] Otaajang Kedikilwe grew up in the 1910s and 1920s in Nekati and Shoshong, where her father, Moruti Seakgano, was stationed. When I pressed her on how people used to join the Church, she thought the question foolish:

> [Was there a book of members' names? -P.L.] No! They [catechumens] were not written down, the congregations just agreed, like you know when a person becomes a Christian he or she goes to confess to the *moruti* and . . . he or she leaves the cattlepost [or wherever], gets dressed, and comes home, and when night has fallen goes to confess herself, do you hear? When she has confessed herself to someone, to you or me or whoever, to a Christian, *each person to whom she confessed* is sent to the *moruti*, so that he may be told about what the person said. Are there not still such confessions today?[46]

There may be, informally. The closeness in small Tswana villages make anything less than cooperation difficult to imagine. Even Church laws might have to be bent in its interest, as was the rule requiring sacramental marriage for couples who were confirmed members. As the Rev. Ramolefhi laughingly told me, when the moment arrives for Communion, "you cannot tell your grandparents they have been living in sin."[47]

Social harmony, like hymnal harmony, helped village congregations span distinct communities, and Mogame and his family benefitted in social and material ways from the Church's ability to trivialize ethnicity. Among Mogame's friends was the Pedi commoner, Lebogang Selato, who provided Mogame a social connection to other Pedi people in the village. Lebogang was a deacon by the mid-1920s and later led the congregation in the decade before his death in 1943.[48] Even before the 1920s, Mogame's people befriended and married with members of Moruti Samuel Maremane's family, further broadening their social and economic networks.

Just as critically, non-Khurutshe Christians helped Mogame farm. Mogame's lands were not close to those of the Pedi majority, and he lacked a plow and a team of oxen for a longer time than other households.[49] It was therefore quite important

---

[45]   LMS SA 89/1, Sandilands to F. H. Hawkins, Serowe 8/1/27, Kgasa extract no. 14.

[46]   Interview: Mrs. Otaajang Kedikilwe, b. 1902, Sefhope, 20 May 1989, my emphasis. Perplexed missionaries told similar stories of enquirers visiting them at night to confess their faith; I am not sure why night was chosen.

[47]   Interview: The Rev. Harsh Ramolefhe, Gaborone 15 June 1989, English, notes taken by hand.

[48]   Interviews: Archbishop (Spiritual Healing Church) Israel Motswasele, Matsiloje, 17 Jan. 1989; Mrs. Bamorago Kgatwane Raditau, b. 1906, Serowe, 18 Jan. 1989; Mr. Oabona Nthobatsang, Serowe, 12 May 1989.

[49]   Norman Mahoney, "Contract and Neighborly Exchange among the Birwa of Botswana," *Journal of African Law* 21, 1 (1977), 55 and 62–63; Duggan, *Economic Analysis*, 109–12; and Interview: Mrs. Balatheo Moloi, Serowe, 17 Nov. 1988.

that other Christians, according to Mogame's daughter, "plowed for my father," and that Christian women came to one another's aid during the cooperative time of harvesting and threshing. "If someone's child was ill, another Christian woman would take her place in the field."[50]

I have already described the evangelical campaigns of the 1920s, and these had an effect in Lerala. Kgosi Ramosoka's youngest wife began attending Church, and several other Pedi enquirers joined their mainly Khurutshe neighbors in the congregation.[51] More than anything, the Ngwato campaigns reassociated with force the ideas of Church, the West, white people (for district officials took a higher profile in the early 1930s), and the king. Such associations allowed Pedi commoners as well as BaKhurutshe to derive prestige from participating in the services in the *kgotla*. Lebogang Selato enjoyed a degree of authority that he, as a commoner, would have never attained through his lineage from *badimo* rituals. The same was true for the few Christian BaKaa in the village.[52] All this amounted to the beginnings of a social transformation. And so, predictably, not all was soft words and acceptance in the village.

Conflicts and Negotiations: Ethnicity, Status, Gender

In the 1920s and 1930s, many villages witnessed the emerging Christian hierarchy clash with other, older configurations of seniority. In Kalamare, near Shoshong, the local *moruti* complained to a conference of Ngwato Church baruti in 1923[53] that his Church had proven "too much" for him. An old evangelist, Sekonopo, had acquired an unhappy influence over the congregation, and "refuses to refrain from preaching, saying [Church] Elders are 'young men.'" Even after Sekonopo's suspension with three other members, he "still rang the bell for services and simply attacked people in his preaching."[54] There appears to have been something like a coup of wealthy senior men over their erstwhile juniors who held senior status in the Kalamare congregation. Before the matter was moved to a secret session, there were accusations of polygynist adultery and false witness.

Similar issues resulted in the suspension of members in Moeng village, in Ratholo, and elsewhere. At Tsienyane, the village chief, Makgala, unilaterally suspended several lay evangelists in the congregation in the absence of their *moruti*, then Monyeki Mashabe. The evangelists then claimed Makgala acted merely because he suspected them of telling Moruti Monyeki "whatever goes on in the

---

50   Interview: Ms. Selebogo Mogame, Lerala, 18 April 1990. Sematlo and Tlotleng Pipedi's mother, Gopolang, was also an early Christian; since Pipedi only come back to Lerala in 1914, as he had fled with Dialwa and others of a foreclosed chiefly lineage, Gopolang's Christianity may well have filled a social need similar to that discussed here; and MmaMotlamma (Ms. Gasewame), Lerala, 17 June 1990.

51   Interview: MmaRramatebele (Mrs. Mapula Ramosoka), b. ca 1908, Lerala, 2 May 1990; and Mr. Joel Tlhalefang, Lerala, 29 May 1990; Mr. Samuel Malete, Lerala, 25 May 1990; and the Rev. Steven Nkgetsi, Lerala, 10 May 1990. There were also some BaPedi, BaKaa, and a few "MaLete" or BaSeleka as well.

52   Interview: Mr. Samuel Malete, Lerala, 25 May 1990.

53   LMS SA 85/2, Minutes of Annual Conference of Mangwato Churches held at Serowe, 3/[2]–7/[2]/23, hereafter LMS SA 85/2, Minutes. Minutes like these were surely felt to be too embarrassing to be reprinted anywhere, and this is the only such record I found.

54   LMS SA 85/2, Minutes, 12; 14–15.

town."[55] Monyeki ordered the reinstatement of the evangelists. In remote villages like Tsienyane in the Kalahari, the *kgosi* was often a deacon; and sometimes, when the *moruti* was absent, deacons dispensed Communion. In such cases, the line between ecclesiastic and community hierarchies vanished and abuses followed.[56]

On the other hand, the resident *moruti* sometimes offended local sensibilities. Thus in 1906, the Rev. Jennings ordered the removal of an evangelist from Makomi in BoKalanga, just as he did Khukhwe Mogodi from Ngamiland. In Makomi the evangelist was a relative of Khama's wife Semane, which led to "many unpleasant hours" of discussion with King Khama.[57] Relationships were thus forged both within villages and in connection with the larger Ngwato Church hierarchy. Although this was a constant and involving process, few Christians wished to recall it later on.

Few people in Lerala chose to remember that in 1923, Moruti Samuel Maremane complained that he could "no longer live in peace" with the Lerala congregation. Samuel had been supervising the catechumen classes of both Seolwane and Lerala. An elder Christian from Seolwane, which lies a few miles to the north of Lerala, went over Samuel's head and told a regional Church conference that Seolwane Christians "refuse to be suspended from Church membership by Samuel, inasmuch as he himself is not without fault and is still in the Church." The Seolwane congregation had been avoiding Lerala and sending their youth north to Maunatlala instead. The senior regional *moruti* (at that time, of Lecheng village) reacted by alluding to two previous complaints against Samuel, and rebuked both him and his accuser.

Perhaps not coincidentally, Samuel moved from Lerala that year. Even before he did so, Lerala's congregation had superseded him in managing their own affairs. By then, greater numbers of Christians and *baruti* were populating the Hills. Kgosi Ramosoka for his part weathered the rise of the new commoner elite with some ambivalence. In the drought of 1921–1923, he sent his son and Dialwa's second son, Kerekang, to the old Gananwa villages in the Transvaal.[58] Although he facilitated commoners' rain prayers, he revealed his unease with the regional Christian hierarchy. Just at the time when Maunatlala, the Birwa village to the north, began to oversee Lerala's Church affairs, Ramosoka "ordered" its ancestor cult to cease beating their drums to make rain: they made noise too early and "frightened away" rainclouds.[59] Ancestral and Church unity were connected in unpredictable ways. Lerala people say that Kgosi Ramosoka had at least one more episode of restlessness with Christian-based rain prayers. The drought of 1933 and 1934 had begun to empty the village by provoking people to live out on their lands.[60] In the 1930s, a travelling prophet claimed to have a connection to Ngwale Nkulu (Mwali),

---

[55]   *Ibid.*, 8. Monyeki was probably away for his ordination of that year, and shortly after returning to Tsienyane he was moved to the more important station at Maunatlala.

[56]   E.g., LMS SA 89/1, Sandilands to Hawkins, Serowe, 8/1/27, Kgasa excerpts Nos. 23, 24.

[57]   LMS SA Reports 4/1, A. Jennings, Serowe for 1906; 4/2, A. Jennings, Serowe for 1909.

[58]   Interviews: Mr. Koolebile Kerekang Dialwa, Lerala, 25 June 1990; Kgosi Mokakapadi (II) a Ramosoka, b. 1907, Lerala, 8 May 1990.

[59]   Interviews: Mr. Mathuba a Madikwe, b. 1901, Mmakgabo village, 24 May 1990; Mr. Samuel Malete, Lerala, 25 May 1990; Mr. Sematlho Pipedi, b. 1914, Lerala, 13 June 1990.

[60]   LMS SA 97/Burns, A. Burns to LMS, Serowe, ?/10/1933; 95/Haile, A. J. Haile to Chirgwin, Tiger Kloof, 25/10/33: an "appalling" drought "still" afflicts. This is when villagers commenced their move from the Gale to Lerala's present site.

the Kalanga God; the prophet often came through Tswapong and "blessed" people's seeds. During a second drought in 1936–1937, Ramosoka sent one of Dialwa's sons to him with a black goat to ask for rain.[61] The resulting deluge spoiled a great deal of the harvest, perhaps as a rebuke to the *kgosi* for deviating from Christian prayer.

From 1910 on, women dominated Lerala's congregation, becoming its presence in the village; Ramosoka had opened the previously male *kgotla* to women for evangelism and ceremony, and they never left.[62] Things did not always go smoothly. Many deacons saw an overwhelmingly female membership as a form of "weakness" (*bokoa*). The Serowe deacons' minutes of 1945 call Mmadinare "weakened because most members are women." In Mookane, there was also trouble, as Moruti Segaise reluctantly[63] told me:

> The leader of the Mookane congregation when I arrived there [in about 1935] was MmaNoko Thabeng. Sephothe was a deacon, from Serowe. Long ago, women had no power—only men. So Sephothe had that mindset and opposed preaching by women.

Recall that Serowe's congregation was largely male as late as 1906. Sephothe opposed MmaNoko's authority on old-fashioned grounds. Sample the intricacies of the case below, without necessarily bothering to sort them out:

> The *kgosi's* wife was also a deacon. MmaNoko Thabeng's husband Thabeng was the uncle of Kgosi Bakwena. Even though the congregation was only ten, these people vied for leadership. Sephothe opposed MmaNoko's dominance and preaching but was stymied from competing with her by me, who was her vice-*moruti*. When I came to Mookane from the cattle post, that is when I preached. The *kgosi* sided with MmaNoko and the women against Sephothe; he [Kgosi Bakwena] himself was only an enquirer, unlike his wife, a deacon.[64]

The entanglement of kin, conflicting notions of seniority, the involvement of the *kgosi* and his wife, the agitation by the Ngwato member of the Church, and the dramatic introduction of Segaise from the veldt turned the Mookane congregation into a cauldron. If this is not enough, a decade later Kgosi Bakwena of Mookane had reversed his position, perhaps after failing to attain the status of member. The Serowe deacon's minutes from February 1945 record that Sepothe and Kgosi Bakwena now joined in barring the largely female congregation from meeting, arguing that women should not preach; the *kgosi* also drove the Ngwato-assigned *moruti* out of the village. According to the latter,

---

61   Interviews: Mr. Koolebile Kerekang Dialwa, Lerala, 25 June 1990, independently giving 1937 as the year; MmaTebo (Rachel) Mathare, Lerala, 2 April 1990; and the entries for "Serowe," LMS, *Report of the L.M.S.*, Vols. 86 (n.s.) (Cape Town, 1936), and 87 (1937).

62   Interviews: Mr. Ditaolo Motlhagodi, Lerala, 2 April 1990; Mrs. Boikanyo Motlhagodi, with Ditaolo Motlhagodi, Lerala, 1 June 1990; Miss Leah Molemoge, Lerala, 3 April 1990; Mrs. Miriam (MmaKgalemang) Tshinye, Lerala, 2 May 1990.

63   Interview: Moruti Modise Segaise (b. ca. 1910) with Mrs. Gasethata Segaise, Serowe, 20 Dec. 1988. I told Segaise that I had read in the forty-five-year old minutes of a man named Sephothe in Mookane, and this spurred his memory.

64   Interview: Moruti Modise Segaise (b. ca. 1910) with Mrs. Gasethata Segaise, Serowe, 29 May 1989, from my notes and not verbatim.

COTTAR'S SATURDAY NIGHT SECWANA VERSION.

Christians posing for W. C. Willoughby, ca. 1897. From *Native Life on the Transvaal Border* (London, n.d. [1899]).

Sephothe and Kgosi Bakwena accuse us and the deacons of being woman-ish. The *kgosi* scattered me and my wife from home in February; we lived in the bush for eight months. Finally the Rev. [Tumedisho] Maruapula came and talked to Sephothe and said, leave the work alone; —he said, if you were not so old, I would cut you off from the Church.[65]

Unfortunately, I found no such specific source for Lerala, although such con-flicts were common enough elsewhere. After Ramosoka's death in 1939, however, most Christians began to hold their rain prayers by a large tree near the present site of the village, "because," one women told me, "the *kgotla* was tainted with past sins."[66]

The Laws of Believers

Most citizens in Lerala grouped Khama's laws and "The Law of God" (or, the Church's laws) together, even if they did not always respect them. The mandatory Sabbath, school and Church fees, the prohibition on Tswana beer, marriage rules, and hut taxes did not fall easily into one or the other category.[67] In small villages, all these laws were enforced, if sporadically, by the local *kgosi*. It was only if he forgot his duty, and word of his lapse reached the central congregation in Serowe, that the long arm of the kingdom entered his territory. Hence when Ramosoka attacked one of his own relatives for failing to pay his hut tax, and the regional tax collector reported to Khama that Ramosoka beat old men after drinking beer, the intervention of a Ngwato regiment seemed frighteningly possible for a while.[68]

It is not easy to gauge the effectiveness of Ngwato laws in peripheral villages, even at the height of the kingdom's power. Certainly, in villages like Bobonong under Modisaotsile, such laws were taken very seriously. Similarly, in Shoshong

Tshekedi Khama as well after the death of Khama, on holy days like Easter and Christmas, when the BaNgwato wished people to go to the church, they sent police to go through the whole village to check those who had put clothes on the line and they took the clothes off, stashed them somewhere, and put those people first in Church. Even on a mere Sunday this might happen.[69]

---

65   UCCSA Papers, Serowe Deacons' Meeting Minutes, 1946–52, 6/2/46, chaired by J. Lenyebe. The same source shows that similar contestations within and between ecclesiastic and village society persisted into the 1950s.

66   Interviews: MmaMotlamma (Ms. Gasewame), Lerala, 17 June 1990; Ms. Selebogo Mogame and MmaWini (Ms. Fetang) and Mr. Tshwene Tshiame, Lerala, 24 June 1990; Mr. Selo Mafoko, b. 1900, Lerala, 11 April 1990.

67   Interviews: Ruth Williams, June 1989, English; Mrs. Dijelwe [Medupe] Moyo, Lerala, 19 April 1990; Mr. Koowetse Molebalwa, b. 1905, Lerala, 9 April 1990; Mr. Selo Mafoko, b. 1900, Lerala, 11 April 1990, and 12 April 1990; Kgosi Shaw Moroka, Lerala, 24 April 1990.

68   Mathuba continued that, after much consternation and rumours that all Lerala's household heads would be summoned to Serowe and fined, a MoNgwato *mophato* (regiment) leader came to scold Lerala. Interview: Mr. Mathuba a Madikwe, b. 1901, Mmakgabo village, 16 June 1990; but there is a lack of agree-ment here: Kgosi Mokakapadi (II) a Ramosoka, b. 1907, Lerala, 24 June 1990, demurs on Ramosoka's earlier problems but says he was arrested for shooting someone; and Mrs. Dijelwe [Medupe] Moyo, Lerala, 19 April 1990, who says beer-brewers were conducted to Serowe in the 1920s by the MaSokola *mophato*.

69   Interview: The Rev. Johane Lenyebe, b. 1917, Serowe, May 1989.

FIGURE 8.1:   The Law

Factors, in rough order of importance, favoring laxness in enforcing *bojalwa* and Sabbath laws	Factors favoring rigorous enforcement

By village:

A Minor Christian presence	A Large Christian presence
B No Ngwato community	B Ngwato community
C No resident governor	C Resident governor

By individual:

A | Discrete | Popular	A |Brazen |Unliked
B *Kgosi*'s descent group	B Other descent group
C Known abstainer or Church-goer	C Known drinker or Sabbath breaker
D | Old | Pliant | Perpetual offender	D | Young | Stubborn | Repeat offender
E Female (sometimes)	E Male commoner

Elsewhere things were not so simple. Let us take the Sabbath and beer laws as examples for Tswapong. In Lerala, those who drink cynically claim that everyone drank, including *baruti*; most people admit beer was brewed, but only in private or on people's outlying lands. Some women in Ratholo told me that on Sundays, every Christian and non-Christian dutifully attended Church; others claimed that one merely had to be discrete while services were going on, and stay indoors, although actual inspanning for plowing was unheard of.[70]

Such ambiguities reflect a mobile dynamic between enforcement and compliance in the 1920s and 1930s in Tswapong. In general, seniority and prestige—whether in the village *kgotla* or congregation—discouraged punishment from within the village. True political crises threw all into flux, but "discovering" infractions was a socially configured phenomenon related to status and social tensions.[71] For instance, a Christian had a great deal to lose if exposed as a drinker, and so tended to abstain; Sunday services often functioned as a catchment for the wayward or middle-status juniors; and children were just beholden to others. On the other hand, the village idiot could do what he wished on Sunday. The schema above indexes factors

---

[70]   Sometimes even horseback riding on Sunday might get one pulled down and beaten. Interviews: Ms. Kadimo Serema, Palapye, 30 Nov. 1988; MmaSentsho Baengoti, and separately, Ms. Setswalo Gobusamang, Ratholo May 1990; The Rev. Tshinamo Molebalwa, Lerala, 28 March 1990; Mr. Selo Mafoko, b. 1900, Lerala, 11 April 1990; Mr. Koowetse Molebalwa, b. 1905, Lerala, 9 April 1990.

[71]   Interviews: Mr. Lewatle Selato, Lerala, 5 April 1990, and Mr. Mathuba a Madikwe, b. 1901, Mmakgabo village, 16 June 1990.

relating to punishment and compulsion in Sabbath and abstinence laws, and so attempts to depict part of the real exercise of power in the realm of the Word.

Brinkmanship, social sanction, and reports to the Ngwato center served to enforce the law. In this as in all other matters, *baruti* served more than one master. Like medieval European priests, however, they more often protected their villages than sought to betray them, especially in the matter of the mandatory tithe. It goes almost without saying that informal *baruti* who served in their home villages rarely turned on them. The small extant correspondence relevant here, most of which certifies couples wishing to marry, warrants this judgement, as *baruti* seem to argue on behalf of their congregations. From Selolwane in 1928, Moruti Solomon Kebothilwe enclosed the following note to the Rev. Kaleakgosi with a young couple wanting to marry. It begins with a verbal gesture:

> The first thing is the boy—this one—he has come to marry ["stand with"] his woman [names and ages given]. The price for them is £1.

He continues in more of an epistolary vein:

> We greet you, *Moruti*—and your people. For our part, we are still living but we see only the sun. We lack even water in the river. Those who planted in November had crops which withered young, and those who planted in December reaped nothing. We have told the congregation about monthly dues [*phalalo*] but we do not know, perhaps by June or July. We all, and my wife, greet you.[72]

Similarly from an unnamed village, "evangelist" Apadile Kedikilwe wrote the Rev. Tumedisho Maruapula in Shoshong: "Sir—concerning the congregation here, we have nothing, and we are weak; no dues [*phalalo*]—we can show you absolutely nothing."[73] Apadile penned a prayer on the reverse.

The fact that informal *baruti* might mean senior male Christians further complicated the authority of the Ngwato regime. The men in Lerala's congregation, for instance, being a clear minority, tended to see themselves as leaders, and many are recalled as *baruti*. Some Christians claimed that these men were "plowed for" like Kgosi Ramosoka and Khama (Khama had an honorary garden outside Lerala up to the 1940s);[74] and Khama and Tshekedi did specifically ask communities to plow and harvest *baruti*'s fields. Some communities complied, but plowing for *baruti* was most often an extension of intracongregational aid and, in any case, was not really an element of law.[75]

72 UCCSA Papers, interleaved in registers (hereafter "loose"), S. Kebothilwe to B. Kaleakgosi, Selolwane 23/3/28, my trans. Note that Selolwane and Seolwane are different villages. The reverse of this letter has notes written in the Rev. Baruti Kaleakgosi's striking script, on five marriages he evidently performed, together with the days of the week in English, and the phrase, in English, "Look at me I am up into the air." I do not know what this means.

73 UCCSA Papers, "loose," in Reg. C, A. Kedikilwe to T. Maruapula (ca. 1939); see also UCCSA Papers, "loose," S. Kebothilwe to B. Kaleakgosi, Francistown Dec. 1935; unsigned to S. Kebothilwe, 26/7/31; Mayala to Kaleakgosi, Madinare 4/10/36; Chief P.T. Moroka to Church, Shashi 29/11/47; A. Jennings et al., *Bogadi*, draft, 12a.

74 Wylie, *A Little God*, 51, mentions one in Chadibe; most old people in Lerala know the precise location of Khama's and Ramosoka's previous *masotlha* in Lerala.

75 Interview: Ms. Kadimo Serema, Palapye, 17 Dec. 1988; LMS SA 85/2, Minutes of Annual Conference, 3/[2]–7/[2]/23, 5–7.

After Christians began praying outside the Lerala *kgotla* in the 1940s, the rest of the BaLerala, Pedi or not, also began to move south to the same area, and the village shifted its site. Moroka II had succeeded to the chiefship, but stayed in his depopulated Gale River village until his death in 1950. He was a weak *kgosi*, and a Christian contingent organized the official removal of Lerala, meaning its *kgotla* and its house of *thuto* (its primary school), from the Gale River to its present location.[76]

The 1940s were a period of sluggish growth for Lerala's congregation. "Khama's laws" weakened. Some men did express new interest in the Church, however, especially men who had labored in South Africa or served in the Second World War. Christianity began to carry a new plurality of associations. Two trends entered Lerala's relationship with Christianity. First, as new paths to Christianity emerged, and with them, several competing visions of *thuto*, enquirers asserted a more personal mode of conversion. They often linked their faith to dreams or illnesses.[77] Secondly, some people sought to introduce alternative and illegal Churches to Lerala and to other Tswapong villages.

Dreams and Personal Choice

Among non-Christians, dreams were the preeminent vehicle for *badimo* to communicate directly with their descendants.[78] Dreams also survived as a narrative idiom for many Christians. In some dreams, *badimo* still spoke, but they might order their grandchildren to Church. Setswalo Gobusamang's mother, for instance, was a strong Christian; after she died in 1944, Setswalo repeatedly dreamt a voice saying, "Go to Church." She could not sleep, and refused, but the voice continued: "Why have you not been baptized?"[79] The Rev. Ms. Kadimo Serema recalled from her experience in (New) Palapye that many converts were motivated by the question, "What will become of me now that my parents are gone, maybe my parents are not happy about my being away from Christianity." Another reason people converted that she remembers is, "I have heard a call, I dreamt [of] my father talking to me saying, 'Be a Christian!'"[80] In Selo Mafoko's dreams, the presence he felt was the Spirit of God.

Selo Mafoko's dreams began when he was in his mining barracks in Johannesburg, in about 1925. Troubled, he at first refused to "go to the *baruti*" of the LMS, who briefly ran a Rand mission. His dreams continued.

> Even in the house that I slept in, when I was taken with sleep—I saw that light, I didn't know what the light was doing with me. I didn't know why it kept coming. Then one day I was asleep, and there was a person near me who had gotten very ill. When he would fall ill, he would bubble forth saliva. Now, this person, when I woke up, I sur-

---

76   Interview: Mr. Ditaolo Motlhagodi with Mrs. Boikanyo Motlhagodi, Lerala, 15 May 1990.

77   J. P. Kiernan discusses the "tactical use of dreams" in Zulu Zionist congregations in KwaMashu, Natal, in *The Production and Management of Therapeutic Power within a Zulu City* (Lewiston, 1990), 190.

78   WCW/762 W. C. Willoughby, "Visions"; Pauw, *Religion in a Tswana Chiefdom*, 26, 37, 198.

79   Interview: Ms. Setswalo Gobusamang, Ratholo May 1990.

80   Interview: Ms. Kadimo Serema, Palapye, 30 Nov. 1988.

prised myself by kneeling and praying. No one had told me to pray for this person. I said, "Amen." . . . When I was through I fell unconscious. In the morning he was no longer ill and we all went to work.[81]

Everybody around Selo was impressed, but significantly, it was only when he returned to settle down in Lerala in the 1930s that he joined Lerala's Ngwato Church congregation and became an important member. His retold experience provided an entrée back into his home community after years of absence.

Selo belongs to a minor commoner lineage. A good way to trace the trends of conversion in the 1940s is to look at the linked fortunes of three family "clusters" of commoner Pedi Tswapong descent: Mathare, Selato, and Molebalwa.[82] Molebalwa was headman of Matalaganye ward at the turn of the century. His senior wife bore him a son named Koowetse. His second wife, Kedisaletswe Mathare, whom he wed around 1910, bore several children, including Tshinamo. When Molebalwa died, Kedisaletswe was blamed for his death: "Matalaganye ward all chased her away as a witch."[83] She returned home to Mathare's yard, where she stayed, and eventually married Nkgetse Ntokwa, a MoKaa resident in Lerala. Both she and Nkgetse shortly joined the congregation and became "deacons," members in good standing.

Koowetse Molebalwa grew up away from the congregation tending his father's cattle, and had a stint on the mines in South Africa. At the age of about thirty-five, he was back at his sleepy cattle post, resting in his dilapidated hut with his fellow herders.

I heard someone call me by my name, "Koowetse, Koowetse, arise and pray." Now I did not know how to pray. The voice said, "Follow after me," and began a prayer, prayed, and then said "Amen." The next day he came again, and did the same; and the third day; until I took my blankets, went outside, and exclaimed that some man was troubling me. So I went off to sleep under some trees. When I reached there, and slept, then that man came again, saying "arise and pray; follow after me," and I did, until he said "Amen." . . . I then ran away, to hide myself! To hide myself! [But it continued . . . until] I then went over there [over the Hills], travelling to where my father's younger sister lived, in Mongala. [Dramatic pause.] I arrived, they were happy to see me, and we eventually went to bed. *As soon as I had gone to bed, the man of the night came again.*

This happened again and again. Finally on Sunday,

I went down with them to Lerala, to Church. I found the Church people, and a man named Lebogang Selato. . . . Now when he began to preach, the Spirit entered me and I flew up! I went up and then came down falling to earth![84]

---

[81]   Interview: Mr. Selo Mafoko, b. 1900, Lerala, 11 April 1990.

[82]   I would not wish, nor in this case think it warranted, to specify precise rules of Tswapong kinship here, but for two useful views, see Adam Kuper, *Wives for Cattle: Bridewealth and Marriage in Southern Africa* (London, 1982), and John L. and Jean Comaroff, "The Management of Marriage" ; both draw on I. Schapera's many works.

[83]   Interview: The Rev. Steven Nkgetsi, Lerala, 10 May 1990.

[84]   Interview: Mr. Koowetse Molebalwa, b. 1905, Lerala, 9 April 1990.

Partial Genealogy of Selato / Molebalwa / Matlhare, Three Prominent Patronymics in Matalaganye Ward, Lerala, Botswana

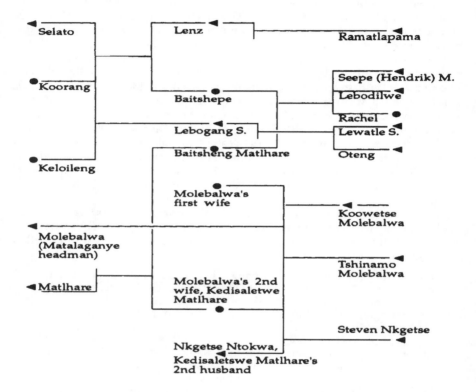

Like Selo Mafoko, Koowetse became a recognized deacon in Lerala. His dream became important because it showed that he was following a calling. The "man from the West," a figure robed in white, was resonant with Jesus.[85] By following him, Koowetse traced his path from cattle post to his father's kinfolk (and his estate), and then to the congregation.

Koowetse never wished to compete with Lebogang Selato's leadership of the congregation in the 1940s. As a first-born son of the leading Matalaganye (Pedi commoner) family, he was likely to become the headman of his own ward. The same was not true of Lenz Selato, Lebogang's elder brother. Like Koowetse and Selo, Lenz was exposed to the diversity of the fervent independent Churches thriving in South Africa, Churches that offered physical and emotional wellness in alien and sometimes frightening work environments.[86] Back in Lerala, however, there was still only the Ngwato Church, which was locally supervised by Lebogang.

---

[85]   *Ibid.*

[86]   E.g., Interview: The Rev. Steven Nkgetsi, Lerala, 10 May 1990: In the mines "there is danger and you must think about the Lord!"

Lenz returned to Lerala in the late 1930s and brought with him his understanding of the Seventh Day Adventist Church, or some Johannesburg emulation of it. He proselytized for his new faith and secured at least one interested person from outside his household to pray with him.[87] After reproaching Lenz, Lebogang went to Serowe to complain to the Ngwato *kgotla*. Word came back that Lenz was to confine his anomalous Saturday worship to his own yard and his immediate family. He prayed in this way until his death, and was never again on good terms with his brother.[88]

Tshinamo Molebalwa, Koowetse's younger half-brother, became an *ngaka* in his youth, but after a stomach sickness, he dreamt of a "big whirlwind" and joined a branch of "Archbishop" Mokaleng's distant Spiritual Healing Church. Steven Nkgetse, the son of Kedisaletswe and Nkgetse Ntokwa, joined a healing Church in the mines in 1943. Both Tshinamo and Steven are now recognized *baruti* in Lerala because of their positions in these Churches, which have ten or twenty active members in Lerala today.[89]

Kedisaletswe Mathare (Tshinamo and Steven's mother) had a younger brother, Baitsheng, who married Lenz Selato's sister, Baitshepe.[90] In 1949 their eldest son Seepe returned from a Transvaal dairy farm with a new Church. It was known as "Brethren" or just "Brothers." His wife then left the Ngwato Church, his daughter Rachel left its catechumenate, and they joined Brothers; even Seepe's parents joined. Seepe healed people with the Holy Spirit and participated in the *kgotla*'s agricultural and rain ceremonies, offending orthodox sensibilities. Despite his boldness, Seepe was not forbidden from worshipping by the Ngwato kingship. To avoid official displeasure, he disallowed *bojalwa* in his Church in accordance with the usual practice of Christians. More importantly, however, by this time the kingship itself was failing.[91]

Next, "Bishop" Modikwa of Ratholo brought the "F.G.A.C." Church ("Faith Gospel After Christ") from its home base in Johannesburg. Such acronyms shared the aura of literacy and officialdom that subordinated so many illiterate migrant miners outside rural villages. F.G.A.C. was not *thuto*, however. Modikwa's adherents thus suffered at the hands of Ratholo's Ngwato Church *kgosi*, who forbade their worship and made a bonfire of their uniforms. In Lerala, Modikwa attempted to make Seepe Mathare his adjunct by asking him to baptize people for the F.G.A.C., but Seepe rejected the overture. Orea Tlhalefang did not; the daughter of an early Khurutshe Christian, and someone who had been healed by Seepe and brought into the Brothers Church, Orea nonetheless wished to brew beer, and so moved to Modikwa's Church. Shortly thereafter, "family troubles" wrecked Seepe's ministry, and the core of his congregation—his own

---

[87] Interview: Mrs. Dijelwe [Medupe] Moyo, Lerala, 19 April 1990, her mother; and MmaTebo (Rachel) Mathare, Lerala, 1 June 1990.

[88] Interview: Mr. Ramatlapama Selato, Lerala, 20 June 1990.

[89] Interviews: The Rev. Steven Nkgetsi, Lerala, 10 May 1990; The Rev. Tshinamo Molebalwa, Lerala, 28 March 1990. The Spiritual Healing Church is based in Matsiloje.

[90] Baitsheng was born in 1889 and celebrated his centennial birthday the year of his death.

[91] Interviews: MmaMachomise (Ms. Otlametse), Lerala, 5 June 1990; MmaTebo (Rachel) Mathare, Lerala, 1 June 1990. Shortly after Seepe began praying in the *kgotla* with Ngwato Church *baruti*, an elderly Christian woman demanded that he doff his mitre, which he refused to do: Mrs. Boikanyo Motlhagodi, with Ditaolo Motlhagodi, Lerala, 1 June 1990.

kin (including his daughter Rachel) and some other Pedi commoners—left for the F.G.A.C., which remains the largest Tswapong-based Church operating in Lerala.[92] Lenz Selato's son Ramatlapana belongs to the F.G.A.C., and he has a strong avuncular relationship with Rachel Mathare's family today. Seepe has since died.

What of the descendants of Dialwa, the excised lineage of the Lerala chiefship once responsible for gathering rain for all Pedi Tswapong? They never "wrote" Dialwa into the graces of the kingship, and they never, in memory, ruled Lerala. Instead, the men in Dialwa's line kept to the east in their heritage and in their outlook. The changes Ramosoka wrought in bringing rain-prayers to his *kgotla*— which saw the attendance of most adults in Lerala, Christian or not—for them meant "doing nothing." From the 1920s, Dialwa's senior son Koboatshwene spent most of his time in self-imposed exile at his cattle post. He sometimes travelled through the forest to water-holes and himself made rain, in a desultory fashion, and Kgosi Moroka II, Ramosoka's successor, occasionally consulted him in this. He was an important man in spite of himself, and in 1951 a faction put his name up for Lerala's chiefship.[93]

His senior son, Bonnetswe Dialwa, went to work for a Boer in an orange grove near Potgeitersrust, Transvaal, in the 1930s. In the grove, he joined a healing Church among the workers, and when he returned to Tswapong around 1941 for four months to recruit labor for his boss, he briefly tried to convert people in Lerala. At that time his evangelism was illegal and unsuccessful; some people recall Bonnetswe kneeling by paths in the veldt, pausing to pray. Today, like his father and uncles before him, Bonnetswe is not a Christian.[94] Women in his extended network of kin, however, belong to independent Churches.

Indeed, by the 1950s, there were soon very many congregations in Lerala. Most of them healed and drew their adherents by healing. They required a very brief period of waiting before confirmation. With the effective demise of the kingship in 1949, described in the last chapter, the Ngwato Church ceased to be an inclusive body. Its remnants amalgamated with other LMS congregations as the United Congregational Church of Southern Africa, or UCCSA: the 1910 Scheme for Church Union come back to life. The UCCSA's Lerala congregation continued to maintain Sunday services in the new Lerala primary school, as befit their lasting hold on *thuto*. By the 1960s, its congregation was aging. Besides some loyal BaKhurutshe and the family members of early "*baruti*," few enquirers attended regular UCCSA services. Lebogang Selato's son Lewatle and Rachel's older brother Lebodilwe are still UCCSA men from the days of the Ngwato Church, but with that Church gone, the vicissitudes of local status, competition, and association have to guide people in deciding on any "religious" affiliation.

---

[92]   Interviews: Mr. Joel Tlhalefang, Lerala, 29 May 1990, and MmaTebo (Rachel) Mathare, Lerala, 22 June 1990.

[93]   This was during the time of conflict over Seretse Khama's marriage to Ruth Williams. TK Papers, M. Sekgoma to Tshekedi, [Moeng College], 4/11/51, and M. Sekgoma to Tshekedi, [Moeng College], 9/11/51; Interview: Kgosi Shaw Moroka, Lerala, 23 April 1990.

[94]   Interviews: Ms. Setswalo Gobusamang, Ratholo May 1990; Mr. Bonnetswe K. Dialwa, b. 1923, Lerala, 22 June 1990; MmaTebo (Rachel) Mathare, Lerala, 2 April 1990; Mr. Ramatlapama Selato, Lerala, 20 June 1990.

The Local View

"Under Magosi's rule, Dialwa as rainmaker would retravel the route of Pedi immigration, that of *badimo*, to bring Tswapong rain." Today, such discussions about *dikgosi* are *ipso facto* both religious and contentious. As they range over the Hills, *badimo* gesture toward the past. Within the single community of Lerala, some people see them gesturing toward the east, and some in other directions. But after ninety years beneath the kingdom's hegemonic Church, the ancestors themselves are ready to make peace. Kgosi Shaw of today's Lerala captured this best for me. In his monologue below, "Mapulana" is the paradigmatic non-Christian settler (and hence part of the *badimo*) in the Tswapong Hills.

> Khama heard of this big war with the MaTebele while in Shoshong. On his part he was a person who liked to go about his villages. In so doing he heard there was an attack, and he said "Ijo-jo-jo!" I mean the war hurt every people, and he went to Rhodesia to ask for a gun from the Englishman, . . .from Livingstone! . . . He then went to ask for England's "Protection," . . . and he came back with the Bible. Then Livingstone and Khama went away, and soon returned with the Hymnbook. [Khama] made a church at Phalapye there. Because [broken English:] "All that chief my grandfather" [i.e., all my forebears, chiefs, my grandfathers] all the way down to father, they all say, "How can we ever thank Khama?"
>
> [Finally] the war ended—it ended by faith [*tumelo*]. Mapulana was made by God as a prayer-of-rain only. . . . He spoke with invisible *badimo*. Now, when he began thus, Khama had asked for self-government of the English, self-government of the Bible, he got faith from England; but still Mapulana worked with the *badimo*. . . . If people understand one another, then rain will fall.[95]

One could scarcely hope for a more succinct summary of the themes underlying this chapter—and much of this book—than this *melangé* monologue by Lerala's *kgosi*. The grouped associations for Lerala, of the West, violence, Christianity, literacy, and the kingdom; the competition between different notions of community; the reinterpretation of the past according to the fluid necessities of life: these were the concerns of Lerala's people themselves, and indeed of everyone in GammaNgwato.

---

[95] Interview: Kgosi Shaw Moroka, Lerala, 24 April 1990.

9

A Realm of the Word: Conclusion and Epilogue

Suppose we wanted a *general* model for the kind of transformation described in this book: a paradigm for viewing the socioreligious history of a quasi-independent (begging the question for a moment) colonized people, like the BaNgwato. It might look like this:

Foreign emissaries linked to a hegemonic state come to a nonliterate society. They present a new religion, and they begin to convey the explicit practices and less explicit behavior that go with it. Like any ideology, the religion is taken up by different sections of the evangelized society, in fits and starts, and through compromises of one kind or another. The discourses and practices within it fragment and change to accommodate the position and ambitions of whatever congeries of social subgroups—economic, gender, ethnic, or political—appropriate it.

Surely this model is not "wrong." Yet this book has been about more than this, about the construction of a regime of power and the sharing of a political/ religious identity through that regime. It has embraced Khama's table settings, impounded cattle, hymns about rain, and the rapes of Birwa women. Christianity repeatedly appeared within the piecemeal construction of power in GammaNgwato, but not as a set of rules or a fragmenting ideology. This is not to say that Christianity may not *also* be represented as a great text of beliefs. But it was more often in its part, its situational adoption, that Tswana voices and pens expressed it.

I have also tried to shift the terrain of explanation away from a story about the actions of missionaries and the reactions of Africans to a story about the orchestration of power based on the elaboration and reverberations of the Word, under an ethos expressed in GammaNgwato as *thuto.* Such a story better fits my understanding of what history is about. In arguing the case for a mobile notion of ethnicity, one set within the dimensions of time as well as space, Ed Wilmsen and Jim Denbow demand that we see history as "the process through which social formations realize their transformations."[1] This book has been about the processual realization of a social formation.

---

[1] Edwin Wilmsen and James Denbow, "Paradigmatic History of San-speaking Peoples and Current Attempts at Revision," *Current Anthropology* 31, 5 (1990), 498.

More exactly, the book has attempted to show the linkages between the bringing-into-being of the Ngwato Kingdom, the Ngwato Church, and colonial overrule. Seen within the social transformations they midwived, these institutions composed a network of power in GammaNgwato. That network I have called the realm of the Word.

The institutional components of this domain, this realm of the Word, were necessary but insufficient in themselves. The Church became the focus of a prolonged contest between missionaries and BaNgwato (Chapter 2), and touched the lives of everyone in GammaNgwato. Technically it was a small body, however, and its active members constituted a fraction of the adult population. The kingdom also was built through contests over meaning: over what sorts of loyalty would triumph in the colonial era, and how political power therein could be defended in its use. The nature of this kingdom, in all its quiddity, was hammered out both at the level of elite politics and in the reevaluations of the communities that composed it. Yet it operated with at best a thin apparatus of enforcement outside the capital town, and its official contact with people in the hinterland was sporadic.

As for the Protectorate government, while surely it hedged the ultimate autonomy of BaTswana, it also prevented the total destruction of their political and productive livelihoods by South African settlers. Much of the time, Protectorate officials had little quotidian presence in Ngwato life, certainly less than the few hundred white traders in GammaNgwato. Although the Ngwato monarchy lost something with the appointment of an activist resident commissioner, Charles Rey, in 1929, the extent of even that change is easily overestimated. Tshekedi Khama's penchant for dramatically engaging Rey in court, on British textual and administrative turf, was after all a component of Protectorate rule.[2] There were conflicting forces at work within the Protectorate; Rey's suspension of Tshekedi from the kingship in 1933 came just after the high commissioner mildly vetted Tshekedi's punishment of Anglican subjects for the crime of being Anglicans (Chapter 7).

The power unifying GammaNgwato was born and reborn through an interplay of all three of these institutions: kingship (developing from *kgosi*-ship), Church, and Protectorate; but also through a subtler interplay of literacy, status, wealth and cattle, abstinence, and attentiveness to *thuto*. Going to school, witnessing evangelical campaigns, hiding and privatizing beer-drinks, and praying by the bedside of the sick were every bit as constitutive of power as was a discussion in the *kgotla*. Wealthy and poor, senior and junior, and men and women negotiated power's enactment in the categories of meaning relevant to them. In this regard, much of the book has turned on the permutations of *thuto* as it touched cattle ownership, gendered and "important" speech, the linkages between fertility and sanctioned authority, and the law. *Thuto* came to embrace the legitimation of writing, of civilized propriety and feminized sobriety, and of both individual attainment and community protection. As an ideal, it drew on the very first signs created by the merchant and capitalist penetration of southern Africa, on hats, books, and tea. It was vaguely enforced by the king, but it was actually brought into play by women and children. It became an elite ideology of national aspiration, but not quite of broad nationhood itself.

---

[2]   See Michael Crowder, *The Flogging of Phineas McIntosh: A Tale of Colonial Folly and Injustice, Bechuanaland, 1933* (New Haven, 1988), and his "Tshekedi Khama and Opposition to the British Administration of the Bechuanaland Protectorate, 1926–1936," *Journal of African History* 26 (1985), 193–214.

The King's Word

The widest argument of the narrative is not difficult to summarize. Khama's domain was a kind of colonial kingdom. GammaNgwato arrived at defined borders, with the northern border at the 22nd meridian, essentially through colonial fiat in 1885. An "Order in Council" in 1890 extended the Protectorate, and so the Ngwato kingdom, north of this line up to its current boundaries. These boundaries were amended by the "railway grant" of (ostensibly) Ngwato land to the British South Africa Company in 1895. Following this expansion, and fearful of incorporation into the Cape and later the Union of South Africa, King Khama III broadened his administration and began staking out his territory with *baruti* and their schoolhouse churches.[3] These Christian and often literate mirrors of his central authority were frequently the only "Ngwato" presence in villages. The critical institution girding his authority was the Christian Church he and fellow Ngwato royals had established in the 1860s and 1870s. It was nominally under the aegis of the London Missionary Society, but missionaries' "control" of the Church was tenuous and narrowly construed.

The king's mode of power blended the old with the new, but it extended the kingdom's reach to new areas. This was so in two dimensions: in sheer territorial expanse, and within the intimate space of personal relations. So far as we know, the Tswana state once had been only the Tswana town, notwithstanding some distant tribute. For the first time in the eastern Kalahari, a realm arose in which a king made laws concerning what men and women should and should not do and pushed their enforcement hundreds of miles beyond his *kgotla*. I have not argued that the Church itself was wholly responsible. The process began with the stabilization of aristocratic BaNgwato's cattle posts in distant villagers' hands. Later on, after those villagers took formal possession of these cattle (and many of them became Christians), the king's repertoire of governance still included devices falling wide of Christians and *baruti* per se. Governors (*baemela kgosi*); both dispatched and locally constituted regiments (*mephato*); hut-tax collectors; the persistent institution of the *lesotla*, or locally cultivated royal field; relations with British magistrates and the Bechuanaland Police; and strong, informal ties to merchants and white ranchers all formed aspects of Ngwato government. From the viewpoint of many Ngwato citizens (and often "emerging BaNgwato"), however, the Protectorate, Ngwato rule, and the Church were very closely bound up as "written" and legitimate authority. People's day-to-day encounters with the centralizing forces of the kingdom transpired with the local *moruti*, wealthy Christians, white traders, and Ngwato officials, who together loomed up like a group. When dissident subjects attempted to disentangle them and secularize a different fealty to the kingdom, the arm of the state, Ngwato or colonial, forcibly insisted on the integral presence of the Church.

The historical framework in which the Protectorate government is said to have held the "real" power in GammaNgwato, and in which mission Churches were "controlled" by missionaries, should be discarded. Moreover, the study of colo-

---

[3]   The 1885 definition occurred on 27 January 1885; the Order in Council dates from 30 June 1890. Edwin Wilmsen argues that the depletion of game and lessening profits from hunting led the Ngwato kingship to force MaSarwa to cattle-post duties, in the 1890s; and that this made MaSarwa the key to Ngwato authority in the expanded domain. I do not grasp the second part of Wilmsen's reasoning. See Wilmsen, *Land Filled with Flies*, 97, 131, 286.

nialism elsewhere in Africa might benefit by demoting similar assumptions to the level of propositions.

Why did Khama succeed in the way he did while by comparison, other Tswana *dikgosi* failed? To begin with, larger historical processes set the stage for the BaNgwato, who seized the moment. Further south, the encroachments of settlers empowered missionaries as Europeans and enervated indigenous rulers as Africans. Thus many BaTswana around Kuruman equated Christianity with a loss of land, cattle, and independence (and unlike Ngwato Church, the Kuruman Church attracted an overwhelmingly female membership from the very start).[4] The resilience of GammaNgwato is shown in that it hardly mattered whether early missionaries blatantly allied themselves to colonial aims: the Rev. Mackenzie did so, the Rev. Hepburn did not, yet both men helped build the realm of the Word. Other Sotho-Tswana polities were ruptured by the effects of Nguni expansion in the 1820s and 1830s, by Boer slave raiding, by the massive exploitation of diamonds and gold in their environs, and by the colonially sponsored advance of larger kingdoms and the capitalization of white farms. Those same afflicted polities also lost the prospect of "religious" coherence.

The Ngwato king and his citizens worked in the political space allotted to them. Elsewhere in the Protectorate, other *dikgosi* failed to make Christianity their own when they had the opportunity. The proportion of their subjects calling themselves Christians (although *not* their Church memberships) reached higher percentages than in GammaNgwato, but their reigns failed to gain thereby. When the Churches in their territories suffered from schisms and defections, they could do little, and they had more trouble regaining their equilibrium after receiving further blows later on.[5]

Among the expanding BaNgwaketse, based in Kanye, an elderly deacon recalled that "Big men [had originally] attended school while boys like myself looked after the cattle." As in GammaNgwato, troubles began when Christians clashed with the ruling house, but in Kanye they never took it over. King Gaseitsiwe objected to the decree that monthly Church dues were to be mandatory: was not the law his own responsibility? The fact that such a distinction existed was the problem. The Rev. James Good, who served in Kanye from 1877, sought to allay the king's fears. Good worked within, and adapted to, the changing political hierarchy and kept his post until the turn of the century. In contrast to his successor, whom few BaNgwaketse liked, Good was remembered as a proper missionary:

> He taught us the Word of God, he taught us the books, he taught our children, he pointed out to us how we could send out children to school. He went about amongst the people . . . and visited the sick, helping them with medicine. He helped the [*kgosi*], both in the town and outside of it. . . .[6]

Help as he might, his purpose had not been woven into the roots of the king's power. When disputes between the LMS and the king flared up, missionaries and officials still had the authority to represent the situation as an opposition between

---

4   LMS SA Reports, 2/3, R. Price and J. Gould, Kuruman for 1893.

5   For instance, at Taungs; see LMS SA Reports 4/2, W. McGee, Taungs, 21/2/09; and J. Cullen, Taungs for 1911. See also Parsons, "Independency and Ethiopianism."

6   LMS SA 67/4, Copy, Kanye Church to LMS, Kanye 2/5/06, *sic* throughout; in translation.

Christian orthodoxy and "certain customs and practices relating to witchcraft," because the king had never appropriated Christianity for himself, his kin, and his people. A renegade *moruti* named Mothowagae split the Ngwaketse Church in half in 1918, but the stage had long been set for him; as one deacon said, "The weakness in the Church was not caused by Mothowagae."[7]

Let us turn to the BaKwena. In the 1850s, King Sechele refused to become a monogamist and had a falling-out with David Livingstone. The reverberations were still felt in 1913, when his grandson Sechele II allied himself to a mixed faction of Kwena non-Christians and Anglicans.[8] This seemed a smart gambit for a while. If the LMS had no real muscle in GammaNgwato, then why would it in Kweneng? The Rev. Haydon Lewis, then living with the BaKwena, was moved to address Sechele (who has here threatened to expel him), as follows:

> [T]he hunter [Lewis] who has fought the lion and conquered it, is not afraid of the cub. I have had many a fight with your father Sebele, and he never beat me, but if you think you are man enough to carry out your threat, do your best, I don't fear you.[9]

Such insolence only crystallized a broad-based opposition against Lewis and, despite his accomplished tenure in Molepolole, he was soon forced to move on to Serowe. It is nevertheless striking that he had come to such a turn. And what was the result? Only that the Protectorate's assistant commissioner excoriated Sechele and his allied *dingaka*, "declared" the LMS church to be mission property, and told the Kwena king that he would thenceforth have no control over the deployment of LMS personnel in his "District."[10]

Consider what might have transpired had the LMS been able to withstand such an adversarial relationship with the BaNgwato; if, in other words, GammaNgwato had not grown into a Christian kingdom. Would not other colonial impositions have followed more swiftly? Is it so hard to imagine that the delegation of the "three chiefs," Khama, Sebele, and Bathoeng (of the BaNgwaketse), might have failed in their purpose in London in 1895, permitting the Protectorate to be handed to Cecil Rhodes' British South Africa Company? Or if not in 1895, then at some later point, that all Bechuanaland would have been incorporated by the Union of South Africa, as Jan Smuts perpetually desired?[11]

Khama was a Christian. The "word" of this king, in the sense of his pronouncements and laws, bore his power in both a negative and positive (or at least active) manner. First, the negative side. Especially after the turn of the century, various common, even banal assumptions became illicit: that only men gathered in the *kgotla*

---

[7]   LMS SA 67/5, W. Cullen to R. W. Thompson, Barkley West, 3/8/06; and L. D. Ngcongco, "Religion and Politics in an African Chiefdom: The Mothowagae Secession Revisited," *Pula* 3, 1 (1983), 59–78; and quote, LMS SA 82/3, E. Dugmore to F. H. Hawkins, Kanye, 8/9/19, on Kanye Conference, 26/2/19.

[8]   This was, incidentally, related to Sechele's marriage to his second wife, the Anglican daughter of Rawe Sekoko; LMS SA Reports 5/1, R. H. Lewis, Molepolole for 1913.

[9]   LMS SA Reports 5/1, R. H. Lewis, Molepolole for 1914.

[10] Ibid.

[11] See Ronald Hyam, "The Politics of Partition in Southern Africa, 1908–61," in Hyam, *Reappraisals in British Imperial History* (Oxford, 1977), Ch. 9. I realize that the fiasco of Cecil Rhodes' "Jameson Raid" on the Transvaal was a major factor in turning the tide against Rhodes, but I am not convinced of the unimportance of other factors.

(Chapter 3), that women brewed beer (Chapter 4), that *dikgosi* directed the vectors of fertility and social continuity even beyond the grave (Chapters 1 and 8). These things became near-heresies, and if they did not diminish or retreat into secrecy, they threatened to traduce the kingdom. The issue was never one in which the enemy of the Ngwato "state" was merely "custom" or "tradition"! After all, as we have seen in Chapter 7, Christian pluralism was the greatest treachery. Rather, deliberate laws made particular modes of association based in the town and village, whether traditional or not, into culpable offenses. If the kingdom's laws came from diverse sources, it was the kingship that laid claim to them and plotted their trajectories.

Moreover, and perhaps more positively, the kingdom construed and constructed a variety of behaviors as *civilized*. Under the regime of the Word, there was an increasingly shared attitude about what "civilized" meant, and here the Church excelled. *Thuto* sanctioned one public mode of association between men and women and provided its language, rites, and leaders. By denigrating beer, nonjuridical chiefly male authority, and the ancestors, *thuto* weakened the underpinnings of ethnic cohesion and removed the autonomy of the village *kgotla*. The medical forays of missionaries and Tswana evangelists attacked the placement of health and wellness in these same non-Christian matrices, attempting to substitute the corporeal body and the congregation (Chapter 5). *Thuto* encoded the church building, with its books, fealty to the capital, and attention to the words of *baruti*, as the privileged domain for achieving wider recognition, public prestige, and personal health. Should outlying villages not have a *moruti* recognized by the central deaconate of the Church in the capital, any informal *moruti*, or for that matter evangelist or senior Church member[12] still carried the *thuto* of the kingdom in him or her. This is what constructed Ngwato-ness. Although even academic specialists continue to read "Ngwato" back into history as a tribe, at the risk of repeating the obvious, it was much more than that.[13]

In Chapter 6 we saw how the vocabulary of *thuto* subordinated Ngamiland to the Ngwato realm of power when missionaries and *baruti* carried it there. The men and women who were present saw this right away, but so did the Ndebele, who stole everybody's Bibles. In GammaNgwato proper, with preexisting local barriers weakened and if necessary rammed flat, *thuto* for a while seemed capable, just possibly, of giving national content to the outline shadow cast by Khama's Word. Khama only saw this toward the close of his long life, and it was too late.

Still this is a falsely autocratic picture. Neither Khama, Sekgoma II, nor Tshekedi acted alone. Their missionaries encouraged sobriety, bureaucratization, and the erasure of "irrational" or "lascivious" community relations in favor of a wider, somehow individuated identity. Khama managed to yoke their ideas and actions to the practices of a Tswana *kgosi*, and to silence their protests about it.

This was only possible because a sufficient number of common men and women—mostly women—made it their job to replicate the king's authority through

---

12   After about 1940, a women might be a *moruti wa sesadi* (woman *moruti*), although there were very few before the 1950s.

13   Recently Roger Charlton, in "The Politics of Elections in Botswana," *Africa* 63, 3 (1993), 348, attributes the consistent success of Seretse Khama's Botswana Democratic Party (BDP) in the Central District (GammaNgwato), as opposed to more confused electoral returns in Ngamiland, to patterns of "simple" versus "complex" ethnicities. But it is a matter of history, not ethnicity.

their personal and communal lives. The authority of the king was then given meaning by the Christians in his land. As Chapter 8 has shown, the entire process blurred secular and spiritual power into a single mode, which, in fact, it had to do to succeed; and neither Ngwato discourse nor British missionaries and officials separated the political from the religious. Inside the Church, however, women's veritable domination resulted from their alliance with the state. Women and the state shared the mutual interest of substituting a new form of status and association for that of the *kgotla*, the male public forum and court. Women's gender had been built around public subordination and their subsistence-level production of private, household foods. Political and economic reforms joined with the realm's particular modes of power to realign many of the components that had defined married womanhood. By participating in the making of the power of the king, Christian women remade themselves. The changes they wrought survived the effective demise of the rule-bound Church in the 1950s and expanded to touch the majority of all women in GammaNgwato, who are today Christians too. It was through Ngwato Churchwomen that the king's Word once embodied civil society in his realm, and their legacy is alive today in Botswana.

Epilogue

The Demise of the Ngwato Kingdom

Perhaps the Ngwato kingdom, if it was such a special case, should have endured the postcolonial world as a desert version of Lesotho. This was not feasible. First, the basis of the kingdom's unified integrity was not firm enough. As we have seen, the potential universality of *thuto* was both strength and weakness almost from the start. As Serowe expanded after 1910, and as young men came back from stints in South Africa and bought new suits and hats, they also acquired different sorts of *thuto*, forcing its referents ever outward. Khama dealt with them by crushing opposition to the exclusivity of the "LMS" Ngwato Church, all the while decrying LMS interference in his affairs. The ire of educated men (like Simon Ratshosa) was then channelled against the mission so as to parallel the feelings of the most conservative non-Christians. In this way, both sets of voices were muted.[14] Ultimately, however, these strategies stopped working. *Thuto* held the seeds of its own ubiquity, and it proved too volatile and fissionable to sustain a national identity in times of crisis. The gate having been opened by Christian pluralists, when Independence neared Botswana, Christians from other parts of the Protectorate easily shared in *thuto*'s discursive domain. Even before this, however, Ngwato identity suffered a crisis in 1948 and 1949 from which it never recovered.

The sudden demise of the kingship is a story in itself.[15] As was then well known, Seretse Khama—the son of Sekgoma II and the heir under his uncle Tshekedi's "regency"—married an Englishwoman, Ruth Williams. Senior Ngwato men then supported Tshekedi in attempting to block Seretse's ascension to the kingship. After a period of hesitancy, Britain's "Commonwealth Relations Office" (or CRO) as the responsible body was now called, also tried to debar Seretse from ruling. The CRO's stance derived from its attention to South African politics. It feared that a mixed-race couple ruling at the Transvaal border under the British flag would propel rightists to power in South Africa, cripple the United Party, and lead the country out of the Commonwealth. In GammaNgwato, however, Tshekedi's position lost its appeal and his people slowly deserted him. On the 21st of June, 1949, a mostly male gathering in the *kgotla* stood and acclaimed Seretse as the new king, and Tshekedi went into internal exile.

After 1949 there would be no more Ngwato "king" at all, if the word has anything near its normal meaning. The CRO exiled Seretse on spurious grounds and would not allow him and Ruth to take their places in Serowe. Tshekedi agitated tirelessly against Seretse, against the CRO's imposition of what some called "direct rule" over GammaNgwato, and against the ascension of anyone else. In one of his

---

14   It was such a coalition that supported a non-LMS "tribal school," which became a pressure valve for the aspirations of an aristocratic elite. Simon became its headmaster, but many of its students had never even attended a regular Church service. See K III C/16/1, Khama to Editor, *Christian Express* (Lovedale), Phalapye, 13/8/02; BNA S.178/1, enclosure, W. C. Willoughby to R. Williams, Serowe, 7/9/02, and Parsons, "Khama III," 259–60, 264.

15   See Michael Dutfield, *A Marriage of Inconvenience: The Persecution of Ruth and Seretse Khama* (London, 1990); my review essay, "The Persecution of Ruth and Seretse Khama," *South African Review of Books* (Jan./Feb., 1991); John Redfern, *Ruth and Seretse: A Very Disreputable Transaction* (London, 1955), and Willie Henderson, Neil Parsons, and Thomas Tlou, *Seretse Khama of Botswana, 1921–1980, A Biography* (forthcoming).

many legal briefs, he prepared a draft of a statement entitled "European Penetration and Miscegenation" in which he argued that Ruth's coming was illegal, as no European had ever "penetrated" GammaNgwato without the consent of both king and people.[16] In truth, Ngwato autonomy was broken; not for that reason, nor even because interim regents like Keaboka Kgamane tended to be inept, but because it was the British who had exiled Seretse. A key part of the realm of the Word was gone.

Beyond this, the debate over Ruth sowed discord everywhere, even in distant villages, and split them along old fault lines. The unity of the kingship was thrown into question. In the midst of the puzzlement and anger that resulted, Tshekedi's generally unpopular local partisans tended disproportionately to be the main bearers of *thuto*, appointed Ngwato governors and old-guard *baruti*. The status of *thuto* and hence the king's Word suffered correspondingly. Khama's church building in Serowe became a tense and divided forum; the resident LMS missionary, the Rev. Seager, inveighed against the marriage from the pulpit and alienated Seretse's sympathizers.[17] Meanwhile Tshekedi's agents bore down on "suspected" supporters of Seretse, intimidating them at night and monitoring their activities; they even opened other people's mail. These agents sent Tshekedi confidential reports on the loyalties of headmen and *dikgosi*. The result of such use of the literate network established by the Ngwato Church was a climate of fear and distrust.

Suddenly the kingship's lock on *thuto* seemed discordant with the postwar world, which it was. Tshekedi's overall reign then began to look increasingly harsh in many people's hindsight; it became difficult to imagine returning to it. A substantial number of young men resented Tshekedi's use of obligatory, regimental labor in the 1940s. Others had served close to Europeans in the recent war, and they questioned anew the premises of British rule, which now seemed partisan to Tshekedi. Moreover the ongoing prohibition on alcohol appeared anachronistic and vain. A growing number of women in railway-line villages such as Palapye and Mahalapye resented Tshekedi's sporadic police efforts to stop them from selling *bojalwa* and *kgadi* to the men travelling south to the mines. They had long ago stopped brewing for an androcentric moral economy: they wanted to earn money.

In hastening the end of the kingdom, Britain ushered itself out of GammaNgwato and ultimately Botswana. In eastern Botswana, colonial overrule had supported the Ngwato realm of the Word for so long that for a while there seemed nothing to do. Some people talked of Oratile, Seretse's sister, becoming "queen," but the popular heir still lived. Eighty years previously, a political crisis in GammaNgwato of similar magnitude had led to the full mobilization of Ngwato men, at which time Khama came to power. Lesser dynastic crises had once been resolved by allowing the polity to divide and separate. Now, however, colonial officials and aristocrats perpetuated the bureaucratic functions of the Ngwato *kgotla* at a time when there should have been no government, no "gathering" whatsoever. The kingship was played false, and as a

---

[16] TK X, Tshekedi Khama, "European Penetration," 1949. Some of Tshekedi's spy reports and communiques to the B.P. police are marked TK/KSM, but are in Box X.

[17] Interview: Ruth Williams Khama, June 1989, Gaborone, English.

result Indirect Rule also began to fail. In October 1952 Tshekedi's nine-room house burned to the ground in sight of the *kgotla*, which was filled with senior men, none of whom intervened. Ngwato policemen refused to interrogate them later. Shortly afterward, "riotous violence" erupted as women, along with a few men, converged on Serowe's *kgotla* to attack the imported police and other officials sent to quell their protests. A man was stoned to death. Many of the rioting women were Christians.[18]

Starting in this period, healing Churches proliferated in GammaNgwato, especially on the margins of the kingdom and on the railway line. As contemporaries remarked, "Zion" Churches grew fastest as the Seretse crisis reached its zenith, and "flourishe[d] in those places where [the kingdom's] control was weak and which the Christian church personnel only rarely visited."[19] The realm of the Word faded. In Serowe, however, invocations of *thuto* and *Lefoko* or Word still echo dimly with power, harking to an identity half-forged and then lost in the colonial age.

The Growth of "Independent" (Healing) Churches

How wrong it would be to depict this late twentieth-century proliferation of independent Churches in Botswana's Ngwato "District" as a process in which Africans rid themselves of missionary control! The history of the Ngwato Church suggests that counterposing independent (Zionist, Ethiopian, healing, schismatic) Churches to their mission forebears risks missing the point. Instead, one must ask who wields power, and how. The few missionaries were after all high-level intermediaries. At the grassroots, people's autonomy of action is not always predicated on whether their institution is tied to a mission. Assuming otherwise flattens the complexity of local constructions of power, and ignores those particular relationships that produce people's gender.

I believe scholars must approach missionaries' teachings through the particular categories constructed in the process of making history. Such a method enables us to see outside the limited bipolar framework of African versus Colonial. The realm of the Word lay across the sum total of those relations of power in GammaNgwato that made and remade the Ngwato kingship as their center. When power—religious, political, and economic—is imagined in this way as its subjects might have felt it, surprising parallels suggest themselves across wide boundaries. Limiting ourselves to Christianity as the reigning sign, we might consider the nineteenth-century Merina kingdom of Madagascar, the Griqua of the Cape, the BaGanda of east-central Africa, even the BaKongo of the seventeenth century.[20] All seem to have successfully blended the secular and religious

---

[18]   Interview: Mr. Dennis Blackbeard, b. 1918, Serowe, 7 Nov. 1988, English; Mrs. Phiri, Serowe, 3 Nov. 1988.

[19]   BNA D.C. North 9/6, Intelligence Report, Ngwato, 12/57; and TK Papers/52, A. E. Seager to Tshekedi, Kent, 15/7/50, remarking the upsurge in Zion Churches.

[20]   The Merina kingdom saw a similar and at times fiercer alliance between affiliation with the LMS's resident Church and allegiance to the king, as Pier Larson has noted to me; regrettably I have not read Françoise Raison-Jourde's *thèse d'etat, Le Bible et Pouvoir à Madagascar au XIX Siècle: Invention d'une Identité Chrétienne et Construction de l'état* (Paris, 1991). See Martin Legassick, "The Northern Frontier to 1840: The Rise and Decline of the Griqua People," in R. Elphick and H. Giliomee, *The Shaping of South African Society, 1652–1840* (Middletown, Conn., 1988), 383–403 esp., on the Griquas' appropriation of evangelism and

under the noses of external Christian bodies. Furthermore, it might be worthwhile to take a new look at "autonomous" missions, from the Anglicans' Masisi
and Catholic White Fathers' Mpala to the west of Lake Tanganyika; to Blantyre,
Livingstonia (and Magomero) in the Shire Highlands; to Zambia's LMS mission
at Kavimbe, the Catholics' mission "chiefdoms," and so on.[21] "Religious" power
shimmered into being and then dissipated—whom did it touch? How was it
reproduced in these places, for non-Christian peasants, ordinary Christians,
evangelists, and for their jural rulers and text-writing teachers? What sort of
power was this, compared to the kind of power redistributed in Africa according to the colors on a map?

Alongside these possible parallels, does not Lekhanyane's massive Zion Christian Church (ZCC), the largest "independent" Church in southern Africa, also fairly
resemble the early Ngwato Church rather than GammaNgwato's fragmentary healing Churches of today? At least in Botswana, the ZCC is largely male. Both Churches
gave individuals an identity broader than that of their village or location and created a network of elites with a pointedly exemplary function. Although the Ngwato
Church differed in having its own territory, the Lekhanyane lineage, the ZCC's
complex at "Morija" in the Transvaal, and the ZCC's repatternings of authority in
all its congregations nonetheless created a shadow state or "realm." There are ZCC
members in every major village, but they form but small groups within them, as
did Ngwato Christians. The notion of a "realm" bridges "state" and "authority,"
does it not? It is not surprising that the Protectorate Government anxiously investigated the "subversive" teachings of branches of South African "Zionist Churches"
in the 1960s.[22]

In contrast to the ZCC, however, the mini-"Churches" now in GammaNgwato
often have few links to any wider body, are based on proximity and kin, and invoke disguised local ancestors. Taken as a whole, however, the great majority of
basadi, married women of all ethnic backgrounds, actively participate in them; their

---

evangelists in expanding their polity even into the domain of the BaTlhaping. See also Michael Twaddle's
discussion in "The Emergence of Politico-Religious Groupings in Late 19th Century Buganda," *Journal of
African History* 29 (1988), 81–92; and John Thornton's suggestions about the possibly critical role of "chapel
boys," in his "The Development of an African Catholic Church in the Kingdom of Kongo, 1491-1750,"
Journal of African History 25 (1984), 165.

[21]   Allen Roberts discusses situational constructions of identity, resonant with my discussion of Ngwato
citizenship, in his "History, Ethnicity and Change in the 'Christian Kingdom' of Southeastern Zaire," in
Leroy Vail, ed., *The Creation of Tribalism in Southern Africa* (Berkeley, 1989), 193–214. See also Peter Hinchliff,
"The Blantyre Scandal: Scottish Missionaries and Colonialism," *Journal of Theology for Southern Africa* 461
(1984). Karen Fields, *Revival and Rebellion in Central Africa*, especially Ch. 2, is clearly apropos here and
has influenced my own thinking; Landeg White, *Magomero, Portrait of an African Village* (Cambridge, 1987),
Ch. 1. This perspective reaches back also to Roland Oliver, *The Missionary Factor in East Africa*, 2nd ed.
(London, 1965), 51–60. In contrast to Oliver's thrust, Robert Rotberg argues that no missionary society
was more committed to the exercise of temporal power than the LMS—at Kavimbe, strict rules and
horsewhippings enforced the Sabbath, etc. Robert I. Rotberg, *Christian Missionaries and the Creation of Northern Rhodesia, 1880–1924* (Princeton, 1965), 56–61. Note also the presence of ecclesiastical language and
procedure in a major political movement of the 1920s in Basutoland, Robert Edgar, *Prophets with Honour:
A Documentary History of Lekhotla la Bafo* (Johannesburg, 1987); see 90 ("catechism"), and 119–27.

[22]   BNA D.7/1092, Police Report, "Zionism/Apostolicism in the B.P.," Office of the Commissioner, B.P.
Police, Mafeking, 12/3/60; courtesy of Neil Parsons. According to Jean Comaroff there were only "a hundred or so" Tshidi BaRolong ZCC members, only a few of whom had been to Morija; this piece of information, seemingly critical, comes only on page 240 of *Body of Power*.

barriers to membership are very few. They offer women a generally supportive (if status-conscious) metacommunity of Christians. They are celebrated by women's public presence in every town and village.[23] These traits were inherited, if expanded, from the Ngwato Church.

A Last Note

Writing history is a quixotic undertaking. It is an attempt to pin and mount lives on the page of a book, like butterflies or rose petals. When the effort is successful, it seems most to suggest elements lying beyond its limited face. I have not avoided fixing the fluidities of meaning in a sort of taxonomy here. My technique, however, has been to try discursively to leave behind, as taxonomic categories, particular notions of power, law, belief, Church, and kingship, in the hope of finding a space from which to recover and retranslate the changing vocabulary of Ngwato experience. I wanted to avoid the artificial clarity of writing about entities I myself had too easily named. Ngwato power, which was amplified and legitimated by the users of the written Word, was best understood through the words thrown forward by those transformations that gave rise to it. The lines between the religious, social, economic, and political, and indeed even between the ideological and the material, were momentarily blurred along the way. The idea was to create a pool of meaning accessible both to historical Tswana experience and to the current reader, who can judge whether I have been successful.

In this spirit, I want to end, as so many begin, with a confession. It may be that the only way truly to privilege Christians' own experiences and expressions is to share in their faith. This my analysis could not do. Any balanced reading, however, must see that when men and women in GammaNgwato prayed to God, they were, so to speak, also praying to God. May their prayers be answered.

---

[23] See Leni Lagerwerf, *"They Pray for You . . ." Independent Churches and Women in Botswana*, IMMO Research Pamphlet No. 6 (London, 1984); O. N. O. Kealotswe, *Healing in the African Independent Churches in Botswana* (Bochum, 1987). Compare Deborah Gaitskell, "'Wailing for Purity': Prayer Unions, African Mothers and Adolescent Daughters, 1912–1940," in Shula Marks and Richard Rathbone, eds., *Industrialization and Social Change in South Africa* (London, 1982).

SOURCES

1. *Archival Holdings*

I kept the British style for dates (day-month-year) in all my citations. After each abbreviation, subdivisions of archives and further abbreviations are given if applicable.

A. LMS: Council for World Mission, London Missionary Society Papers; formerly at Rhodes Livingstone House, now housed at the School of Oriental and African Studies, University of London.

    a South[ern] Africa Incoming Letters: LMS SA, followed by box and file number, e.g. LMS/SA 71/4. After 1930, alphabetized names locate box numbers, e.g. LMS SA/Bur.

    b South[ern] Africa Reports: LMS SA Reports, and box and file number

    c Africa Personals: LMS SA Personals or LMS SA P/ and box, file

    d LMS Candidates Papers, series 1 and 2, alphabetic

    e SAEC and SADC Minutes of Assemblies

    f London Committee Meetings

In addition, and noted separately:

    g The published "Private and Confidential" deputations' reports, London

    h The published *Reports of the London Missionary Society*, London

    i The published *The Chronicle of the London Missionary Society*, London

B. K III, S II, TK: Khama III Memorial Museum, Serowe, Botswana. The first three designations include correspondence in SeTswana between the royal Ngwato secretariat and merchants, officials, governors, spies, *baruti,* and friends and kinspeople.

    a Khama III Papers: K III, followed by lettered subsection, and numbered box and file.

    b Sekgoma II Papers: S II, same.

    c Tshekedi Khama Papers: TK, same.

In addition, BHP and QNP/WCW, also at the Museum:

    d Bessie Head Papers: BHP followed by a notebook number. I did not make use of her "personal" correspondence.

    e [Q.] N. Parsons' deposited photocopies, some of which are lost in the original: QNP/WCW "additional documents"

C. WCW: William C. Willoughby Papers, Selly Oaks College, Birmingham, U.K. There are over 800 files, and they are cited WCW/ followed by the file number and specifics. Notably, however, there are

a Notes from Willoughby's days in GammaNgwato
b Drafts of Willoughby's essays
c WCW/804, containing Tiger Kloof examination statements from Bible students; I have labelled these in brackets, "[Confessions]," followed by the name of the author.

D. BNA: Botswana National Archives, Gaborone.
a District Commissioner series: D.
b Resident Magistrate series: RM.
c Serowe series: S.
d Miscellaneous other designations, including:
The Rev. J. H. L. Burns' Papers on microfiche
The Rev. Arthur Sandilands' Papers
Bamangwato Tribal Assembly Papers.

E. UCCSA: United Congregational Church of South Africa, Serowe, Papers. I have deposited copies of some material at the Khama Memorial Museum (see *B.* above). Other papers still reside with the UCCSA congregation in Serowe.
a Baptismal Registers (numbered)
b Marriage Registers (numbered)
c Deacons' Minutes, 1946–1952
d Miscellaneous, including medical texts and loose correspondence ("loose").

F. ZKM: Moeding College, Z. K. Matthews Library; Tiger Kloof Missionary College material. These texts are cited by following the filing numbers, adopted by the Z. K. Matthews library, a somewhat ideal list of which is available in the CWM collection at SOAS, University of London.

G. JR: Papers of the Rev. Dr. John Rutherford, in his possession in Greystoke, near Penrith, Cumbria, England.
In the late 1970s, Dr. Rutherford had access to W. C. Willoughby's registers of catechumens and Communion-takers. He took thorough notes especially of Willoughby's interrogations of Christians in Phalapye for the turn of the century. The originals were among the Serowe church's voluminous papers, most of which were appropriated by the Rev. Albert Locke when he departed Serowe. (He let stay the material marked "UCCSA" above.) They were eventually deposited with the UCCSA in Gaborone in 1979. Their whereabouts today are unknown, and my citations follow Dr. Rutherford's in the hope that they turn up:
JR LMS/S [Box] 3, Register "[name]".

H. RDM: *Rand Daily Mail* from 1922, cited as *RDM* followed by the date.

I. Miscellaneous Documents: Cited as below and identified
a Material courtesy of Isaac Schapera, including:
i. Public Record Office, CO/417/141, Annexure A. Enclosures in Despatch No. 136.G 24/7/1895; Phalapye, 21 and 24/6/1895. Cited as PRO 24/7/1895 after explanation in note.
ii. Rhodesian National Archives (now Zimbabwe National Archives), "Phalapye, March 23, 1894," marked "[29]" and "handwriting of W. C. Willoughby, apparently copied from ms. by Tiro." My translation. Cited as RNA 23/3/1894 after explanation in note.

b Neil Parsons/Michael Crowder photocopied material, some from the late Michael Crowder's academic papers.

c Material courtesy of Dennis Blackbeard, an old letter from his father and a medical book (see "Chase" in Section 3 below).

2. Cited Interviews: Orally Transmitted Information

Below, people are called by the names and titles by which they identified themselves to me, with these exceptions: (1) I have bestowed "Mr." on men simply to show they are men. (2) In the cases where Ms. is given, women did not specify Mrs., Miss, or "Mma-," which signifies "mother of" and hence substitutes for all other three titles. Interviews are in SeTswana unless specified "English" at the end of the entry. Serowe and Lerala as locations here embrace their surrounding fields and cattle posts. The interviews in 1988–89 often depended heavily on the translating of Mr. Pro Nthobatsang and Mr. Gabriel Selato, less so toward June of 1989. Those in 1990 relied more on my own language ability, but still depended heavily on the diplomatic skill of Mr. Baruteng Onamile.

Mr. Dennis Blackbeard, b. 1918, Serowe, 7 Nov. 1988, English.
Mrs. Setuhile Sebina, Serowe, 28 Feb. 1989.
Mrs. Balatheo Moloi, Serowe, 17 Nov. 1988.
Mr. Modengwa Koothupile, b. 1910, Serowe, Jan. 1989.
Mrs. Ruth Williams Khama, Gaborone, June 1989, English.
Mrs. B. M. Sebina, Serowe, 1 Dec. 1989.
Ms. Bokutso Mele, Serowe, 6 Nov. 1988.
Ms. Tsologela Rakgamanyane, Serowe, 20 Nov. 1988.
The Rev. Harsh Ramolefhe, Gaborone 15 June 1989, English.
The Rev. Phethu Sekgoma, b. 1922, Bobonong 2 May 1989.
Mr. and Mrs. Lebogang Bolokeng, b. 1920, Serowe, n.d.
Miss Dichetiso Balang, b. 1908, Serowe, 3 Nov. 1988.
MmaBotlhale (Ditsenyo) Kesianye, b. 1912, Serowe, 9 Jan. 1989.
The Rev. Johane Lenyebe, b. 1917, Serowe, May 1989.
Ms. Maretha Masheto, Radisele 18 April 1989.
Mr. (Deacon) Padiko Mathodi, b. 1928, Serowe, 2 Dec. 1988.
Moruti Maatlametlo Mokobi, b. 1901, Mahalapye 20 Jan. 1989.
Mrs. Maatlametlo Mokobi, b. 1910, Mahalapye 14 Jan. 1989.
Archbishop (Spiritual Healing Church) Israel Motswasele, Matsiloje, 17 Jan. 1989.
Mrs. Ogaletse Phiri, Serowe, 1 and 3 Nov. 1988.
Mr. Radiphofu Moloi Sekgoma, b. 1902, Serowe, 20 Nov. 1988.
Moruti Modise Segaise (b. ca. 1910) with Mrs. Gasethata Segaise, Serowe, 20 Dec. 1988.
Moruti Modise Segaise (b. ca. 1910) with Mrs. Gasethata Segaise, Serowe, 29 May 1989.
Ms. Oathokwa Samoele, b. 1918, Radisele 18 Feb. 1989.
Mrs. Peter Mazebe Sebina, b. 1905, Serowe, 2 Dec. 1988.
Mrs. Barophi Ratshosa, b. 1918, Serowe, 9 Nov. 1988, English.
Miss Bernice N. Sebina, Serowe, 4 Nov. 1988.

Mr. Steven M., b. 1917, Palapye 19 Dec. 1988.
Ms. Kadimo Serema, Palapye, 30 Nov. and 17 Dec. 1988.
Mrs. Tsogang Serema, b. 1901, Palapye, 7 Dec. 1988.
Mr. Jenamo Tebape, Serowe, 24 Nov. 1988, English.
Mr. Radikabari R. Thedi, b. 1903, Palapye 19 Dec. 1988.
Mrs. Botsanyang Ramatsela, b. 1908, Serowe, 10 Nov. 1988.
Ms. Gabotepele Ntsosa, b. 1910, Serowe, 27 Feb. 1989.
Mr. L. G. Baruti, b. 1902, Baruti ward, Serowe, 8 Nov. 1988, English.
Mrs. Bamorago Kgatwane Raditau, b. 1906, Serowe, 18 Jan. 1989.
Mrs. Obolokile Sekga, b. approx. 1903, Serowe, 12 Nov. 1988.
Mrs. Otaajang Kedikilwe, b. 1902, Sefhope, 20 May 1989.
Mr. Oabona Nthobatsang, Serowe, 9 May 1989, and Serowe, 12 May 1989.
The Rev. B. R. Tshipa, b. 1902, Serowe, 17 and 22 Feb. 1989, English.
The Rev. Father Haskins Sekgoma, b. 1903, Serowe, 19 Feb. and 31 May 1989,
   English.
Headman Mokgobelela, Serowe, 14 Feb. 1989.
MmaSentsho Baengoti, Ratholo May 1990.
MmaNgala Mompisi, Ratholo May 1990.
Ms. Setswalo Gobusamang, Ratholo May 1990.
Ms. Ngele Thusa, Ratholo May 1990.
Mr. Ditaolo Motlhagodi, Lerala, 2 April and 14 May 1990.
Mr. Ditaolo Motlhagodi with Mrs. Boikanyo Motlhagodi, Lerala, 15 May 1990.
Mrs. Boikanyo Motlhagodi, with Ditaolo Motlhagodi, Lerala, 17 May and 1
   June 1990.
Mr. Bonnetswe K. Dialwa and Mr. Rrawesi Dialwa, Lerala, 4 April 1990.
Mr. Rrawesi Dialwa, Lerala, 23 April 1990.
Mr. Bonnetswe K. Dialwa, b. 1923, Lerala, 2, 15, and 17 May, and 22 June
   1990.
Mr. Koolebile Kerekang Dialwa, Lerala, 25 June 1990.
Mrs. Dijelwe [Medupe] Moyo, Lerala, 19 April 1990.
Mr. Joel Tlhalefang, Lerala, 29 May 1990.
Mr. Kereeditse Sesinye, b. approx. 1908, on the road to Ratholo, 20 April 1990.
Mr. Koowetse Molebalwa, b. 1905, Lerala, 9 April and 16 June 1990.
Miss Leah M., Lerala, 3 April 1990.
Mr. Lekgaritha Mokakapadi and wife, 19 May 1990, Moremi village.
Mr. Lewatle Selato, Lerala, 5 April 1990.
Mr. Makwesa Leso, Lerala, 20 June 1990; with notebook, from father, ca. 1986.
Mr. Mathuba a Madikwe, b. 1901, Mmakgabo village, 24 May and 16 June
   1990.
Mrs. Mathuba, Serowe, 8 Nov. 1988.
MmaMachomise (Ms. Otlametse), Lerala, 5 June 1990.
MmaMotlamma (Ms. Gasewame), Lerala, 17 June 1990.
MmaRramatebele (Mrs. Mapula Ramosoka), b. ca 1908, Lerala, 2 and 3 May
   1990.
Ms. Sekibi Ramosoka, and MmaRramatebele, Lerala, 7 May 1990.
MmaTebo (Rachel) Mathare, Lerala, 2 April 1990, 7 May , 1 June , and 22 June
   1990.

Kgosi Mokakapadi (II) a Ramosoka, b. 1907, Lerala, 28 March, 8 May , and 24 June 1990.
Mr. Molaodi Thakeng, b. 1901, Lerala, 12 June 1990.
Mrs. Moswamasimo Molebalwa, Lerala, 27 March 1990.
Mr. Samuel Malete, Lerala, 25 May 1990.
Mr. Sebele Gaborone, b. 1903, Lerala, 2 May and 11 June 1990.
Mrs. Gobuamang Sebele, Lerala, 3 May 1990.
Ms. Selebogo Mogame, Lerala, 18 April 1990.
Ms. Selebogo Mogame and MmaWini (Ms. Fetang), Lerala, 22 April 1990.
Ms. Selebogo Mogame and MmaWini (Ms. Fetang) and Mr. Tshwene Tshiame, Lerala, 24 June 1990.
Mr. Selo Mafoko, b. 1900, Lerala, 11 and 12 April 1990.
Mr. Sematlho Pipedi, b. 1914, Lerala, 13 and 22 June 1990.
Senior women singing, 19 May 1990, GooMoremi.
Mr. Shagadi Ramosoka, b. approx. 1908, Lerala, 13 June 1990.
The Rev. Steven Nkgetsi, Lerala, 10 May 1990.
Mr. Tlotleng Pipedi, Lerala, 12 June 1990.
The Rev. Tshinamo Molebalwa, Lerala, 28 March 1990.
Mrs. Miriam (MmaKgalemang) Tshinye, Lerala, 2 May 1990.
Kgosi Shaw Moroka, Lerala, 23 and 24 April 1990.
MmaShaw Moroka, n.d. informal, Lerala, June.
Mr. Ramatlapana Selato, Lerala, 20 June 1990.
MmaNjalwa (Kesenntsang) Kerekang, b. approx. 1890, Lerala, 10 June 1990.
Mr. Ralekau Mokone, Lerala, 19 April 1990.
The Rev. John Rutherford and Olive Rutherford, Greystoke, Cumbria, 3–5 August 1993.

3. Books, Articles, and Theses Cited

Alverson, Hoyt. *Mind in the Heart of Darkness*. New Haven, Conn., 1978.
Adler, Marianna. "From Symbolic Exchange to Commodity Consumption." In *Drinking*, edited by Susan Barrows and R. Room, 376–98. Berkeley, 1991.
Alnaes, Kirsten. "Living with the Past: The Songs of the Herero in Botswana." *Africa* 59, 3 (1989), 267–99.
Ambler, R. W. "From Ranters to Chapel Builders." In *Voluntary Religion*, edited by W. J. Sheils and D. Wood, 319–37. Worcester, 1986.
Ambler, Charles H. "Alcohol and Disorder in Precolonial Africa." *Working Papers in African Studies* No. 126, Boston University, 1987.
_____. "Drunks, Brewers and Chiefs: Alcohol Regulation in Colonial Kenya, 1900–1939." In *Drinking*, S. Barrows and R. Room, eds., 165–83. Berkeley, 1991.
Anderson, Benedict. *Imagined Communities,*. rev. ed. New York, 1991.
Atkins, Keletso. "'Kafir Time': Preindustrial Temporal Concepts and Labour Discipline in 19th Century Colonial Natal." *Journal of African History* 29 (1988), 229–44.
Barfield, Owen. "The Meaning of 'Literal'." In *The Rediscovery of Meaning, and Other Essays*, Owen Barfield, ed., 32–43. Middletown, Conn., 1977.
_____. *History, Guilt and Habit*. Middletown, Conn., 1979.
Barrett, David. *Schism and Renewal in Africa*. Nairobi, 1968.

Barrows, Susan, and R. Room, eds. *Drinking: Behavior and Belief in Modern History.* Berkeley, 1991.

Beidelman, T. O. *Colonial Evangelism: A Socio-Historical Study of an East African Mission at the Grassroots.* Bloomington, Ind., 1982.

Belfield, E. M. G. *The Boer War.* London, 1975.

Belsey, Mark. "The Epidemiology of Infertility: A Review . . . Sub-Saharan Africa." *Bulletin of the World Health Organization,* 54 (1976), 319–41.

Benson, Mary. *Tshekedi Khama.* London, 1960.

Bhabha, Homi. "Of Mimicry and Man: The Ambivalence of Colonial Discourse." *October,* 28 (1984), 125–33.

Binsbergen, Wim van. *Religious Change in Zambia: Exploratory Studies.* London, 1981.

Boas, Frantz. "The Aim of Ethnography" [1888]. In F. Boas, *Race, Language and Culture.* New York, 1940.

Bobeng, Modisanyane. "The Bangwato–Babirwa Conflict in the Late 19th and Early Twentieth Centuries." B.A. Thesis, University of Botswana, Lesotho, and Swaziland, 1976.

Bonner, Philip L. "Liquor, Prostitution and the Migration of BaSotho Women to the Rand, 1920–1945." In *Women and Gender in Southern Africa,* edited by Cherryl Walker, 221–50. London, 1990.

Borges, Georges Luis. "The Library of Babel." In G. L. Borges, *Labyrinths.* New York, 1964.

Borker, Ruth. "To Honor Her Head: Hats as a Symbol of Women's Position in Three Evangelical Churches in Edinburgh, Scotland." Chap. 4 of *Women and Ritual and Symbolic Roles,* J. Hoch-Smith and A. Spring, eds. New York, 1978.

Bourdieu, Pierre. *Distinction: A Social Critique of the Judgement of Taste.* Trans. R. Nice. London, 1984.

Bozzoli, Belinda. "Marxism, Feminism and South African Studies." *Journal of Southern African Studies* 9, 2 (1983).

Bozzoli, Belinda, with the assistance of Mmantho Nkosoe. *Women of Phokeng. Consciousness, Life Strategy, and Migrancy in South Africa, 1900–1983.* Portsmouth, NH, 1991.

Bradford, Helen. "We Are Now the Men: Women's Beer Protests in the Natal Countryside, 1929." In *Class, Community and Conflict: South African Perspectives,* edited by Belinda Bozzoli, 292–323. Johannesburg, 1984.

Brandel-Syrier, Mia. *Black Women in Search of God.* London, 1962.

Breutz, P. L. "Tribes of the Marico District." *Ethnological Publication No. 30.* Pretoria, 1955.

Briggs, D. R., and J. Wing. *The Harvest and the Hope: The Story of Congregationalism in Southern Africa.* Johannesburg, 1970.

British War Office, Transvaal Dept. of Native Affairs. *The Native Tribes of the Transvaal.* London, 1905.

Brown, Barbara. "Facing 'The Black Peril': The Politics of Population Control in South Africa." *Journal of Southern African Studies* 13, 3 (1987), 256–73.

Brown, J. Tom. *Dilo tse di Chwanetseng go Itsiwe.* [Things That Should Be Known]. London, n.d. [1920?]

Brown, J. Tom. *The Apostle of the Marshes: The Story of Shomolekae.* London, 1925.

_____. *Setswana Dictionary.* Cape Town, 1923.

Burke, Tim. "Lifebuoy Men, Lux Women." Ph.D. dissertation, Johns Hopkins, 1992.

_____. "'Nyamarira That I Loved': Commoditization, Consumption, and the Social History of Soap in Zimbabwe." *Collected Papers on the Societies of Southern Africa in the 19th and 20th Centuries*, Vol 17. London, 1991.

Burns, J. L. H., and J. Sandilands. *A Hundred Years of Christianity among the Bamangwato*. Lobatsi, Bechuanaland Protectorate, 1962.

Callaway, Henry. *The Religious System of the AmaZulu*. Cape Town, 1970, 2nd printing.

Chapman, J. *Travels in the Interior of South Africa*. London, 1868.

Charlton, Roger. "The Politics of Elections in Botswana." *Africa* 63, 3 (1993), 330–70.

_____. "Texts, Printing, Readings." In *The New Cultural History*, edited by Lynn Hunt, 154–75. Berkeley, 1989.

Chase, [Not given]. *Dr. Chase's Last and Complete Recipe Book and Household Physician*. London, 1884.

Chirenje, J. Mutero. *Chief Kgama and his Times, c. 1835–1923*. London, 1978.

_____ . "Chief Sekgoma Letsholathebe II: Rebel or 20th Century Nationalist?" *Botswana Notes and Records*, 3 (1971), 64–69.

_____ . *A History of Northern Botswana*. London, 1977.

Clayton, W. C. *Ipswich Temperance Tracts, No. 228* [ca. 1850]. In *Religion in Victorian Society, a Sourcebook of Documents*, edited by R. J. Helmstadter and P. T. Philips, 341. Lanham, Md., 1985.

Cliffe, L., and R. Moorsom. "Rural Class Formation and Ecological Collapse in Botswana." *Review of African Political Economy* 15–16 (1980), 35–52.

Coan, J. R. "The Expansion of Missions of the African Methodist Episcopal Church in South Africa, 1896–1908." Ph.D. dissertation, Hartford Seminary Foundation, 1961.

Cobbing, Julian. "The Mfecane as Alibi: Thoughts on Dithakong and Mbolompo." *Journal of African History* 29 (1988), 487–519.

Cobbing, Julian. "The Ndebele State." In *Before and After Shaka: Papers in Nguni History*, edited by J. B. Peires, 166–77. Grahamstown, 1981.

Cohen, David William, and E. S. Atieno Odhiambo. *Burying SM: The Politics of Knowledge and the Sociology of Power in Africa*. Portsmouth, N.H., 1992.

_____. *Siaya: The Historical Anthropology of an African Landscape*. Athens, Ohio, 1989.

Comaroff, Jean. "Bodily Reform as Historical Practice: The Semantics of Resistance in Modern South Africa." *International Journal of Psychology* 20 (1985), 541–67.

Comaroff, Jean. *Body of Power, Spirit of Resistance*. Chicago, 1985.

_____. "Healing and Cultural Transition: The Tswana of Southern Africa." *Social Science and Medicine*, 15B (1981), 367–78.

Comaroff, Jean, and John L. Comaroff. "Christianity and Colonialism in South Africa." *American Ethnologist* 13 (1986), 1–22.

_____. "Home-Made Hegemony: Modernity, Domesticity, and Colonialism in South Africa." In *African Encounters with Domesticity*, edited by Karen Tranberg Hansen, 37–74. New York, 1992.

_____. "The Management of Marriage in a Tswana Chiefdom." In *Essays on African Marriage in Southern Africa*, edited by E. Krige and J. L. Comaroff. Cape Town, 1981.

_____. *Of Revelation and Revolution: Christianity, Colonialism and Consciousness in South Africa*, Vol. 1. Chicago, 1991.

Comaroff, John L. "Dialectical Systems, History and Anthropology: Units of Study and Questions of Theory." *Journal of Southern African Studies* 8 (1982), 143–72.
_____. "Images of Empire, Contests of Conscience: A Model of Colonial Domination in South Africa." *American Ethnologist* 16, 4 (1989), 661–85.
Comaroff, John L., and Simon Roberts. "Rules and Rulers: Political Processes in a Tswana Chiefdom." *Man* (n.s.) 13, 1 (1978), 1–20.
_____. *Rules and Processes: The Cultural Logic of Dispute in an African Context.* Chicago, 1981.
Coplan, David. "Eloquent Knowledge: Lesotho Migrants' Songs and the Anthropology of Experience." *American Ethnologist* 14, 3 (1987), 413–33.
_____. *In the Time of Cannibals: Word Music of South Africa's Basotho Migrants.* Chicago, 1994.
Corkish, J. D. "Some Notes on Children's Skipping Rhymes." *Botswana Notes and Records* 3 (1972), 37–39.
Croston, Julie. "Crocodile Snatch the Boer Child's Hat: Historical Use of Tswana Praise-Poems." Unpub. paper, ASA meeting, Denver, Colo., 19 Nov., 1987.
_____. "An Economic and Social History of the Freehold Land Tenure District of Bechuanaland Protectorate (Botswana), 1903–1966." Ph.D. dissertation, Boston University, 1993.
Crowder, Michael. *The Flogging of Phineas McIntosh: A Tale of Colonial Folly and Injustice, Bechuanaland, 1933.* New Haven, Conn., 1988.
_____. "The Succession Crisis over the Illness and Death of Kgosi Sekgoma II of the Bangwato, 1925." In *Succession to High Office in Botswana*, edited by Jack Parson, 33–72. Athens, Ohio, 1990.
_____. "Tshekedi Khama and Opposition to the British Administration of the Bechuanaland Protectorate, 1926–1936." *Journal of African History* 26 (1985), 193–214.
Crush, Jonathan, Alan Jeeves, and David Yudelman. *South Africa's Labor Empire: A History of Black Migrancy to the Gold Mines.* Boulder, Colo., 1991.
Currie, R., A. Gilbert, and L. Horsley. *Churches and Churchgoers: Patterns of Church Growth in the British Isles since 1700.* Oxford, 1977.
Curtin, Philip D. *The Image of Africa: British Ideas and Action, 1780–1850.* Madison, Wis., Wis., 1964.
Curtis, D. "Cash Brewing in a Rural Economy." *Botswana Notes and Records* 5 (1973).
_____. "The Social Organization of Ploughing." *Botswana Notes and Records* 4 (1972).
Cuthbertson, G. "Missionary Imperialism and Colonial Warfare: LMS Attitudes to the South African War, 1899–1902." *South African Historical Journal* [Johannesburg] 19 (1987), 93–114.
Dachs, Anthony J. "Functional Aspects of Religious Conversion among the Sotho-Tswana." In *Christianity South of the Zambezi*, Vol. 2, edited by A. J. Dachs and M. F. C. Bourdillon, Gwelo [Zimbabwe], 1977.
_____. *Papers of John Mackenzie.* Johannesburg, 1975.
_____. "Missionary Imperialism: The Case of Bechuanaland." *Journal of African History* 13 (1972), 647–58.
Daneel, Martinus. *The Quest for Belonging: An Introduction to the Study of African Independent Churches.* Gweru, Zimbabwe, 1987.
Dennis, C. [F. Seeley]. "The Role of *Dingaka tsa Setswana* from the 19th Century to the Present." *Botswana Notes and Records* 10 (1978), 53–67.

Depelchin, H., and Charles Croonenberghs. *Journey to Gubuluwayo: Letters of Frs. H. Depelchin and C. Croonenberghs*. Buluwayo, 1979.

Devitt, Leonard, ed. *Individual Church Studies: Religion in Botswana Project*, Vol. 3. Gaborone, privately published by the University of Botswana, 1984.

Dimpe, Motswaedi. "Batswapong-Bangwato Relations: The Politics of Subordination and Exploitation, 1895–1949." University of Botswana Student Research Essay, 1986.

Dixon, R., and S. Mathesias. *Victorian Architecture*. London, 1978.

Douglas, Mary. *Evans-Pritchard*. London, 1980.

_____. *Purity and Danger*. London, 1967.

Douglas, Mary, ed. *Constructive Drinking: Perspectives on Drink from Anthropology*. Cambridge, 1987.

Drechsler, Horst. *Let Us Die Fighting: subtitle needed*. London, 1980.

Duggan, William. *An Economic Analysis of Southern African Agriculture*. New York, 1986.

Dutfield, Michael. *A Marriage of Inconvenience: The Persecution of Ruth and Seretse Khama*. London, 1990.

Edgar, Robert. *Prophets with Honour: A Documentary History of Lekhotla la Bafo*. Johannesburg, 1987.

Eliade, Mircea. *A History of Religious Ideas, Vol. 1*. Trans. by W. R. Trask. New York, 1981.

_____. *The Sacred and the Profane*. Chicago, 1959.

Ellenberger, Vivian. "DiRobaroba Matlhakolatsa ga Masodi-a-Phela." *Transactions of the Royal Soc. of South Africa* XXV, 1 (1937), 1–72.

Elphick, Richard. "Africans and the Christian Campaign in Southern Africa." In *The Frontier in History, North America and Southern Africa Compared*, edited by H. Lamar and L. Thompson, 270–308. New Haven, Conn., 1981.

Etherington, Norman. "Missionary Doctors and African Healers in Mid-Victorian South Africa." *South African Historical Journal* 19 (1987), 77–92.

_____. *Preachers, Peasants and Prophets in Southeast Africa, 1835–1880*. London, 1978.

Fako, Thabo. "Historical Processes and African Health Systems: The Case of Botswana." Ph.D. dissertation, 1984, University of Wisconsin–Madison.

Feierman, Steven. "African Therapeutic Systems." *Social Science and Medicine* 13 B (1979), 277–84.

_____. *Peasant Intellectuals: Anthropology and History in Tanzania*. Madison, Wis., 1990.

_____. *The Shambaa Kingdom: A History*. Madison, Wis., 1974.

_____. "Struggles for Control: The Social Roots of Health and Healing in Modern Africa." *African Studies Review*, 28, 2/3 (June/Sept. 1985), 73–147.

_____. "Therapy as a System-in-Action in Northeastern Tanzania." *Social Science and Medicine*, 15B (1981), 353–60.

Fernandez, James. *Bwiti: An Ethnography of the Religious Imagination in Africa*. Princeton, 1982.

Fields, Karen. *Revival and Rebellion in Central Africa*. Princeton, 1985.

Ford, John. *The Role of Trypanosomiasis in African Ecology*. Oxford, 1971.

Foucault, Michel. *The Birth of the Clinic*. London, 1976.

_____. *Discipline and Punish, The Birth of the Prison.* Trans. by A. Sheridan. New York, 1979.

_____. *A History of Sexuality, Vol. 1: An Introduction.* New York, 1990.

_____. *Power/Knowledge.* New York, 1980.

Fox, David M. *Health Policies, Health Politics: The British and American Experiences, 1911–1965.* Princeton, 1986.

Gaitskell, Deborah. "Devout Domesticity? A Century of African Women's Christianity in South Africa." In *Women and Gender in Southern Africa,* edited by Cherryl Walker, 251–72. London, 1990.

_____. "Housewives, Maids or Mothers? Some Contradictions of Domesticity for Christian Women in Johannesburg, 1903–1939." *Journal of African History* 24 (1983).

_____. "'Wailing for Purity': Prayer Unions, African Mothers and Adolescent Daughters, 1912–1940." In *Industrialization and Social Change in South Africa,* edited by Shula Marks and Richard Rathbone. London, 1982.

Gallagher, Thomas, and Catherine Laqueur, eds. *The Making of the Modern Body: Sexuality and Society in the Nineteenth Century.* Berkeley, 1987.

Gates, Henry Louis. *Figures in Black.* Oxford, 1987.

Geary, Christraud. "Photographs as Materials for African History." *History in Africa* 13 (1986), 89–116.

Gellner, Ernest. "The Mightier Pen?" review of Edward Said, *Culture and Imperialism* (London, 1992), in the *Times Literary Supplement,* Feb. 19, 1993.

Genovese, Eugene. *Roll, Jordan, Roll: The World the Slaves Made.* New York, 1972.

Gluckmann, E. "The Tragedy of the Ababirwas." Six-part series. In *The Rand Daily Mail,* Johannesburg, 10–14 and 16 May 1922.

Giedion, Siegfried. *Mechanization Takes Command: A Contribution to Anonymous History* [1948]. New York, 1975.

Gifford, Caroline de S. "Women in Social Reform Movements." In *Women and Religion in America, Vol 1: The 19th Century,* edited by R. R. Ruether and R. S. Keller, Chap 7. New York, 1981.

Goodall, Norman. *A History of the London Missionary Society, 1895–1945.* Oxford, 1954.

Goody, Jack. *The Domestication of the Savage Mind.* Cambridge, 1978.

Gould, Stephen J. "The Hottentot Venus." In Stephen J. Gould, *The Flamingo's Smile: Reflections in Natural History.* New York, 1985.

Gray, Richard. *Black Christians, White Missionaries.* New Haven, 1990.

_____. "Christianity." In *The Cambridge History of Africa,* Vol. 7, edited by A. Roberts, 140–90. Cambridge, 1986.

_____. "Christianity and Social Change in Africa." *African Affairs* 77, 306 (1978).

Grove, Richard. "Scottish Missionaries, Evangelical Discourses and the Origins of Conservationist Thinking in Southern Africa, 1820–1900." *Journal of Southern African Studies* 15, 2 (1989).

Gusfield, J. "Benevolent Repression: Popular Culture, Social Structure and the Control of Drinking." In *Drinking, Behavior and Belief,* edited by Susan Barrows and R. Room, 399–424.

Guthrie, Malcolm. "Bantu Word Division." In Malcolm Guthrie, *Collected Papers on Bantu Linguistics,* 1–31. Middlesex, 1970.

_____. *Comparative Bantu.* 4 vols. Farnborough, 1967–70.

Guy, Jeff. "Analysing Precapitalist Societies in Southern Africa." *Journal of Southern African Studies* 10, 1 (1983), 39–54.

Haley, Bruce. *The Healthy Body in Victorian Culture.* Cambridge, Mass., 1978.

Hall, David D. *Worlds of Wonder, Days of Judgment: Popular Religious Belief in Early New England.* Cambridge, Mass., 1989.

Hall, Kenneth. "Humanitarianism and Racial Subordination: John Mackenzie and the Transformation of Tswana Society." *International Journal of African Historical Studies* 8 (1975), 97–110.

Harris, J. C. *Khama the Great African Chief.* London, 1922.

Nancy Hartsock. "Foucault on Power: A Theory for Women?" In *Feminism/ Postmodernism*, edited by Linda J. Nicholson, 157–76. New York, 1990.

la Hausse, Paul. *Brewers, Beerhalls and Boycotts, A History of Liquor in South Africa.* Johannesburg, 1988.

Hawkins, F. H. *Through Lands That Were Dark: Being a Record of a Year's Missionary Journey.* London, 1914.

Hay, Margaret Jean. "Queens, Prostitutes and Peasants: Historical Perspectives on African Women, 1971–1986." Boston University, African Studies Center, Working Paper No. 130, 1988.

Head, Bessie. *Serowe, Village of the Rain Wind.* London, 1981.

Henige, David. *The Chronology of Oral Tradition: The Quest for a Chimera.* Oxford, 1974.

Hepburn, James D. *Twenty Years in Khama's Country.* London, 1895.

Hepburn, Mrs. J. D. *Jottings.* London, 1928.

Hilton, B. *The Age of Atonement.* Oxford, 1980.

Hinchliff, Peter. "The Blantyre Scandal: Scottish Missionaries and Colonialism." *Journal of Theology for Southern Africa*, 461 (1984).

_____. "Voluntary Absolutism: British Missionary Societies in the 19th Century." In *Voluntary Religion*, edited by W. J. Sheils, 363–80.

Hobsbawm, Eric J. *Primitive Rebels* [c. 1959]. New York, 1965.

Hodgson, Janet. *The God of the Xhosa.* Cape Town, 1982.

Hofmeyr, Isabel. *"We Spend Our Years as a Tale That is Told": Oral Historical Narrative in a South African Chiefdom.* Portsmouth, NH, 1993.

Holdrege, Barbara. "Introduction: Towards a Phenomenology of Power." *Journal of Ritual Studies* 4, 2 (Summer, 1990).

Hollander, Anne. *Seeing Through Clothes.* New York, 1978.

Holub, Emil. *Seven Years in South Africa: Travels, Researches, and Hunting Adventures, between the Diamond-Fields and the Zambesi (1872–79).* 2 vols. Trans. E. E. Frewer. Boston, 1881.

Horton, Robin. "African Conversion." *Africa*, 41, 2 (1971), 85–108.

_____. "African Traditional Thought and Western Science." *Africa* 37, 1 (1967), 50–71; and 37, 2 (1967), 155–187.

_____. "On the Rationality of Conversion, Part I." *Africa* 45 (1975).

Hunt, Nancy Rose. "Domesticity and Colonialism in Belgian Africa: Usumbura's *Foyer Social*, 1946–1960." *Signs* 15, 3 (1990), 447–73.

_____. "Noise Over Camouflaged Polygyny: Colonial Morality Taxation and a Woman-Naming Crisis in Belgian Congo," *Journal of African History*, 32, 3 (1991), 471–94.

Hunt, William. *The Puritan Moment*. Cambridge, 1983.

Hyam, Ronald. *Reappraisals in British Imperial History*. Oxford, 1977.

Iliffe, John. *The African Poor: A History*. Cambridge, 1987.

Jacobson-Widding, Anita. *Red-White-Black as a Mode of Thought*. Uppsala, 1979.

James, W., and D. Johnson. "Introduction." *Vernacular Christianity*. New York, 1988.

Janson, Tore, and Joseph Tsonope. *Birth of a National Language: The History of Setswana*. Gaborone, 1991.

Janzen, John M. *Ngoma: Discourses of Healing in Central and Southern Africa*. Berkeley, 1992.

Janzen, John M., with Louis Arkinstall. *The Quest for Therapy: Medical Pluralism in Lower Zaire*. Berkeley, 1978.

Jeeves, Alan. "Migrant Labor and South African Expansion, 1920–1950." *South African Historical Journal* 18 (1986), 73–92.

Jennings, Albert E. *Bogadi: A Study of the Marriage Laws and Customs of the Bechuana Tribes of South Africa*. Tiger Kloof, 1933.

Jewsiewicki, Bogumil. "African Historical Studies: Academic Knowledge as 'Usable Past,' and Radical Scholarship." Address to the African Studies Association, Denver, Colo., 20 Nov., 1987.

Karp, Ivan. "Beer Drinking and Social Experience in an African Society: An Essay in Formal Sociology." In *Explorations in African Systems of Thought*, edited by Ivan Karp and Charles Bird, 83–119. Bloomington, Ind., 1980.

Kealotswe, O. N. O. *Healing in the African Independent Churches in Botswana*. Bochum, 1987.

Kebonang, B. B. "The History of the Herero in Mahalapye, Central District, 1922–84." *Botswana Notes and Records* 21 (1989), 43–52.

Keegan, Tim. *Facing the Storm: Portraits of Black Lives in Rural South Africa*. Athens, Ohio, 1988.

Kerr, Walter. *The Far Interior*. London, 1886.

Kgasa, M. L. A. *Thuto Ke Eng* [What is Learning?]. Lovedale, 1939.

Kiernan, J. P. *The Production and Management of Theraputic Power within a Zulu City*. Lewiston, NY, 1990.

_____. "Prophet and Preacher: An Essential Partnership in the Work of Zion." *Man*, (n.s.) 11 (1976).

_____. "The Work of Zion: An Analysis of an African Zionist Ritual." *Africa*, 46, 4 (1976), 340–55.

_____. "Where Zionists Draw the Line." *African Studies*, 33, 2 (1974), 79–90.

Kinsman, Margery. "'Beasts of Burden': the Subordination of Southern Tswana Women, 1800–1840." *Journal of Southern African Studies* 10, 1 (1983).

Kiyaga-Mulindwa, David, ed. *Tswapong Historical Texts*. 3 vols. University of Botswana Project, 1980. Published by photocopy for limited circulation.

Knight-Bruce, Louise. "Kame." *Murray's Magazine* V, 28 (1889), 452–65.

Kunzle, David. "The Art of Pulling Teeth in the Seventeenth and Nineteenth Centuries: From Public Martyrdom to Private Nightmare and Political Struggle?" In *Zone 5: Fragments for a History of the Human Body, Part Three*, edited by Michael Feher. New York, 1989.

Kuper, Adam. *South Africa and the Anthropologist*. London, 1987.

_____. *Wives for Cattle: Bridewealth and Marriage in Southern Africa*. London, 1982.

Kuper, Hilda. "Costume and Identity." *Comparative Studies in Society and History* 15 (1973).

Lagerwerf, Leni. *"They Pray for You . . ." Independent Churches and Women in Botswana: IMMO Research Pamphlet No. 6.* London, 1984.

Lan, David. *Guns and Rain.* Berkeley, 1985.

Landau, Paul. "The Making of Christianity in a Southern African Kingdom: GammaNgwato, ca. 1870 to 1940." Ph.D. dissertation, University of Wisconsin–Madison, Wis., 1992.

_____. "The Persecution of Ruth and Seretse Khama." *South African Review of Books,* Jan./Feb., 1991.

_____. "Preacher, Chief, and Prophetess." *Journal of Southern African Studies* 17, 1 (March 1991), 1–22.

_____. "When Rain Falls: Rainmaking and Community in a Tswana Village, ca. 1870 to Recent Times." *International Journal of African Historical Studies* 26, 1 (1993), 1–29.

_____. "Zulu Zionism and Social Health in South Africa." M.A. thesis, University of Wisconsin–Madison, Wis., 1986.

Legassick, Martin. "The Northern Frontier to 1840: The Rise and Decline of the Griqua People." In *The Shaping of South African Society, 1652–1840,* edited by Richard Elphick and H. Giliomee. Middletown, Conn., 1988.

Lesotlho, J. "*Badimo* in the Tswapong Hills: A Traditional Institution in Action." *Botswana Notes and Records* 15 (1982), 7–8.

Lewis, I. M. *Ecstatic Religion.* Middlesex, 1971.

Lévi-Strauss, Claude. *The Savage Mind.* London, 1966.

Lieta, the Reverend R. "The Origin of the Anglican Church in Botswana." In University of Botswana, *Religion in Botswana Project,* Vol. 3 (1984), 32–50.

Livingstone, David. *Family Letters, 1841–56.* Vol. I, edited by Isaac Schapera. London, 1959.

_____. *Livingston's Private Journals, 1851–1853,* edited by Isaac Schapera. Cape Town, 1960.

_____. *Missionary Correspondence, 1841–1856,* edited by Isaac Schapera. London, 1961.

_____. *Missionary Travels and Researches in South Africa.* London, 1857.

_____. *South African Papers, 1849–1853,* edited by Isaac Schapera. Cape Town, 1974.

Lloyd, Edwin. *Three Great African Chiefs.* London, 1895.

London Missionary Society. *Bibela e e Boitshepo* [Holy Bible, 1908].] Goodwood, South Africa, 1986 .

_____. *Dihela* [Hymns.] Cape Town, 1973.

_____. *Dihela Tsa Tihelo ea Modimo* [Hymns of God's Work]. Kuruman, 1894.

_____. *The MaSarwa (Bushmen): Report of an Inquiry by the SADC.* Cape Town, 1935.

Long, Una, ed. *The Journals of Elizabeth Lees Price.* London, 1956.

Loos, Adolph. "Ornament and Crime." First published as a manifesto in 1908. In *Programs and Manifestoes on 20th Century Architecture,* edited by U. Conrads. Cambridge, Mass., 1970.

Loudon, J. B. "Psychogenic Disorder and Social Conflict among the Zulu." In *Culture and Mental Health,* edited by M. K. Opler. New York, 1959.

Lovegrove, Deryck. "Idealism and Association in Early 19th Century Dissent." In *Voluntary Religion*, edited by W. J. Sheils, 303–18.

Lovett, R. *The History of the London Missionary Society, 1795–1895*. 2 vols. Oxford, 1899.

Lutheran Theological College (Mapumulo, Natal, South Africa). "The Report of the Umpumulo Consultation on the Healing Ministry of the Church." Typescript, 19–27/9/67.

MacGaffey, Wyatt. *Religion and Society in Central Africa*. Chicago, 1986.

Mackenzie, William D. *John Mackenzie: South African Missionary and Statesman*. London, 1902.

Mackenzie, John. *Austral Africa: Ruling it or Losing it*. 2 Vols. London, 1887.

_____. *Day-Dawn in Dark Places*. London, 1883.

_____. *Ten Years North of the Orange River: A Story of Everyday Life and Work among the South African Tribes*. London, 1871.

Mackenzie, John M. "The Natural World and the Popular Consciousness in Southern Africa: The European Appropriation of Nature." In *Cultural Struggle and Development in Southern Africa*, edited by Preben Kaarsholm, 13–32. Portsmouth, NH, 1991.

Maggs, Tim, and G. Whitelaw. "A Review of Recent Archaeological Research on Food-Producing Communities in Southern Africa." *Journal of African History* 32, 1 (1991).

Mahoney, Norman. "Contract and Neighborly Exchange among the Birwa of Botswana." *Journal of African Law* 21, 1 (1977).

Majno, Guido., M.D. *The Healing Hand: Man and Wound in the Ancient World* [1975]. Cambridge, Mass., 1991.

Mandala, Elias C. *Work and Control in a Peasant Economy*. Madison, Wis., 1990.

Mann, Kristin. *Marrying Well: Marriage, Status and Social Change among Educated Elites in Colonial Lagos*. Cambridge, 1985.

Marks, Shula, and N. Andersson. "Typhus and Social Control: South Africa 1917–1950." In *Disease, Medicine and Empire*, edited by Roy Macleod and Milton Lewis, 257–83. New York, 1988.

Massey, M. "A Case of Colonial Collaboration: The Hut Tax and Migrant Labour." *Botswana Notes and Records* 10 (1978), 95–98.

Mauss, Marcel. *The Gift*. Trans. I. Cunnison. London, 1966.

May, Joan. *Zimbabwean Women in Colonial and Customary Law*. Gweru, Zimbabwe, 1983.

Maylam, Paul. *Rhodes, the Tswana, and the British*. Westport, Conn., 1980.

Mbiti, John. *African Religions and Philosophy*. New York, 1969.

McCracken, John. "Colonialism, Capitalism and Ecological Crisis in Malawi: A Reassessment." In *Conservation in Africa*, edited by David Anderson and Richard Grove. Cambridge, 1987.

Meillassoux, Claude. "'The Economy' in Agricultural Self-Sustaining Societies: A Preliminary Analysis." In *Relations of Production: Marxist Approaches to Economic Anthropology*, edited by David Seddon. London, 1978.

_____. *Maidens, Meal and Money: Capitalism and the Domestic Community*. Cambridge, 1981.

Meintjes, Sheila. "Family and Gender in the Christian Community at Edendale, Natal in Colonial Times." In *Women and Gender in Southern Africa*, edited by Cheryl Walker. London, 1990.

Memmi, Albert. *The Colonizer and the Colonized*. Boston, 1967.

Methuen, Henry. *Life in the Wilderness or, Wanderings in South Africa*. London, 1846.

Mgadla, Part Themba. "Missionary and Colonial Education among the Bangwato, 1862–1948." Ph.D. dissertation, Boston University, 1986.

Miers, Suzanne, and Michael Crowder. "The Politics of Slavery in Bechuanaland: Power Struggles and the Plight of the Basarwa in the Bamangwato Reserve, 1926–1940." In *The End of Slavery in Africa*, edited by Suzanne Miers and Richard Roberts. Madison, Wis., 1988.

Mignon, Andrea. "'Ein Vorkolonialer Missionsversuch in Botswana,' Eine ethnohistorische Studies zur Geschichte der Hermannsburger Mission bei den Balete/Botswana im 19. Jhd." Ph.D. dissertation, University of Vienna, 1989.

Miller, Joseph C., ed. *The African Past Speaks*. Folkstone, 1980.

Mockford, Julian. *Khama King of the Bamangwato*. Oxford, 1931.

Moffat, Robert. *Missionary Labours and Scenes in Southern Africa*. New York, 1847.

_____ . *The Matabele Journals of Robert Moffat, 1829–1860*, edited by J. P. R. Wallis. London, 1945.

Mongwa, Mbako D. K. "The Struggle between BakaNswazwi under John Madawo Nswazwi and the Bangwato under Tshekedi Khama, 1926–1932." B.A. thesis, U. of Botswana, 1977.

Monnig, H. O. *The Pedi*. Pretoria, 1967.

Mooko, Tjuma. "The Role of Women in Bangwato Politics." B.A. thesis, University of Botswana, 1985.

Moorhouse, Geoffrey. *The Missionaries*. Philadelphia, 1973.

Mort, Frank. *Dangerous Sexualities: Medico-Moral Politics in England since 1830*. New York, 1987.

Morton, Fred, and Jeff Ramsay, eds. *The Birth of Botswana: A History of the Bechuanaland Protectorate from 1910 to 1966*. Gaborone, 1987.

Motzafi-Haller, Pnina. "Transformations in the Tswapong Region, Central Botswana: National Policies and Local Realities." Ph.D. dissertation (Anthropology), Brandeis University, 1988.

Mtutuki, M. J. "The Mwali Cult in Northern Botswana (Some Oral Traditions, c. 1893–1976)." B.A. thesis, University of Botswana, Lesotho, and Swaziland, 1976.

Murray, James. *Life in Scotland A Hundred Years Ago as Reflected in the Old Statistical Act of Scotland, 1791–1799*. Paisley, UK, 1900.

Muzorewa, F. D. "Through Prayer to Action: The Rukwadzano Women of Rhodesia." In *Themes in the Christian History of Central Africa*. Terence O. Ranger and J. Weller, eds. London, 1975.

Nettleton, G. E. "BaNgwato" (in SeTswana). In *Ditirafalo tsa Merafe ye Batswana ba Lefatshe la Tshireletso*, edited by Isaac Schapera. Cape Town, 1954.

Nettleton, Sarah. *Power, Pain and Dentistry*. Philadelphia, 1992.

_____ . "Protecting a Vulnerable Margin: Towards an Analysis of How the Mouth Came to be Separated from the Body." *Sociology of Health and Illness* 10, 2 (1988), 156–69.

Ngcongco, Leonard D. "Religion and Politics in an African Chiefdom: The Mothowagae Secession Revisited." *Pula*, 3, 1 (May, 1983), 59–78.

_____ . "Tswana Political Tradition: How Democratic?" In *Democracy in Botswana*, edited by J. Holm and P. Molutsi. Athens, Ohio, 1989.

Ngubane, Harriet. *Body and Mind in Zulu Medicine*. London, 1977.

Nicholson, S. E. "The Historical Climatology of Africa." In *Climate and History*, edited by T. M. Wigley. Cambridge, 1981.

Oliver, Roland. *The Missionary Factor in East Africa*, 2nd ed. London, 1965.

Oosthuizen, Gerhardus C. "The Aetiology of Spirit in Southern Africa." In *Afro-Christianity: Religion and Healing in Southern Africa*, edited by G. C. Oosthuizen et al. Lewiston, NY, 1989.

_____. *The Theology of a South African Messiah: An Analysis of the Hymnal of "The Church of the Nazarites"*. Leiden, 1967.

"Our South African Ally–King Khama." [Anon.] *Pall Mall Gazette*. London. Saturday, 21 Oct. 1893.

Packard, Randall. *Chiefship and Cosmology: An Historical Study of Political Competition*. Bloomington, 1981.

_____. *White Plague, Black Labor: Tuberculosis and the Political Economy of Health and Disease in South Africa*. Berkeley, 1989.

Parsons, Neil. "The Economic History of Khama's Country in Botswana, 1844 to 1930." In *The Roots of Rural Poverty in Central and Southern Africa*, edited by R. Palmer and N. Parsons, 113–43. London, 1977.

_____. "Education and Development in Pre-Colonial and Colonial Botswana to 1965." In *Education for Development*, edited by Michael Crowder. Symposium, Gaborone, 15–19 August, 1983. Gaborone, 1984.

_____. "Franz or Klikko, the Wild Dancing Bushman: A Case of Koisan Stereotyping." *Botswana Notes and Records* 20 (1988), 71–76.

_____. "The Image of Khama the Great–1868 to 1970." *Botswana Notes and Records* 3 (1971).

_____. "Independency and Ethiopianism among the Tswana in the Late 19th and Early 20th Centuries." *Collected Seminar Papers on the Societies of Southern Africa in the 19th and 20th Centuries*, Vol. 1. London, 1971.

_____. "Khama III, the Bamangwato and the British, with special reference to 1895–1923." Ph.D. dissertation, University of Edinburgh, 1973.

_____. *A New History of Southern Africa*. London, 1982.

_____. "Settlement in East-Central Botswana, ca. 1800–1920." In *Settlement in Botswana*, edited by R. Renee Hitchcock and Mary R. Smith. Gaborone, 1980.

_____. "Shots for a Black Republic? Simon Ratshosa and Botswana Nationalism." *African Affairs* 73, 293 (Oct. 1974), 449–58.

_____. *The Word of Khama*. Lusaka, Zambia, 1972.

Pauw, B. A. *Religion in a Tswana Chiefdom*. Cape Town, 1961.

Peel, J. D. Y. *Aladura: A Religious Movement among the Yoruba*. London, 1968.

_____. "The Pastor and the Babalawo: The Interaction of Religions in 19th c. Yorubaland." *Africa* 60, 3 (1990).

Pelling, Margaret. "Appearance and Reality: Barber-surgeons, the Body and Disease." In *London 1500–1700*, edited by A. L. Beier and Roger Finley, 82–112. London, 1986.

Peters, Jeane. *The Medical Profession in Mid-Victorian London*. Berkeley, 1978.

Peters, Pauline. "Gender, Development Cycles and Historical Processes: A Critique of Recent Research on Women in Botswana." *Journal of Southern African Studies* 10, 1 (1983), 100–22.

Pinney, Christopher. "Colonial Anthropology." In *The Raj: India and the British, 1600–1947* [exhibition catalogue], edited by Christopher A. Bayly. London: National Portrait Gallery, 1991.

Plaatje, Solomon. *The Boer War Diaries of Sol Plaatje*, edited by John L. Comaroff. Cape Town, 1973.

_____ . *Sechuana Proverbs with Literal Translations and their European Equivalents*. London, 1916.

Price, Elizabeth Lees. *The Journals of Elizabeth Lees Price*. Una Long, ed. London, 1956. [Also listed under U. Long.]

Prickett, S. *Words and The Word: Language, Poetics and Biblical Interpretation*. Cambridge, 1986.

Prins, Gwyn. *The Hidden Hippopotamus: Reappraisal in African History*. Cambridge, 1980.

Radcliffe-Brown, A. R. "On Social Structure," in *Structure and Function in Primitive Society*. New York, 1952.

Rae, Colin. *Malaboch or Notes from my Diary on the Boer Campaign of 1894*. Cape Town, 1898.

Raison-Jourde, Françoise. *Le Bible et pouvoir à Madagascar au XIX siècle: Invention d'une identité chrétienne et construction de l'état*. Paris, 1991.

Ramsay, F. Jeffress. "The Rise and Fall of the Kwena Dynasty of South-Central Botswana, 1820–1940." 2 Vols. Ph.D. dissertation, Boston University, 1991.

Ranger, Terence O. "Godly Medicine: The Ambiguities of Medical Mission in Southeast Tanzania, 1900–1945." *Social Science and Medicine* 15B (1981), 261–77.

_____ . "Missionary Adaptation of African Religious Institutions: The Masasi Case." In *The Historical Study of African Religion*, edited by T. O. Ranger and I. N. Kimambo. Berkeley, 1972.

_____ . "Religious Movements and Politics in Sub-Saharan Africa." *African Studies Review* 29, 2 (1986), 1–71.

Rey, Sir Charles. *Monarch of All I Survey: Bechuanaland Diaries 1929–37*, edited by Neil Parsons and M. Crowder. Gaborone, 1988.

Richards, Audrey I. *Land, Labour and Diet in Northern Rhodesia*. Oxford, 1939.

Ricoeur, Paul. "The Model of the Text: Meaningful Action Considered as a Text." *Social Research* 38 (1971), 529–62. Reprinted as Ch. 7 in P. Ricoeur, *From Text to Action, Essays in Hermeneutics II*. Evanston, 1991.

Roberts, Allen. "History, Ethnicity and Change in the 'Christian Kingdom' of Southeastern Zaire." In *The Creation of Tribalism in Southern Africa*, edited by Leroy Vail, 193–214. Berkeley, 1989.

Roberts, Noel. "The Bagananoa or Ma-Laboch." *South African Journal of Science* 12 (1915), 241–56.

Roberts, Simon. "Tswana Government and Law in the Time of Seepapitso, 1910–1916." In *Law in Colonial Africa*, edited by Richard Roberts and Kristin Mann, 167–84. Portsmouth, NH, 1991.

Rossiter, Frank M., M.D. *The Practical Guide to Health* [1908]. Nashville, Texas, 1913.

Rotberg, Robert I. *Christian Missionaries and the Creation of Northern Rhodesia, 1880–1924*. Princeton, 1965.

Rutherford, John. "William C. Willoughby of Bechuanaland, Missionary Practitioner and Scholar." Ph.D. dissertation (Theology), University of Birmingham, 1981.

Said, Edward. "Opponents, Audiences, Constituencies and Community." In *The Anti-Aesthetic, Essays on Postmodern Culture*, edited by Hal Foster. Port Townsend, Wash., 1983.

Said, Edward. *Orientalism*. New York, 1978.

Sales, Jane. *The Planting of the Churches in South Africa*. Grand Rapids, Mich., 1971.

Sanneh, Lamin. *West African Christianity: The Religious Impact*. Maryknoll, NY, 1983.

Scarry, Elaine. *The Body in Pain: The Making and Unmaking of the World*. Oxford, 1985.

Schapera, Isaac. *Bogwera: Kgatla Initiation*. Gaborone, 1978.

_____ . "Christianity and the Tswana." *Journal of the Royal Anthropological Institute* 83 (1958), 1–9.

_____ . "The Early History of the Khurutshe." *Botswana Notes and Records* 2 (1970), 1–5.

_____ . *Ethnic Origins of Tswana Tribes*. London, 1952.

_____ . *Handbook of Tswana Law and Custom* [1938]. London, 1955.

_____ . *Married Life in an African Tribe*. Harmondsworth, 1971.

_____ . *Migrant Labour and Tribal Life*. Oxford, 1947.

_____ . *Native Land Tenure in the Bechuanaland Protectorate*. Cape Town, 1943.

_____ . "The Political Organization of the Ngwato of Bechuanaland Protectorate." In *African Political Systems*, edited by M. Fortes and E. E. Evans-Pritchard. London, 1940.

_____ . *Praise-Poems of Tswana Chiefs*. London, 1965.

_____ . *Rainmaking Rites of Tswana Tribes*. Cambridge, 1971.

_____ . "Report and Recommendations Submitted to the Bechuanaland Protectorate Administration on the Native Land Problem in the Tati District, 1943." [Reprinted in] *Botswana Notes and Records* 3 (1971), 219–68.

_____ . *Tribal Innovators: Tswana Chiefs and Social Change, 1795–1940*. London, 1970.

_____ . *The Tswana* [1953]. London, 1966.

Schapera, Isaac, ed. *Livingstone's Private Journals, 1851–1853*. Cape Town, 1960.

Schmidt, Elizabeth. *Peasants, Traders and Wives: Shona Women in the History of Zimbabwe*. Portsmouth, NH, 1992.

Schoffeleers, J. Matthew. "Oral History and the Retrieval of the Distant Past." In *Theoretical Explorations in African Religion*, edited by M. Schoffeleers and Wim van Binsbergen. London, 1985.

_____ . "Ritual Healing and Political Acquiescence: The Case of the Zionist Churches in Southern Africa." *Africa* 60, 1 (1991).

_____ . *River of Blood: The Genesis of a Martyr Cult in Southern Malawi, c. 1600*. Madison, Wis., 1992.

Scott, Joan Wallach. "Gender: A Useful Category of Historical Analysis." In Joan W. Scott, *Gender and the Politics of History*. New York, 1988.

Seeley, C. F. "The Reaction of the BaTswana to the Practice of Western Medicine." M.Phil, London School of Economics, 1973.

Setel, Philip. "'A Good Moral Tone,' Victorian Ideals of Health and the Judgement of Persons in Nineteenth Century Travel and Mission Accounts from East Africa." *Boston University Working Papers in African Studies*, No. 150 (1991).

Setiloane, G. *African Theology, an Introduction*. Cape Town, 1986.

_____ . *The Image of God Among the Sotho-Tswana*. Rotterdam, 1976.

Shamukuni, D. M. "The BaSubiya." *Botswana Notes and Records*, 4 (1972), 161–84.

Sheils, W. J., and D. Wood, eds. *Voluntary Religion: Studies in Church History, Vol 23.* Worcester, 1986.

Shillington, Kevin. *The Colonization of the Southern Tswana, 1870–1900.* Johannesburg, 1985.

Shiman, Lilian. *The Crusade Against Drink in Victorian England.* London, 1988.

Sillery, Anthony. *Founding a Protectorate.* The Hague, 1965.

_____ . *History of the Bechuanaland Protectorate.* Oxford, 1952.

_____ . *John Mackenzie of Bechuanaland, a Study in Humanitarian Imperialism.* Cape Town, 1971.

_____ . *Sechele: The Story of an African Chief.* London, 1954.

South African Native Affairs Commission (SANAC). *Minutes of the South African Native Affairs Commission, 1903–5, Vol. 4.* Cape Town, 1904.

Smith, E. W. *Great Lion of Bechuanaland: The Life and Times of Roger Price, Missionary.* London, 1957.

Staugard, Franz. *Traditional Healers: Traditional Medicine in Botswana.* Gaborone, 1985.

Stoler, Ann. "Making Empire Respectable: The Politics of Race and Sexual Morality in 20th Century Colonial Culture." *American Ethnologist* 16, 4 (1989), 634–60.

Strobel, Margaret. *European Women and the Second British Empire.* Bloomington, Ind., 1991.

Sundkler, Bengt. *Bantu Prophets in South Africa* [1948]. London, 1961.

Tambiah, Stanley J. "The Magical Power of Words." *Man* (n.s.) 3 (1968).

Tapela, H. M. "The Tati District of Botswana." Ph.D. dissertation, University of Sussex, 1976.

Taussig, Michael. "Reification and the Consciousness of the Patient." *Social Science and Medicine* 14B (1980), 3–13.

Thema, B. C. "A History of Native Education in the Bechuanaland Protectorate, 1840–1946." M.Ed. thesis, University of South Africa, 1948.

Thomas, Keith. *Religion and the Decline of Magic.* New York, 1973.

Thompson, E. P. "The Moral Economy of the English Crowd in the 18th Century." *Past and Present* 50 (1971), 76–136.

Thompson, Leonard. *Survival in Two Worlds: Moshoeshoe of Lesotho, 1786–1870.* Oxford, 1970.

Thomas, Nicholas. "Colonial Conversions: Difference, Hierarchy and History in Evangelical Propaganda." *Comparative Studies in Society and History* 34 (1992), 366–89.

Thomas, Thomas M. *Eleven Years in Central Africa* [1873]. Bulawayo, 1970.

Thornton, John. "The Development of an African Catholic Church in the Kingdom of Kongo, 1491–1750." *Journal of African History* 25 (1984), 147–67.

Tlou, Thomas. "The Batawana of Northwestern Botswana and Christian Missionaries, 1877–1906." *Transafrican Journal of History* 3, 1 and 2 (1973), 112–20.

_____ . *A History of Ngamiland, 1750–1906: The Formation of an African State.* Gaborone, 1985.

_____ . "Khama III–Great Reformer and Innovator." *Botswana Notes and Records* 2 (1970).

_____ . "*Melao ya ga Kgama*: Transformation in the 19th c. Ngwato State." M.A. thesis, Univ. of Wisconsin, 1969.

_____ . "Servility and Political Control: Batlhanka Among the BaTawana in Northwestern Botswana, ca. 1750-1906." In *Slavery in Africa*, edited by Suzanne Miers and Igor Kopytoff, 367–90. Madison, Wis., 1977.

Truschel, Louis W. "Political Survival in Colonial Botswana: The Preservation of Khama's State and the Growth of the Ngwato Monarchy," *Transafrican Journal of History* 4, 1 and 2 (1974), 71–93.

Turner, Victor. *The Forest of Symbols: Aspects of Ndembu Ritual*. Ithaca, 1967.

Turshen, Meredith. *The Political Ecology of Disease in Tanzania*. New Brunswick, N. J., 1984.

Twaddle, Michael. "The Emergence of Politico-Religious Groupings in Late 19th Century Buganda." *Journal of African History* 29 (1988), 81–92.

Tyrell, Ian. "Women's Temperance in International Perspective: The World's WCTU, 1880s–1920s." In *Drinking, Behavior and Belief*, edited by Susan Barrow and R. Room, 217–42.

Vansina, Jan. *Oral Tradition as History*. London and Madison, Wis., 1985.

_____ . *Paths Through the Rainforest*. Madison, Wis., 1991.

Vaughan, Megan. *Curing their Ills: Colonial Power and African Illness*. Stanford, 1991.

_____ . "Directions in the Social History of Medicine in Africa." Unpub. paper, SOAS African history seminar, 24/1/90.

Vail, Leroy, and Landeg White. *Power and the Praise Poem: Southern African Voices in History*. Charlottesville, 1991.

Virilio, Paul. *Vitesse et Politique*. Paris, 1977.

Waite, Gloria. "Public Health in Precolonial East-Central Africa." *Social Science and Medicine* 24, 3 (1987), 197–208.

Walker, Cherryl, ed. *Women and Gender in Southern Africa to 1945*. London, 1990.

Wallis, J. P. R., ed. *The Matebele Mission: A Selection from the Correspondence of John and Emily Moffat and David Livingstone and Others, 1858–1878*. London, 1945.

van Warmelo, N.J. "The Ndebele of J. Kekana," *Ethnological Publication No. 18*. Pretoria, 1950.

_____ . *Transvaal Ndebele Texts, Ethnological Publications, Vol. I*. Pretoria, 1930.

van Warmelo, N. J., ed. *The Copper Miners of Musina and the Early History of the Zoutspansberg*. Pretoria, 1940.

Warren, Allen. "'Mothers for Empire?' The Girl Guides Association in Britain, 1909–39." In *Making Imperial Mentalities, Socialization and British Imperialism*, edited by J. A. Mangan, 96–109. New York, 1990.

Warwick, Peter. *Black People and the South African War, 1899–1902*. Johannesburg, 1983.

Werbner, Richard. "The Argument of Images: from Zion to the Wilderness in African Churches." In *Theoretical Explorations in African Religion*, edited by Wim van Binsbergen and M. Schoffeleers. London, 1985.

_____ . "Land and Chiefship in the Tati Concession." *Botswana Notes and Records* 2 (1970), 6–13.

_____ . "Making the Hidden Seen: Tswapong Divination." Chapter 1 in *Ritual Passage, Sacred Journey*. Washington, D.C., 1989.

_____ . "The Political Economy of Bricolage." *Journal of Southern African Studies* 13, 1 (1986).

_____ . "Regional Cult of the God Above." In Richard Werbner, *Ritual Passage, Sacred Journey*. Washington, D.C., 1989.

West, Martin. *Bishops and Prophets in a Black City*. Cape Town, 1975.

White, Haydon. *Tropics of Discourse*. Baltimore, 1978.

White, Landeg. *Magomero: Portrait of an African Village*. Cambridge, 1987.

Whitehouse, J. O. *Register of Missionaries*. London, 1877.

Willoughby, W. C. "Khama: A Bantu Reformer." *International Review of Missions* (Jan. 1924), 74–6.

_____. *Native Life on the Transvaal Border*. London: n.d. [1899].

_____. *Nature Worship and Taboo*. Hartford, Conn. 1932.

_____. "Notes on the Initiation Ceremonies of the Becwana." *Journal of the Royal Anthropological Institute*, 39 (1909), 228–45.

_____. "Notes on the Totemism of the Becwana." *Journal of the Royal Anthropological Institute* 35 (1905), 302–3.

_____. *The Soul of the Bantu*. New York, 1928.

_____. *Tiger Kloof: The L.M.S.'s Native Institution in South Africa*. London, 1912.

Wilmsen, Edwin. *Land Filled With Flies: A Political Economy of the Kalahari*. Chicago, 1989.

_____. "The Real Bushman is the Male One: Labour and Power in the Creation of Ethnicity." *Botswana Notes and Records* 22 (1990), 21–35.

Wilmsen, Edwin, and Denbow, James. "Paradigmatic History of San-speaking Peoples and Current Attempts at Revision." *Current Anthropology* 31, 5 (1990), 489–523.

Wilson, Kenneth. "Science, Authority and Ecology: On the Colonial Endeavor in Africa." Unpub. paper, Nuffield College, Oxford, 10/3/90.

Wilson, Monica, and Godfrey Wilson. *The Analysis of Social Change*. Cambridge, 1945.

Wittgenstein, Ludwig. *On Certainty*. Trans. by G. Anscombe. Oxford, 1967.

_____. *Philosophical Investigations*. Trans. by G. Anscombe. New York, 1958.

_____. *Zettel*. Trans. by G. Anscombe. Oxford, 1967.

Wookey, Alfred J. *First Steps in English for Becwana Scholars, Part 1*. London, 1915.

Wookey, Alfred J., ed. *Dinwao Leha e le Diplolelo kaga Dico tsa Secwana (History of the Bechuana)*. Vryburg, South Africa, 1913.

Wright, John. "Control of Women's Labour in the Zulu Kingdom." In *Before and After Shaka: Papers in Nguni History*, edited by J. B. Peires, 82–99. Grahamstown, S.A., 1981.

Wright, Marcia. "Technology, Marriage and Women's Work in the History of Maize-Growers in Mazabuka, Zambia: A Reconnaissance." *Journal of Southern African Studies* 10, 1 (1983), 71–85.

Wylie, Diana. *A Little God: The Twilight of Patriarchy in a Southern African Chiefdom*. Hanover, NH, 1990.

Zikmund, Barbara. "The Struggle for the Right to Preach." In *Women and Religion in America, Vol. 1: The 19th Century*, edited by R. R. Ruether and R. S. Keller. New York, 1981.

INDEX

DATE DUE

5/1/06			